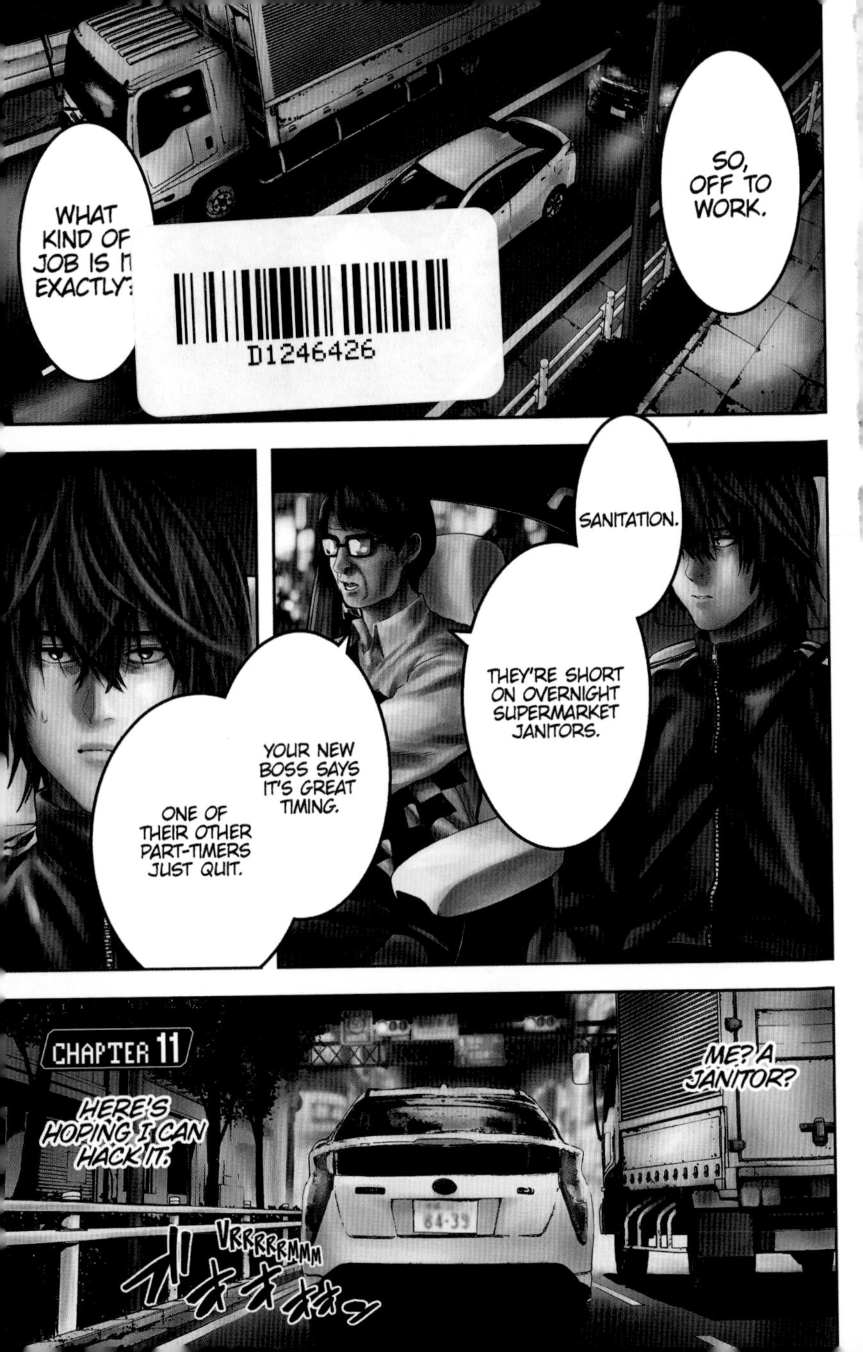
SO, OFF TO WORK.
WHAT KIND OF JOB IS I EXACTLY?
SANITATION.
THEY'RE SHORT ON OVERNIGHT SUPERMARKET JANITORS.
YOUR NEW BOSS SAYS IT'S GREAT TIMING.
ONE OF THEIR OTHER PART-TIMERS JUST QUIT.
ME? A JANITOR?
CHAPTER 11
HERE'S HOPING I CAN HACK IT.
VRRRRRMMM

THE NPCs IN THIS VILLAGE SIM GAME MUST BE REAL! 3

Original Story: Hirukuma
Manga Adaptation: Kazuhiko Morita
Character Designs: Namako

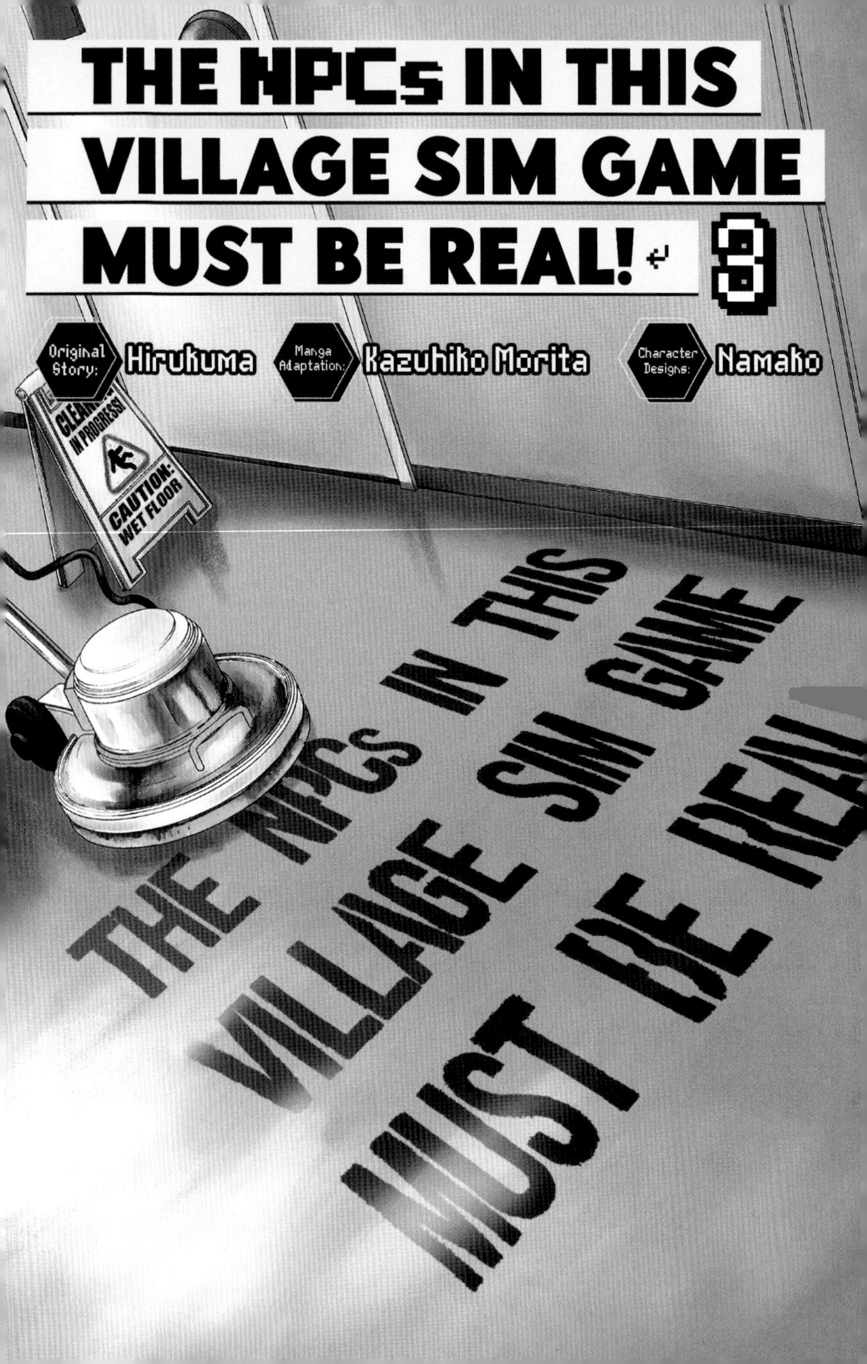
IN PROGRESS!
CAUTION: WET FLOOR
THE NPCs IN THIS
VILLAGE SIM GAME
MUST BE

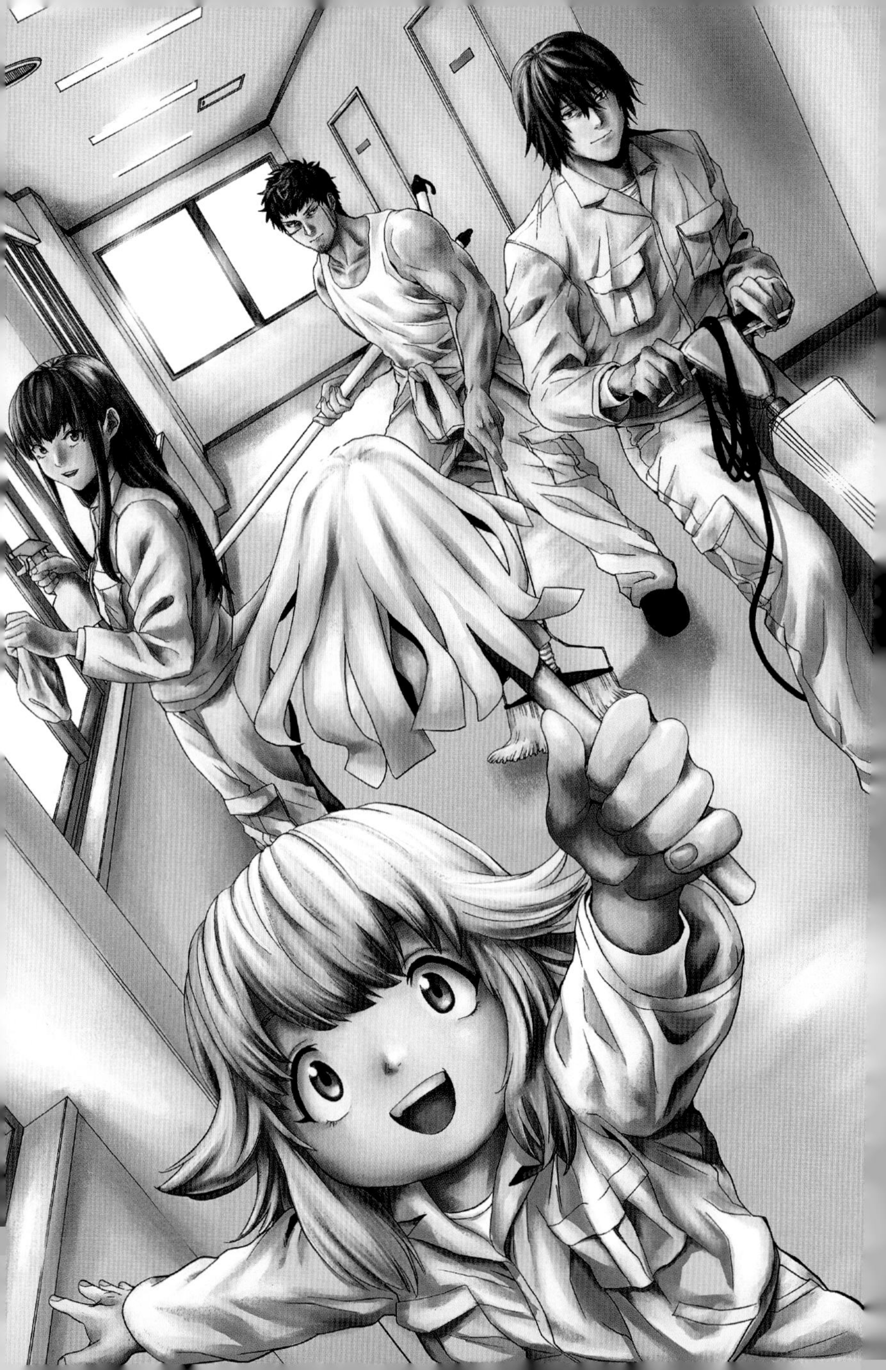

THE NPCs IN THIS VILLAGE SIM GAME MUST BE REAL! ↵

3

CONTENTS

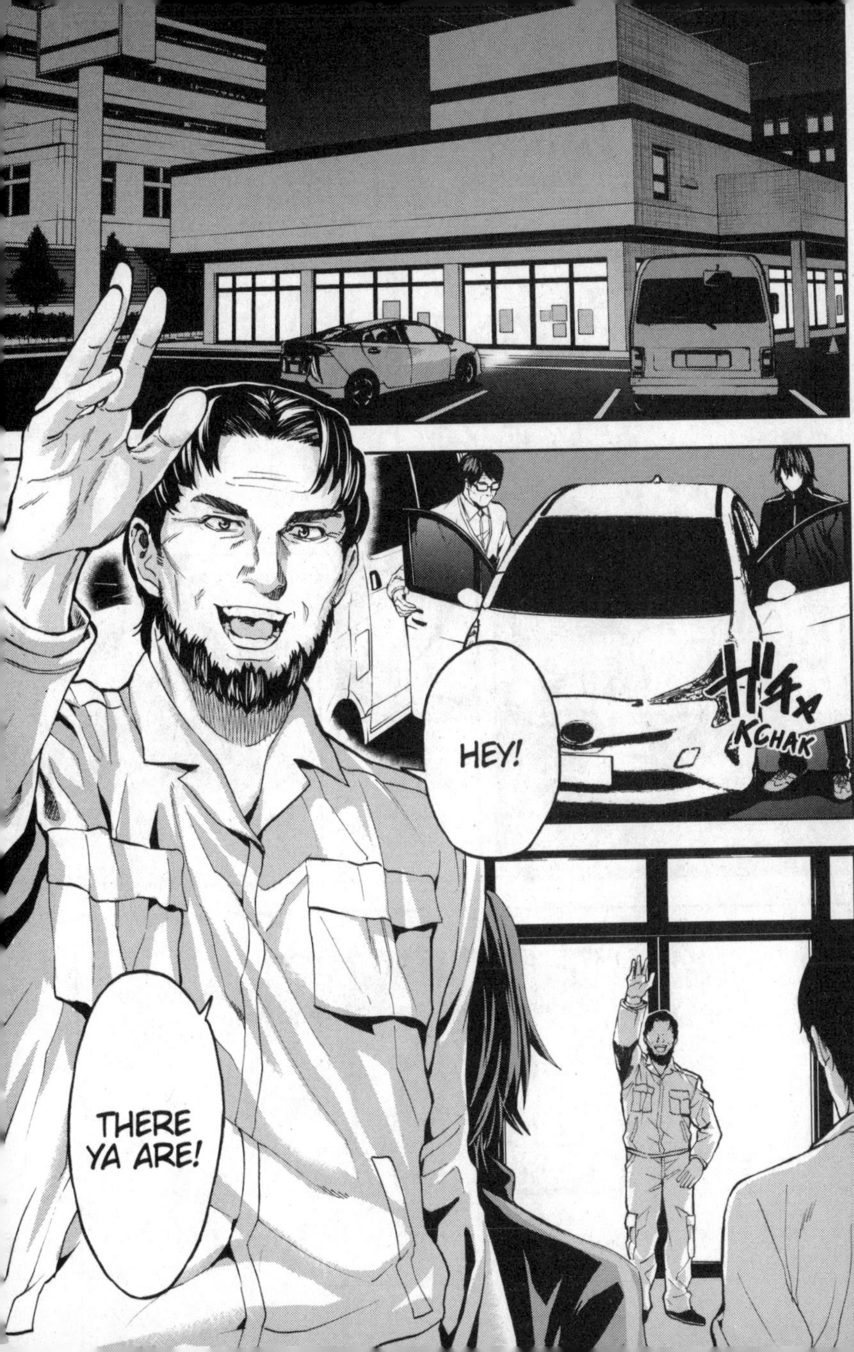
ガチャ
KCHAK
HEY!
THERE YA ARE!

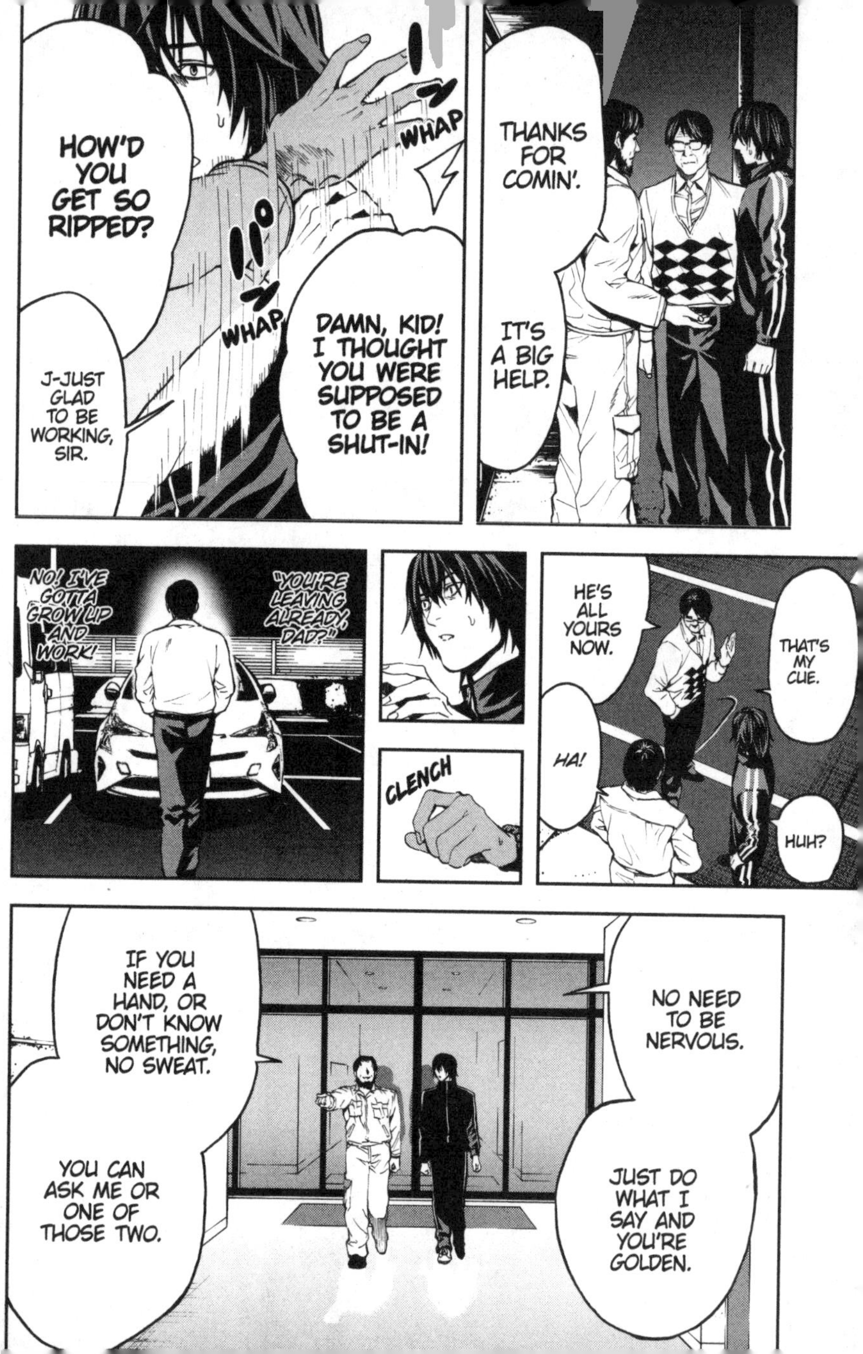
THANKS FOR COMIN'.
IT'S A BIG HELP.
WHAP
WHAP
DAMN, KID! I THOUGHT YOU WERE SUPPOSED TO BE A SHUT-IN!
HOW'D YOU GET SO RIPPED?
J-JUST GLAD TO BE WORKING, SIR.
HE'S ALL YOURS NOW.
THAT'S MY CUE.
HA!
HUH?
CLENCH
"YOU'RE LEAVING ALREADY, DAD?"
NO! I'VE GOTTA GROW UP AND WORK!
NO NEED TO BE NERVOUS.
JUST DO WHAT I SAY AND YOU'RE GOLDEN.
IF YOU NEED A HAND, OR DON'T KNOW SOMETHING, NO SWEAT.
YOU CAN ASK ME OR ONE OF THOSE TWO.

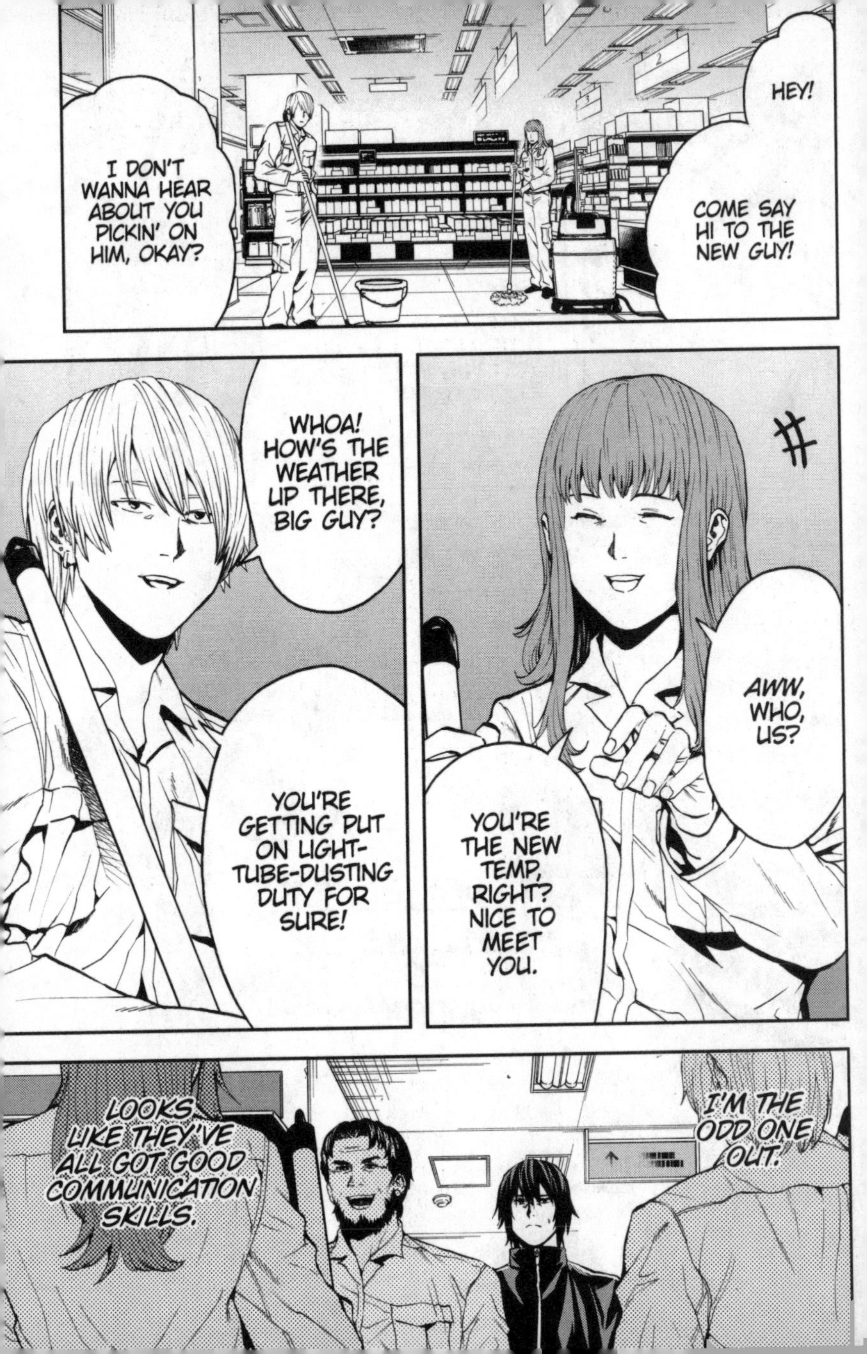
HEY!
COME SAY HI TO THE NEW GUY!
I DON'T WANNA HEAR ABOUT YOU PICKIN' ON HIM, OKAY?
AWW, WHO, US?
YOU'RE THE NEW TEMP, RIGHT? NICE TO MEET YOU.
WHOA! HOW'S THE WEATHER UP THERE, BIG GUY?
YOU'RE GETTING PUT ON LIGHT-TUBE-DUSTING DUTY FOR SURE!
I'M THE ODD ONE OUT.
LOOKS LIKE THEY'VE ALL GOT GOOD COMMUNICATION SKILLS.

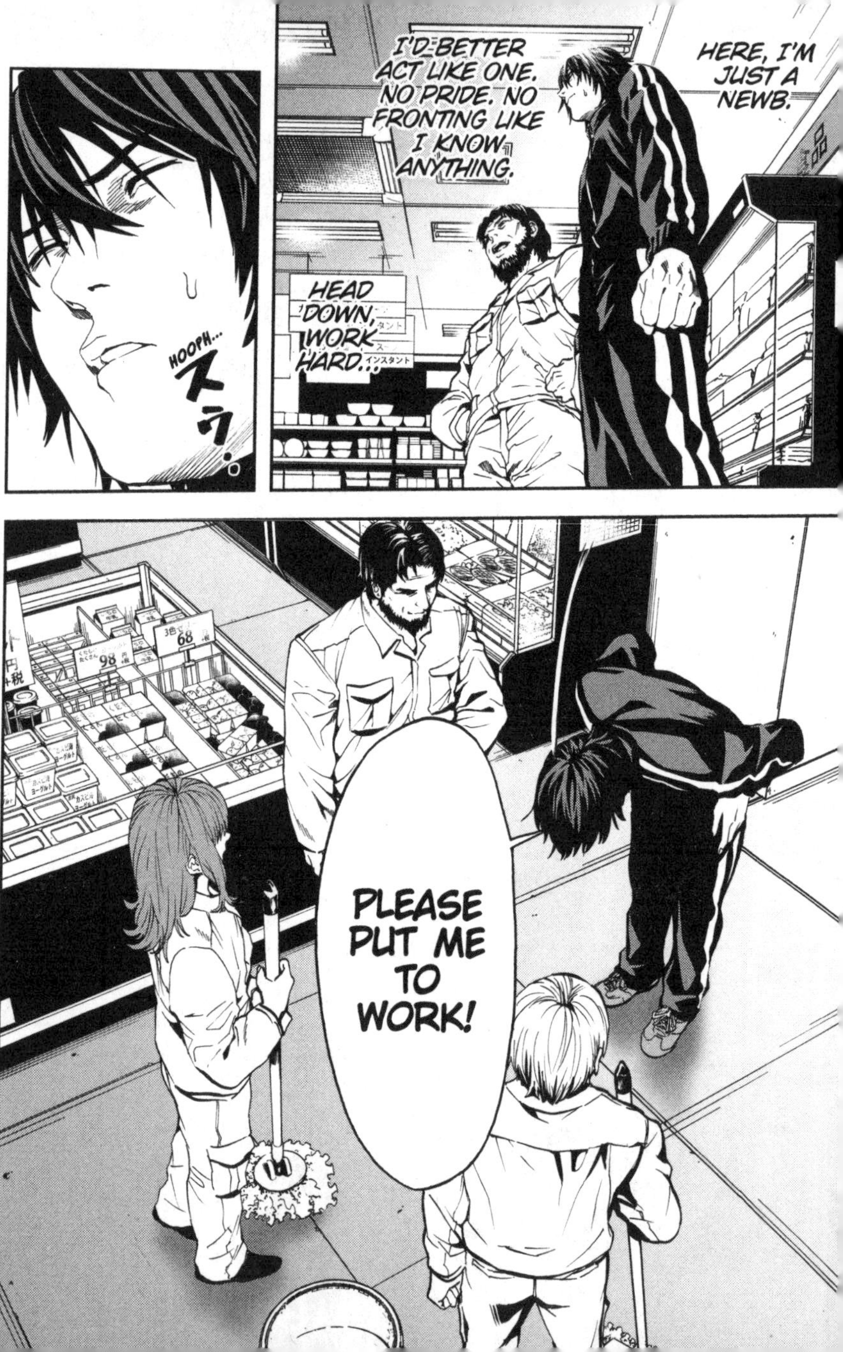
HERE, I'M JUST A NEWB.
I'D BETTER ACT LIKE ONE. NO PRIDE. NO FRONTING LIKE I KNOW ANYTHING.
HEAD DOWN, WORK HARD...
HOOPH...
スゥ
PLEASE PUT ME TO WORK!

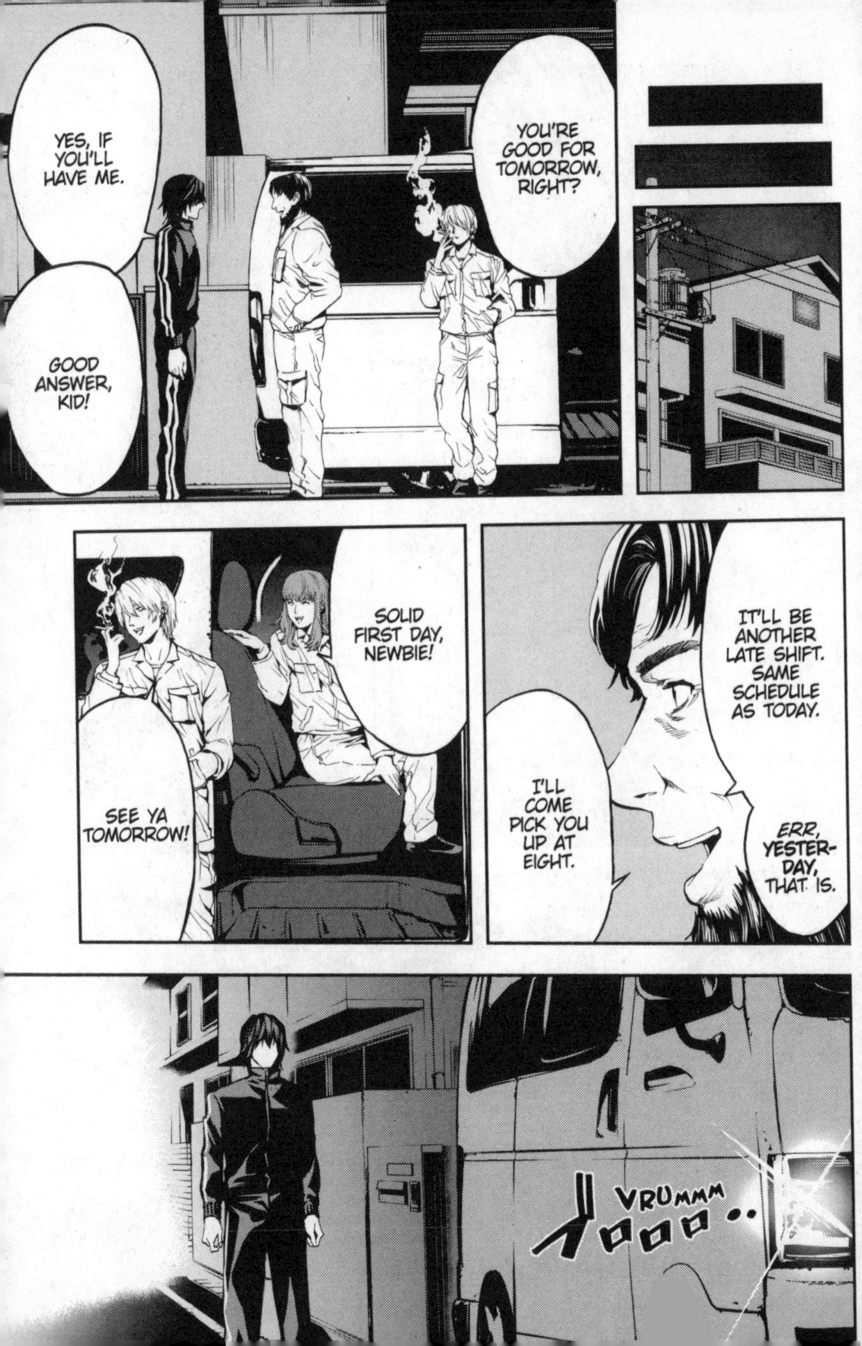
YOU'RE GOOD FOR TOMORROW, RIGHT?
YES, IF YOU'LL HAVE ME.
GOOD ANSWER, KID!
IT'LL BE ANOTHER LATE SHIFT. SAME SCHEDULE AS TODAY.
ERR, YESTER-DAY, THAT IS.
I'LL COME PICK YOU UP AT EIGHT.
SOLID FIRST DAY, NEWBIE!
SEE YA TOMORROW!
VRUMMM ..

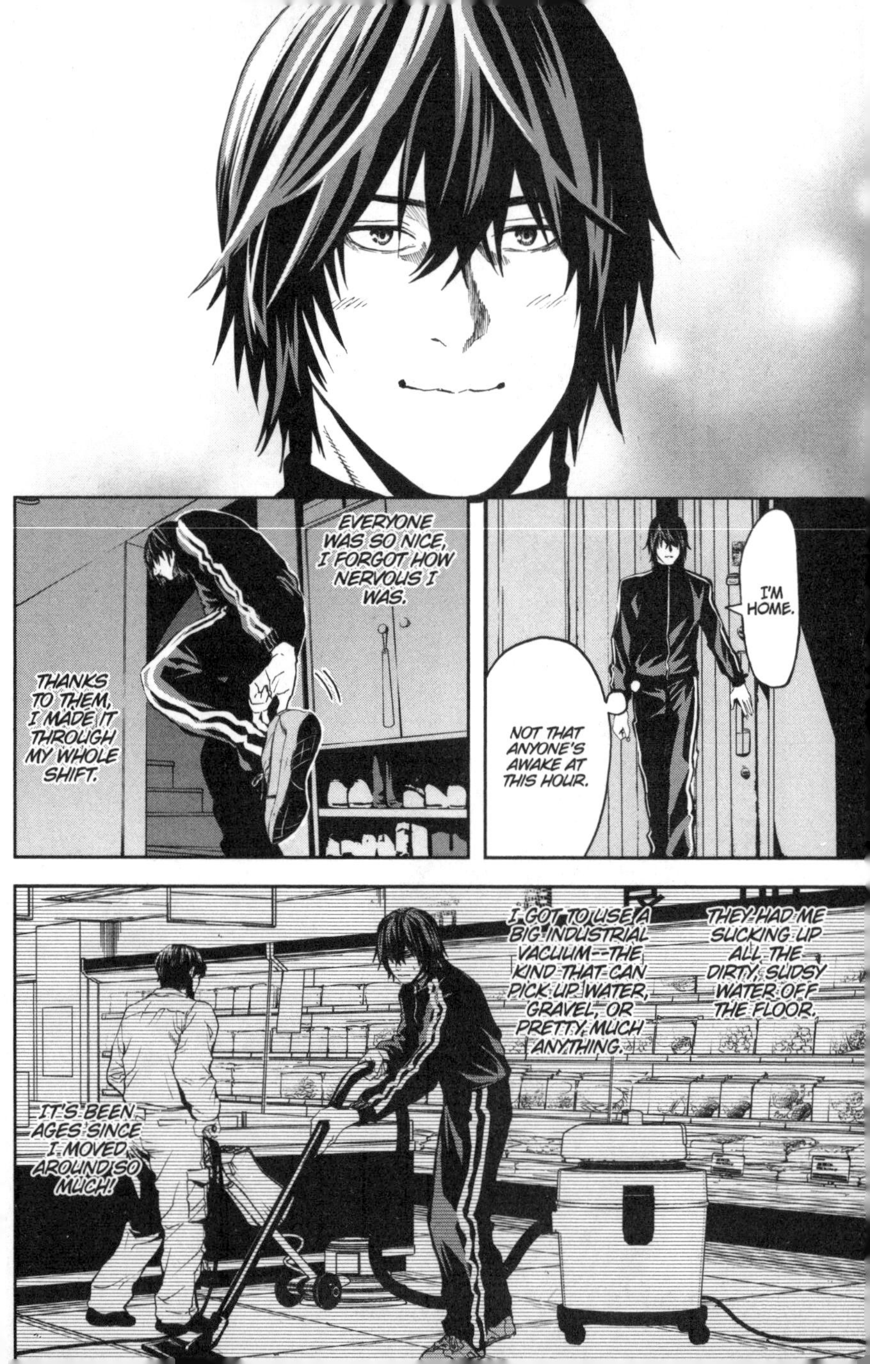
I'M HOME.
NOT THAT ANYONE'S AWAKE AT THIS HOUR.
EVERYONE WAS SO NICE, I FORGOT HOW NERVOUS I WAS.
THANKS TO THEM, I MADE IT THROUGH MY WHOLE SHIFT.
THEY HAD ME SUCKING UP ALL THE DIRTY, SUDSY WATER OFF THE FLOOR.
I GOT TO USE A BIG INDUSTRIAL VACUUM--THE KIND THAT CAN PICK UP WATER, GRAVEL, OR PRETTY MUCH ANYTHING.
IT'S BEEN AGES SINCE I MOVED AROUND SO MUCH!

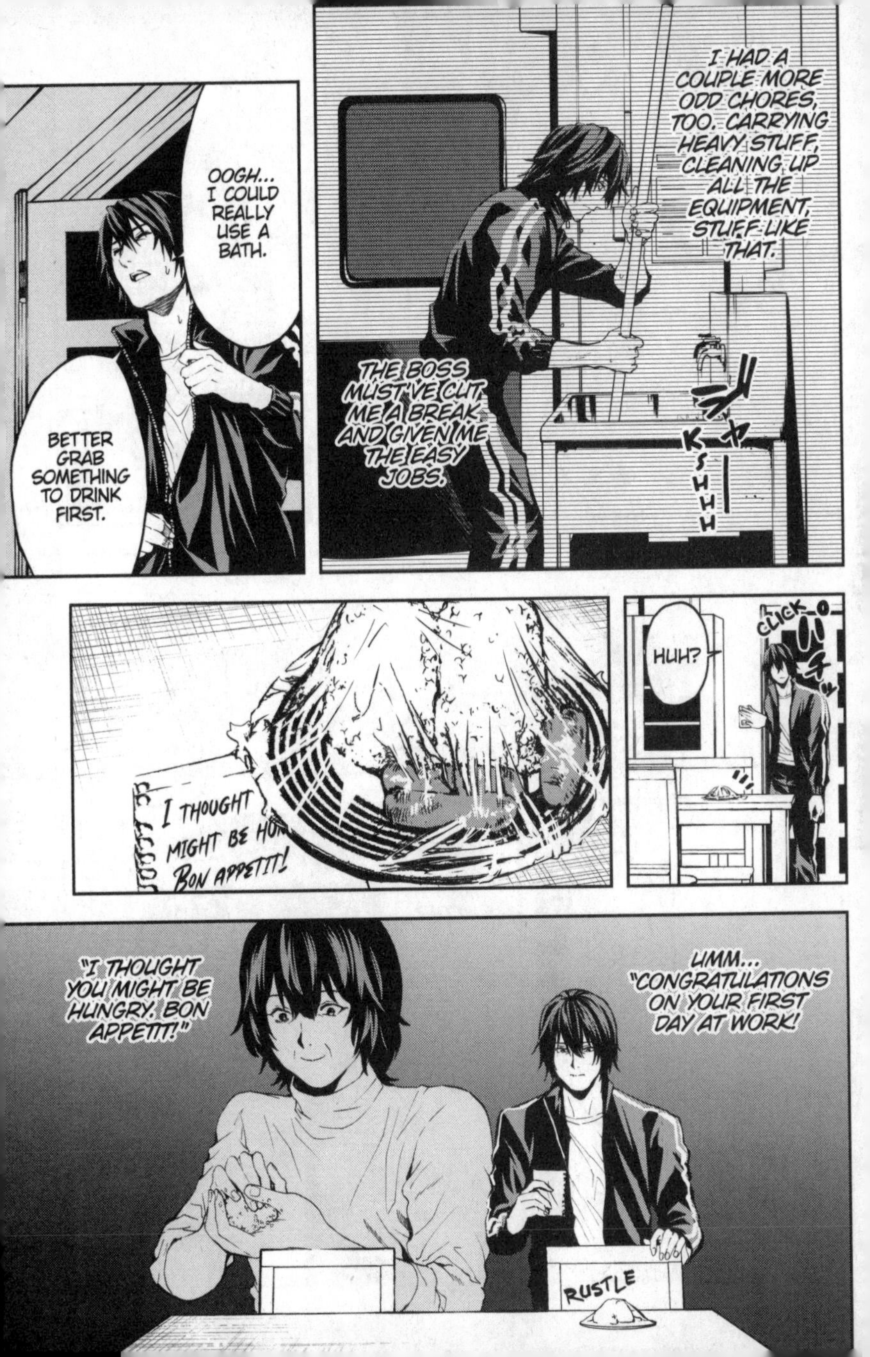

I HAD A COUPLE MORE ODD CHORES, TOO. CARRYING HEAVY STUFF, CLEANING UP ALL THE EQUIPMENT, STUFF LIKE THAT.
THE BOSS MUST'VE CUT ME A BREAK AND GIVEN ME THE EASY JOBS.
KSHHH
OOGH... I COULD REALLY USE A BATH.
BETTER GRAB SOMETHING TO DRINK FIRST.
CLICK
HUH?
I THOUGHT
MIGHT BE
BON APPETIT!
UMM... "CONGRATULATIONS ON YOUR FIRST DAY AT WORK!
"I THOUGHT YOU MIGHT BE HUNGRY. BON APPETIT!"
RUSTLE

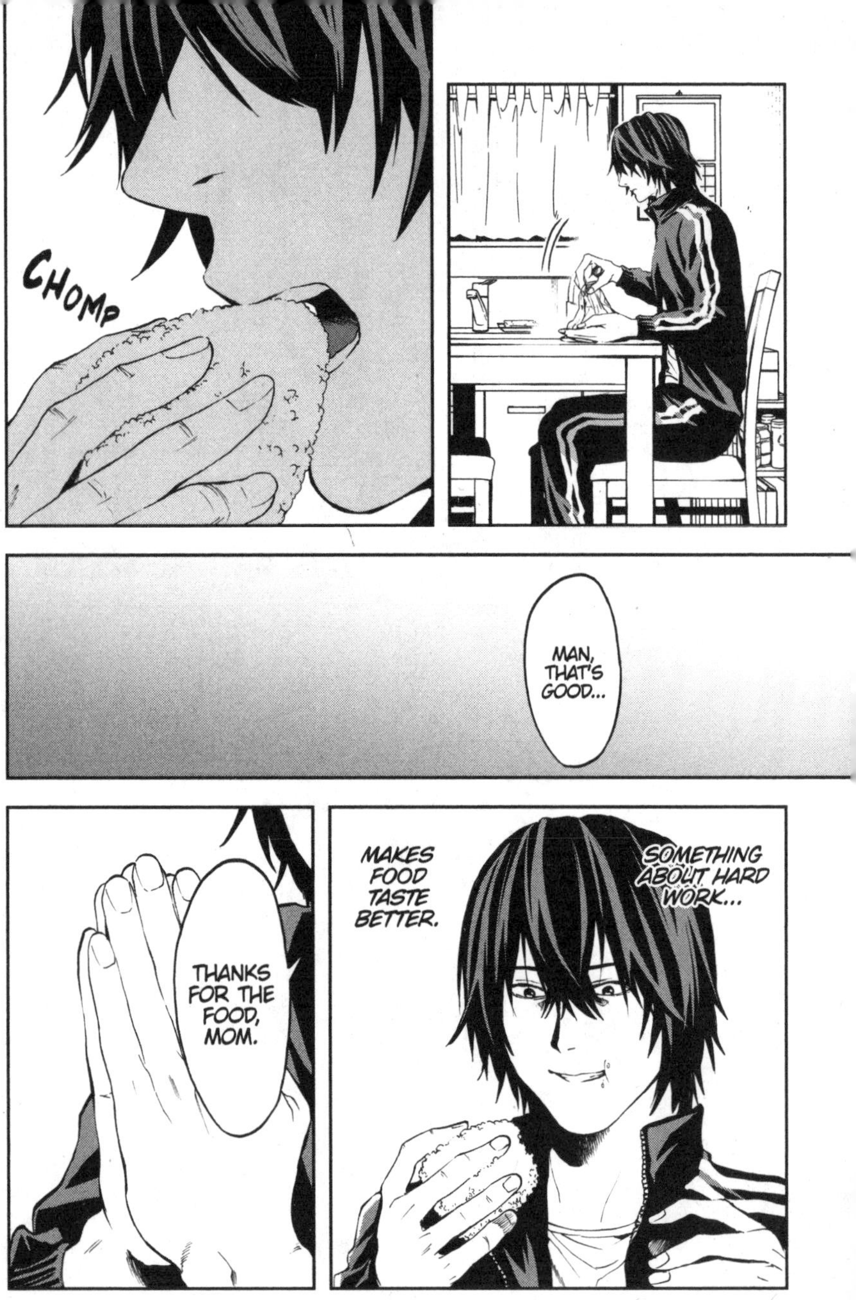
CHOMP
MAN, THAT'S GOOD...
SOMETHING ABOUT HARD WORK...
MAKES FOOD TASTE BETTER.
THANKS FOR THE FOOD, MOM.

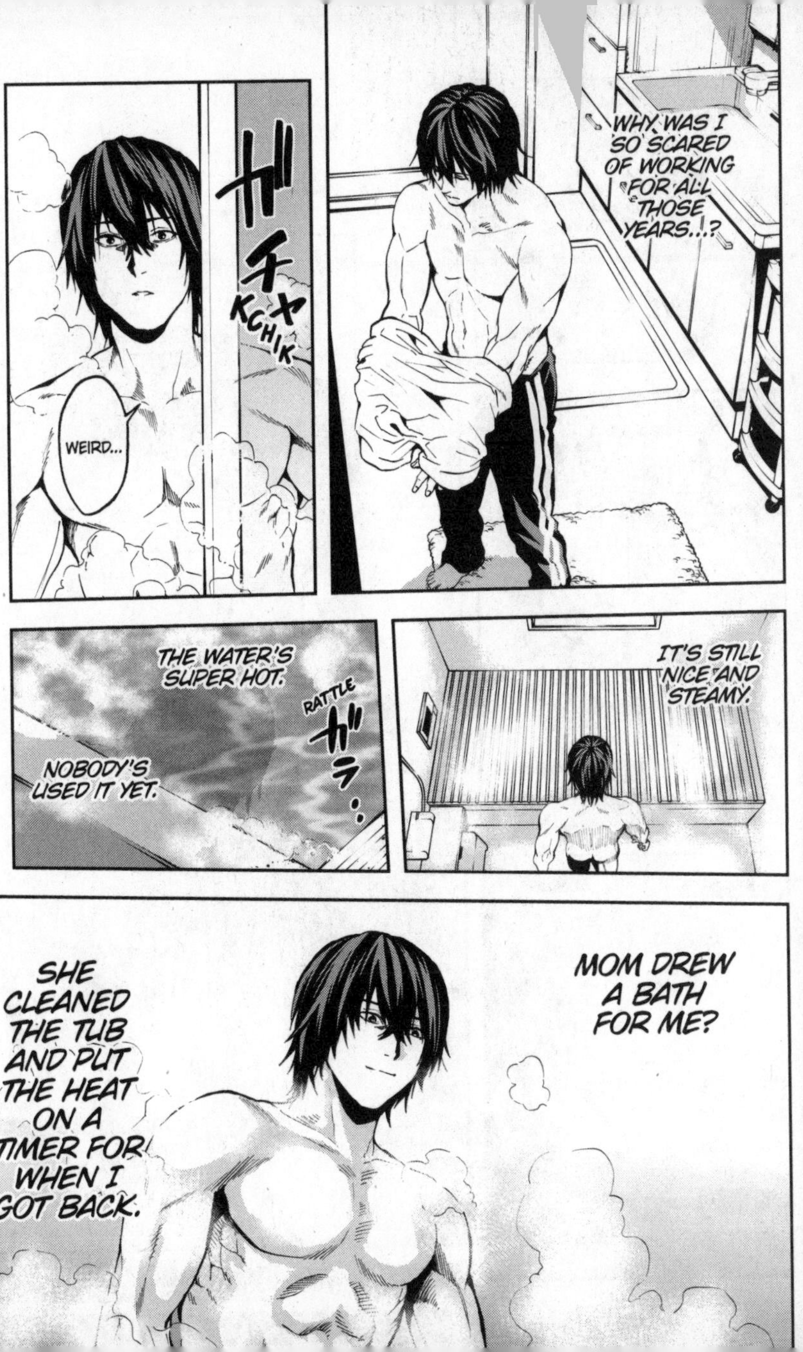
WHY WAS I SO SCARED OF WORKING FOR ALL THOSE YEARS...?
ガチャ
KCHIK
WEIRD...
IT'S STILL NICE AND STEAMY.
RATTLE
ガラ..
THE WATER'S SUPER HOT.
NOBODY'S USED IT YET.
MOM DREW A BATH FOR ME?
SHE CLEANED THE TUB AND PUT THE HEAT ON A TIMER FOR WHEN I GOT BACK.

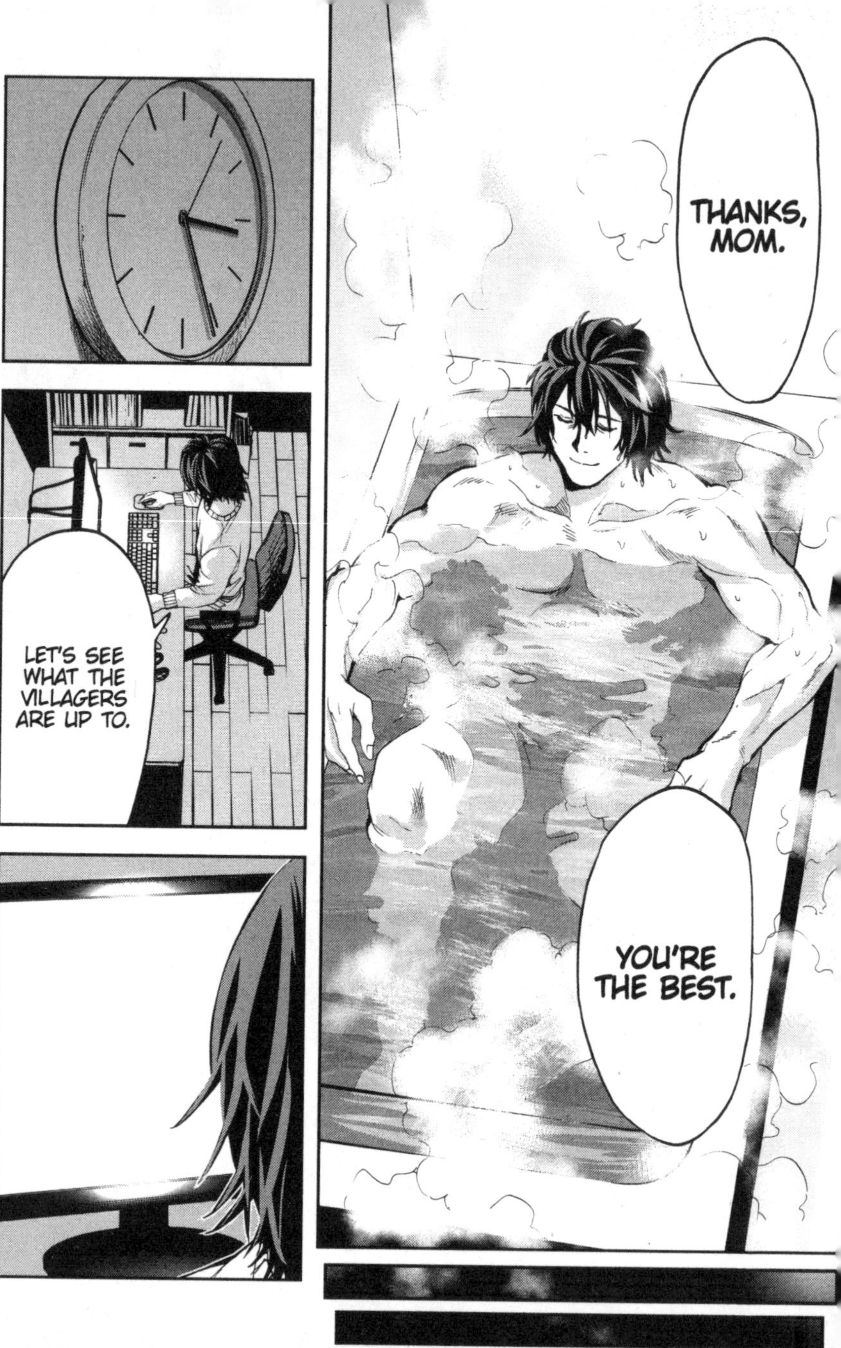
THANKS, MOM.
YOU'RE THE BEST.
LET'S SEE WHAT THE VILLAGERS ARE UP TO.

FIGURES.

EVERYONE'S FAST ASLEEP.

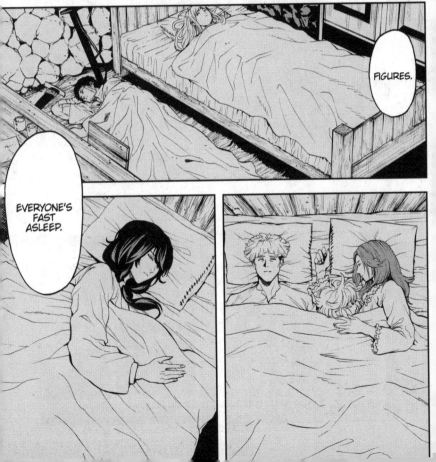

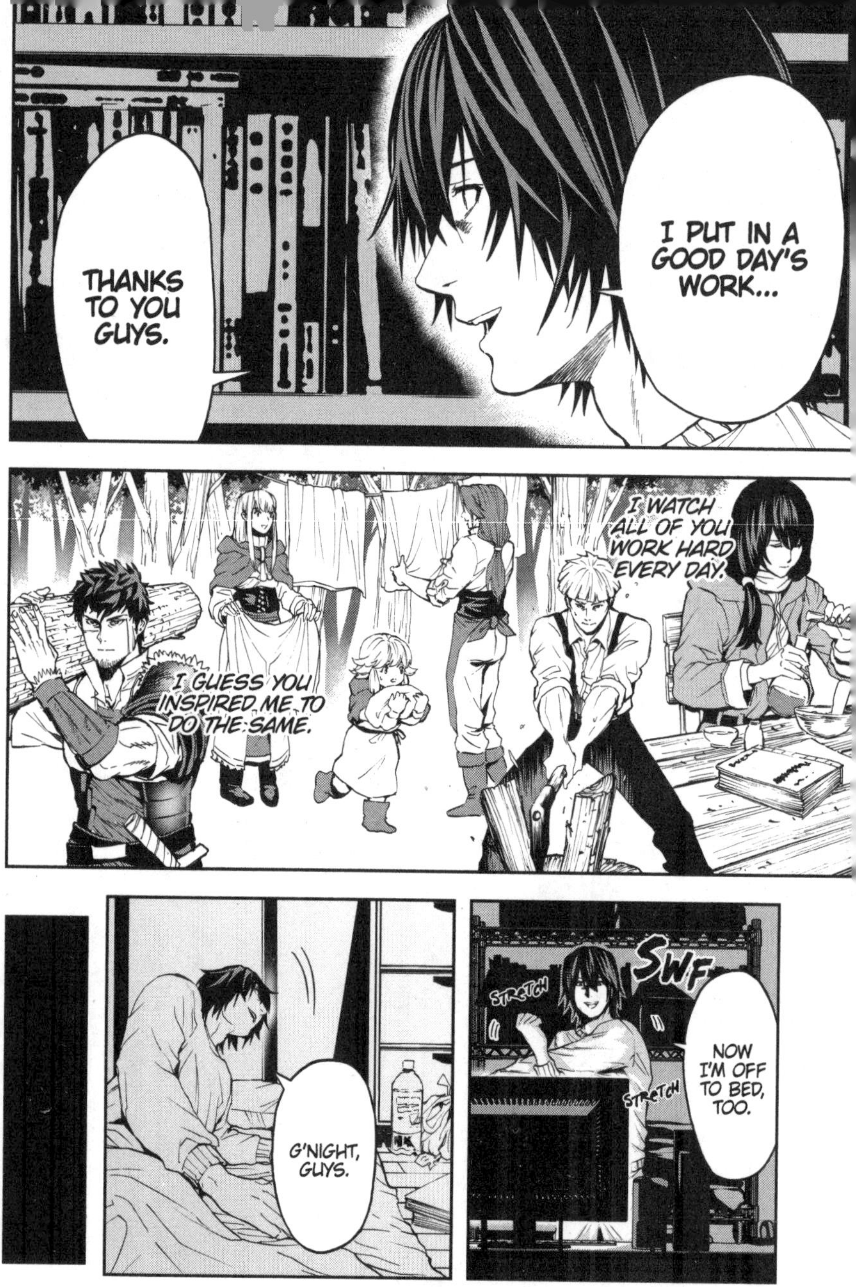
I PUT IN A GOOD DAY'S WORK...
THANKS TO YOU GUYS.
I WATCH ALL OF YOU WORK HARD EVERY DAY.
I GUESS YOU INSPIRED ME TO DO THE SAME.
SWF
STRETCH
STRETCH
NOW I'M OFF TO BED, TOO.
G'NIGHT, GUYS.

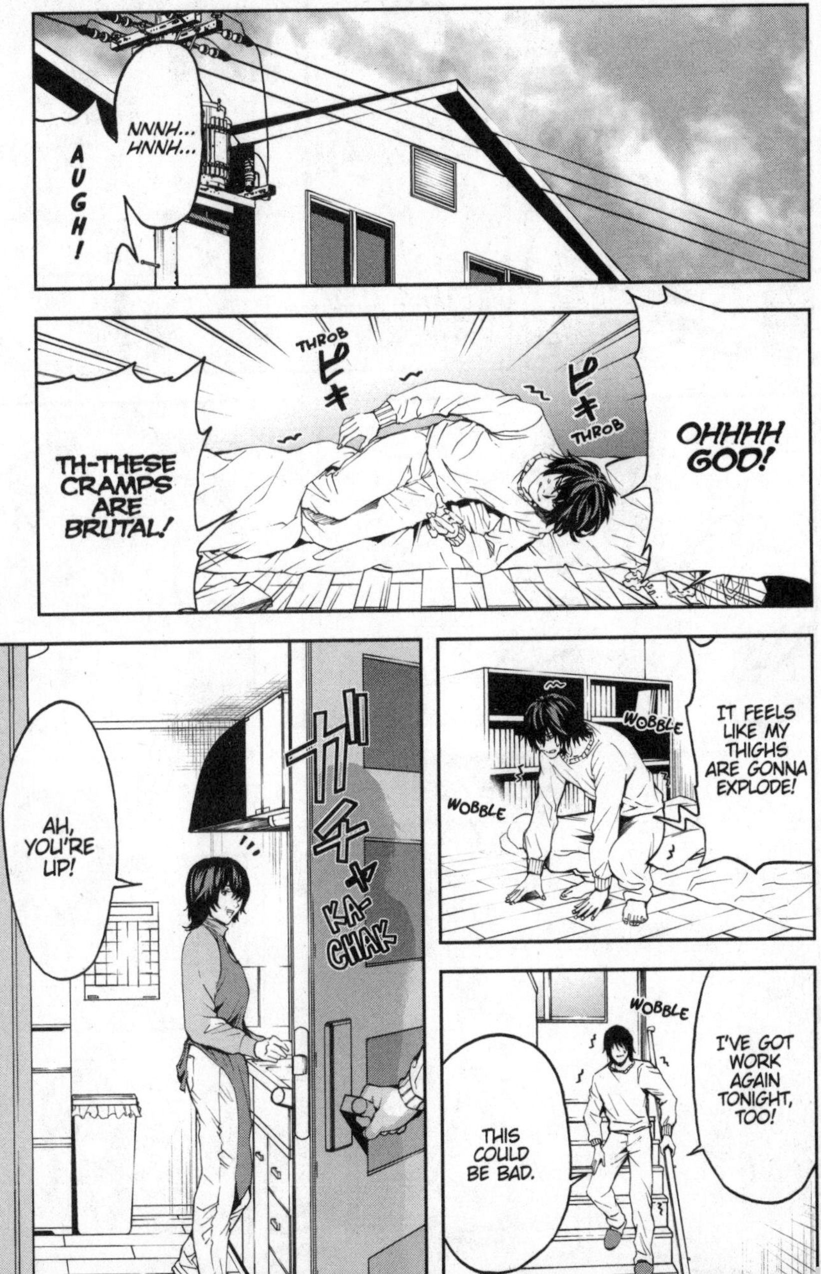
NNNH... HNNH...
AUGH!
OHHHH GOD!
ピキ
THROB
ピキ
THROB
TH-THESE CRAMPS ARE BRUTAL!
IT FEELS LIKE MY THIGHS ARE GONNA EXPLODE!
WOBBLE
WOBBLE
I'VE GOT WORK AGAIN TONIGHT, TOO!
WOBBLE
THIS COULD BE BAD.
ガチャ
KA-CHAK
AH, YOU'RE UP!

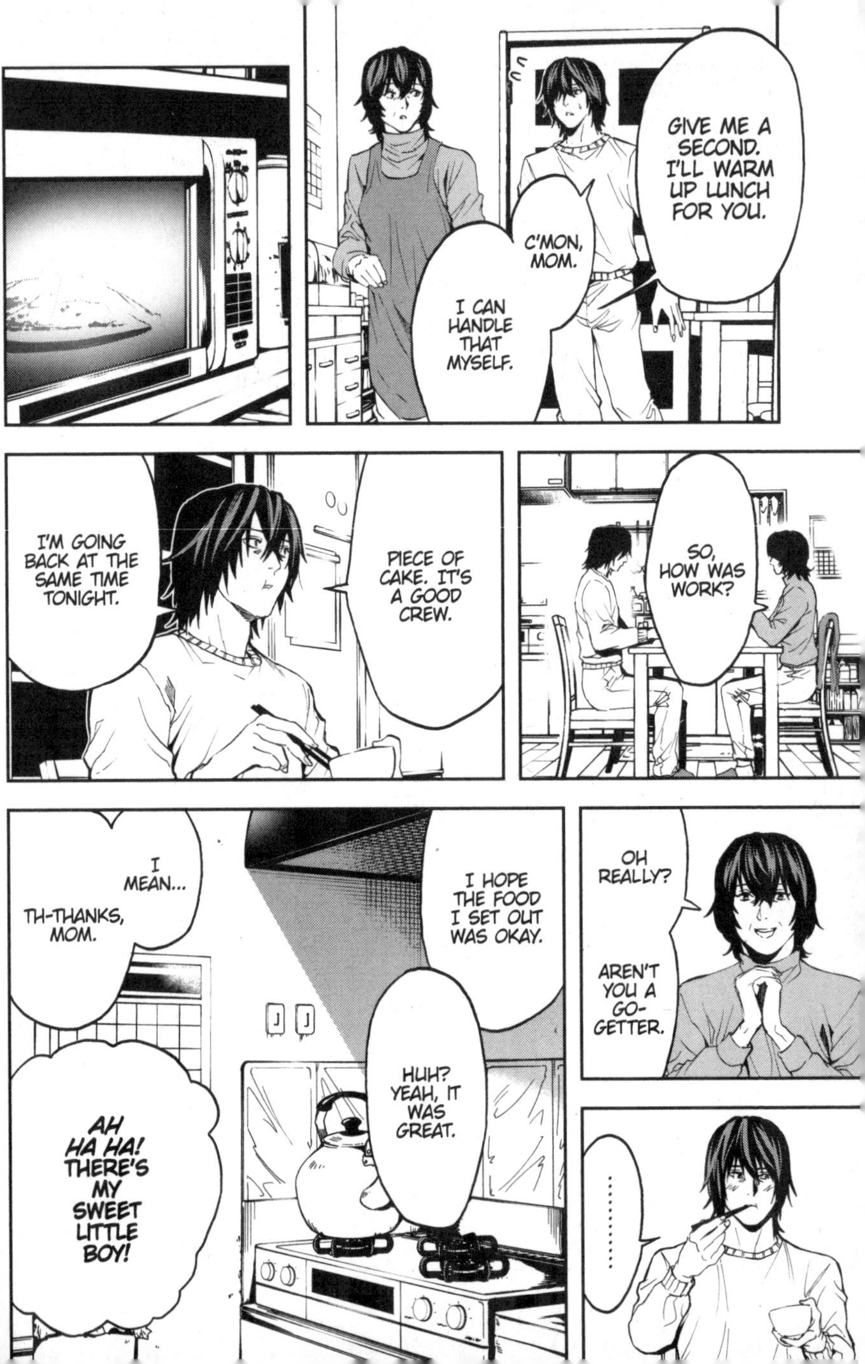
GIVE ME A SECOND. I'LL WARM UP LUNCH FOR YOU.
C'MON, MOM.
I CAN HANDLE THAT MYSELF.
SO, HOW WAS WORK?
PIECE OF CAKE. IT'S A GOOD CREW.
I'M GOING BACK AT THE SAME TIME TONIGHT.
OH REALLY?
AREN'T YOU A GO-GETTER.
......
I HOPE THE FOOD I SET OUT WAS OKAY.
HUH? YEAH, IT WAS GREAT.
I MEAN...
TH-THANKS, MOM.
AH HA HA! THERE'S MY SWEET LITTLE BOY!

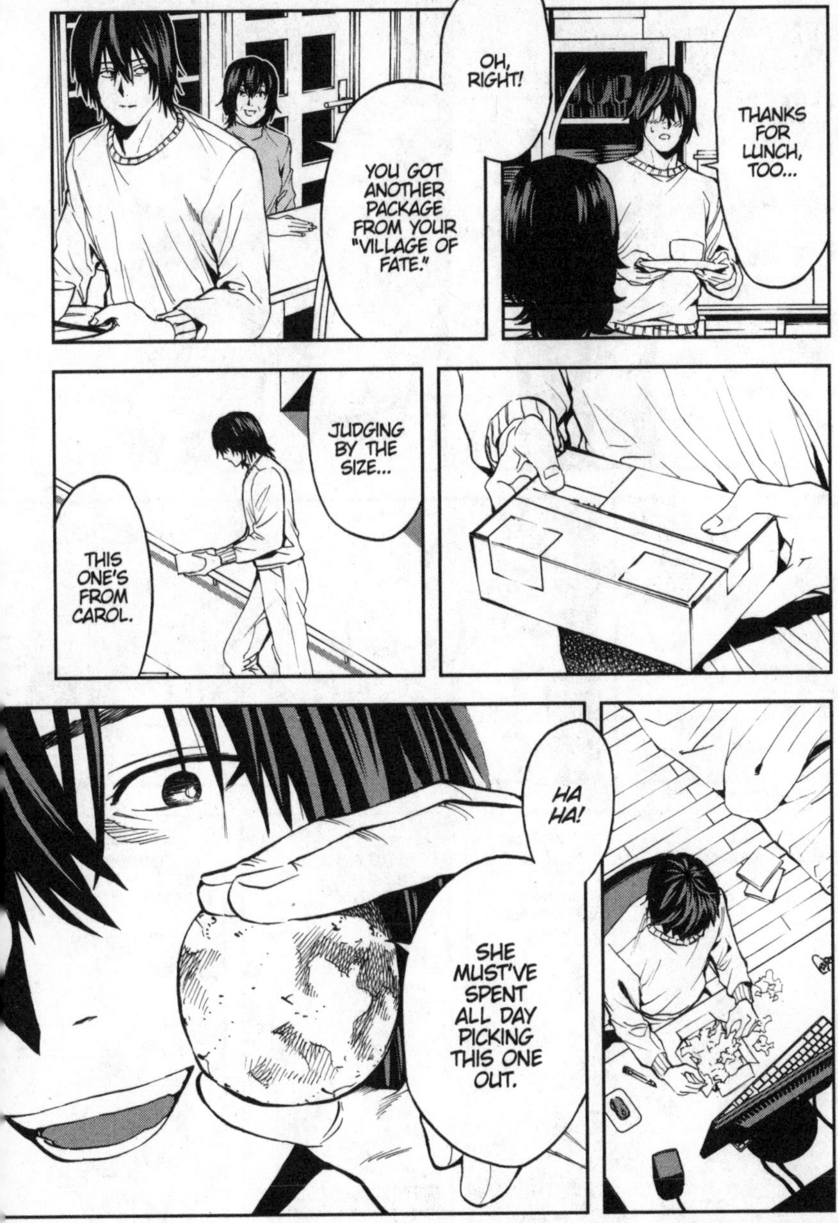
THANKS FOR LUNCH, TOO...
OH, RIGHT!
YOU GOT ANOTHER PACKAGE FROM YOUR "VILLAGE OF FATE."
JUDGING BY THE SIZE...
THIS ONE'S FROM CAROL.
HA HA!
SHE MUST'VE SPENT ALL DAY PICKING THIS ONE OUT.

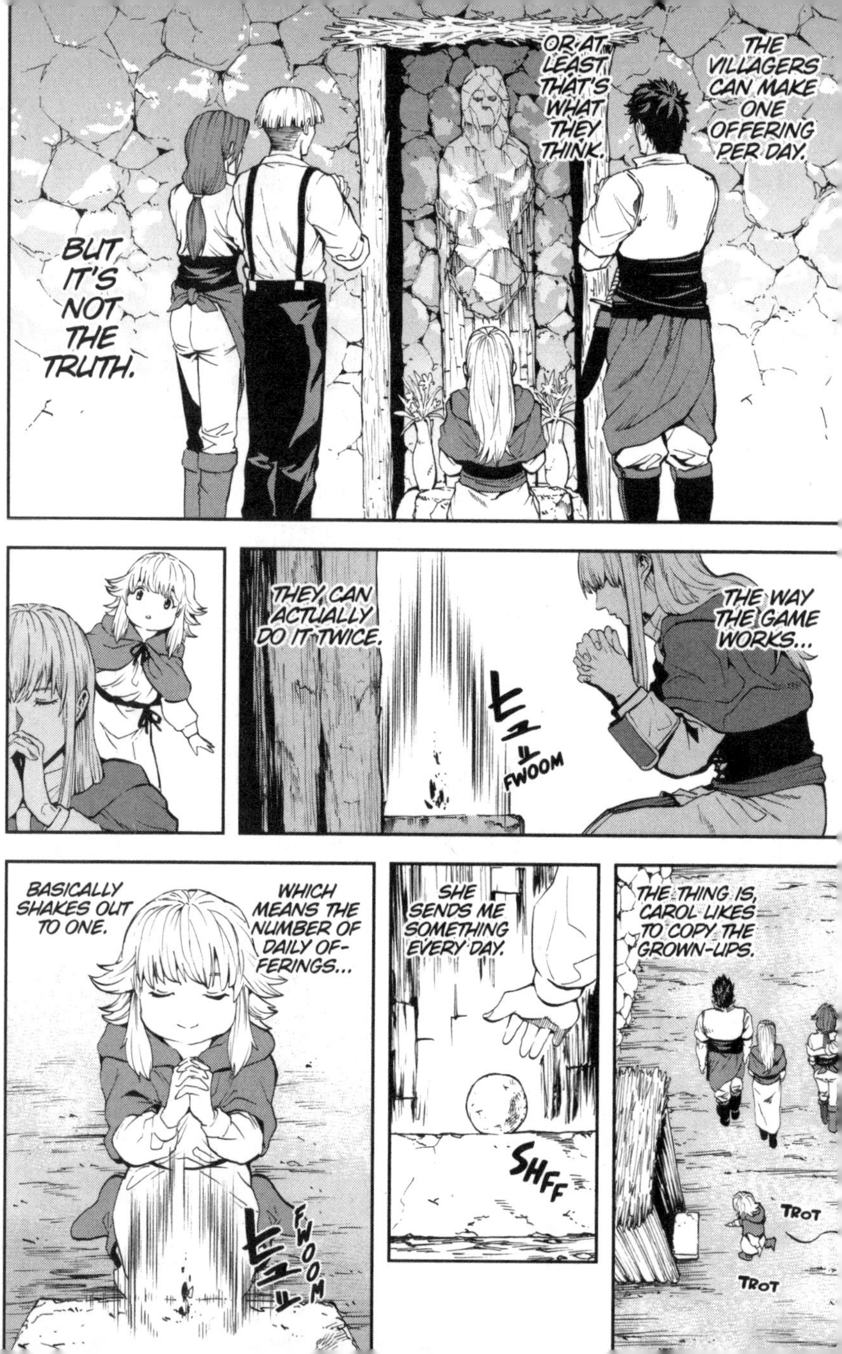
THE VILLAGERS CAN MAKE ONE OFFERING PER DAY.
OR AT LEAST THAT'S WHAT THEY THINK.
BUT IT'S NOT THE TRUTH.
THE WAY THE GAME WORKS...
THEY CAN ACTUALLY DO IT TWICE.
FWOOM
THE THING IS, CAROL LIKES TO COPY THE GROWN-UPS.
TROT
TROT
SHE SENDS ME SOMETHING EVERY DAY.
SHFF
WHICH MEANS THE NUMBER OF DAILY OF-FERINGS...
BASICALLY SHAKES OUT TO ONE.
FWOOM

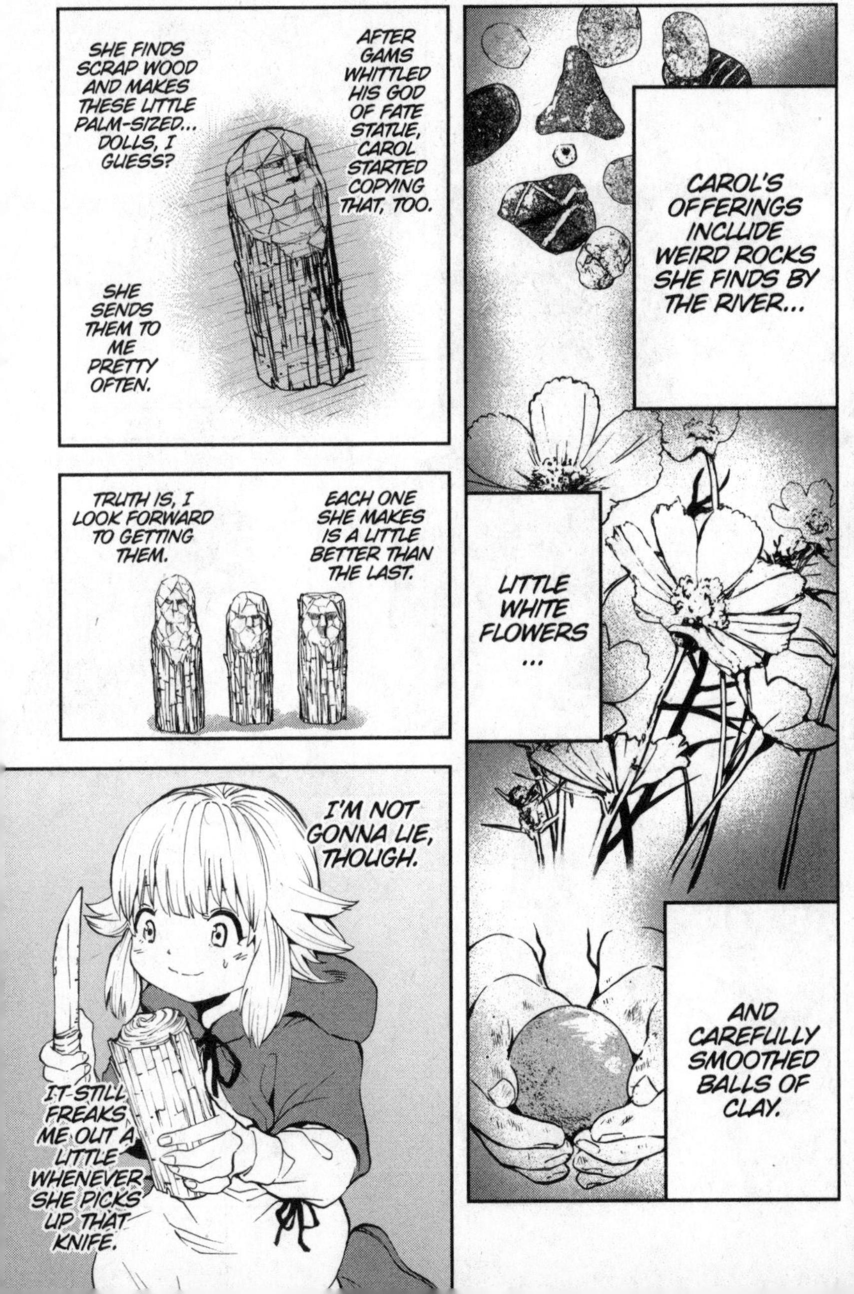
CAROL'S OFFERINGS INCLUDE WEIRD ROCKS SHE FINDS BY THE RIVER...
LITTLE WHITE FLOWERS ...
AND CAREFULLY SMOOTHED BALLS OF CLAY.
AFTER GAMS WHITTLED HIS GOD OF FATE STATUE, CAROL STARTED COPYING THAT, TOO.
SHE FINDS SCRAP WOOD AND MAKES THESE LITTLE PALM-SIZED... DOLLS, I GUESS?
SHE SENDS THEM TO ME PRETTY OFTEN.
EACH ONE SHE MAKES IS A LITTLE BETTER THAN THE LAST.
TRUTH IS, I LOOK FORWARD TO GETTING THEM.
I'M NOT GONNA LIE, THOUGH.
IT STILL FREAKS ME OUT A LITTLE WHENEVER SHE PICKS UP THAT KNIFE.

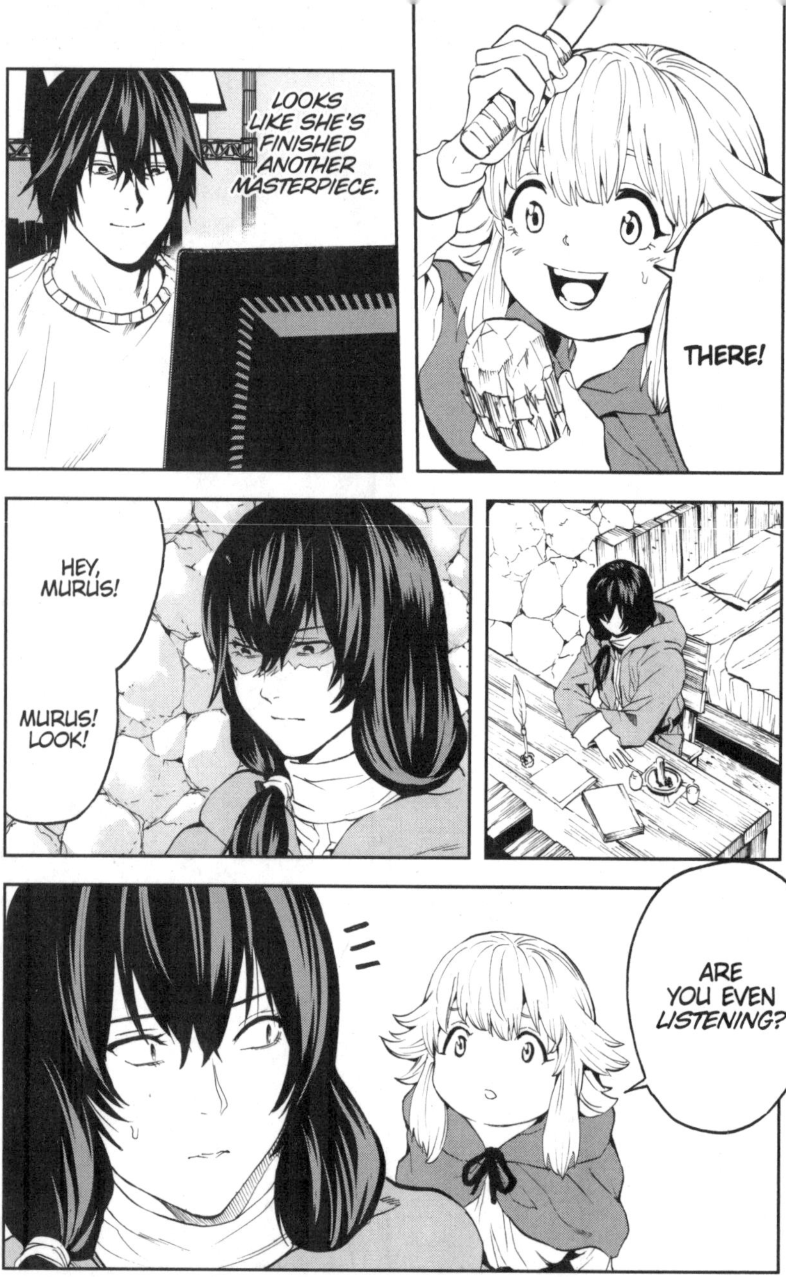
THERE!
LOOKS LIKE SHE'S FINISHED ANOTHER MASTERPIECE.
HEY, MURUS!
MURUS! LOOK!
ARE YOU EVEN LISTENING?

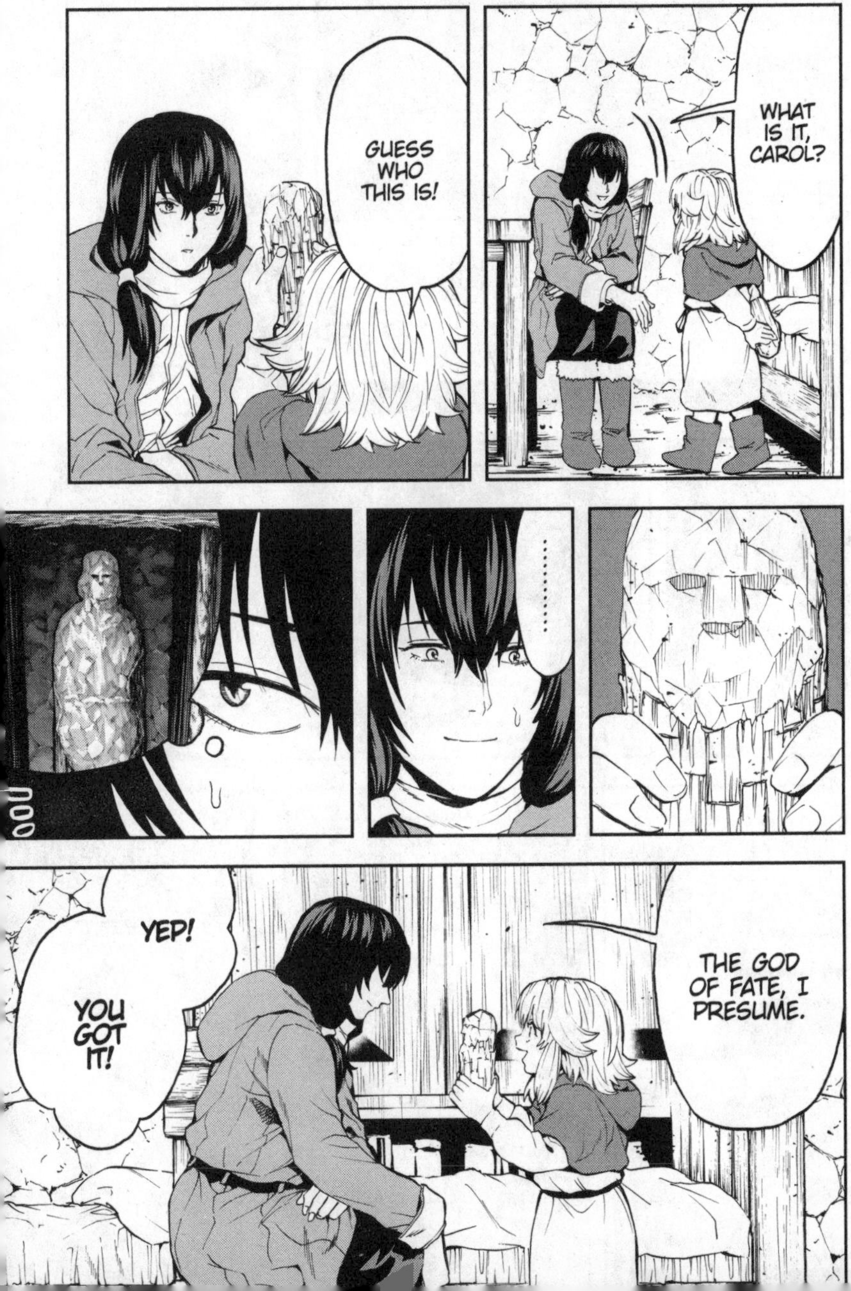
WHAT IS IT, CAROL?
GUESS WHO THIS IS!
......
THE GOD OF FATE, I PRESUME.
YEP!
YOU GOT IT!

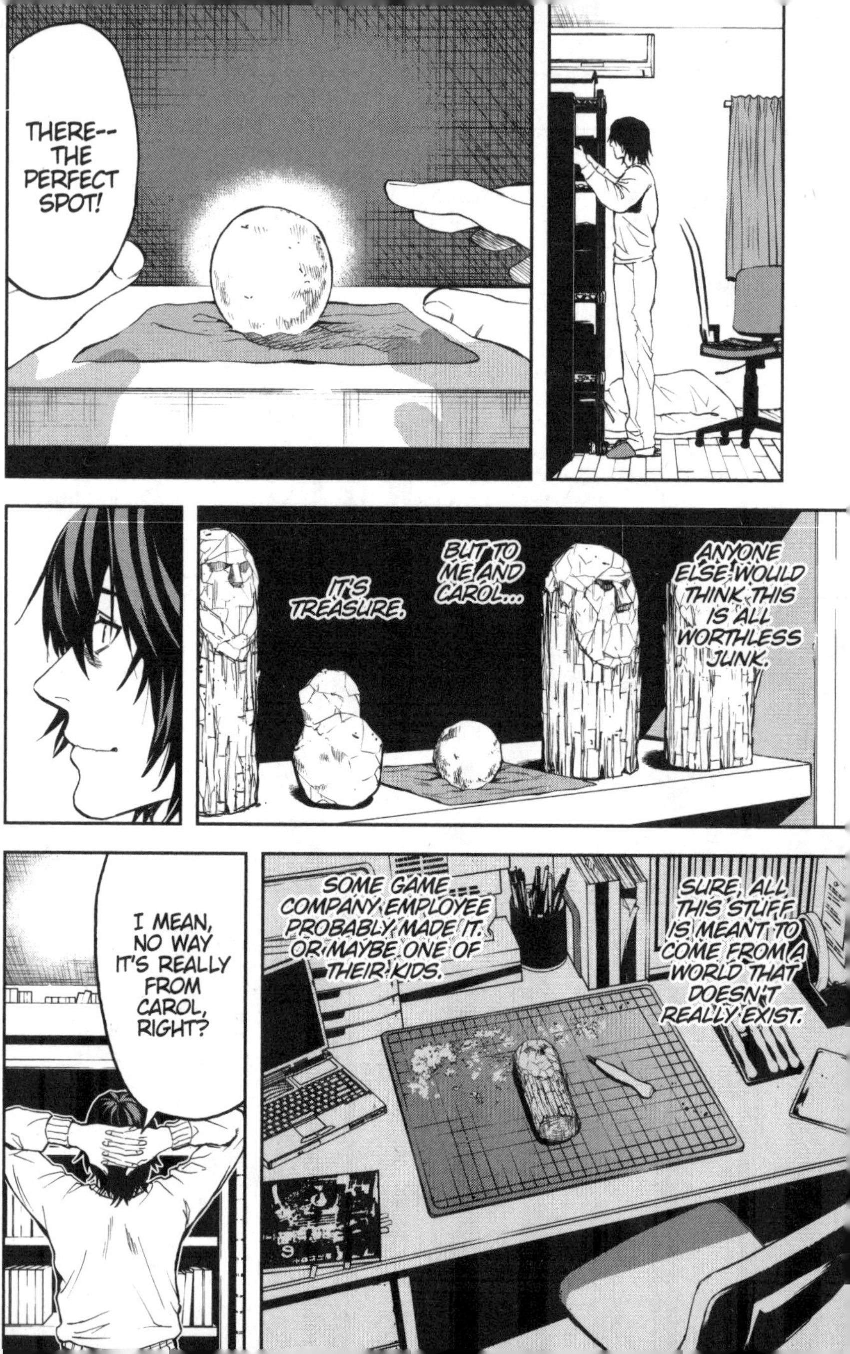
THERE-- THE PERFECT SPOT!
ANYONE ELSE WOULD THINK THIS IS ALL WORTHLESS JUNK.
BUT TO ME AND CAROL...
IT'S TREASURE.
SURE, ALL THIS STUFF IS MEANT TO COME FROM A WORLD THAT DOESN'T REALLY EXIST.
SOME GAME COMPANY EMPLOYEE PROBABLY MADE IT. OR MAYBE ONE OF THEIR KIDS.
I MEAN, NO WAY IT'S REALLY FROM CAROL, RIGHT?

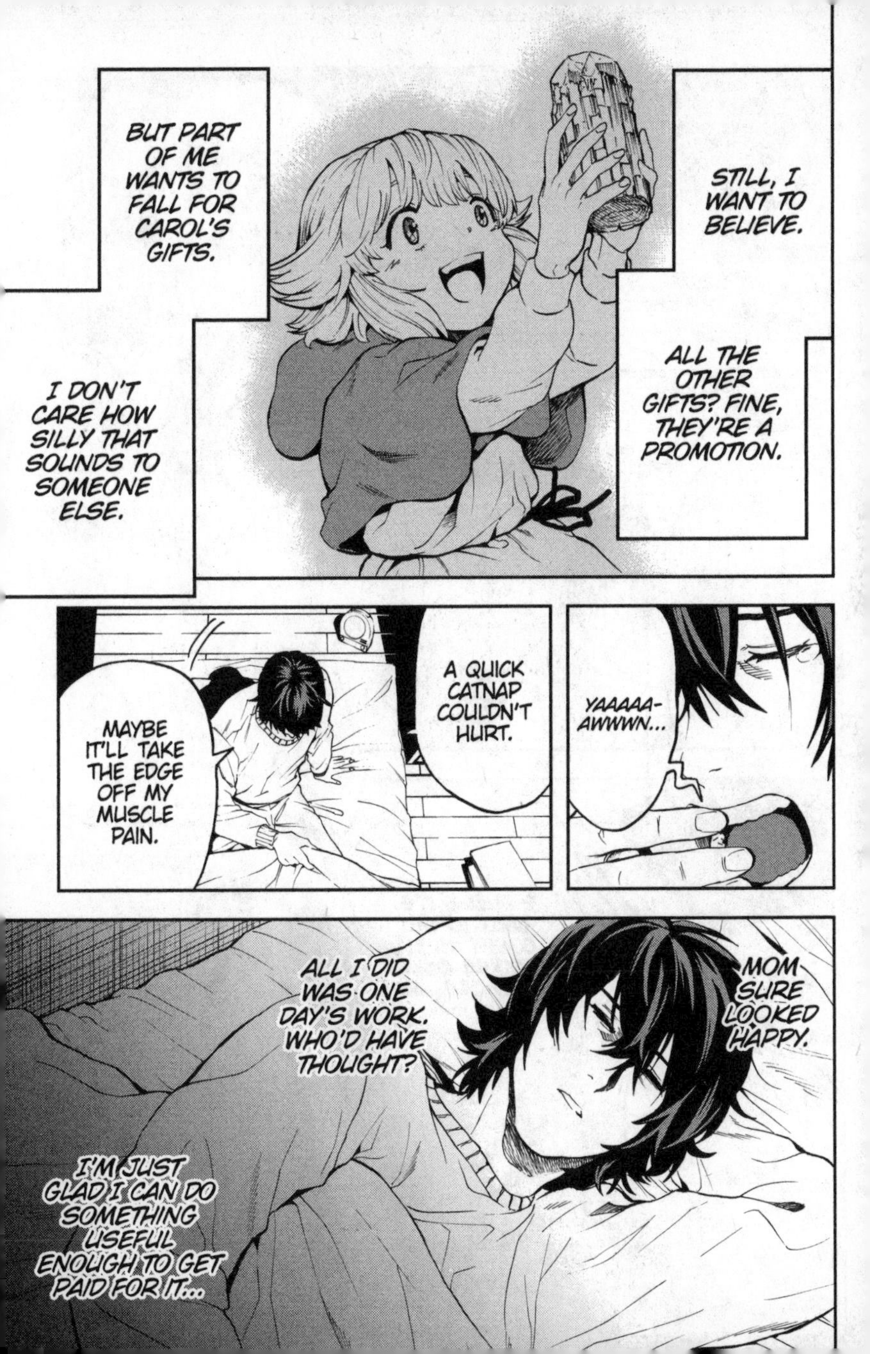
STILL, I WANT TO BELIEVE.
ALL THE OTHER GIFTS? FINE, THEY'RE A PROMOTION.
BUT PART OF ME WANTS TO FALL FOR CAROL'S GIFTS.
I DON'T CARE HOW SILLY THAT SOUNDS TO SOMEONE ELSE.
YAAAAA-AWWWN...
A QUICK CATNAP COULDN'T HURT.
MAYBE IT'LL TAKE THE EDGE OFF MY MUSCLE PAIN.
MOM SURE LOOKED HAPPY.
ALL I DID WAS ONE DAY'S WORK. WHO'D HAVE THOUGHT?
I'M JUST GLAD I CAN DO SOMETHING USEFUL ENOUGH TO GET PAID FOR IT...

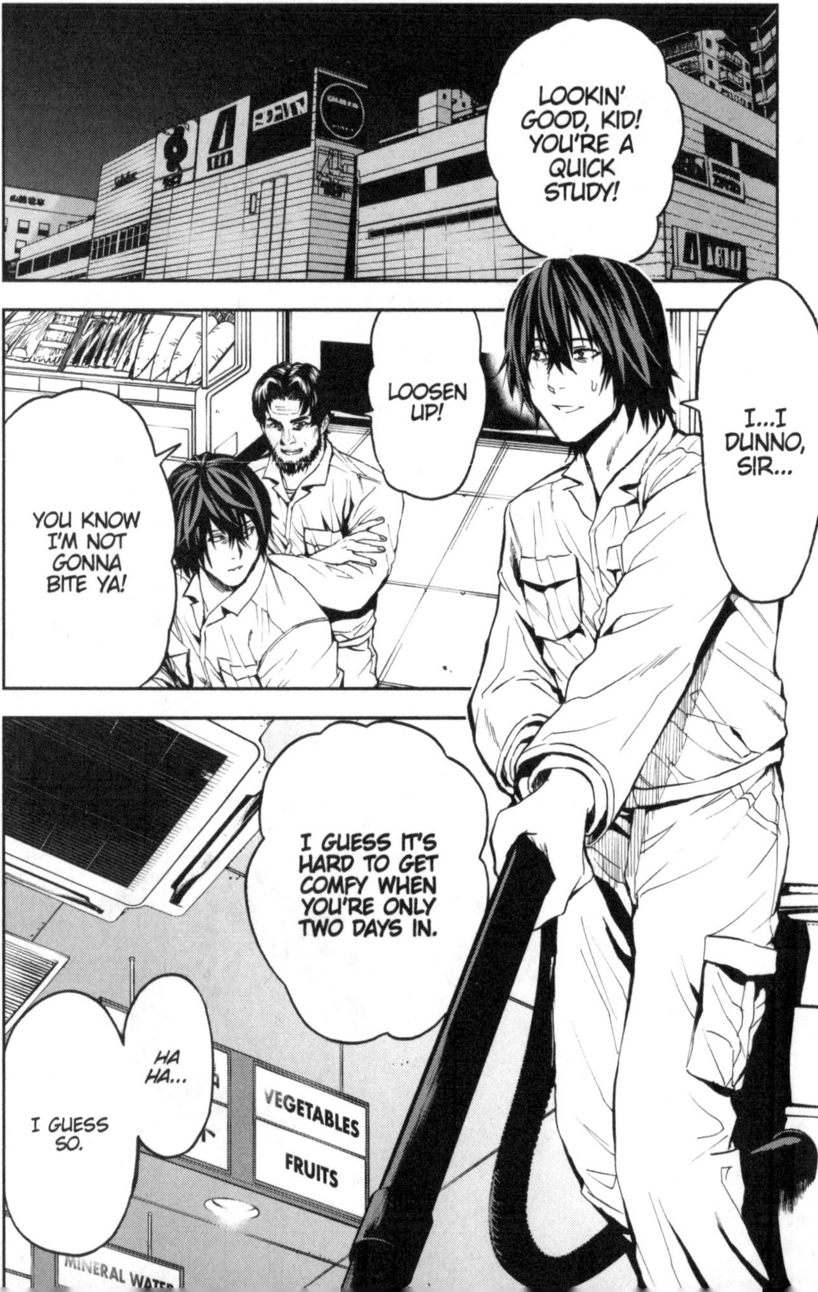
LOOKIN' GOOD, KID! YOU'RE A QUICK STUDY!
I...I DUNNO, SIR...
LOOSEN UP!
YOU KNOW I'M NOT GONNA BITE YA!
I GUESS IT'S HARD TO GET COMFY WHEN YOU'RE ONLY TWO DAYS IN.
HA HA...
I GUESS SO.
VEGETABLES
FRUITS

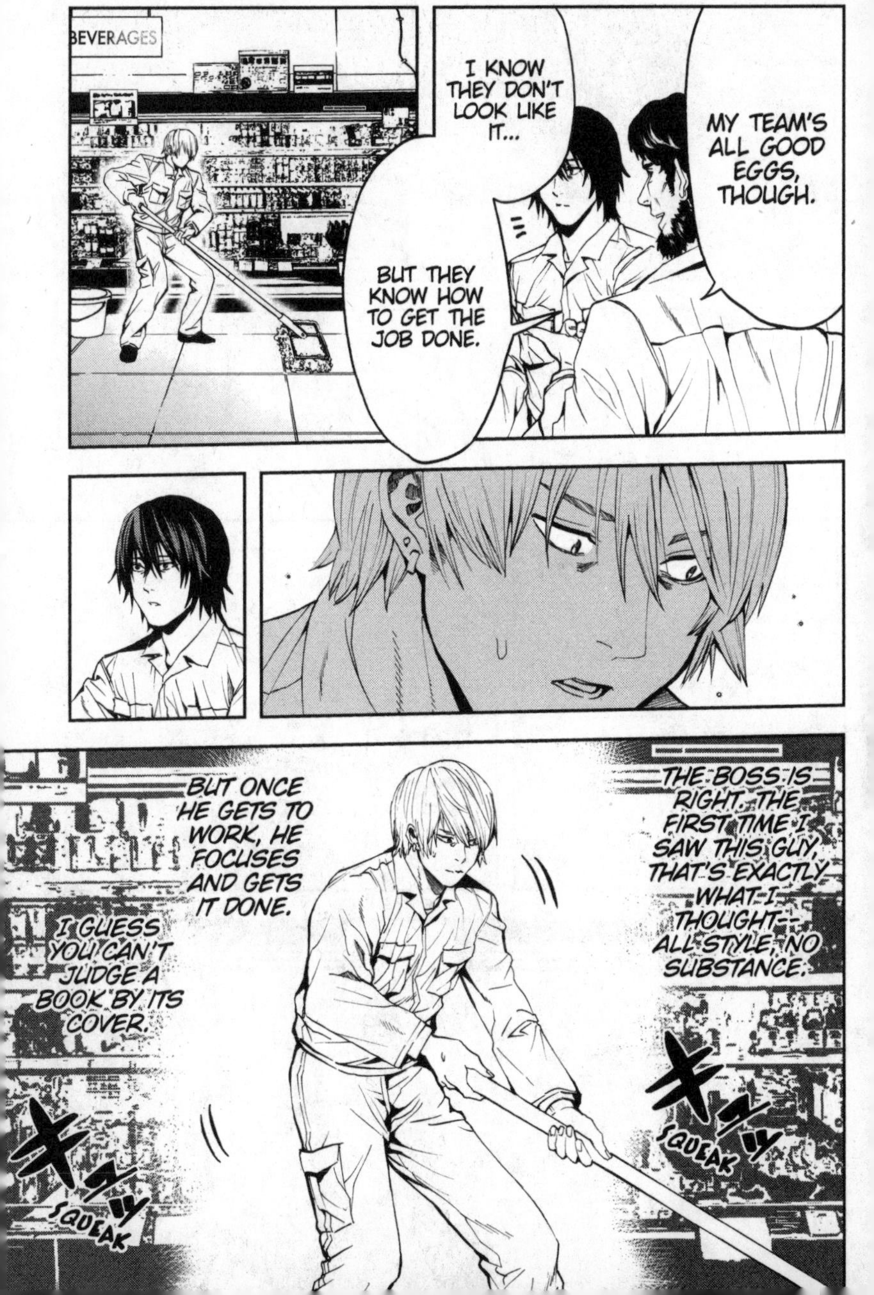
MY TEAM'S ALL GOOD EGGS, THOUGH.
I KNOW THEY DON'T LOOK LIKE IT...
BUT THEY KNOW HOW TO GET THE JOB DONE.
BEVERAGES
THE BOSS IS RIGHT. THE FIRST TIME I SAW THIS GUY, THAT'S EXACTLY WHAT I THOUGHT-- ALL STYLE, NO SUBSTANCE.
BUT ONCE HE GETS TO WORK, HE FOCUSES AND GETS IT DONE.
I GUESS YOU CAN'T JUDGE A BOOK BY ITS COVER.
SQUEAK
SQUEAK

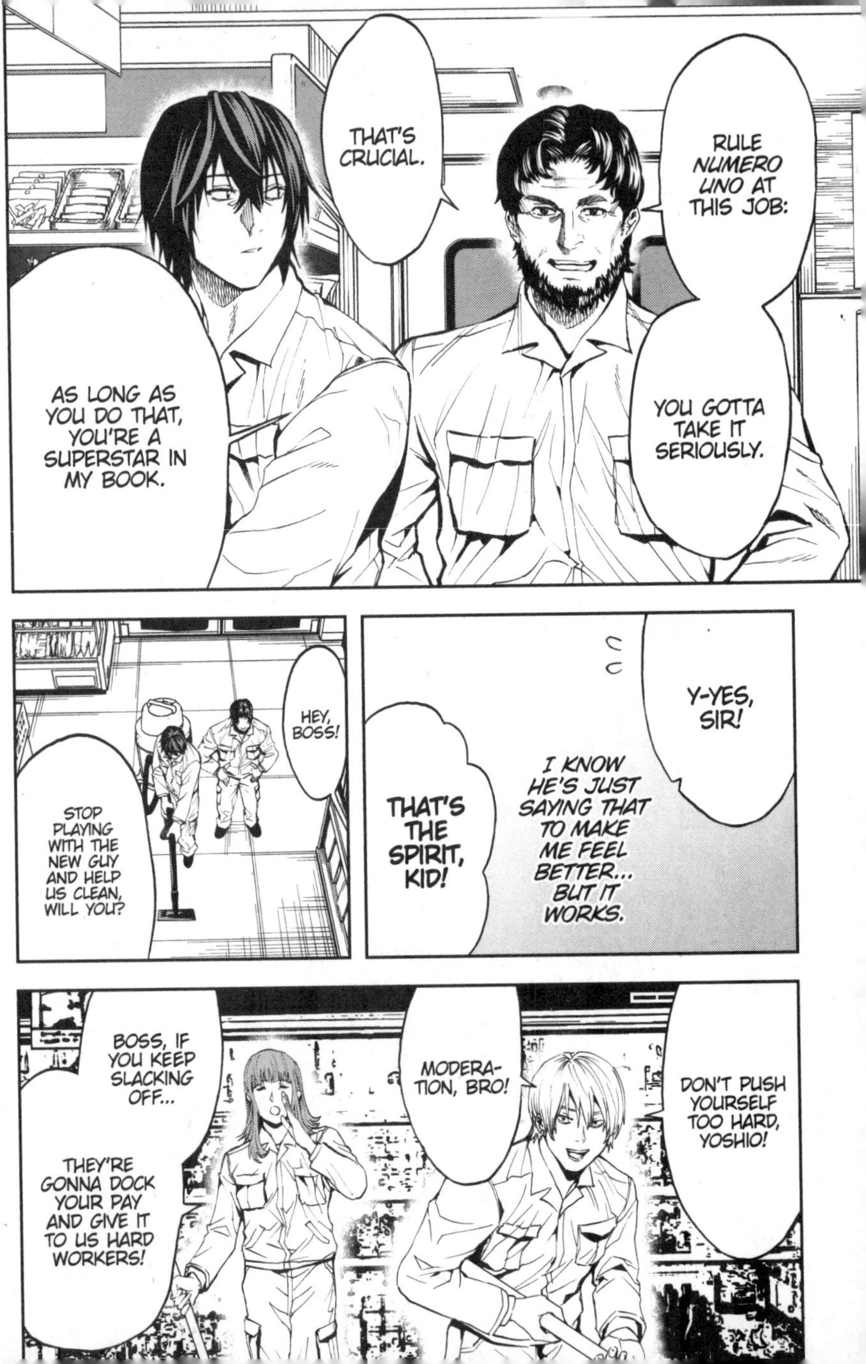
RULE NUMERO UNO AT THIS JOB:
YOU GOTTA TAKE IT SERIOUSLY.
THAT'S CRUCIAL.
AS LONG AS YOU DO THAT, YOU'RE A SUPERSTAR IN MY BOOK.
Y-YES, SIR!
I KNOW HE'S JUST SAYING THAT TO MAKE ME FEEL BETTER... BUT IT WORKS.
THAT'S THE SPIRIT, KID!
HEY, BOSS!
STOP PLAYING WITH THE NEW GUY AND HELP US CLEAN, WILL YOU?
DON'T PUSH YOURSELF TOO HARD, YOSHIO!
MODERA-TION, BRO!
BOSS, IF YOU KEEP SLACKING OFF...
THEY'RE GONNA DOCK YOUR PAY AND GIVE IT TO US HARD WORKERS!

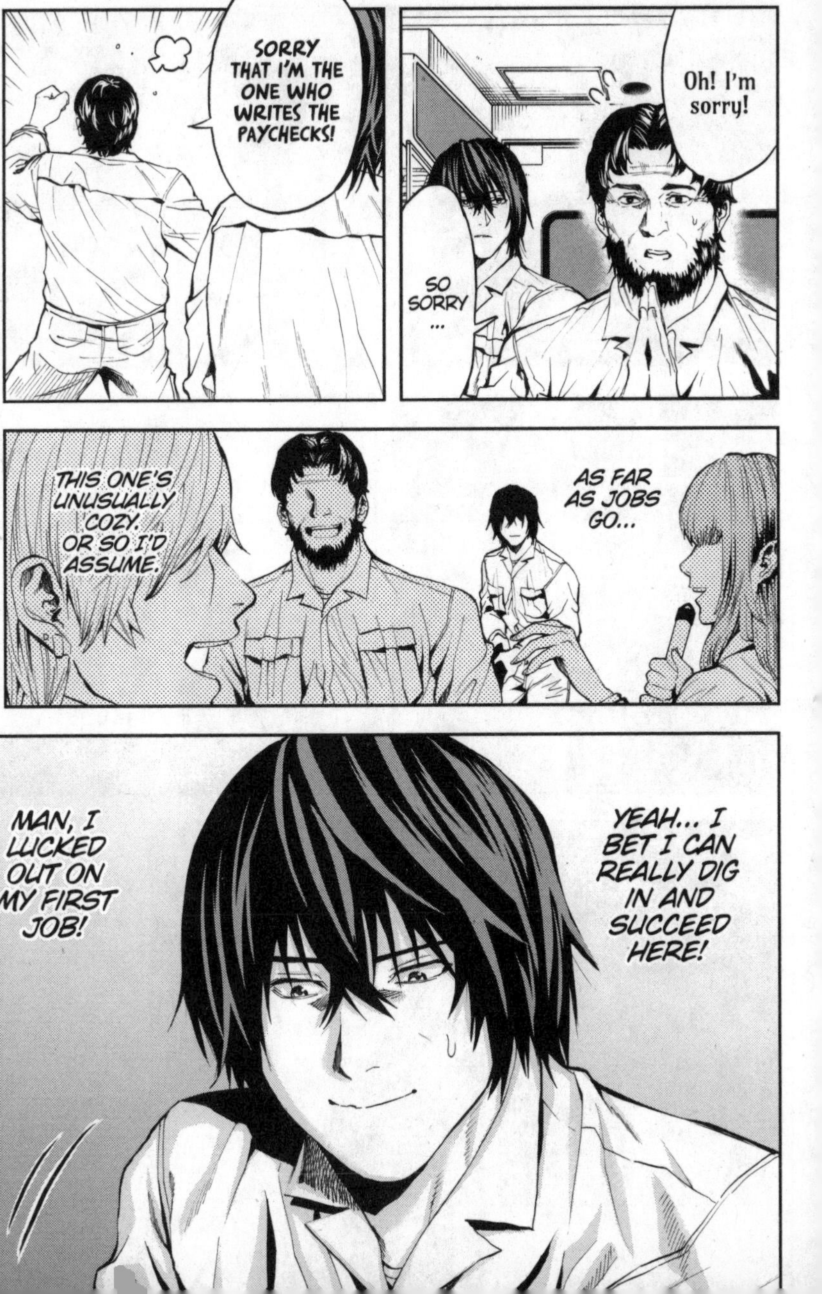
Oh! I'm sorry!
SO SORRY ...
SORRY THAT I'M THE ONE WHO WRITES THE PAYCHECKS!
AS FAR AS JOBS GO...
THIS ONE'S UNUSUALLY COZY. OR SO I'D ASSUME.
YEAH... I BET I CAN REALLY DIG IN AND SUCCEED HERE!
MAN, I LUCKED OUT ON MY FIRST JOB!

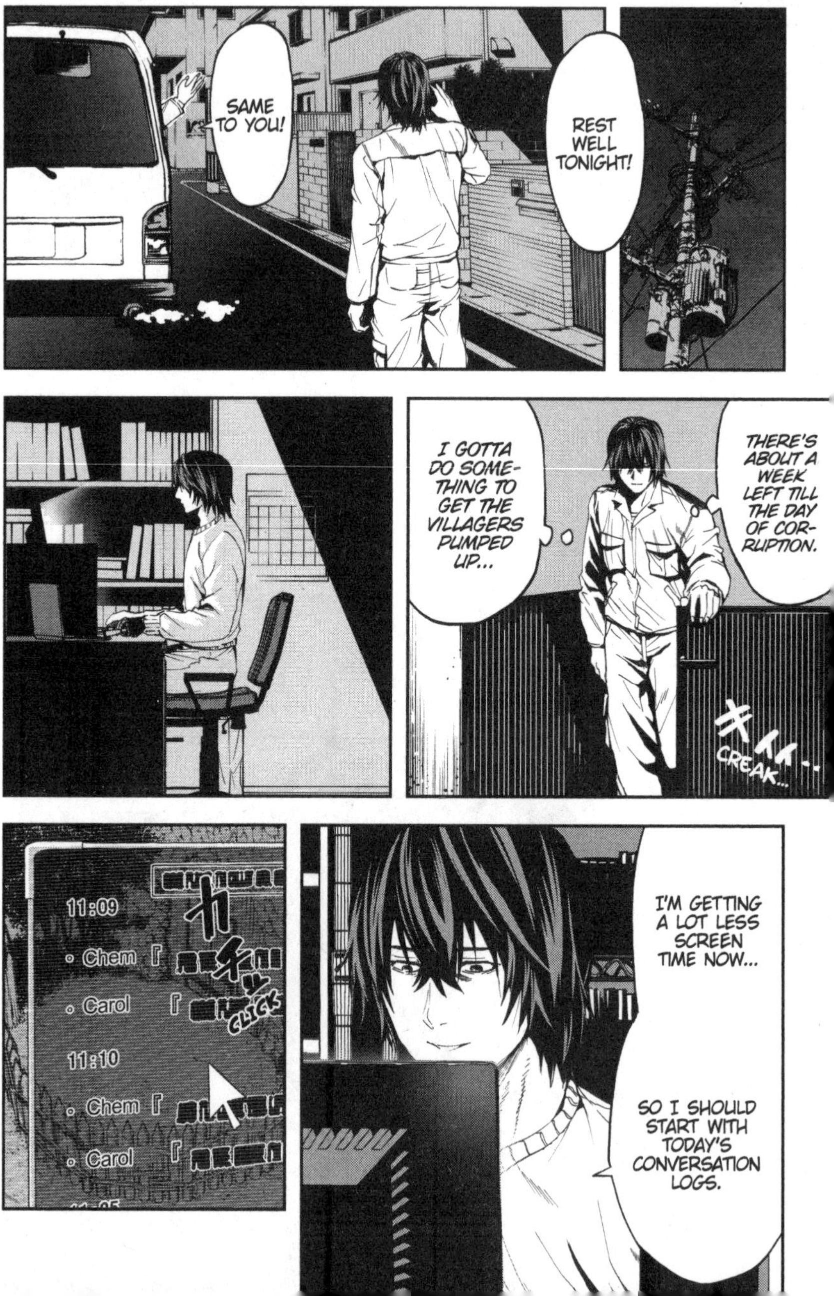
REST WELL TONIGHT!
SAME TO YOU!
THERE'S ABOUT A WEEK LEFT TILL THE DAY OF CORRUPTION.
I GOTTA DO SOMETHING TO GET THE VILLAGERS PUMPED UP...
CREAK...
I'M GETTING A LOT LESS SCREEN TIME NOW...
SO I SHOULD START WITH TODAY'S CONVERSATION LOGS.
11:09
Chem
Carol
CLICKS
11:10
Chem
Carol

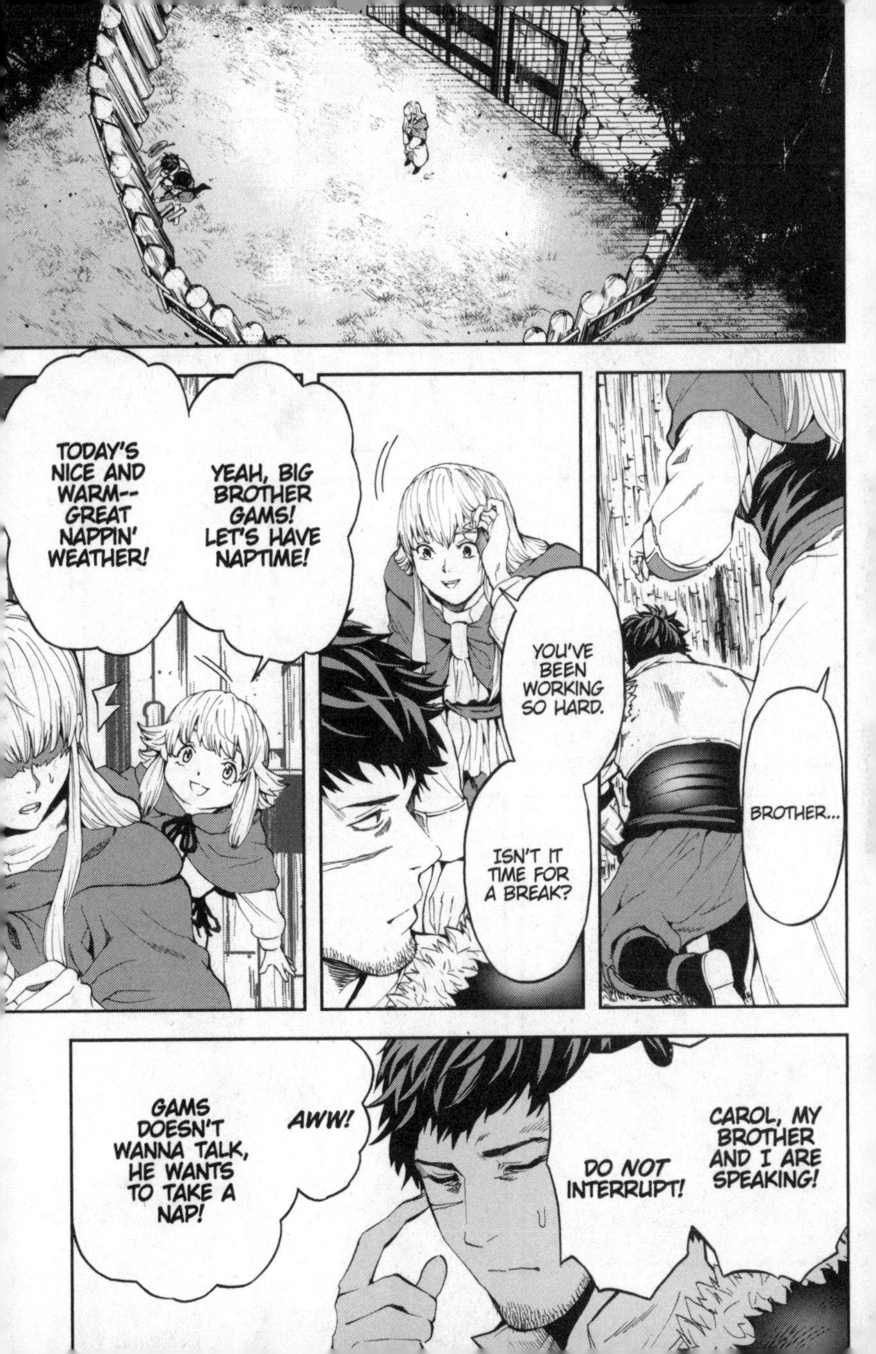
BROTHER...
YOU'VE BEEN WORKING SO HARD.
ISN'T IT TIME FOR A BREAK?
YEAH, BIG BROTHER GAMS! LET'S HAVE NAPTIME!
TODAY'S NICE AND WARM-- GREAT NAPPIN' WEATHER!
CAROL, MY BROTHER AND I ARE SPEAKING!
DO NOT INTERRUPT!
AWW!
GAMS DOESN'T WANNA TALK, HE WANTS TO TAKE A NAP!

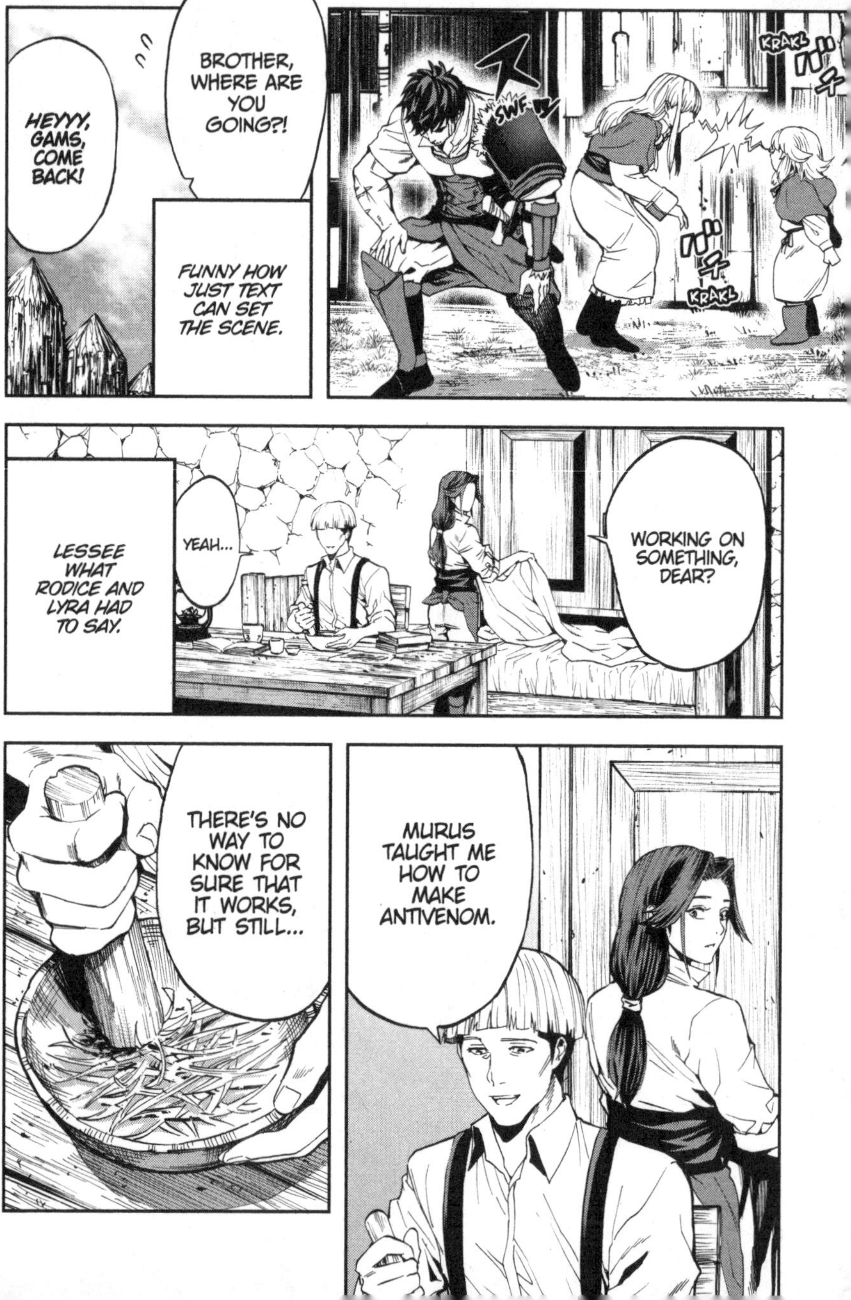
KRAKL
SWF
KRAKL
BROTHER, WHERE ARE YOU GOING?!
HEYYY, GAMS, COME BACK!
FUNNY HOW JUST TEXT CAN SET THE SCENE.
WORKING ON SOMETHING, DEAR?
YEAH...
LESSEE WHAT RODICE AND LYRA HAD TO SAY.
MURUS TAUGHT ME HOW TO MAKE ANTIVENOM.
THERE'S NO WAY TO KNOW FOR SURE THAT IT WORKS, BUT STILL...

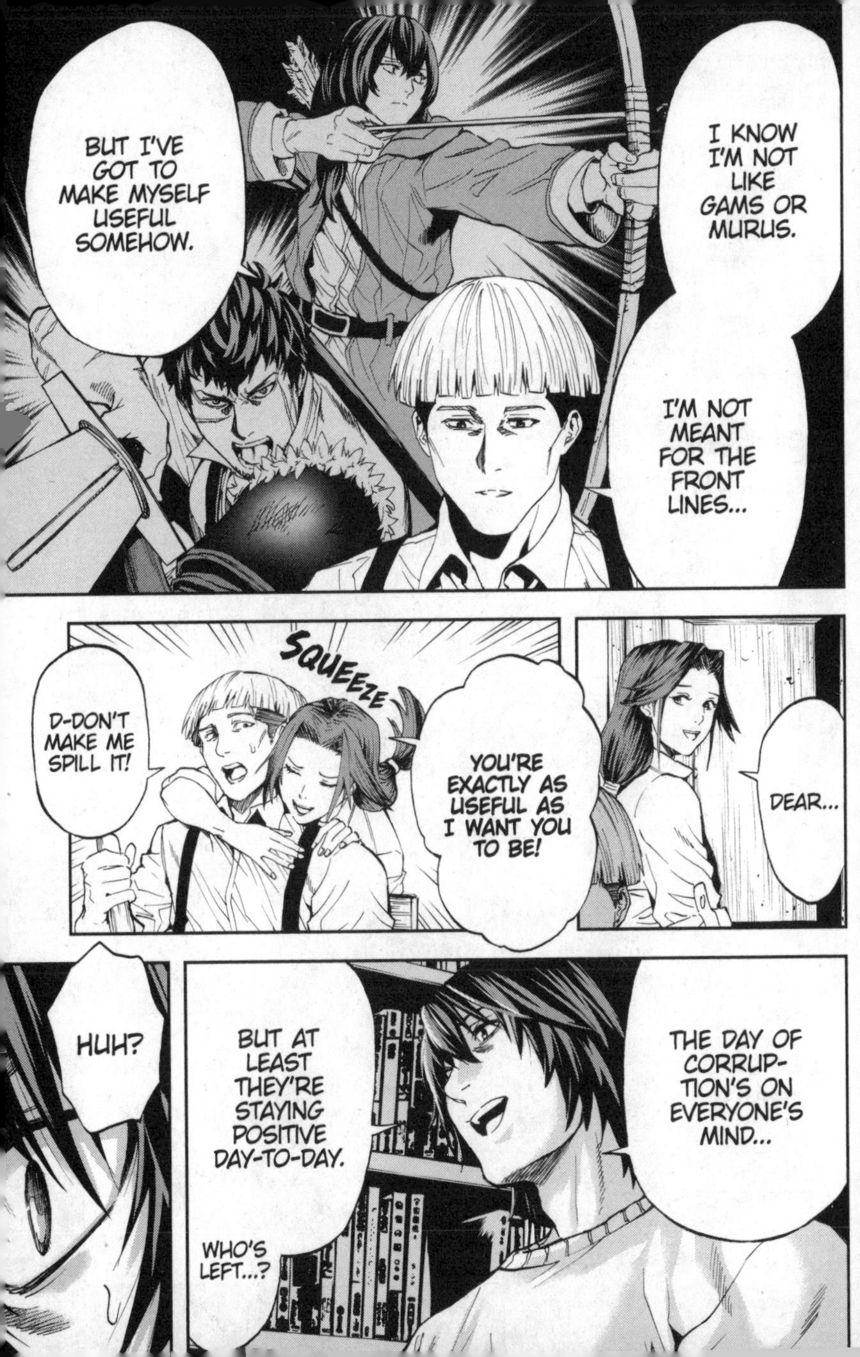
I KNOW I'M NOT LIKE GAMS OR MURUS.
I'M NOT MEANT FOR THE FRONT LINES...
BUT I'VE GOT TO MAKE MYSELF USEFUL SOMEHOW.
DEAR...
YOU'RE EXACTLY AS USEFUL AS I WANT YOU TO BE!
SQUEEZE
D-DON'T MAKE ME SPILL IT!
THE DAY OF CORRUPTION'S ON EVERYONE'S MIND...
BUT AT LEAST THEY'RE STAYING POSITIVE DAY-TO-DAY.
WHO'S LEFT...?
HUH?

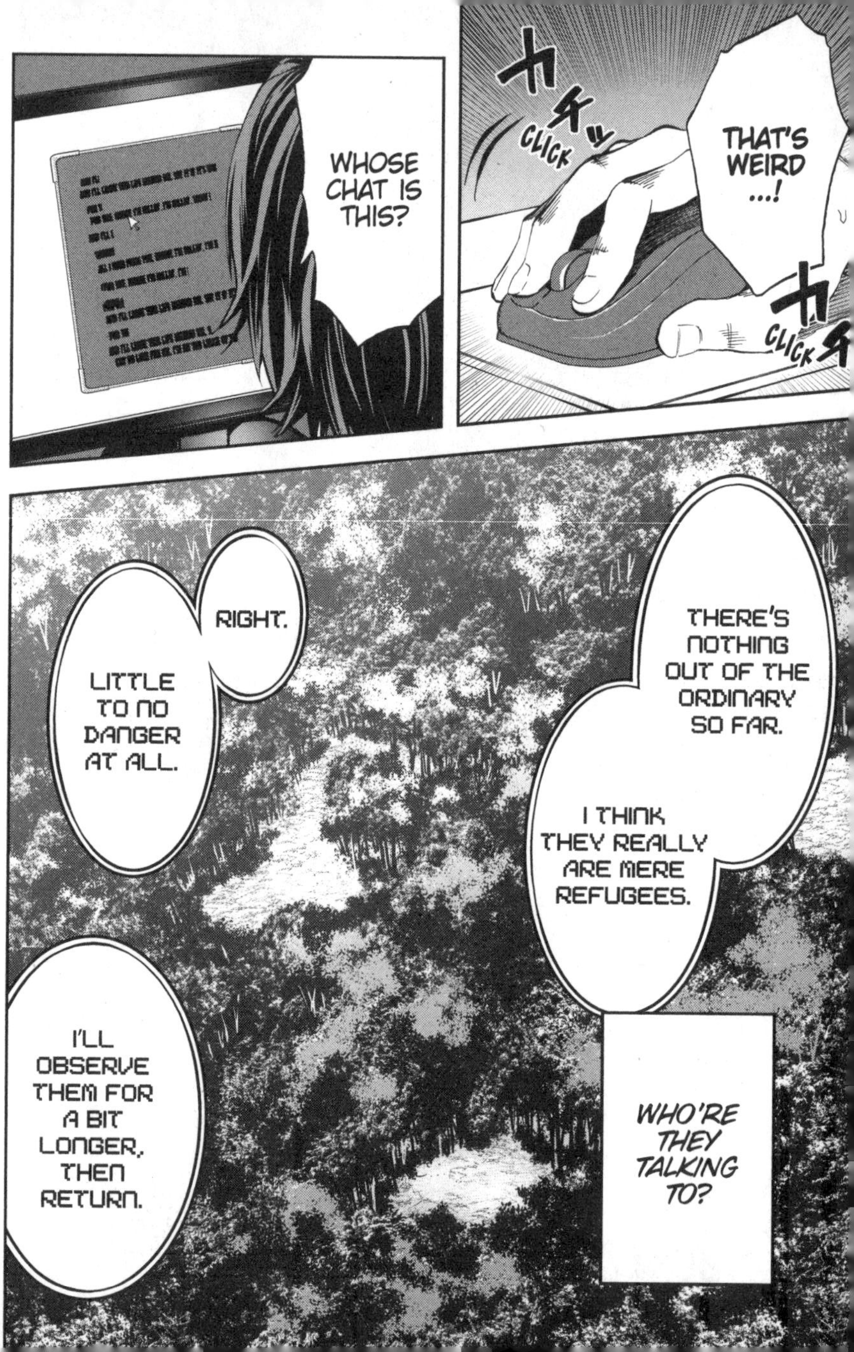
カチッ
CLICK
THAT'S WEIRD ...!
カチ
CLICK
WHOSE CHAT IS THIS?
THERE'S NOTHING OUT OF THE ORDINARY SO FAR.
RIGHT.
LITTLE TO NO DANGER AT ALL.
I THINK THEY REALLY ARE MERE REFUGEES.
WHO'RE THEY TALKING TO?
I'LL OBSERVE THEM FOR A BIT LONGER, THEN RETURN.

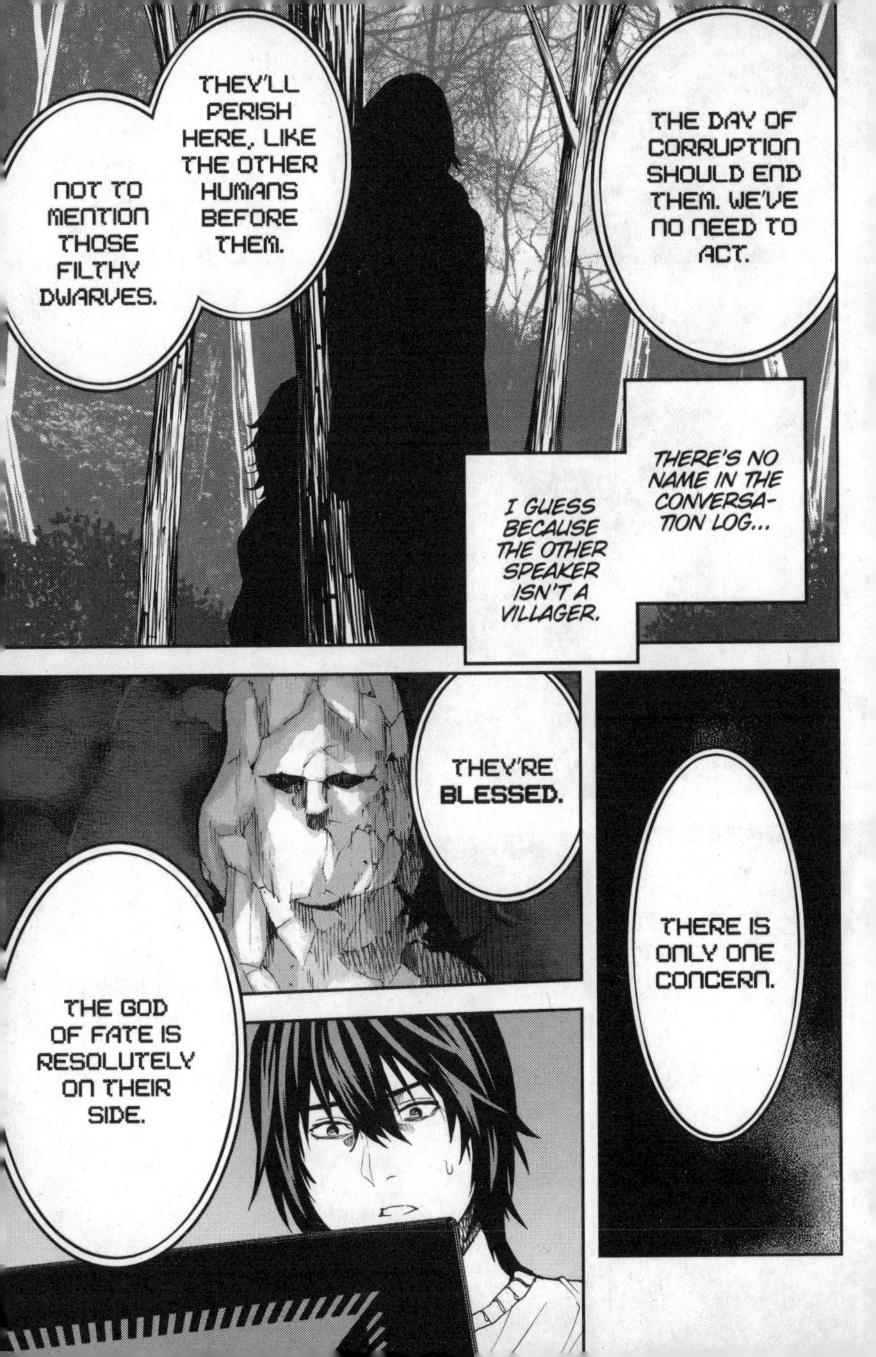
THE DAY OF CORRUPTION SHOULD END THEM. WE'VE NO NEED TO ACT.
THEY'LL PERISH HERE, LIKE THE OTHER HUMANS BEFORE THEM.
NOT TO MENTION THOSE FILTHY DWARVES.
THERE'S NO NAME IN THE CONVERSA-TION LOG...
I GUESS BECAUSE THE OTHER SPEAKER ISN'T A VILLAGER.
THERE IS ONLY ONE CONCERN.
THEY'RE BLESSED.
THE GOD OF FATE IS RESOLUTELY ON THEIR SIDE.

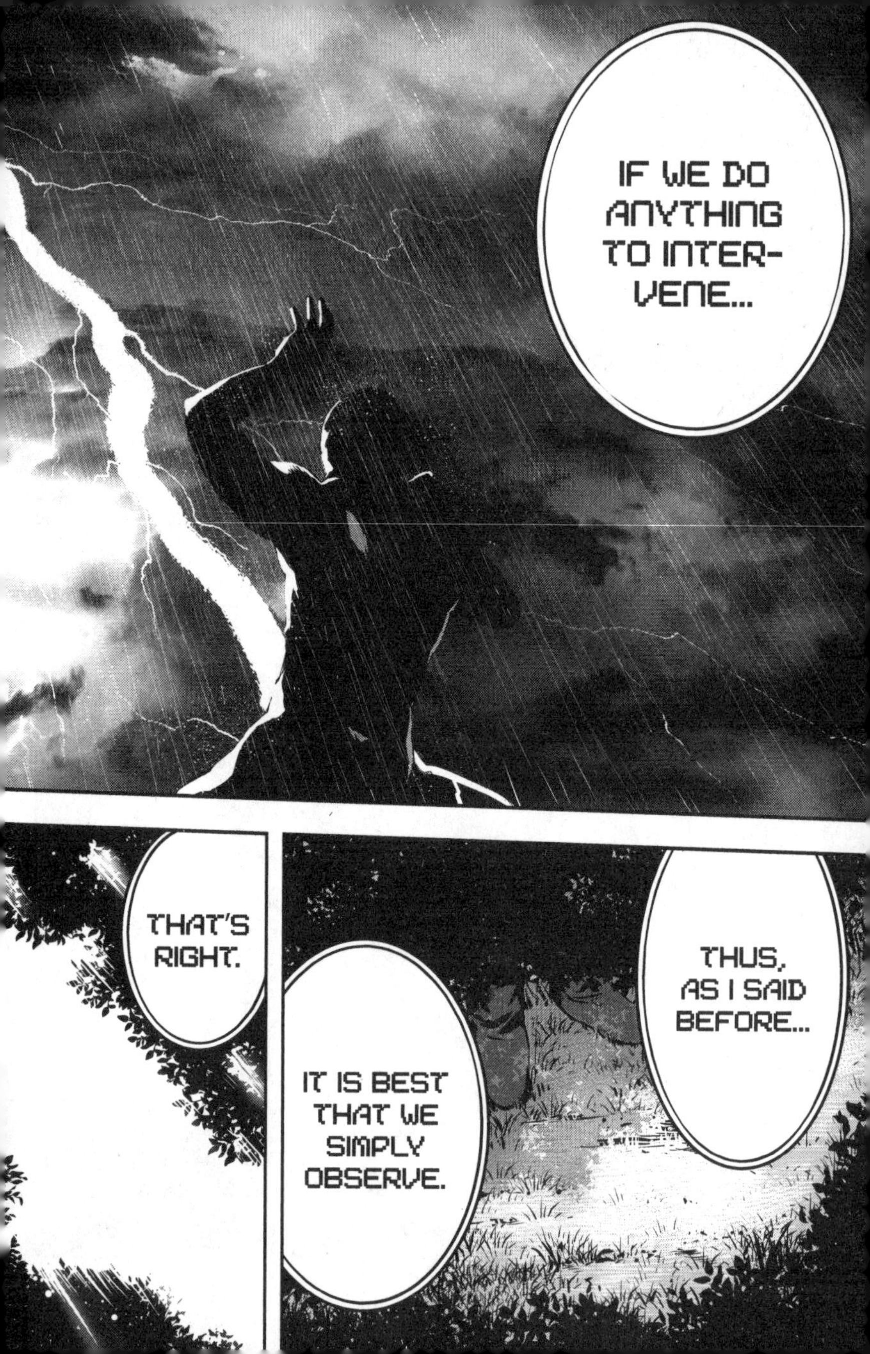
IF WE DO ANYTHING TO INTER-VENE...
THUS, AS I SAID BEFORE...
IT IS BEST THAT WE SIMPLY OBSERVE.
THAT'S RIGHT.

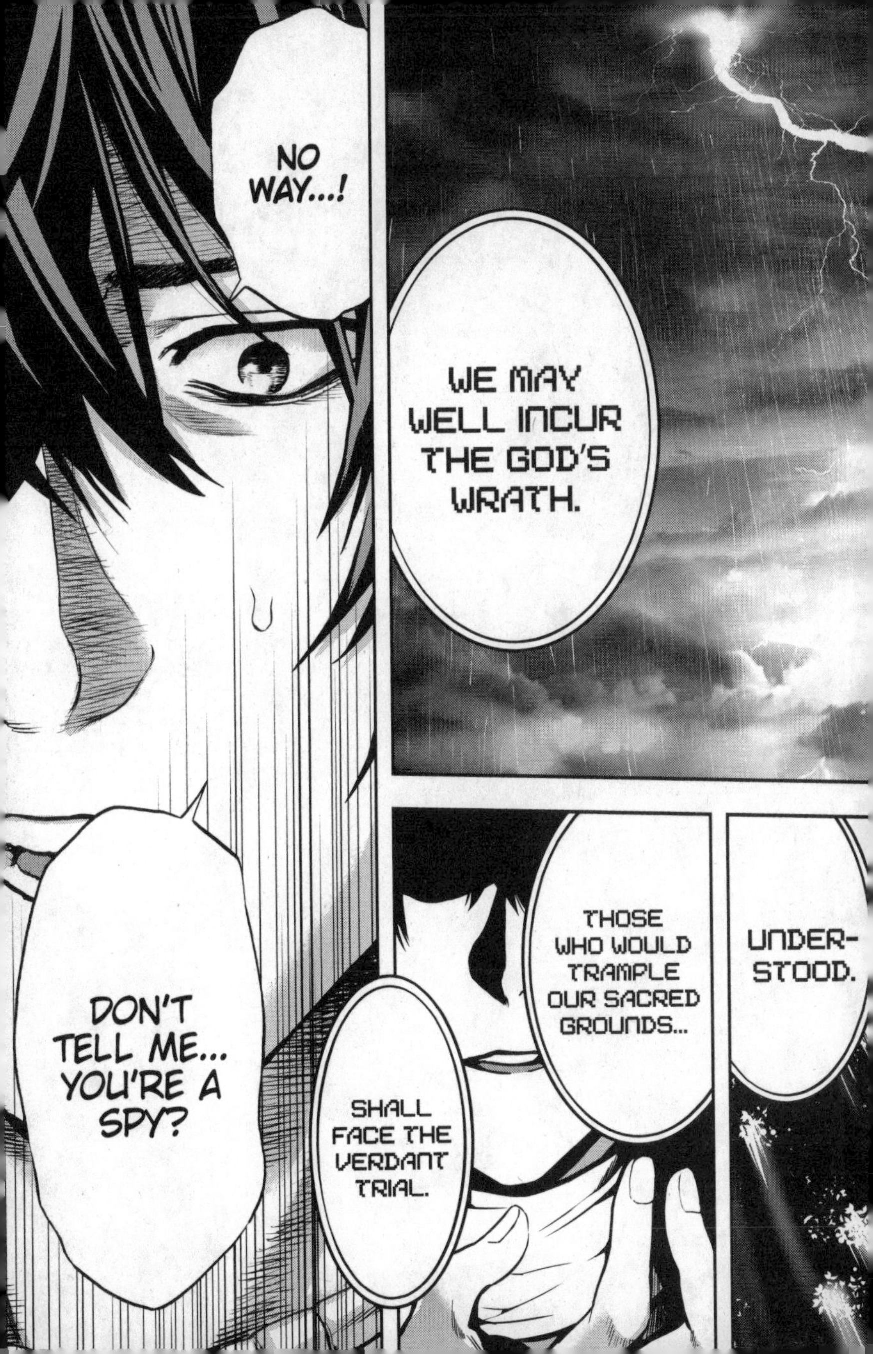
WE MAY WELL INCUR THE GOD'S WRATH.
NO WAY...!
UNDER-STOOD.
THOSE WHO WOULD TRAMPLE OUR SACRED GROUNDS...
SHALL FACE THE VERDANT TRIAL.
DON'T TELL ME... YOU'RE A SPY?

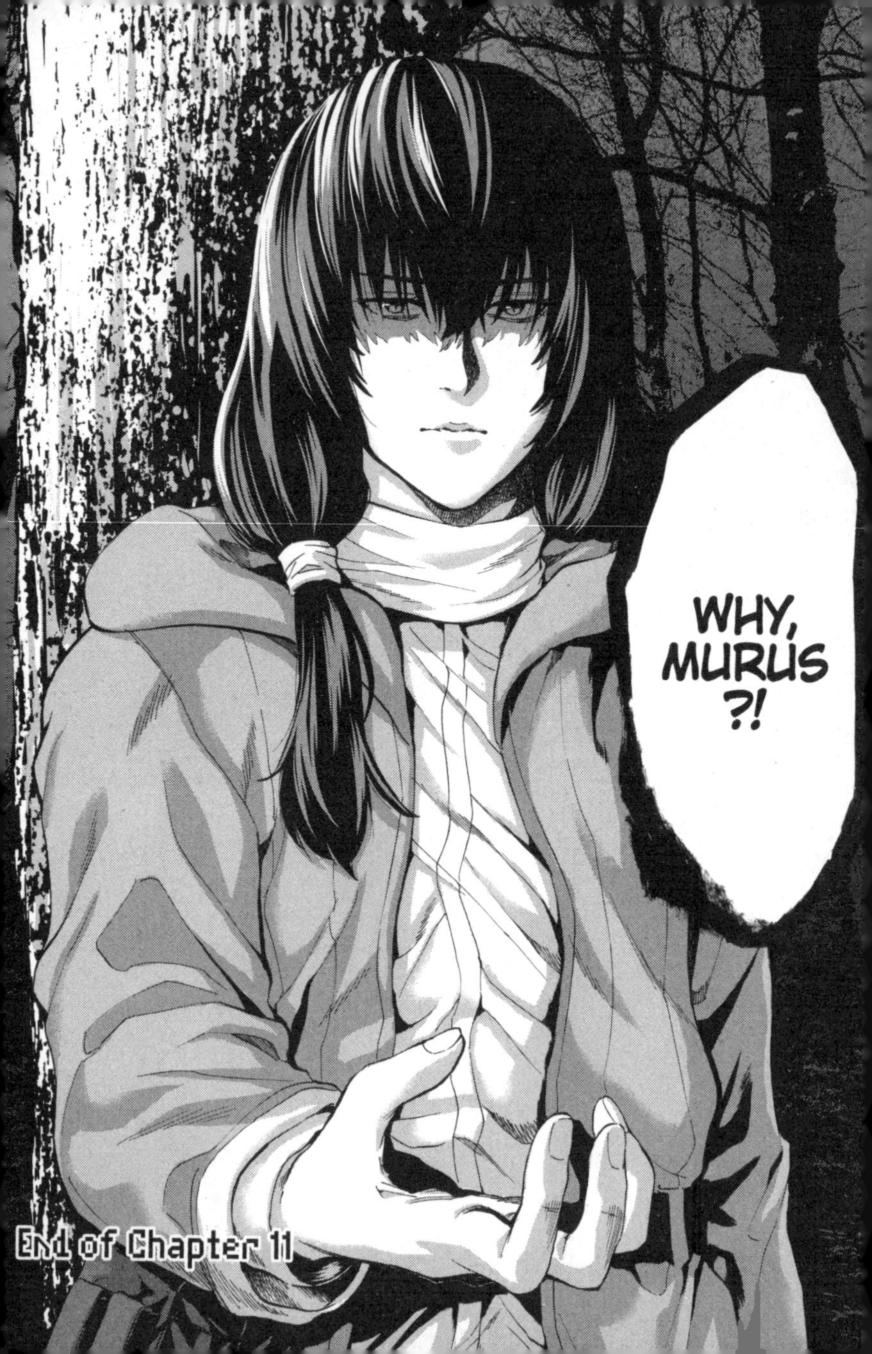
WHY, MURUS ?!
End of Chapter 11

Character

Murus

▶ Gender: ???

Class: Physician

E : Bow and arrows

E : Cloth armor

E : Medicinal herbs

THE NPCs IN THIS VILLAGE SIM GAME MUST BE REAL!

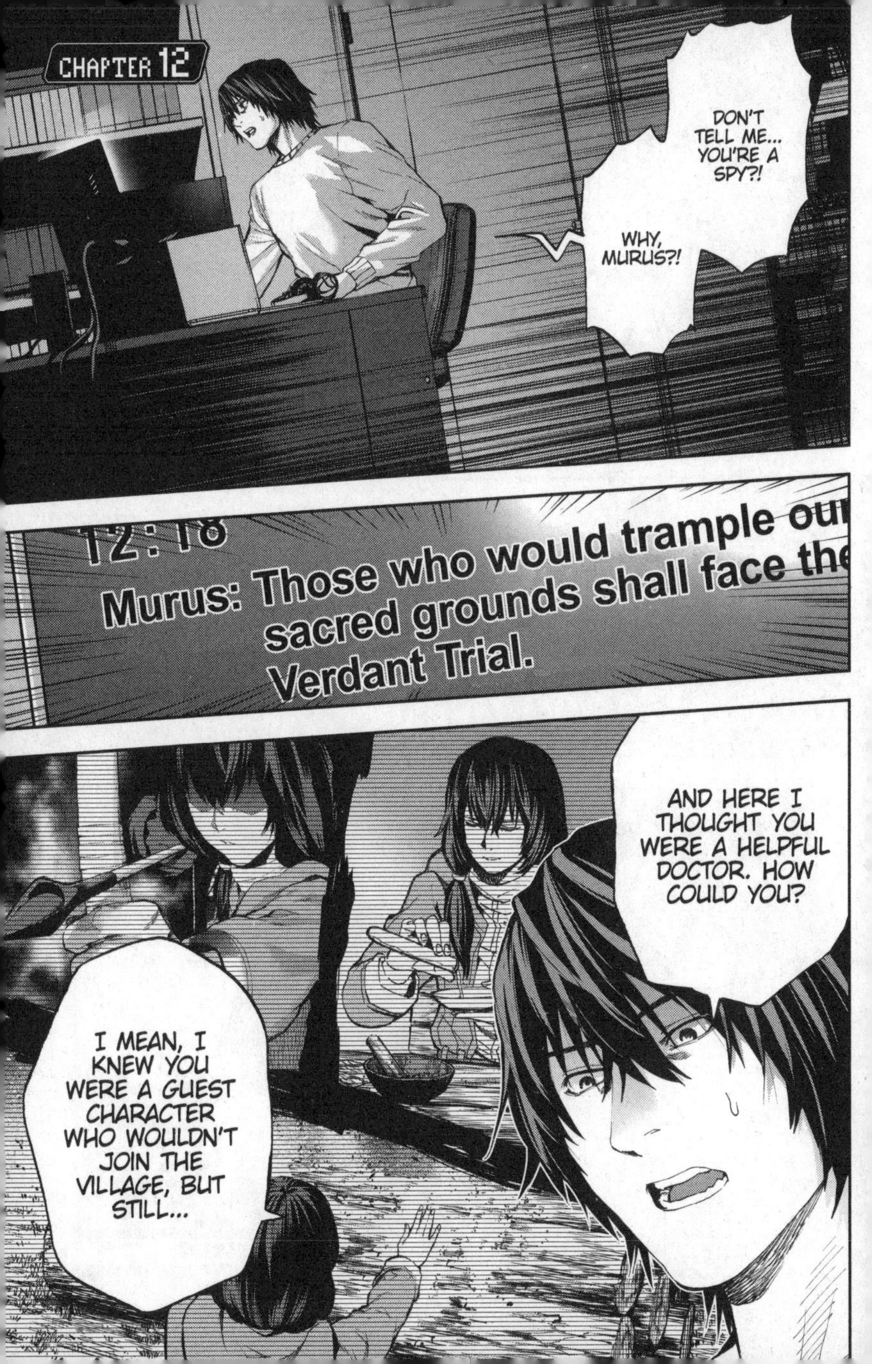
CHAPTER 12
DON'T TELL ME... YOU'RE A SPY?!
WHY, MURUS?!
12:18
Murus: Those who would trample ou
sacred grounds shall face the
Verdant Trial.
AND HERE I THOUGHT YOU WERE A HELPFUL DOCTOR. HOW COULD YOU?
I MEAN, I KNEW YOU WERE A GUEST CHARACTER WHO WOULDN'T JOIN THE VILLAGE, BUT STILL...

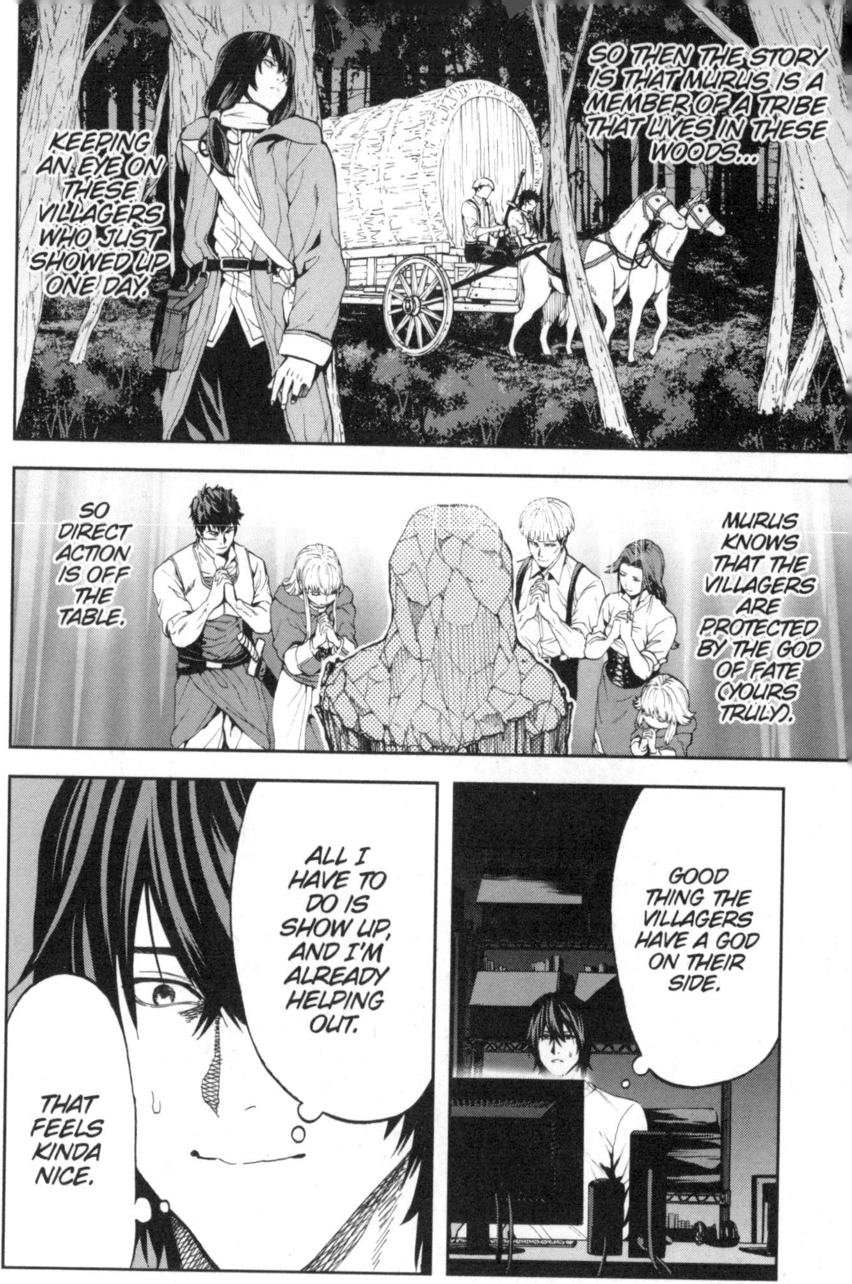
SO THEN THE STORY IS THAT MURUS IS A MEMBER OF A TRIBE THAT LIVES IN THESE WOODS...
KEEPING AN EYE ON THESE VILLAGERS WHO JUST SHOWED UP ONE DAY.
MURUS KNOWS THAT THE VILLAGERS ARE PROTECTED BY THE GOD OF FATE (YOURS TRULY).
SO DIRECT ACTION IS OFF THE TABLE.
GOOD THING THE VILLAGERS HAVE A GOD ON THEIR SIDE.
ALL I HAVE TO DO IS SHOW UP, AND I'M ALREADY HELPING OUT.
THAT FEELS KINDA NICE.

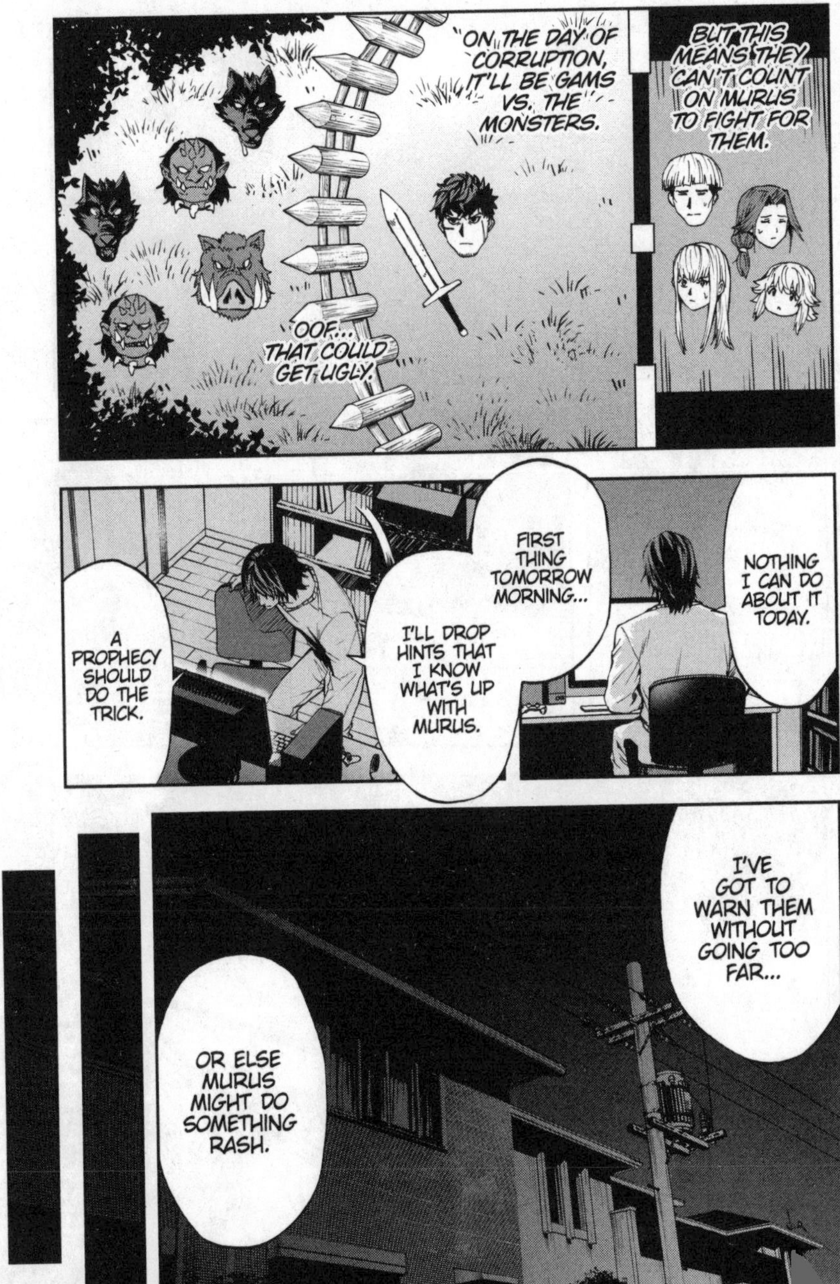
BUT THIS MEANS THEY CAN'T COUNT ON MURUS TO FIGHT FOR THEM.
"ON THE DAY OF CORRUPTION, IT'LL BE GAMS VS. THE MONSTERS."
OOF... THAT COULD GET UGLY.
NOTHING I CAN DO ABOUT IT TODAY.
FIRST THING TOMORROW MORNING...
I'LL DROP HINTS THAT I KNOW WHAT'S UP WITH MURUS.
A PROPHECY SHOULD DO THE TRICK.
I'VE GOT TO WARN THEM WITHOUT GOING TOO FAR...
OR ELSE MURUS MIGHT DO SOMETHING RASH.

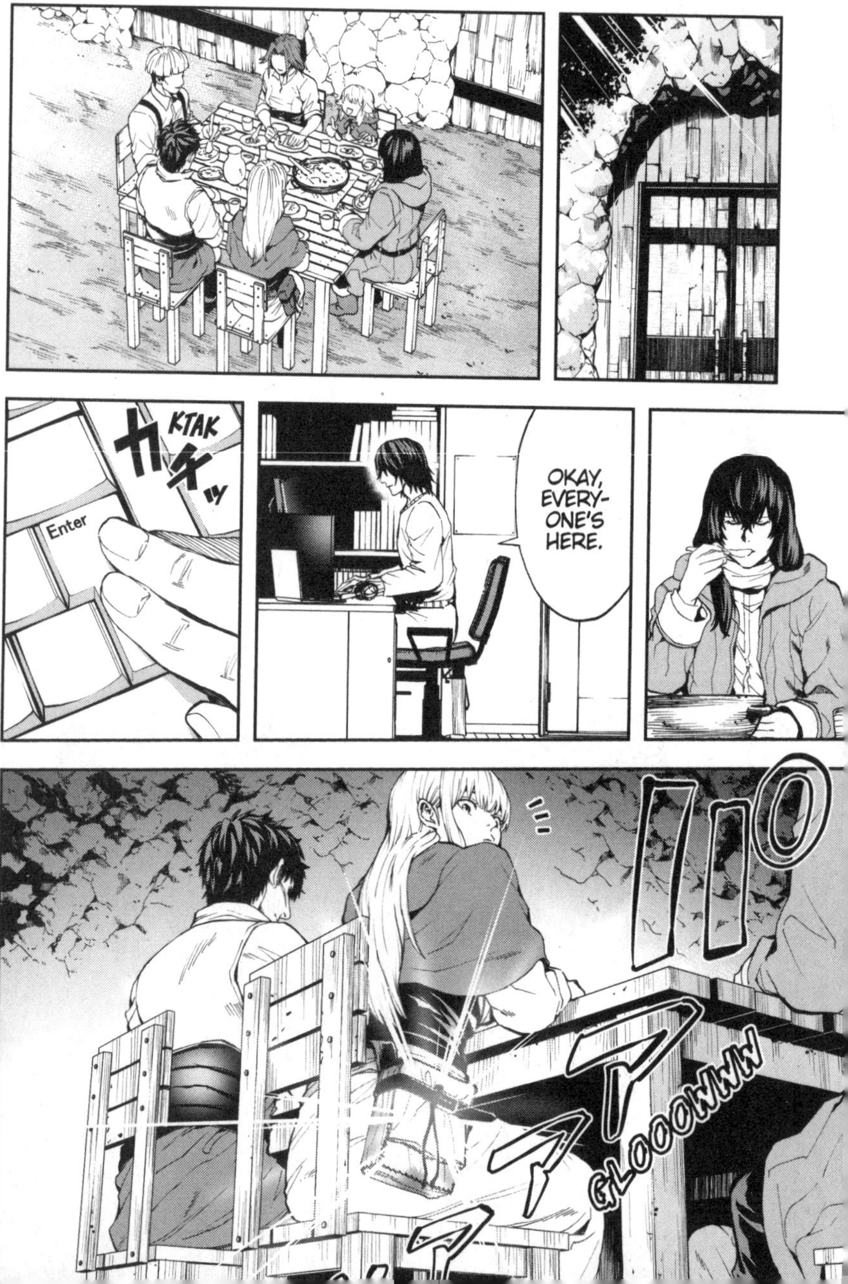
OKAY, EVERY-ONE'S HERE.
KTAK
GLOOOWWW

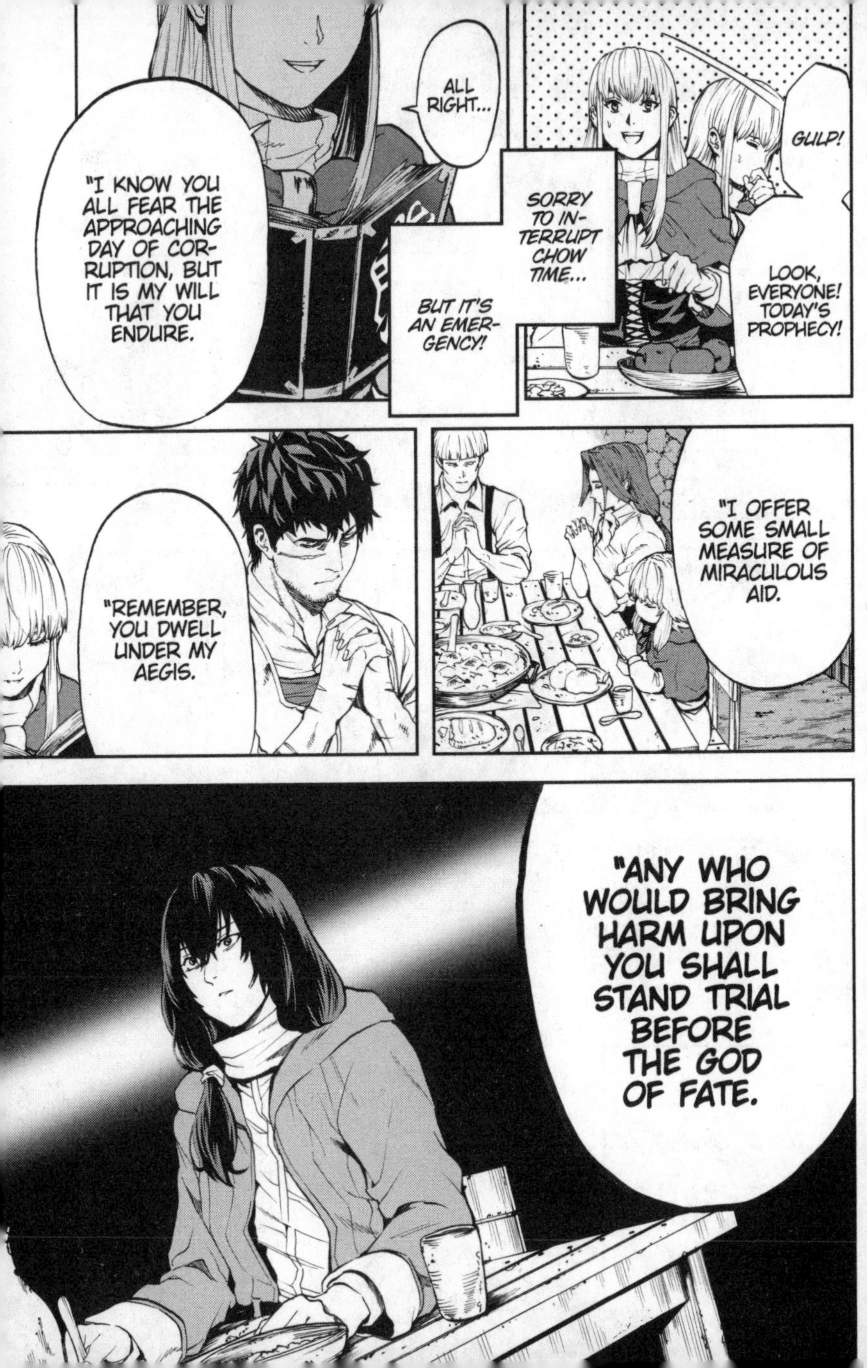
GULP!
LOOK, EVERYONE! TODAY'S PROPHECY!
SORRY TO IN-TERRUPT CHOW TIME...
BUT IT'S AN EMER-GENCY!
ALL RIGHT...
"I KNOW YOU ALL FEAR THE APPROACHING DAY OF COR-RUPTION, BUT IT IS MY WILL THAT YOU ENDURE.
"I OFFER SOME SMALL MEASURE OF MIRACULOUS AID.
"REMEMBER, YOU DWELL UNDER MY AEGIS.
"ANY WHO WOULD BRING HARM UPON YOU SHALL STAND TRIAL BEFORE THE GOD OF FATE.

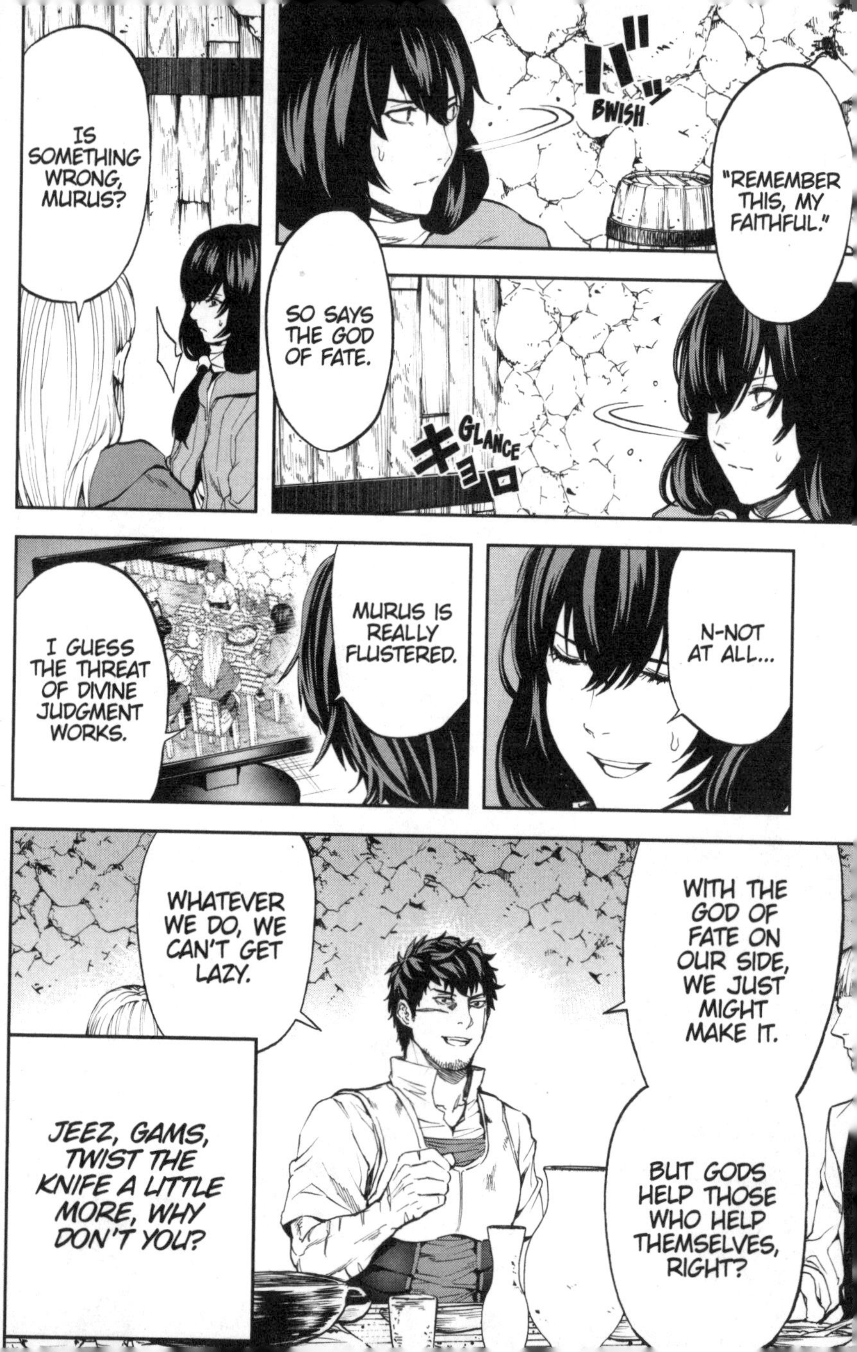

BWISH
"REMEMBER THIS, MY FAITHFUL."
SO SAYS THE GOD OF FATE.
GLANCE
IS SOMETHING WRONG, MURUS?
N-NOT AT ALL...
MURUS IS REALLY FLUSTERED.
I GUESS THE THREAT OF DIVINE JUDGMENT WORKS.
WITH THE GOD OF FATE ON OUR SIDE, WE JUST MIGHT MAKE IT.
BUT GODS HELP THOSE WHO HELP THEMSELVES, RIGHT?
WHATEVER WE DO, WE CAN'T GET LAZY.
JEEZ, GAMS, TWIST THE KNIFE A LITTLE MORE, WHY DON'T YOU?

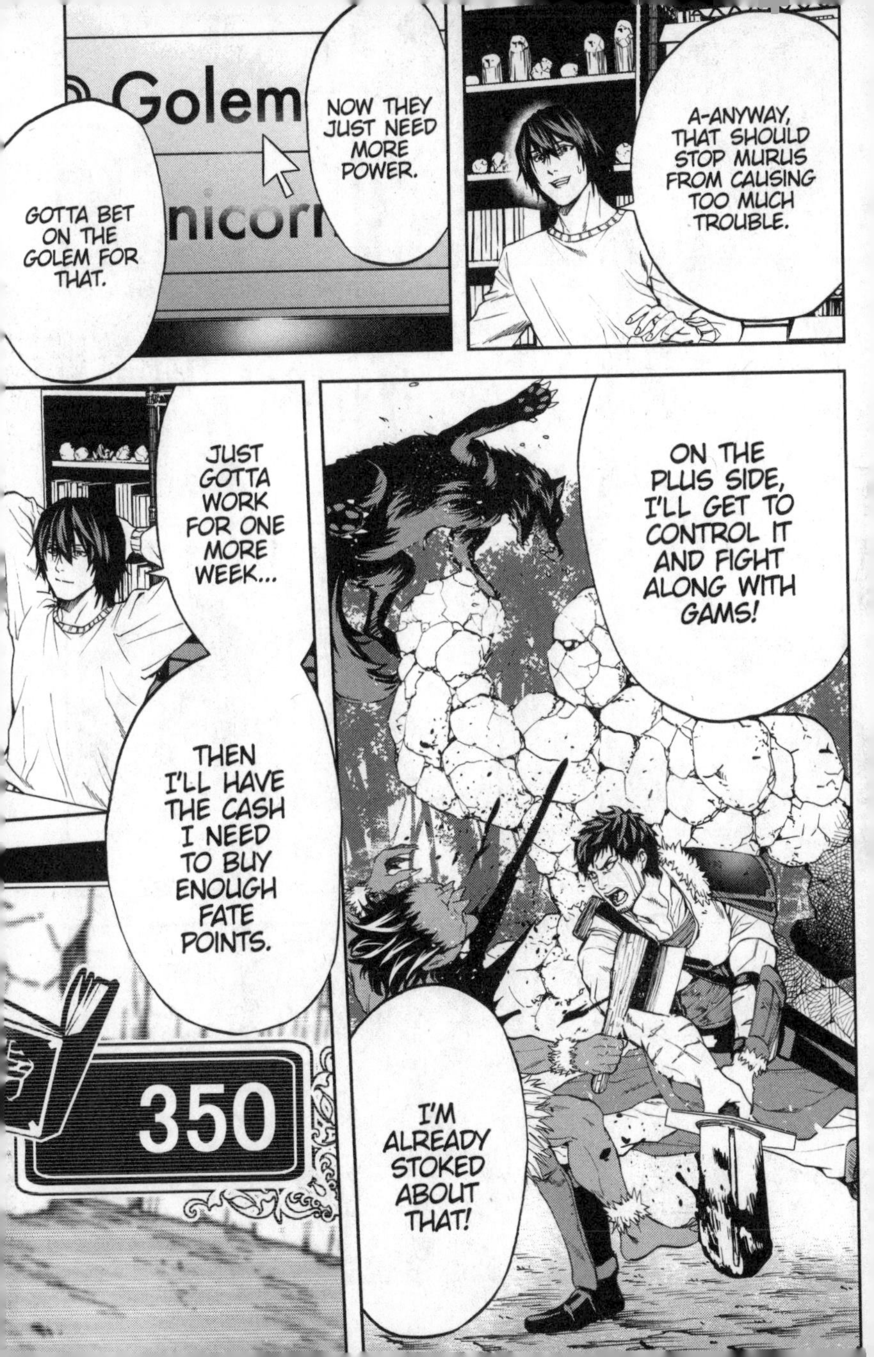
A-ANYWAY, THAT SHOULD STOP MURUS FROM CAUSING TOO MUCH TROUBLE.
NOW THEY JUST NEED MORE POWER.
Golem
GOTTA BET ON THE GOLEM FOR THAT.
ON THE PLUS SIDE, I'LL GET TO CONTROL IT AND FIGHT ALONG WITH GAMS!
I'M ALREADY STOKED ABOUT THAT!
JUST GOTTA WORK FOR ONE MORE WEEK...
THEN I'LL HAVE THE CASH I NEED TO BUY ENOUGH FATE POINTS.
350

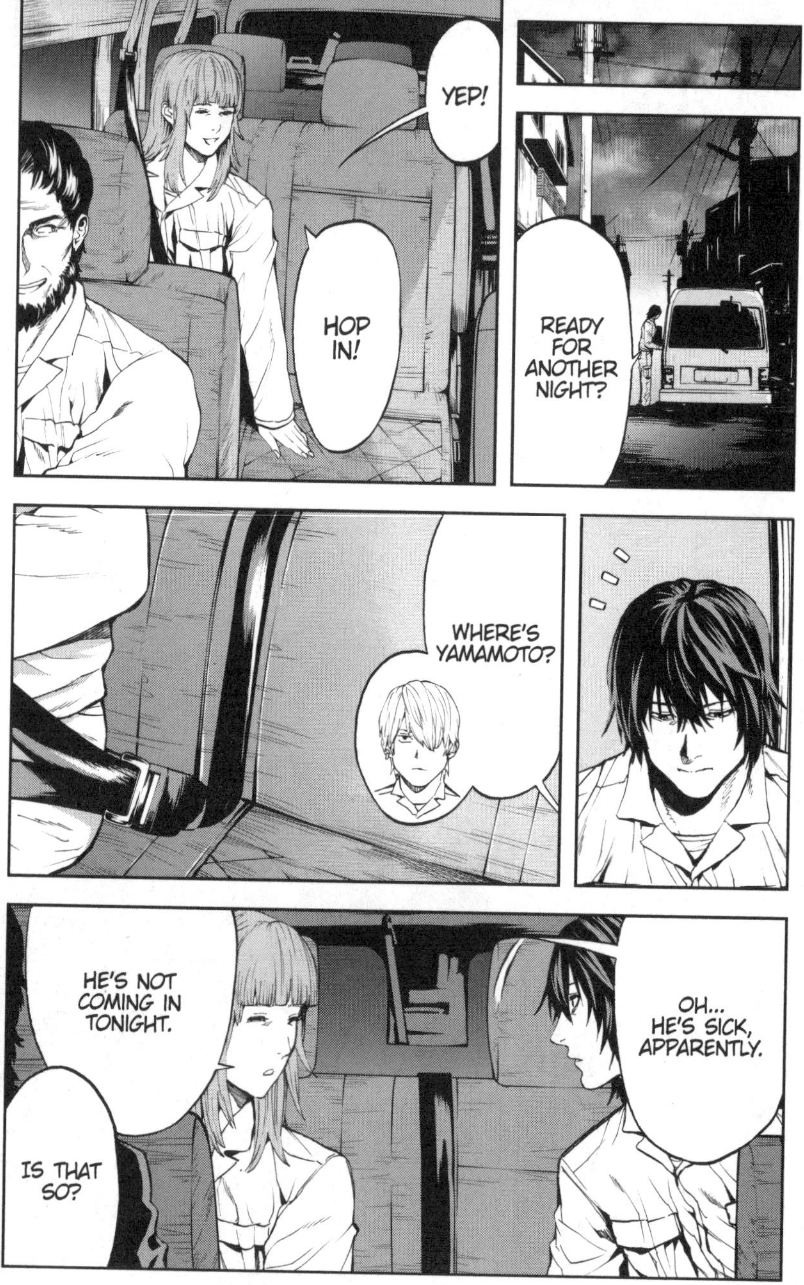
READY FOR ANOTHER NIGHT?
YEP!
HOP IN!
WHERE'S YAMAMOTO?
OH... HE'S SICK, APPARENTLY.
HE'S NOT COMING IN TONIGHT.
IS THAT SO?

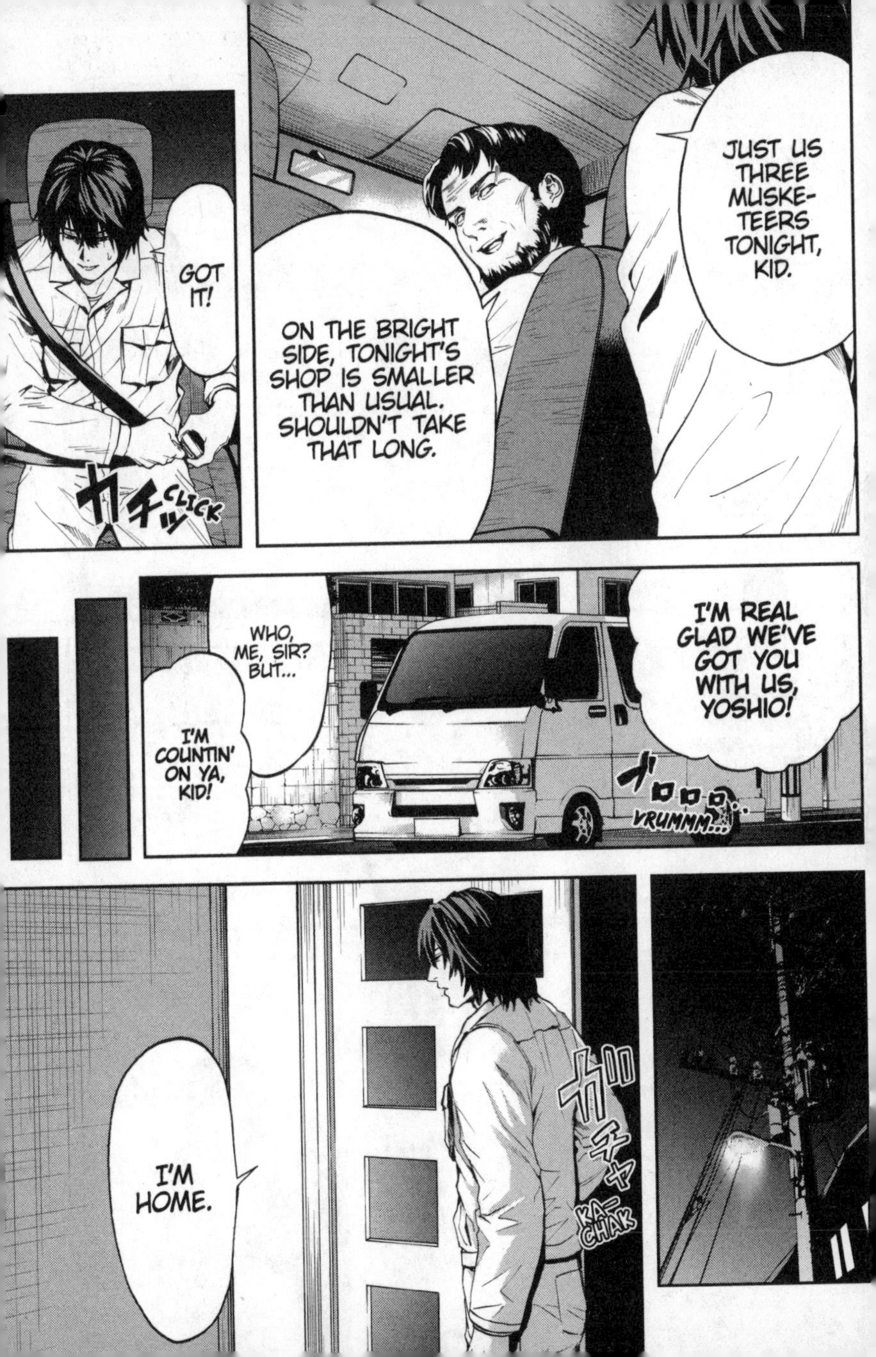
JUST US THREE MUSKETEERS TONIGHT, KID.
ON THE BRIGHT SIDE, TONIGHT'S SHOP IS SMALLER THAN USUAL. SHOULDN'T TAKE THAT LONG.
GOT IT!
カチッ
CLICK
I'M REAL GLAD WE'VE GOT YOU WITH US, YOSHIO!
ガロロロ…
VRUMMM...
WHO, ME, SIR? BUT...
I'M COUNTIN' ON YA, KID!
ガチャ
KA-CHAK
I'M HOME.

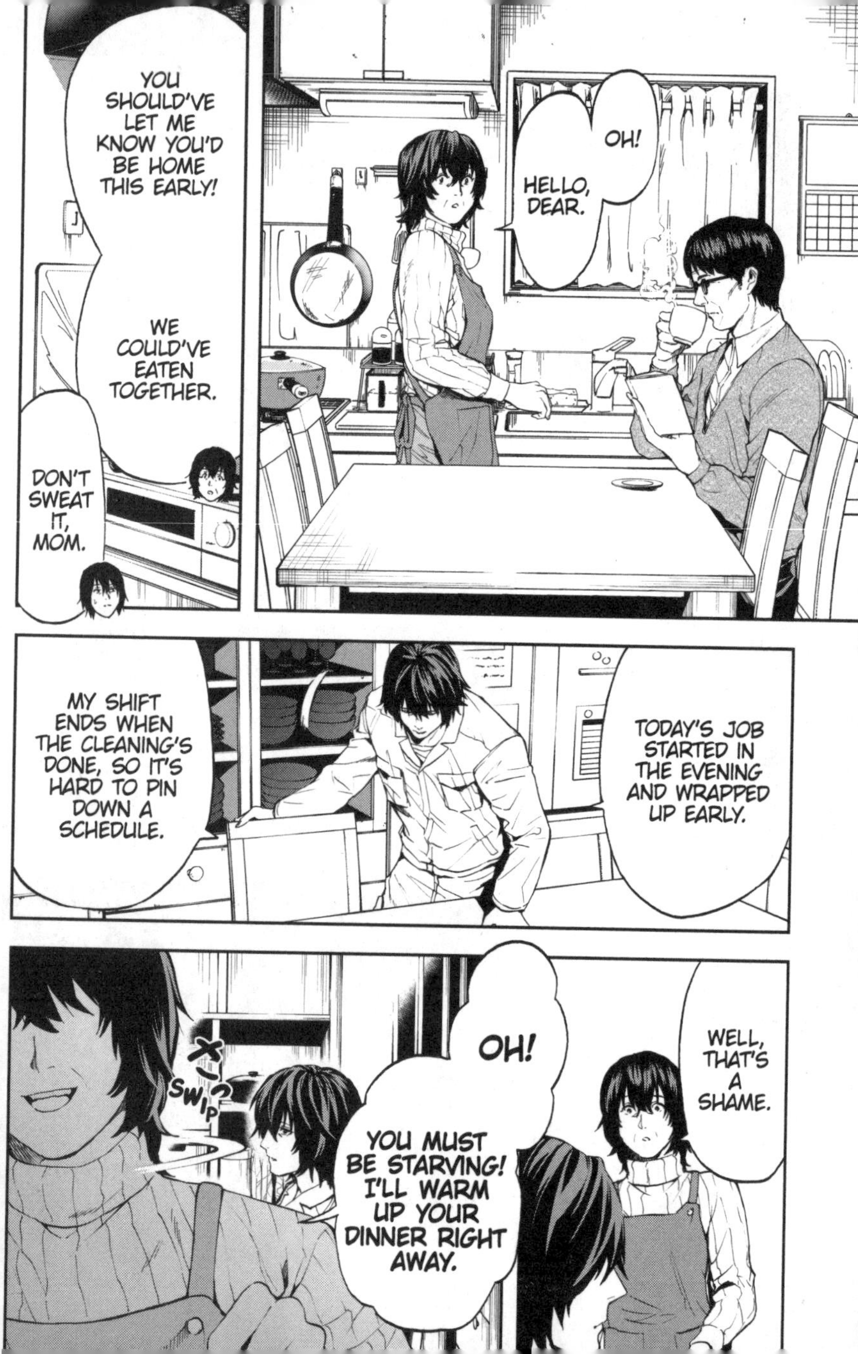
OH!
HELLO, DEAR.
YOU SHOULD'VE LET ME KNOW YOU'D BE HOME THIS EARLY!
WE COULD'VE EATEN TOGETHER.
DON'T SWEAT IT, MOM.
TODAY'S JOB STARTED IN THE EVENING AND WRAPPED UP EARLY.
MY SHIFT ENDS WHEN THE CLEANING'S DONE, SO IT'S HARD TO PIN DOWN A SCHEDULE.
WELL, THAT'S A SHAME.
OH!
YOU MUST BE STARVING! I'LL WARM UP YOUR DINNER RIGHT AWAY.
SWIP

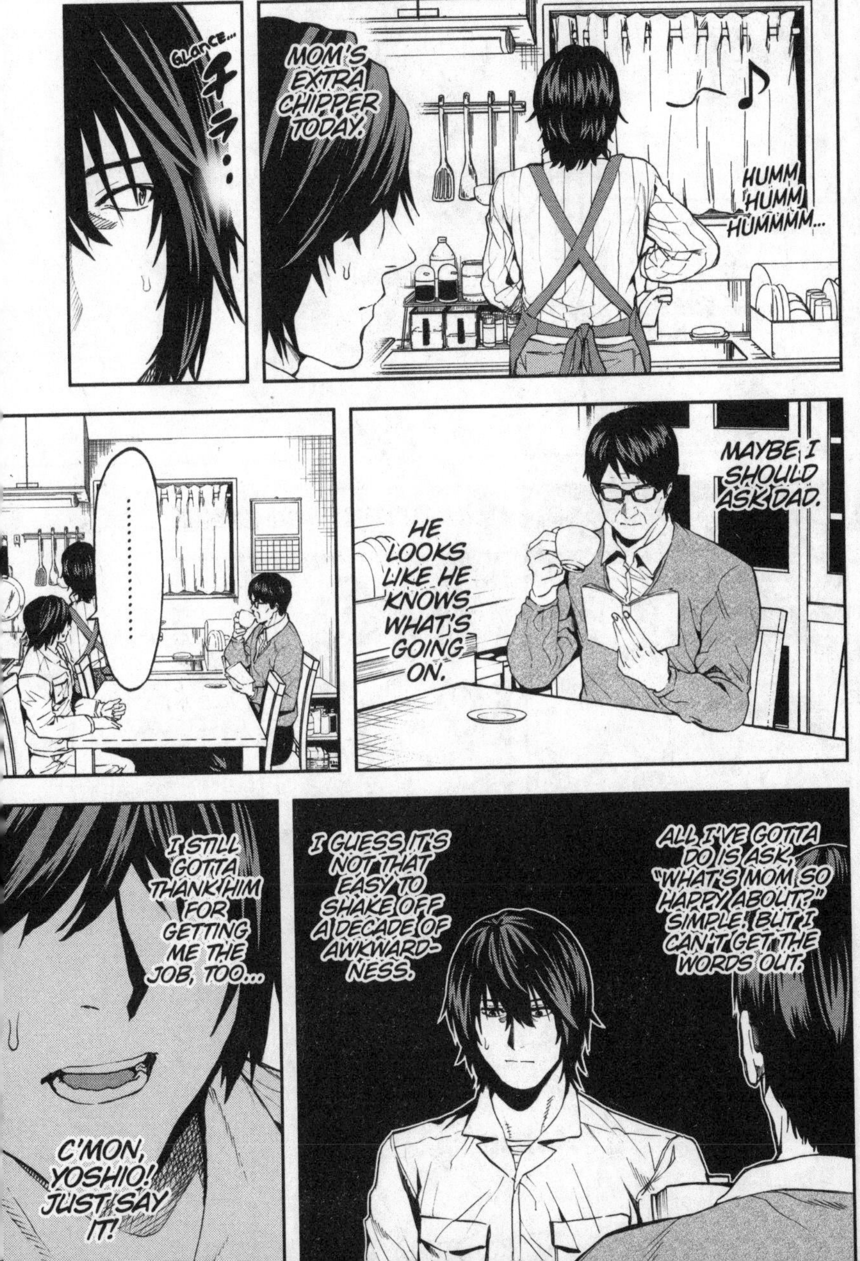
HUMM HUMM HUMMMM...
MOM'S EXTRA CHIPPER TODAY.
GLANCE...
チラ...
MAYBE I SHOULD ASK DAD.
HE LOOKS LIKE HE KNOWS WHAT'S GOING ON.
......
ALL I'VE GOTTA DO IS ASK, "WHAT'S MOM SO HAPPY ABOUT?" SIMPLE! BUT I CAN'T GET THE WORDS OUT.
I GUESS IT'S NOT THAT EASY TO SHAKE OFF A DECADE OF AWKWARDNESS.
I STILL GOTTA THANK HIM FOR GETTING ME THE JOB, TOO...
C'MON, YOSHIO! JUST SAY IT!

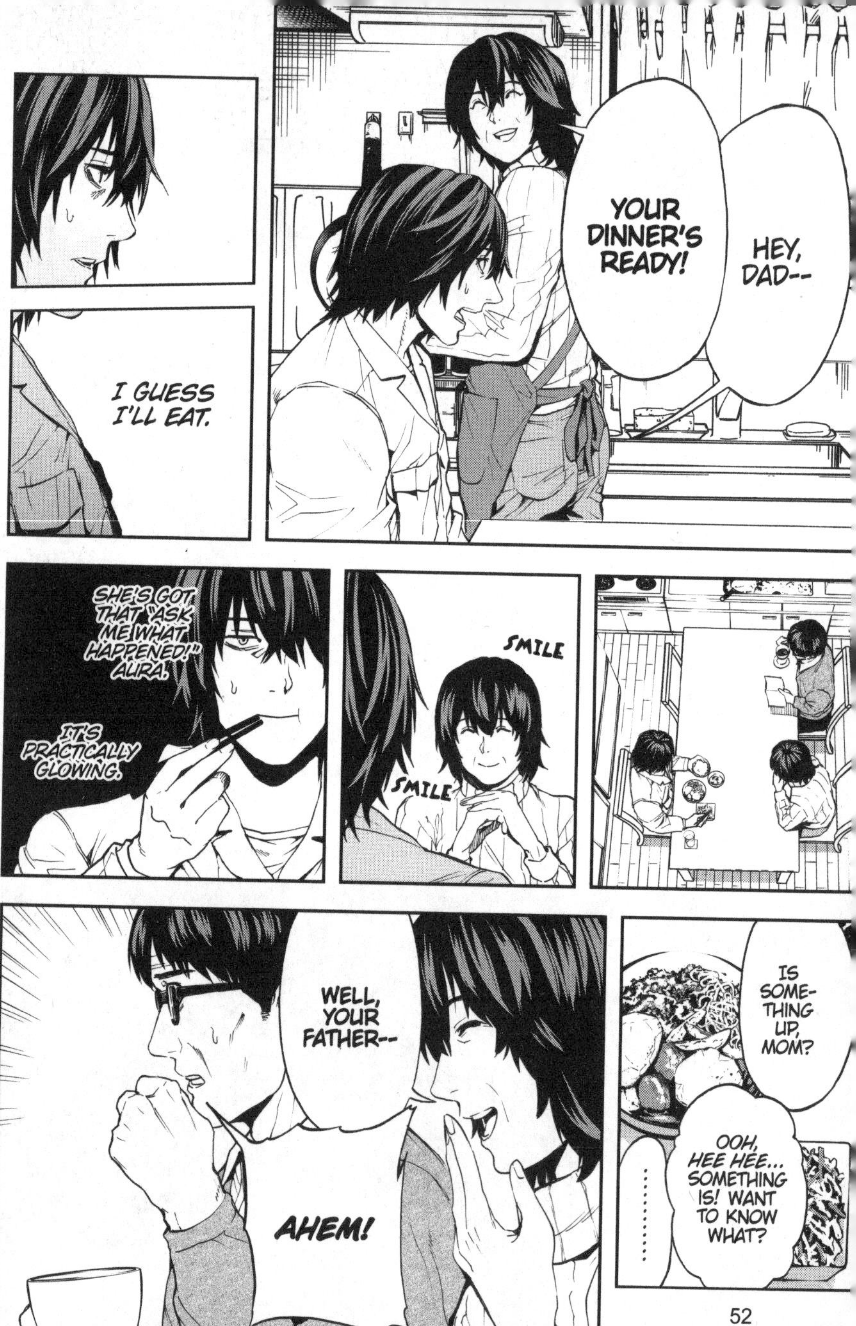
HEY, DAD--
YOUR DINNER'S READY!
I GUESS I'LL EAT.
SMILE
SMILE
SHE'S GOT THAT "ASK ME WHAT HAPPENED!" AURA.
IT'S PRACTICALLY GLOWING.
IS SOME-THING UP, MOM?
OOH, HEE HEE... SOMETHING IS! WANT TO KNOW WHAT?
......
WELL, YOUR FATHER--
AHEM!

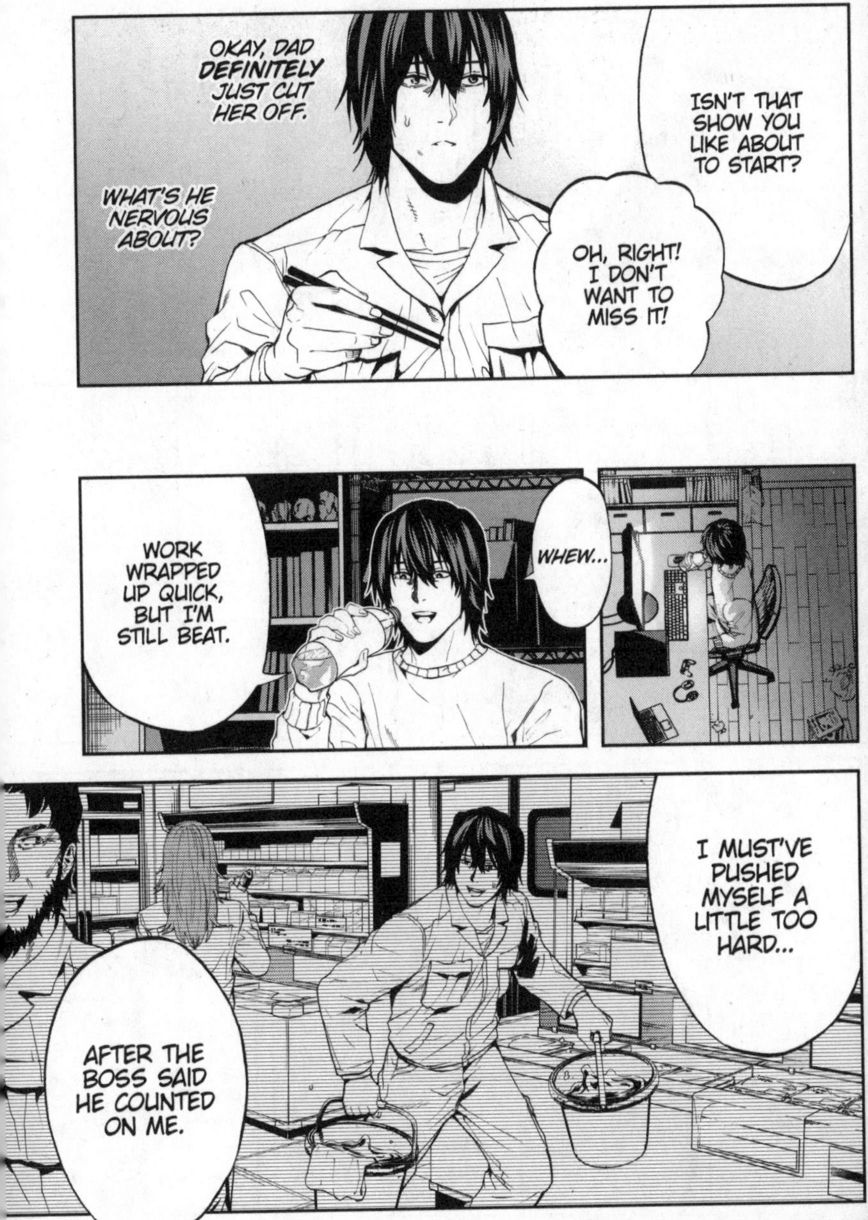
ISN'T THAT SHOW YOU LIKE ABOUT TO START?
OH, RIGHT! I DON'T WANT TO MISS IT!
OKAY, DAD DEFINITELY JUST CUT HER OFF.
WHAT'S HE NERVOUS ABOUT?
WHEW...
WORK WRAPPED UP QUICK, BUT I'M STILL BEAT.
I MUST'VE PUSHED MYSELF A LITTLE TOO HARD...
AFTER THE BOSS SAID HE COUNTED ON ME.

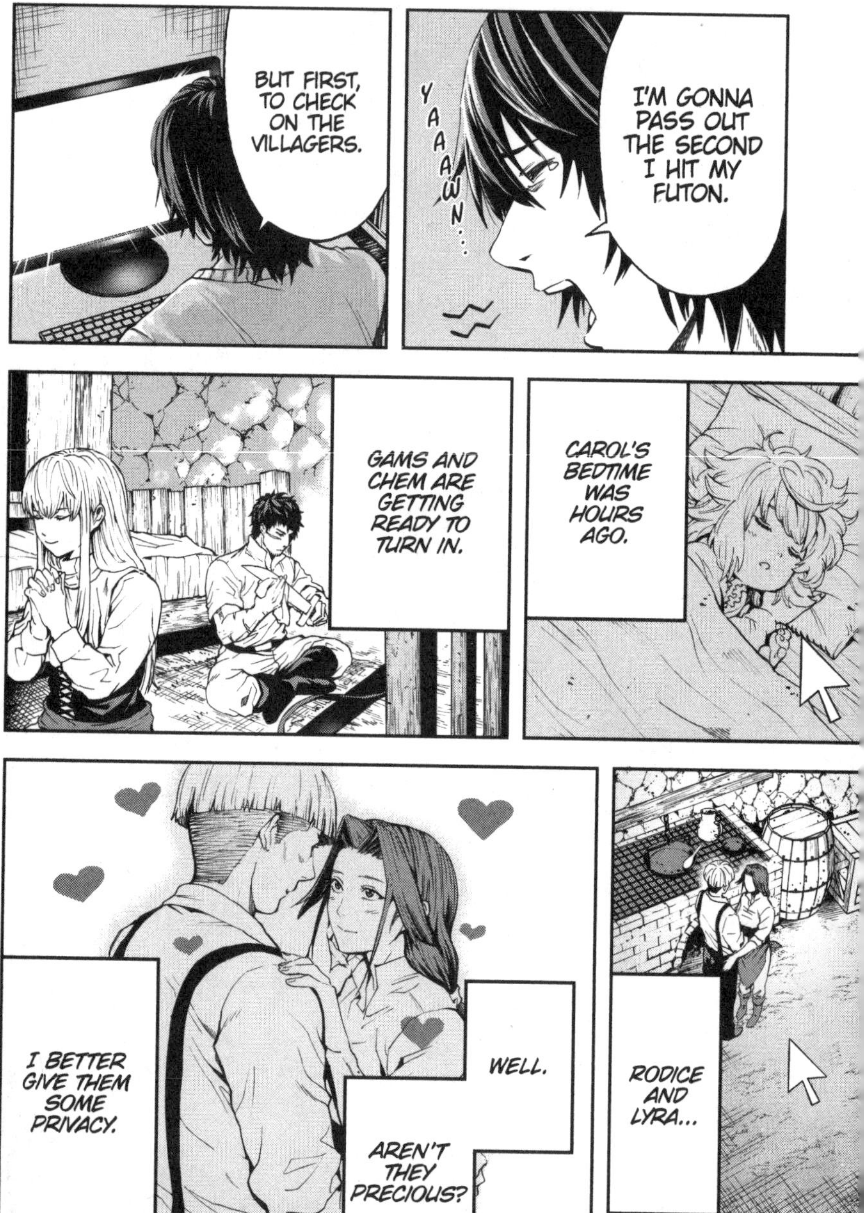
I'M GONNA PASS OUT THE SECOND I HIT MY FUTON.
YAAAWN...
BUT FIRST, TO CHECK ON THE VILLAGERS.
CAROL'S BEDTIME WAS HOURS AGO.
GAMS AND CHEM ARE GETTING READY TO TURN IN.
RODICE AND LYRA...
WELL.
AREN'T THEY PRECIOUS?
I BETTER GIVE THEM SOME PRIVACY.

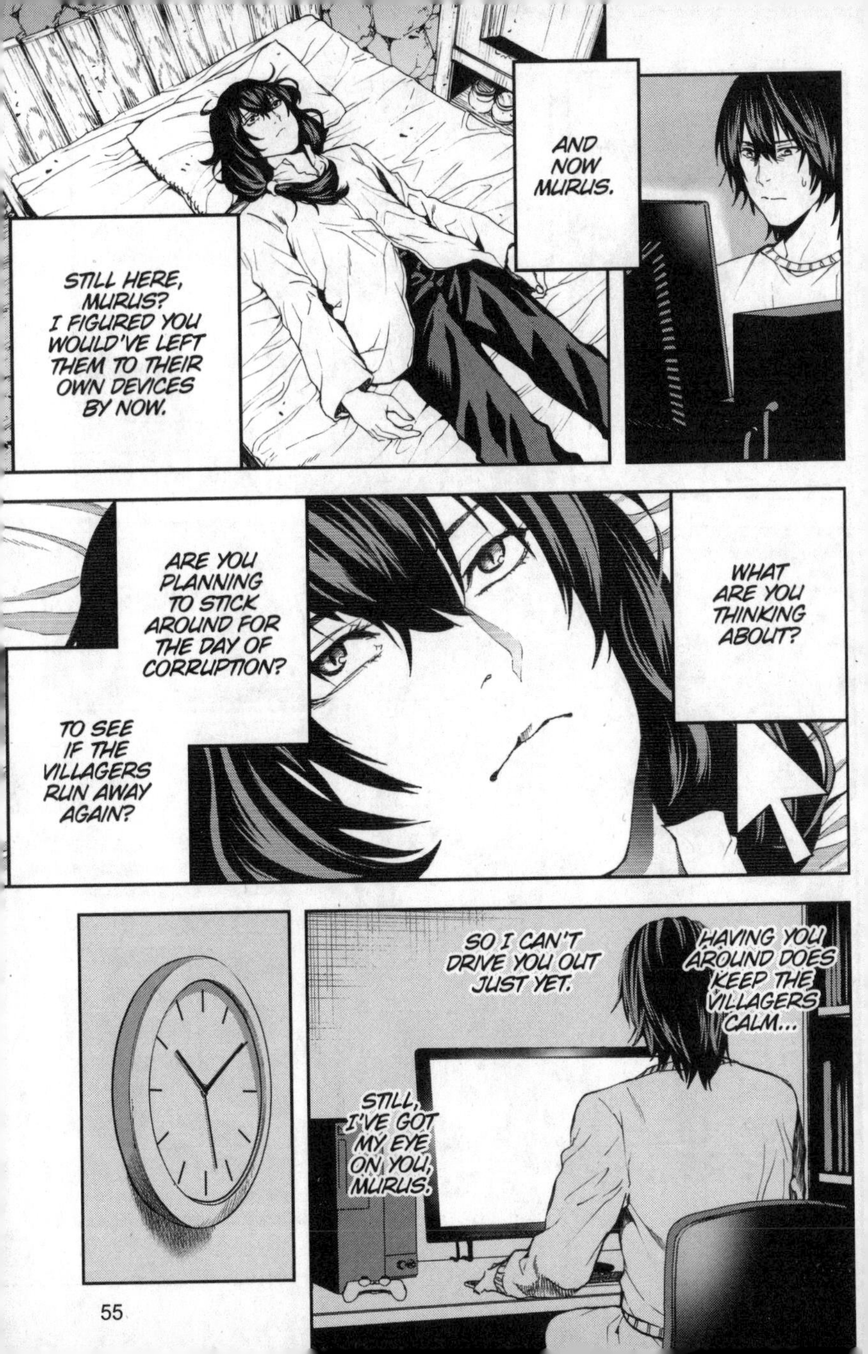
AND NOW MURUS.
STILL HERE, MURUS? I FIGURED YOU WOULD'VE LEFT THEM TO THEIR OWN DEVICES BY NOW.
WHAT ARE YOU THINKING ABOUT?
ARE YOU PLANNING TO STICK AROUND FOR THE DAY OF CORRUPTION?
TO SEE IF THE VILLAGERS RUN AWAY AGAIN?
HAVING YOU AROUND DOES KEEP THE VILLAGERS CALM...
SO I CAN'T DRIVE YOU OUT JUST YET.
STILL, I'VE GOT MY EYE ON YOU, MURUS.

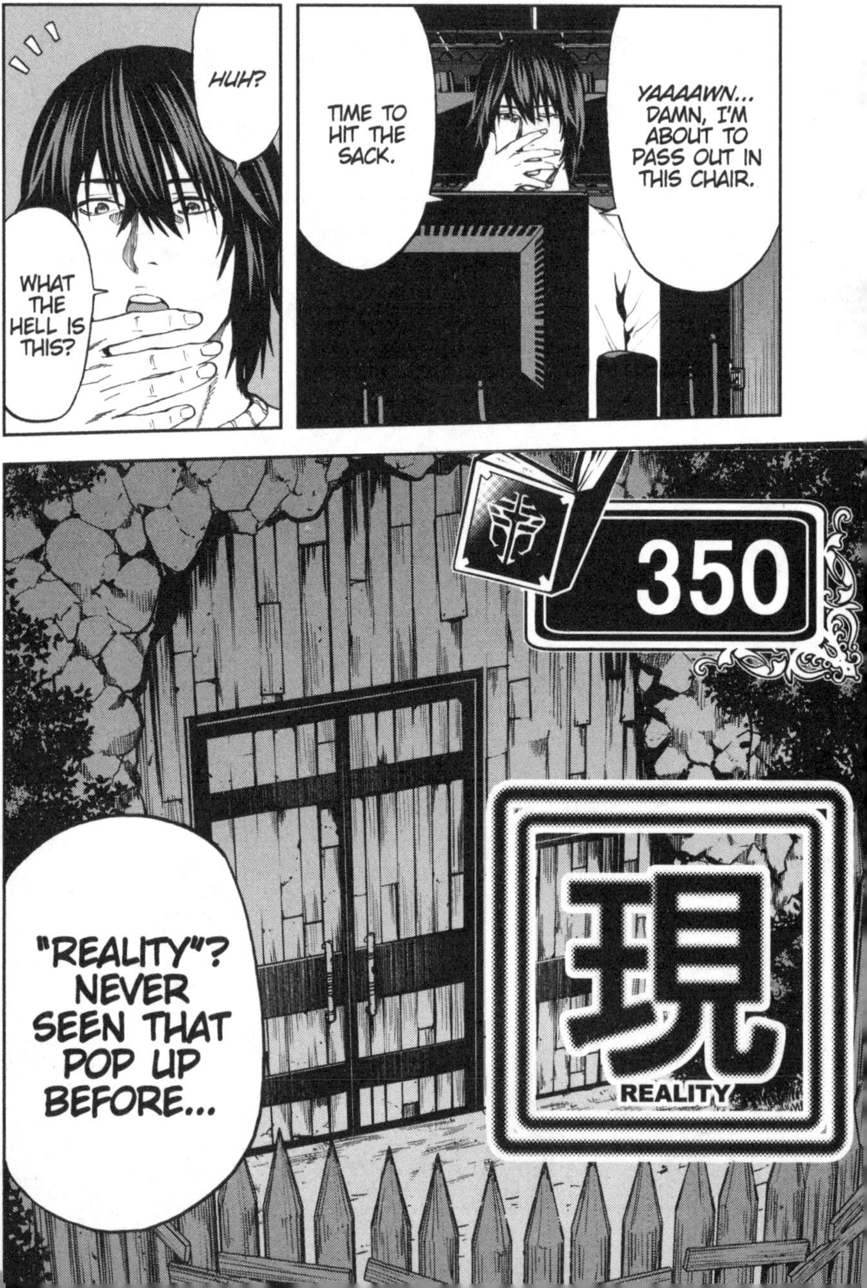
YAAAAWN... DAMN, I'M ABOUT TO PASS OUT IN THIS CHAIR.
TIME TO HIT THE SACK.
HUH?
WHAT THE HELL IS THIS?
350
現
REALITY
"REALITY"? NEVER SEEN THAT POP UP BEFORE...

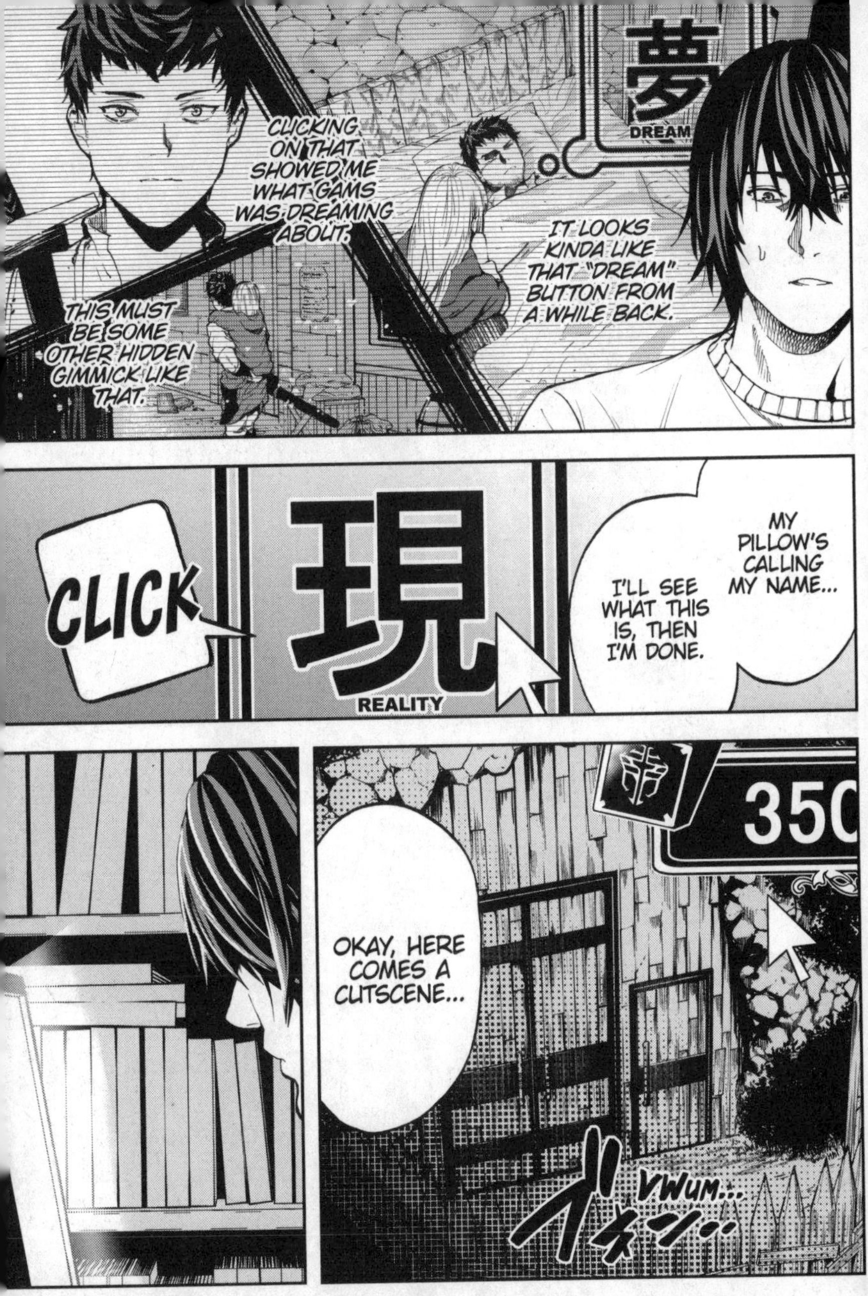
夢
DREAM
IT LOOKS KINDA LIKE THAT "DREAM" BUTTON FROM A WHILE BACK.
CLICKING ON THAT SHOWED ME WHAT GAMS WAS DREAMING ABOUT.
THIS MUST BE SOME OTHER HIDDEN GIMMICK LIKE THAT.
MY PILLOW'S CALLING MY NAME...
I'LL SEE WHAT THIS IS, THEN I'M DONE.
現
REALITY
CLICK
350
OKAY, HERE COMES A CUTSCENE...
VWUM...

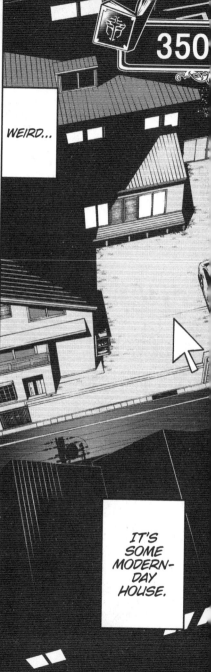

WEIRD...

IT'S SOME MODERN-DAY HOUSE.

AHA, THERE'S STILL MOUSE CONTROL.

I CAN ZOOM IN AND OUT AND MOVE AROUND, JUST LIKE ALWAYS.

THE ENTRANCE.

THE HALL-WAY.

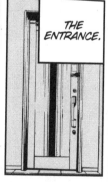

THE KITCHEN.

WAIT A SEC...

THE CRAP-PER.

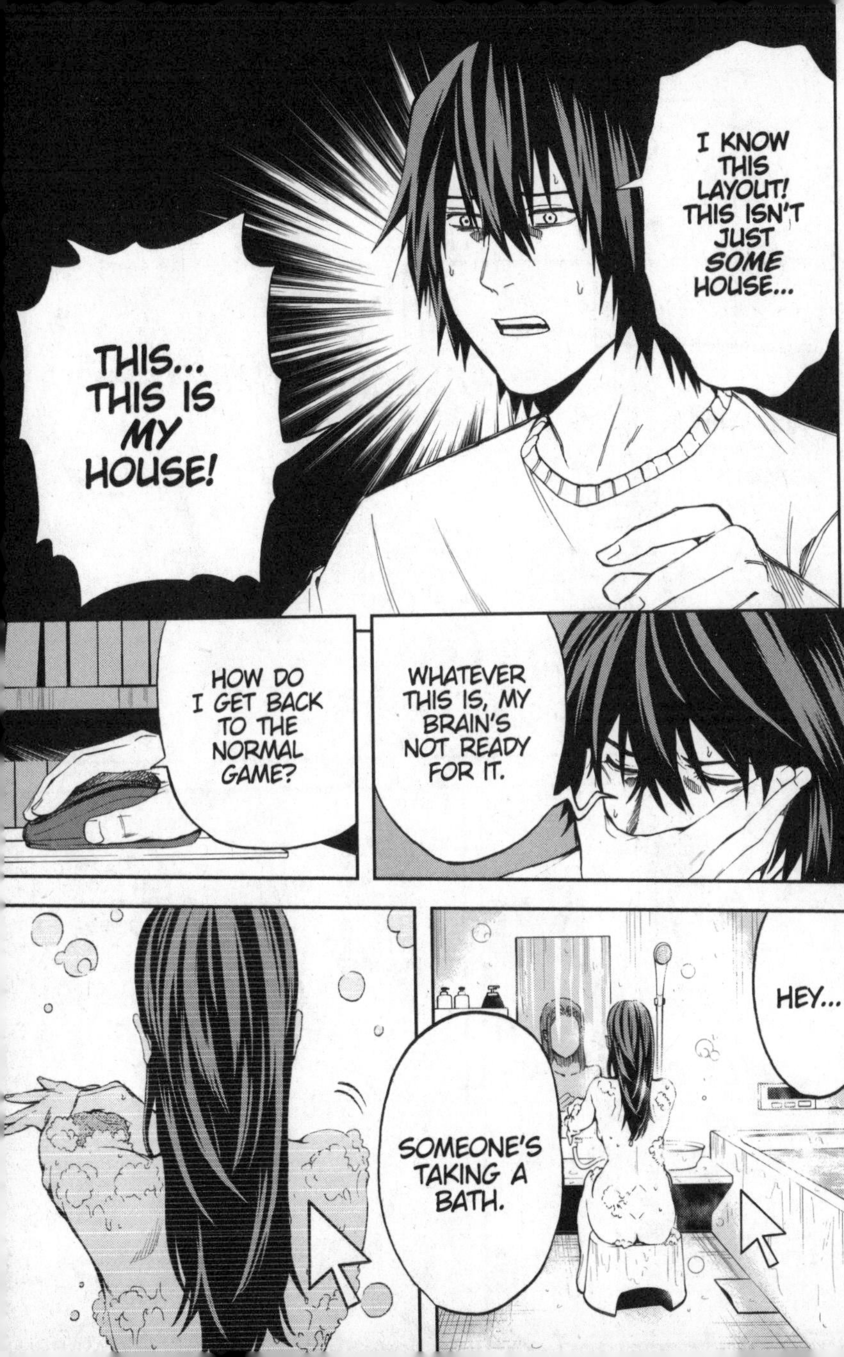
I KNOW THIS LAYOUT! THIS ISN'T JUST *SOME* HOUSE...
THIS... THIS IS *MY* HOUSE!
WHATEVER THIS IS, MY BRAIN'S NOT READY FOR IT.
HOW DO I GET BACK TO THE NORMAL GAME?
HEY...
SOMEONE'S TAKING A BATH.

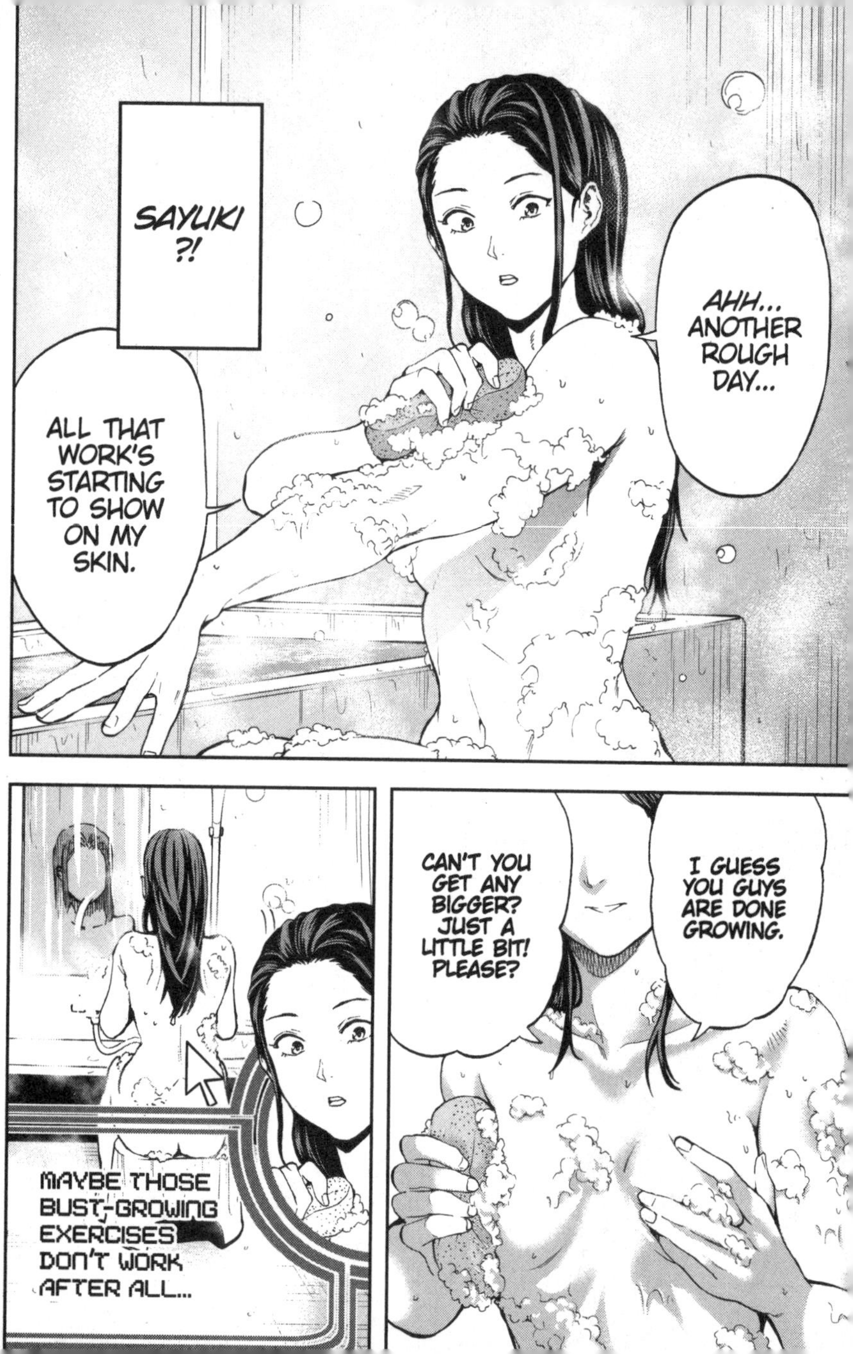
AHH... ANOTHER ROUGH DAY...
SAYUKI ?!
ALL THAT WORK'S STARTING TO SHOW ON MY SKIN.
I GUESS YOU GUYS ARE DONE GROWING.
CAN'T YOU GET ANY BIGGER? JUST A LITTLE BIT! PLEASE?
MAYBE THOSE BUST-GROWING EXERCISES DON'T WORK AFTER ALL...

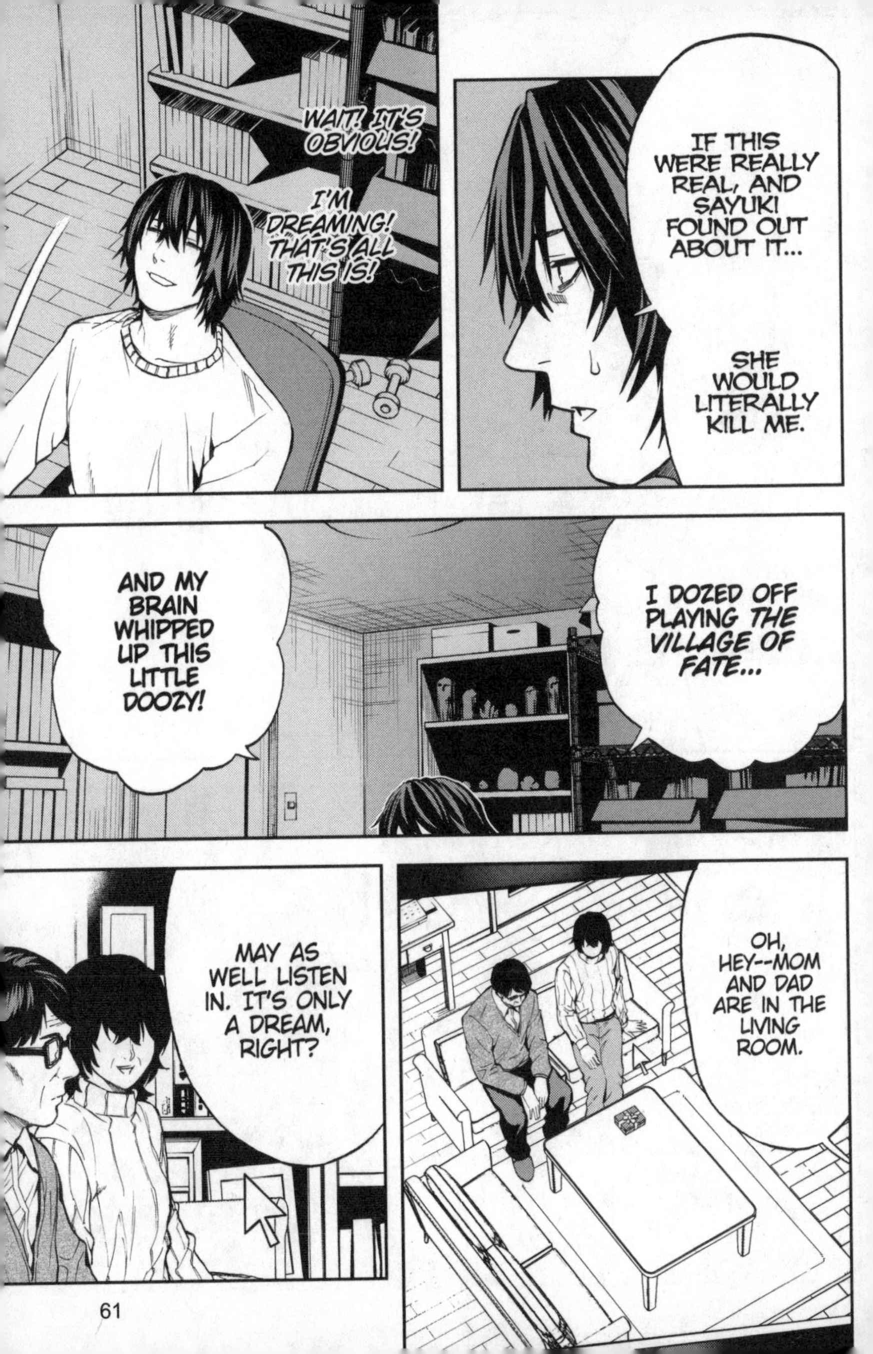
IF THIS WERE REALLY REAL, AND SAYUKI FOUND OUT ABOUT IT...
SHE WOULD LITERALLY KILL ME.
WAIT! IT'S OBVIOUS!
I'M DREAMING! THAT'S ALL THIS IS!
I DOZED OFF PLAYING *THE VILLAGE OF FATE*...
AND MY BRAIN WHIPPED UP THIS LITTLE DOOZY!
OH, HEY--MOM AND DAD ARE IN THE LIVING ROOM.
MAY AS WELL LISTEN IN. IT'S ONLY A DREAM, RIGHT?

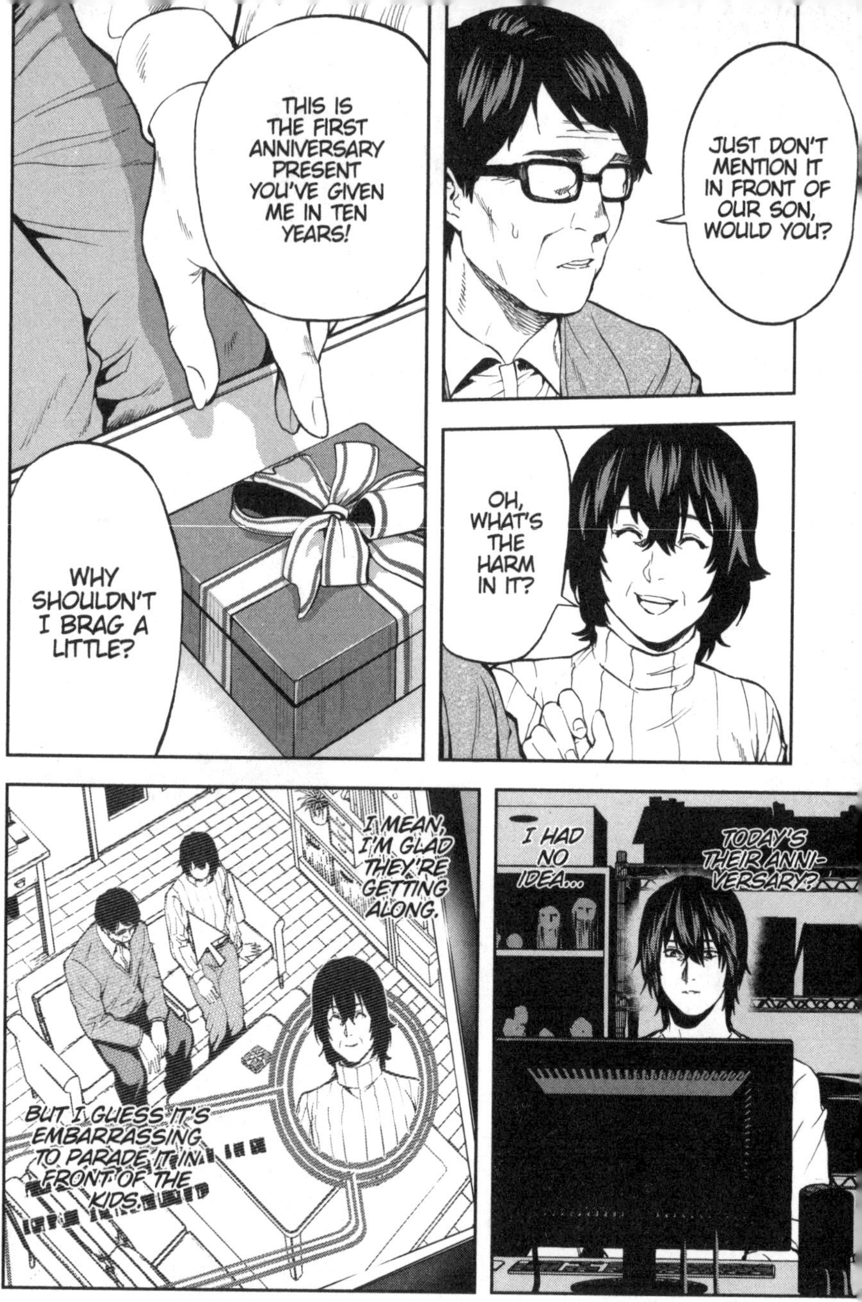
JUST DON'T MENTION IT IN FRONT OF OUR SON, WOULD YOU?
OH, WHAT'S THE HARM IN IT?
THIS IS THE FIRST ANNIVERSARY PRESENT YOU'VE GIVEN ME IN TEN YEARS!
WHY SHOULDN'T I BRAG A LITTLE?
TODAY'S THEIR ANNI-VERSARY?
I HAD NO IDEA...
I MEAN, I'M GLAD THEY'RE GETTING ALONG.
BUT I GUESS IT'S EMBARRASSING TO PARADE IT IN FRONT OF THE KIDS.

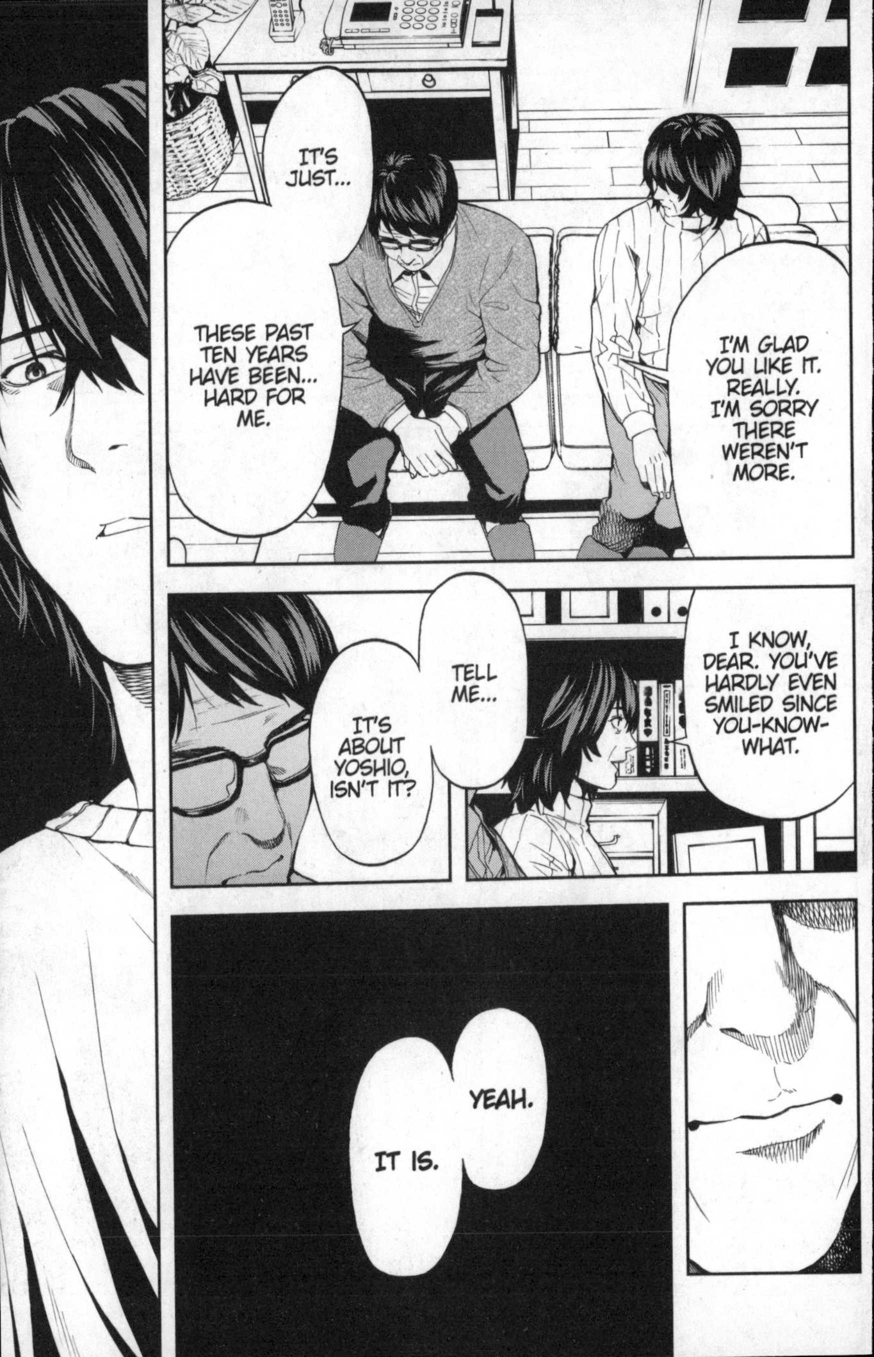
I'M GLAD YOU LIKE IT. REALLY. I'M SORRY THERE WEREN'T MORE.
IT'S JUST...
THESE PAST TEN YEARS HAVE BEEN... HARD FOR ME.
I KNOW, DEAR. YOU'VE HARDLY EVEN SMILED SINCE YOU-KNOW-WHAT.
TELL ME...
IT'S ABOUT YOSHIO, ISN'T IT?
YEAH.
IT IS.

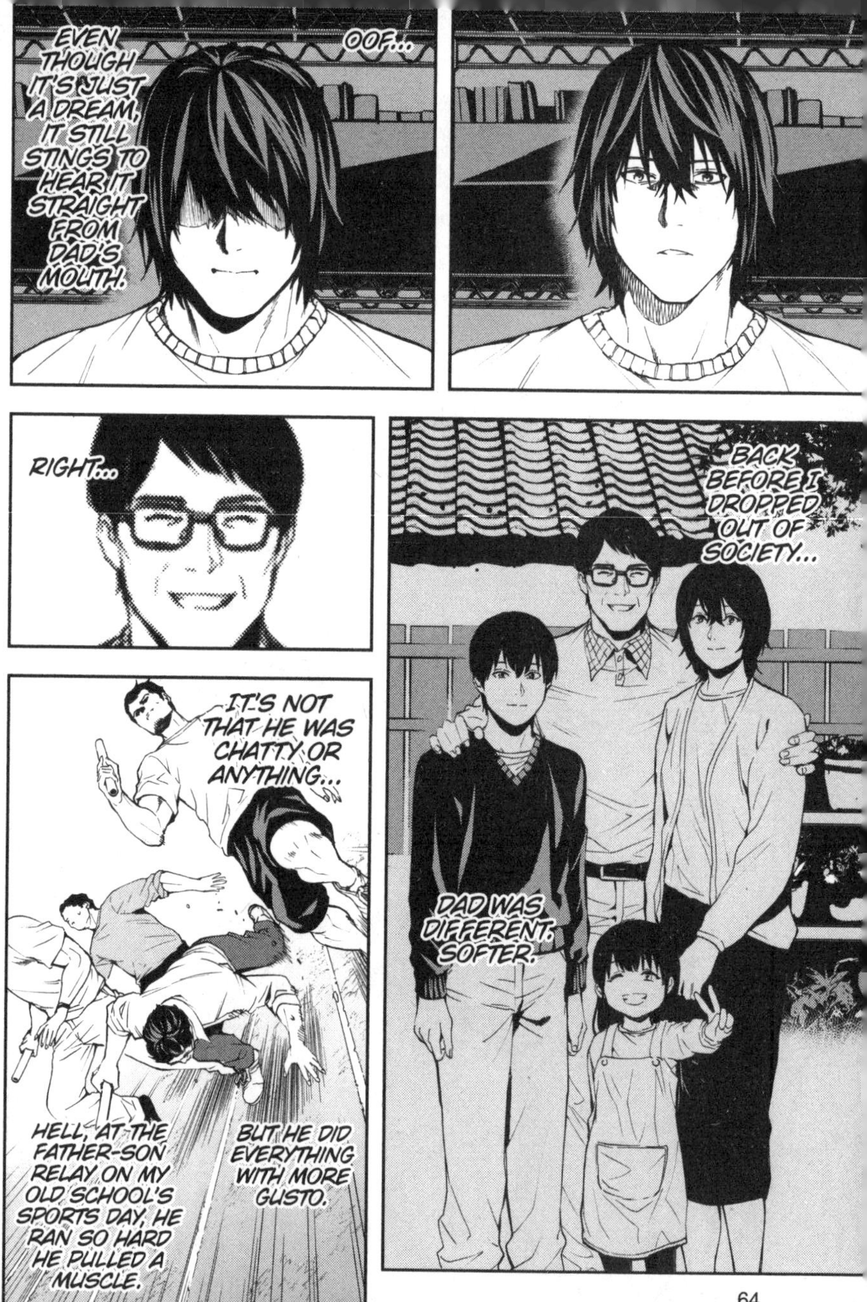
OOF...
EVEN THOUGH IT'S JUST A DREAM, IT STILL STINGS TO HEAR IT STRAIGHT FROM DAD'S MOUTH.
BACK BEFORE I DROPPED OUT OF SOCIETY...
DAD WAS DIFFERENT. SOFTER.
RIGHT...
IT'S NOT THAT HE WAS CHATTY OR ANYTHING...
BUT HE DID EVERYTHING WITH MORE GUSTO.
HELL, AT THE FATHER-SON RELAY ON MY OLD SCHOOL'S SPORTS DAY, HE RAN SO HARD HE PULLED A MUSCLE.

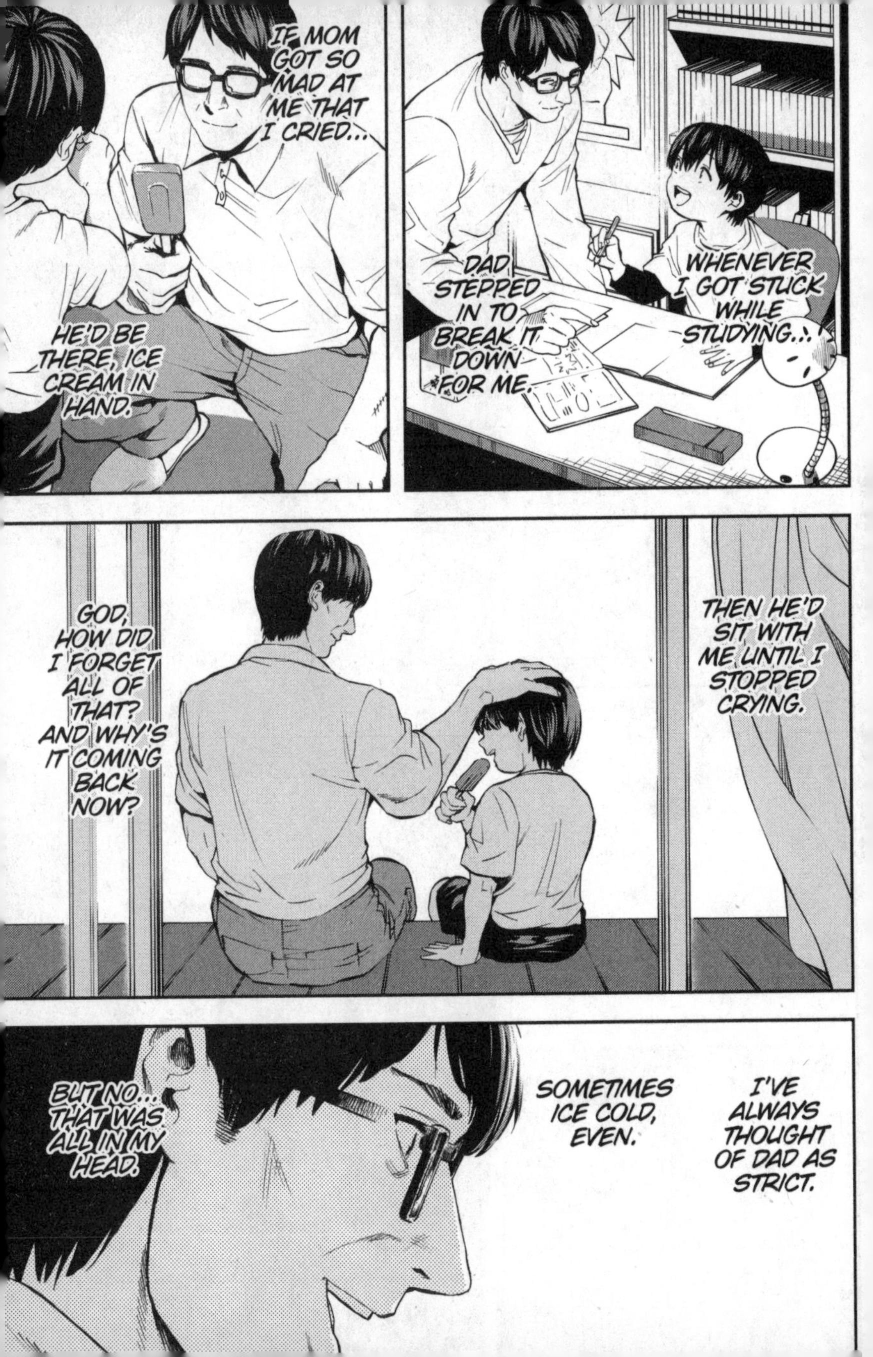
WHENEVER I GOT STUCK WHILE STUDYING...
DAD STEPPED IN TO BREAK IT DOWN FOR ME.
IF MOM GOT SO MAD AT ME THAT I CRIED...
HE'D BE THERE, ICE CREAM IN HAND.
THEN HE'D SIT WITH ME UNTIL I STOPPED CRYING.
GOD, HOW DID I FORGET ALL OF THAT? AND WHY'S IT COMING BACK NOW?
I'VE ALWAYS THOUGHT OF DAD AS STRICT.
SOMETIMES ICE COLD, EVEN.
BUT NO... THAT WAS ALL IN MY HEAD.

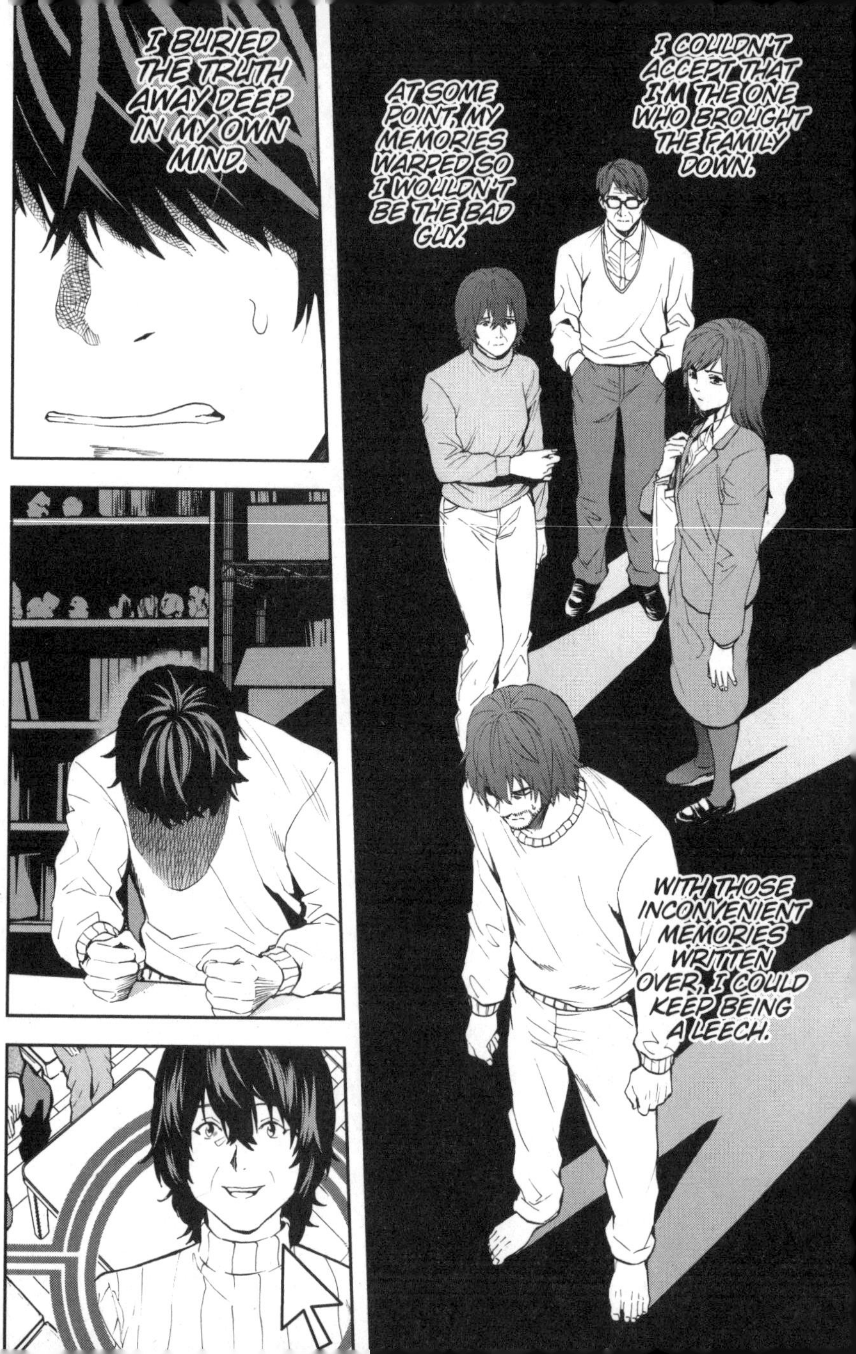
I COULDN'T ACCEPT THAT I'M THE ONE WHO BROUGHT THE FAMILY DOWN.
AT SOME POINT, MY MEMORIES WARPED SO I WOULDN'T BE THE BAD GUY.
WITH THOSE INCONVENIENT MEMORIES WRITTEN OVER, I COULD KEEP BEING A LEECH.
I BURIED THE TRUTH AWAY DEEP IN MY OWN MIND.

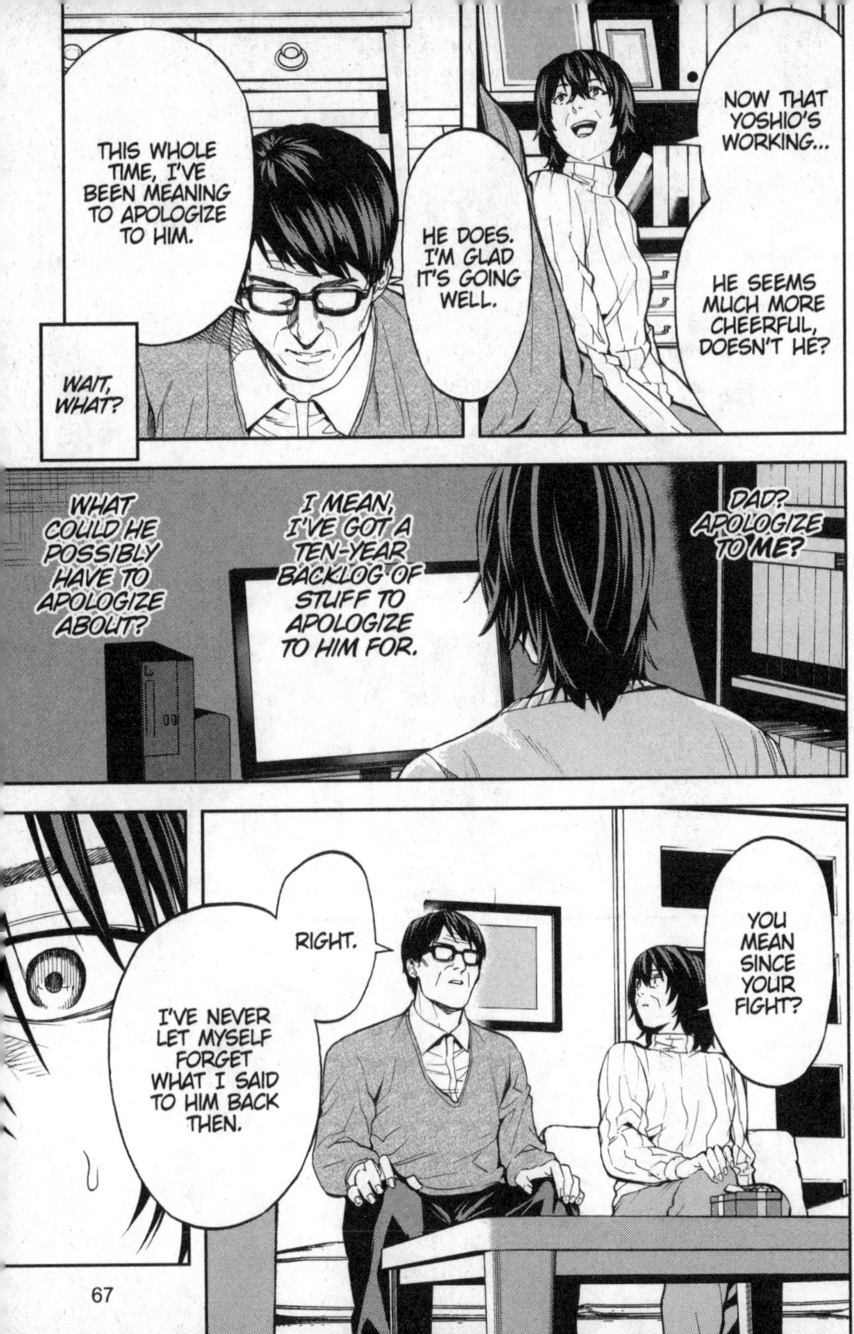

NOW THAT YOSHIO'S WORKING...
HE SEEMS MUCH MORE CHEERFUL, DOESN'T HE?
HE DOES. I'M GLAD IT'S GOING WELL.
THIS WHOLE TIME, I'VE BEEN MEANING TO APOLOGIZE TO HIM.
WAIT, WHAT?
DAD? APOLOGIZE TO ME?
I MEAN, I'VE GOT A TEN-YEAR BACKLOG OF STUFF TO APOLOGIZE TO HIM FOR.
WHAT COULD HE POSSIBLY HAVE TO APOLOGIZE ABOUT?
YOU MEAN SINCE YOUR FIGHT?
RIGHT.
I'VE NEVER LET MYSELF FORGET WHAT I SAID TO HIM BACK THEN.

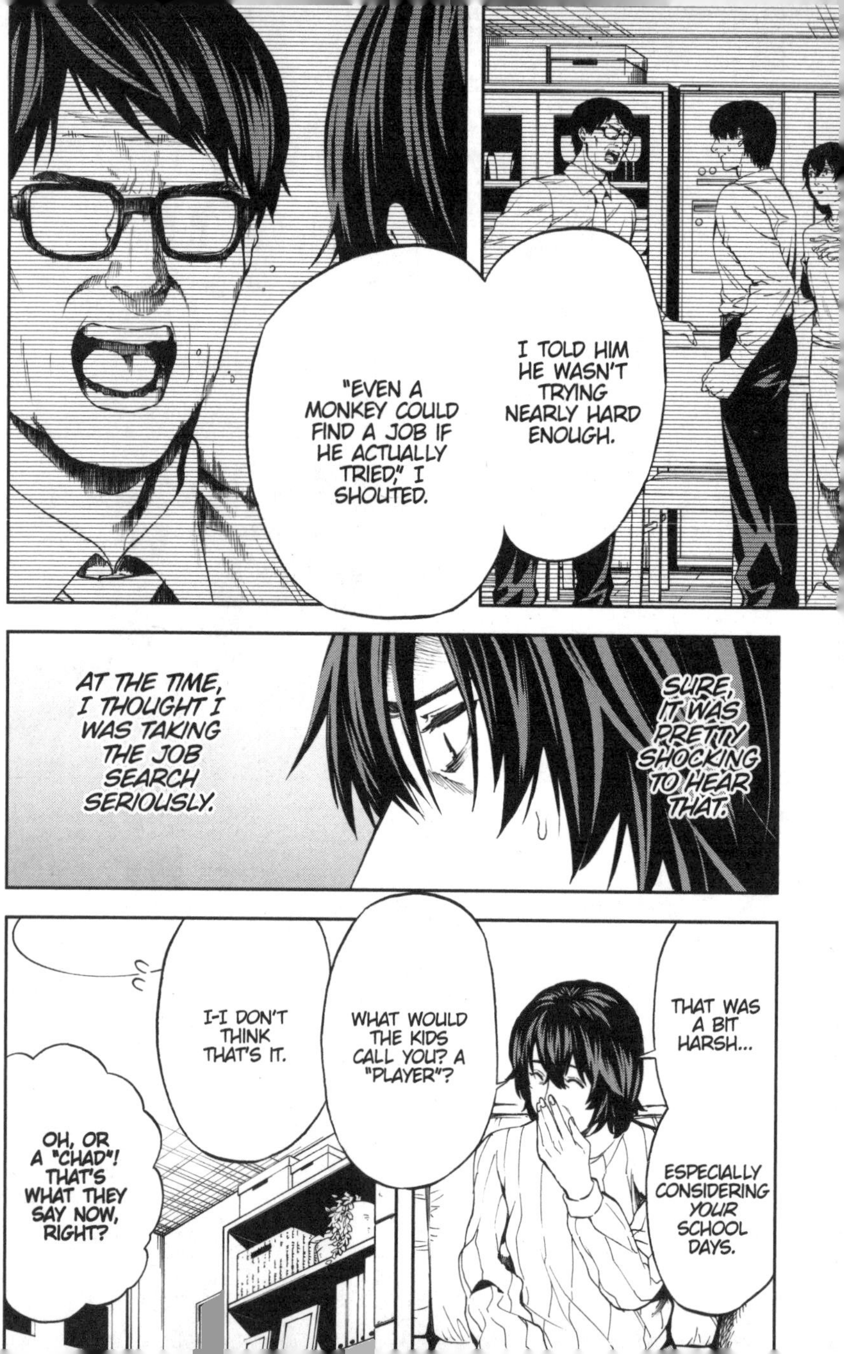
I TOLD HIM HE WASN'T TRYING NEARLY HARD ENOUGH.
"EVEN A MONKEY COULD FIND A JOB IF HE ACTUALLY TRIED," I SHOUTED.
SURE, IT WAS PRETTY SHOCKING TO HEAR THAT.
AT THE TIME, I THOUGHT I WAS TAKING THE JOB SEARCH SERIOUSLY.
THAT WAS A BIT HARSH...
ESPECIALLY CONSIDERING *YOUR* SCHOOL DAYS.
WHAT WOULD THE KIDS CALL YOU? A "PLAYER"?
I-I DON'T THINK THAT'S IT.
OH, OR A "CHAD"! THAT'S WHAT THEY SAY NOW, RIGHT?

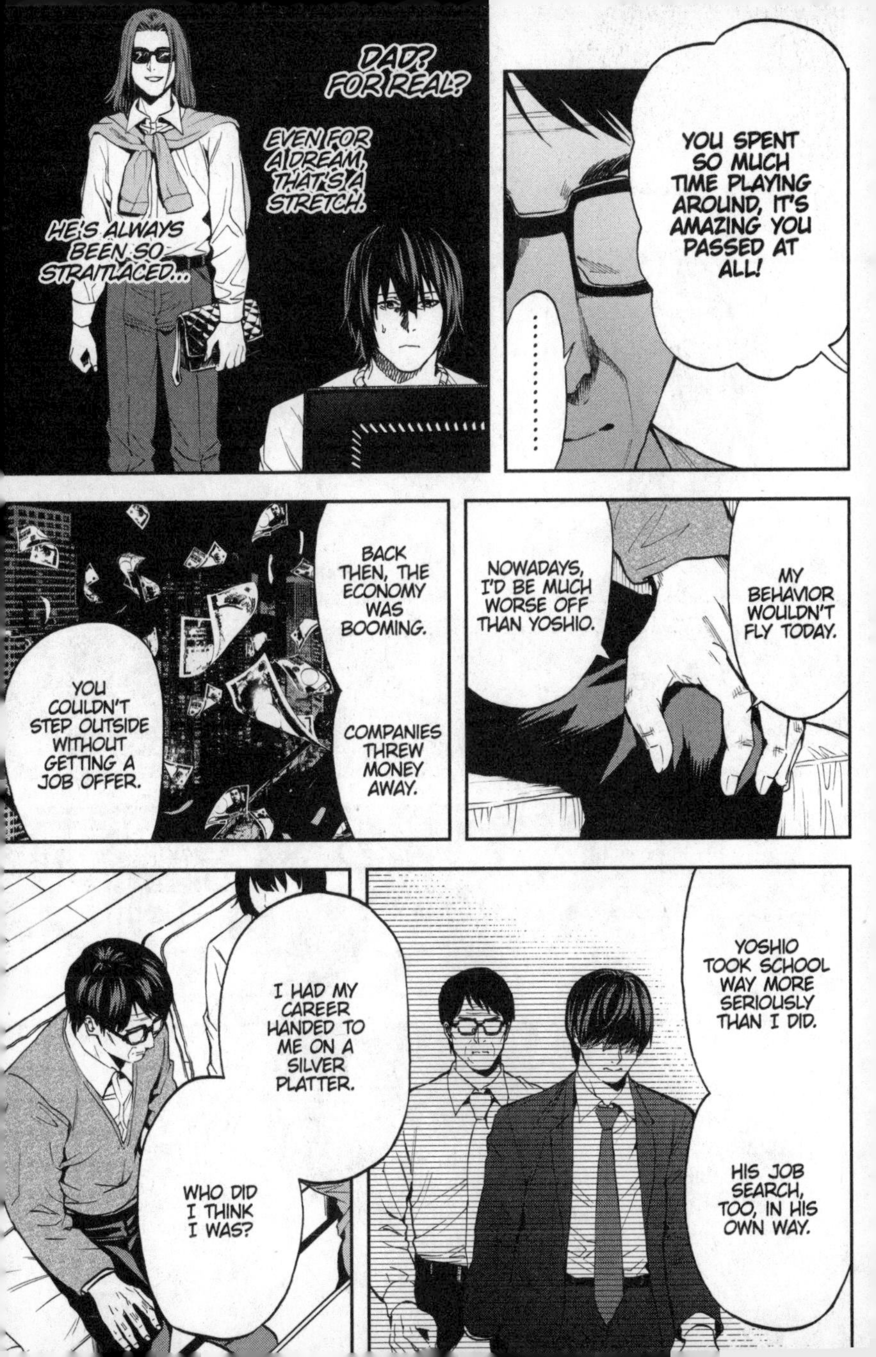
YOU SPENT SO MUCH TIME PLAYING AROUND, IT'S AMAZING YOU PASSED AT ALL!
......
DAD? FOR REAL?
EVEN FOR A DREAM, THAT'S A STRETCH.
HE'S ALWAYS BEEN SO STRAITLACED...
MY BEHAVIOR WOULDN'T FLY TODAY.
NOWADAYS, I'D BE MUCH WORSE OFF THAN YOSHIO.
BACK THEN, THE ECONOMY WAS BOOMING.
COMPANIES THREW MONEY AWAY.
YOU COULDN'T STEP OUTSIDE WITHOUT GETTING A JOB OFFER.
YOSHIO TOOK SCHOOL WAY MORE SERIOUSLY THAN I DID.
HIS JOB SEARCH, TOO, IN HIS OWN WAY.
I HAD MY CAREER HANDED TO ME ON A SILVER PLATTER.
WHO DID I THINK I WAS?

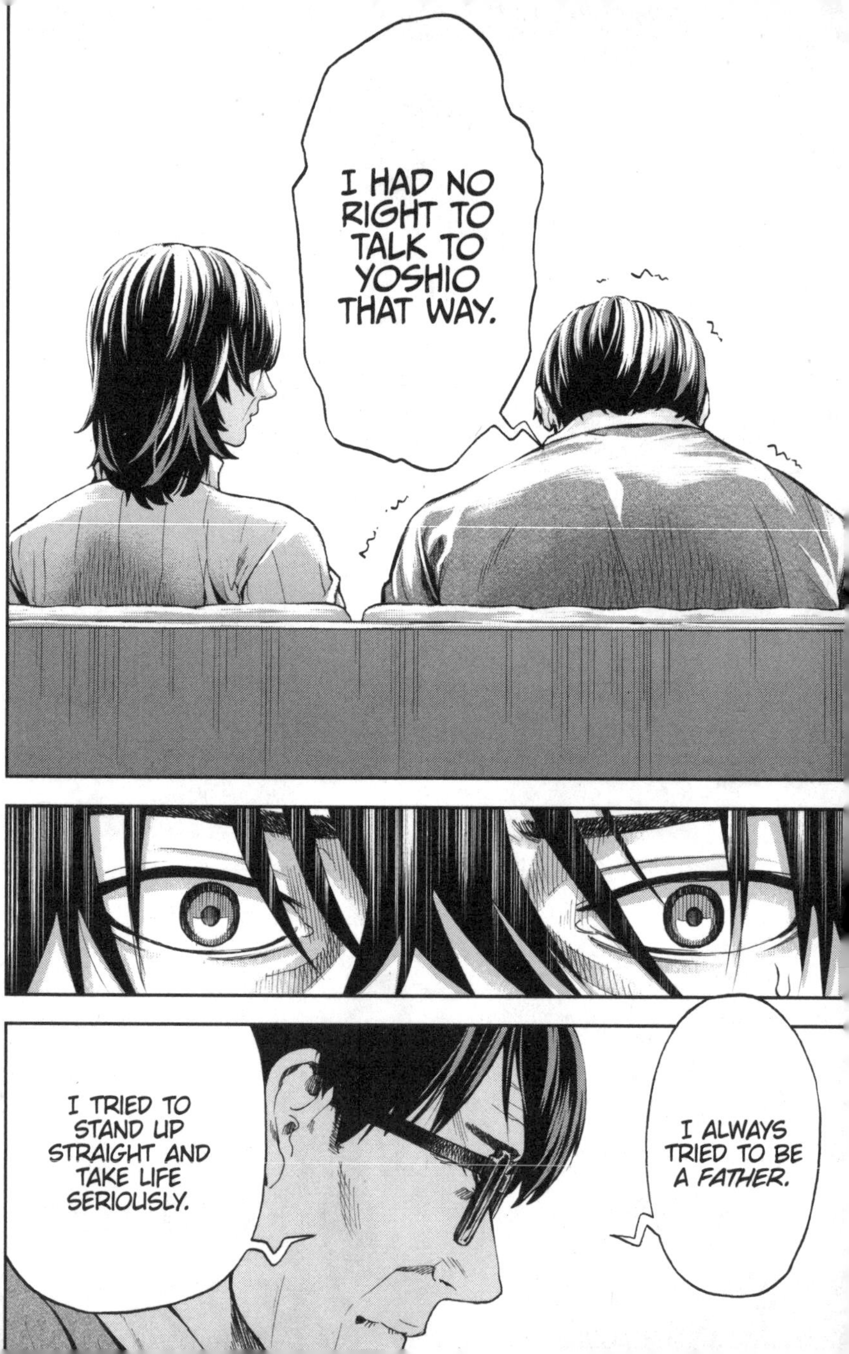
I HAD NO RIGHT TO TALK TO YOSHIO THAT WAY.
I ALWAYS TRIED TO BE A *FATHER.*
I TRIED TO STAND UP STRAIGHT AND TAKE LIFE SERIOUSLY.

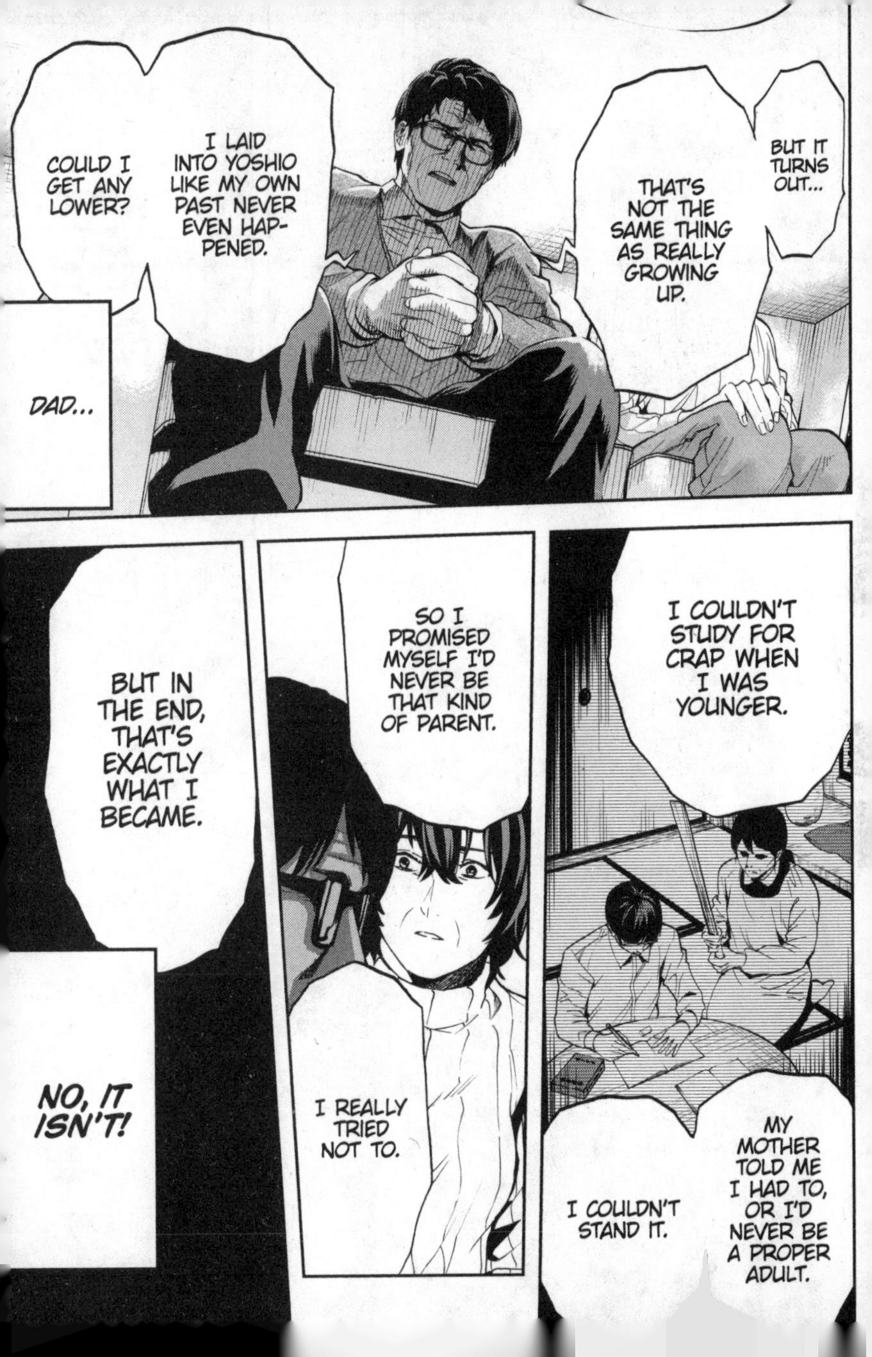
BUT IT TURNS OUT...
THAT'S NOT THE SAME THING AS REALLY GROWING UP.
I LAID INTO YOSHIO LIKE MY OWN PAST NEVER EVEN HAPPENED.
COULD I GET ANY LOWER?
DAD...
I COULDN'T STUDY FOR CRAP WHEN I WAS YOUNGER.
MY MOTHER TOLD ME I HAD TO, OR I'D NEVER BE A PROPER ADULT.
I COULDN'T STAND IT.
SO I PROMISED MYSELF I'D NEVER BE THAT KIND OF PARENT.
I REALLY TRIED NOT TO.
BUT IN THE END, THAT'S EXACTLY WHAT I BECAME.
NO, IT ISN'T!

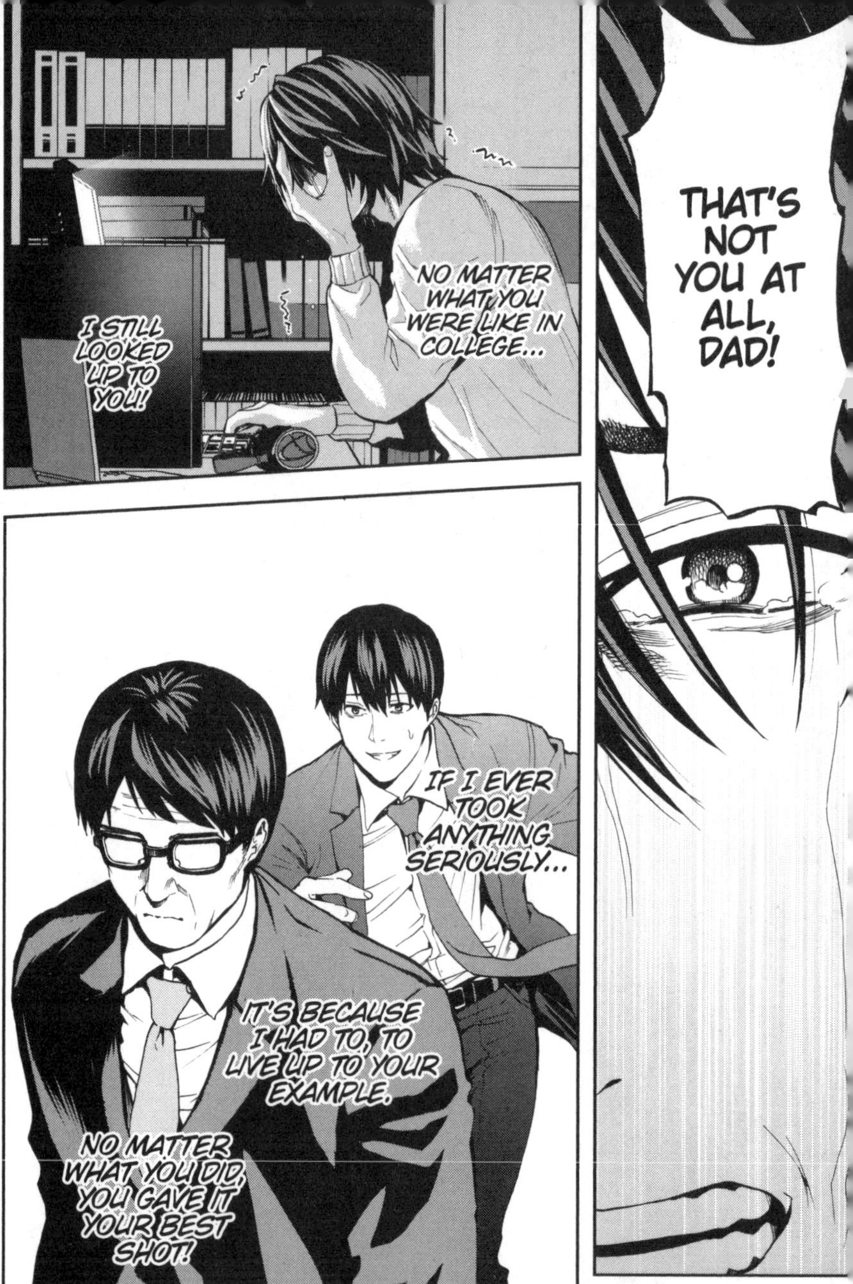
THAT'S NOT YOU AT ALL, DAD!
NO MATTER WHAT YOU WERE LIKE IN COLLEGE...
I STILL LOOKED UP TO YOU!
IF I EVER TOOK ANYTHING SERIOUSLY...
IT'S BECAUSE I HAD TO, TO LIVE UP TO YOUR EXAMPLE.
NO MATTER WHAT YOU DID, YOU GAVE IT YOUR BEST SHOT!

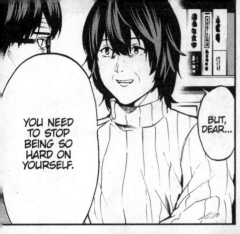

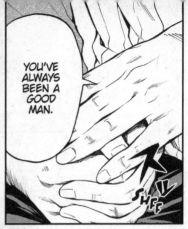

YOU'VE ALWAYS BEEN A GOOD MAN.
SHFF
BUT, DEAR...
YOU NEED TO STOP BEING SO HARD ON YOURSELF.
SURE, YOU AND I ARE GETTING OLD. OUR CHILDREN ARE ALL GROWN UP.
BUT THE ONLY THING THAT SEPARATES PARENTS FROM THEIR CHILDREN IS A FEW MORE YEARS OF EXPERIENCE.
JUST BEING A PARENT DOESN'T MAKE SOMEONE A "PROPER ADULT."
BACK WHEN I WAS A KID...
I THOUGHT PARENTS AND ADULTS WERE ALL OWED RESPECT.
SO DID I.
BUT, DEAR, WE'RE BOTH STILL GROWING.

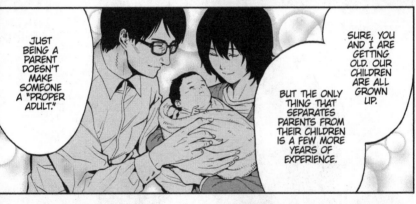

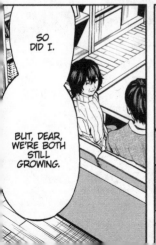

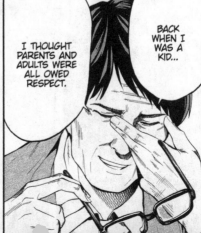

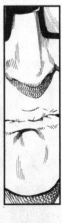

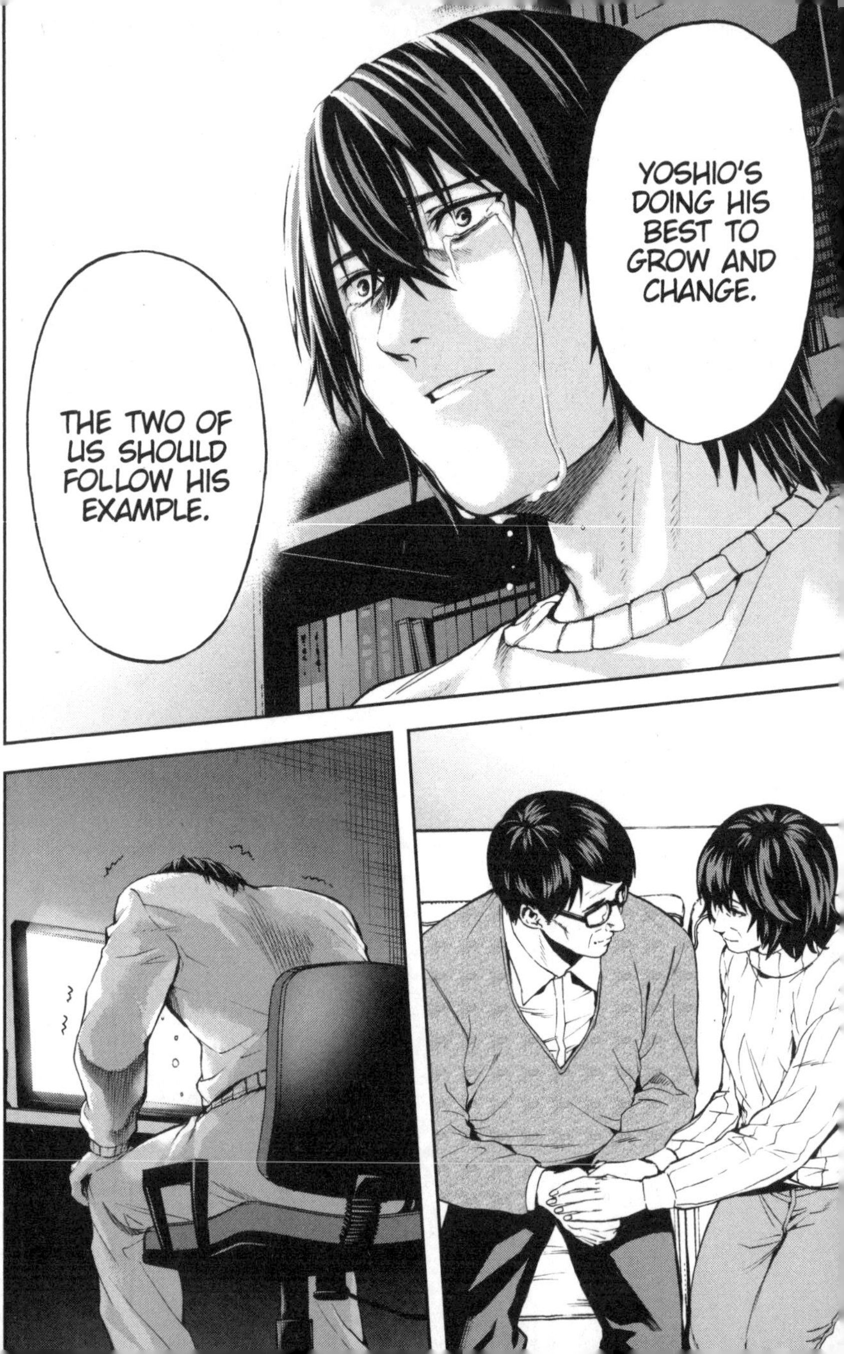
YOSHIO'S DOING HIS BEST TO GROW AND CHANGE.
THE TWO OF US SHOULD FOLLOW HIS EXAMPLE.

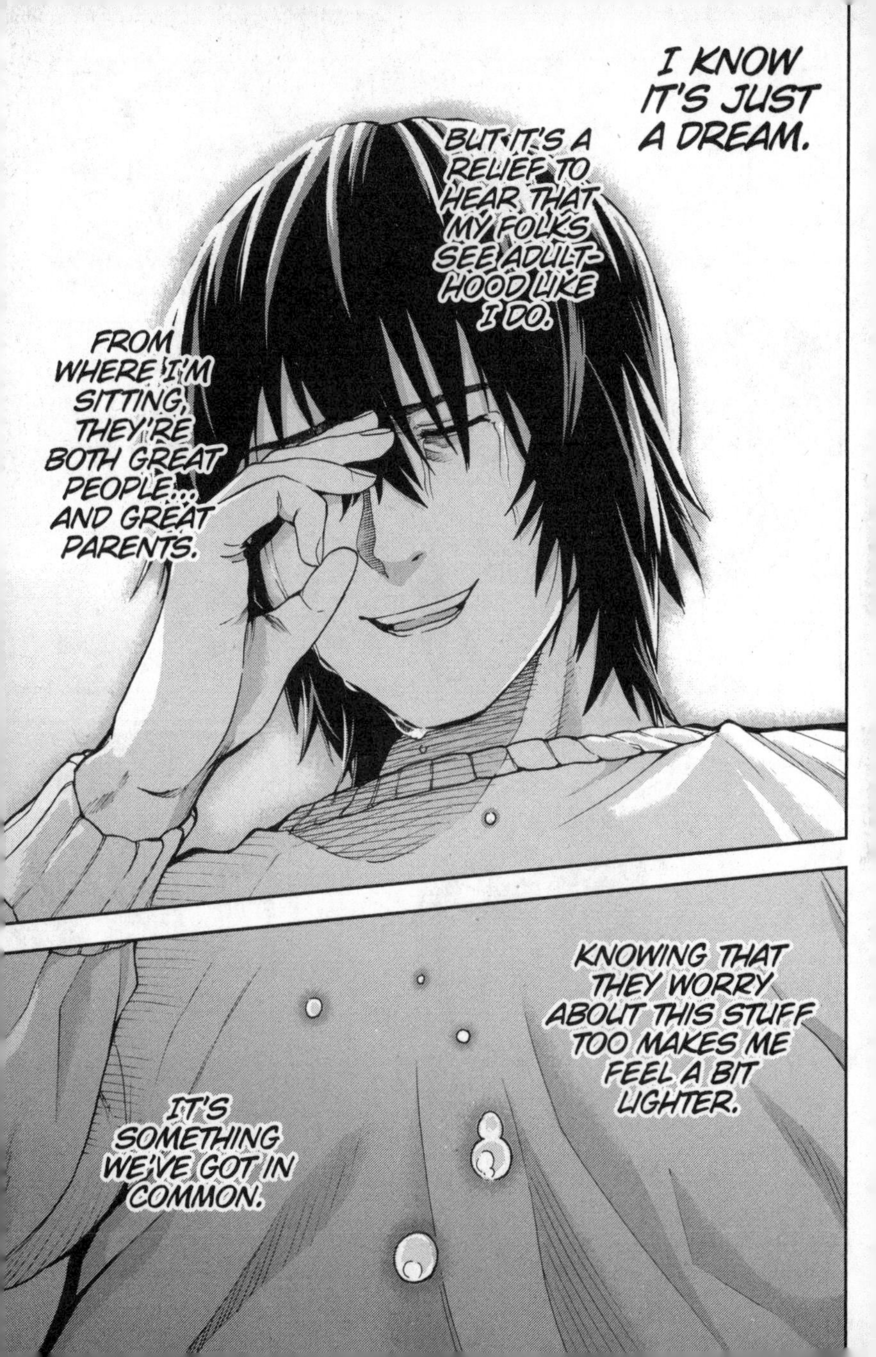
I KNOW IT'S JUST A DREAM.
BUT IT'S A RELIEF TO HEAR THAT MY FOLKS SEE ADULT-HOOD LIKE I DO.
FROM WHERE I'M SITTING, THEY'RE BOTH GREAT PEOPLE... AND GREAT PARENTS.
KNOWING THAT THEY WORRY ABOUT THIS STUFF TOO MAKES ME FEEL A BIT LIGHTER.
IT'S SOMETHING WE'VE GOT IN COMMON.

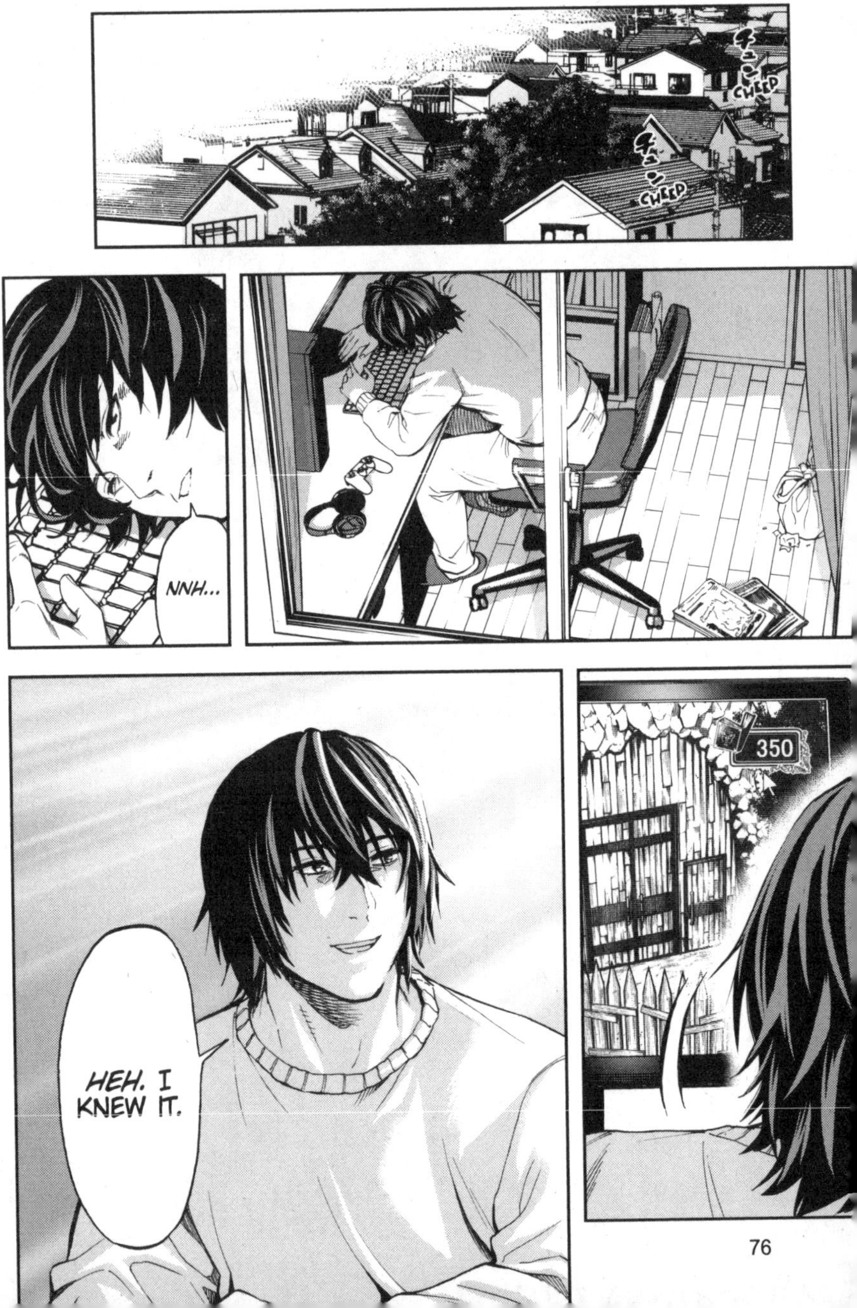

チュン
CHEEP
チュン
CHEEP
NNH...
350
HEH. I KNEW IT.

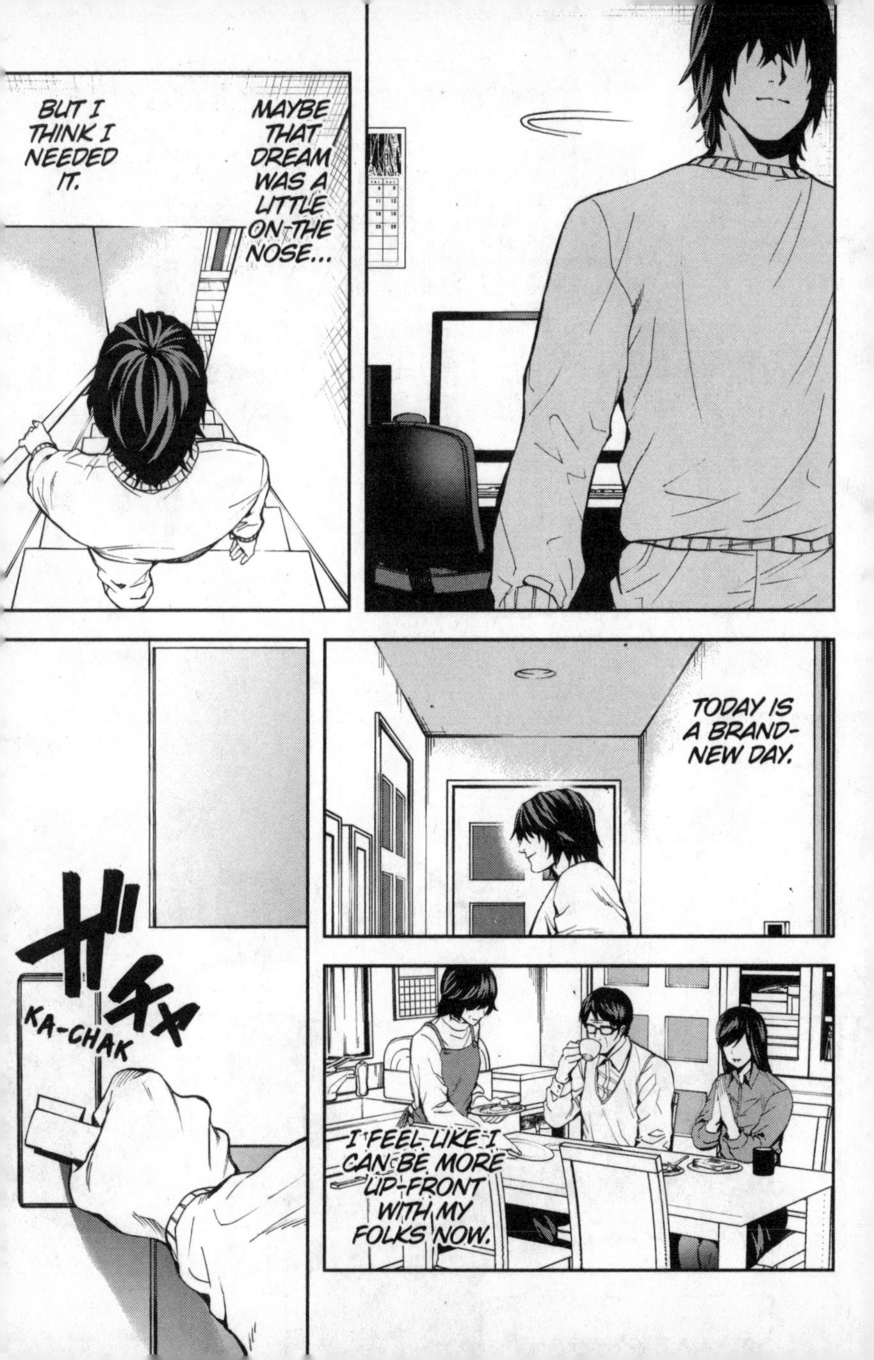
MAYBE THAT DREAM WAS A LITTLE ON-THE NOSE...
BUT I THINK I NEEDED IT.
TODAY IS A BRAND-NEW DAY.
I FEEL LIKE I CAN BE MORE UP-FRONT WITH MY FOLKS NOW.
ガチャ
KA-CHAK

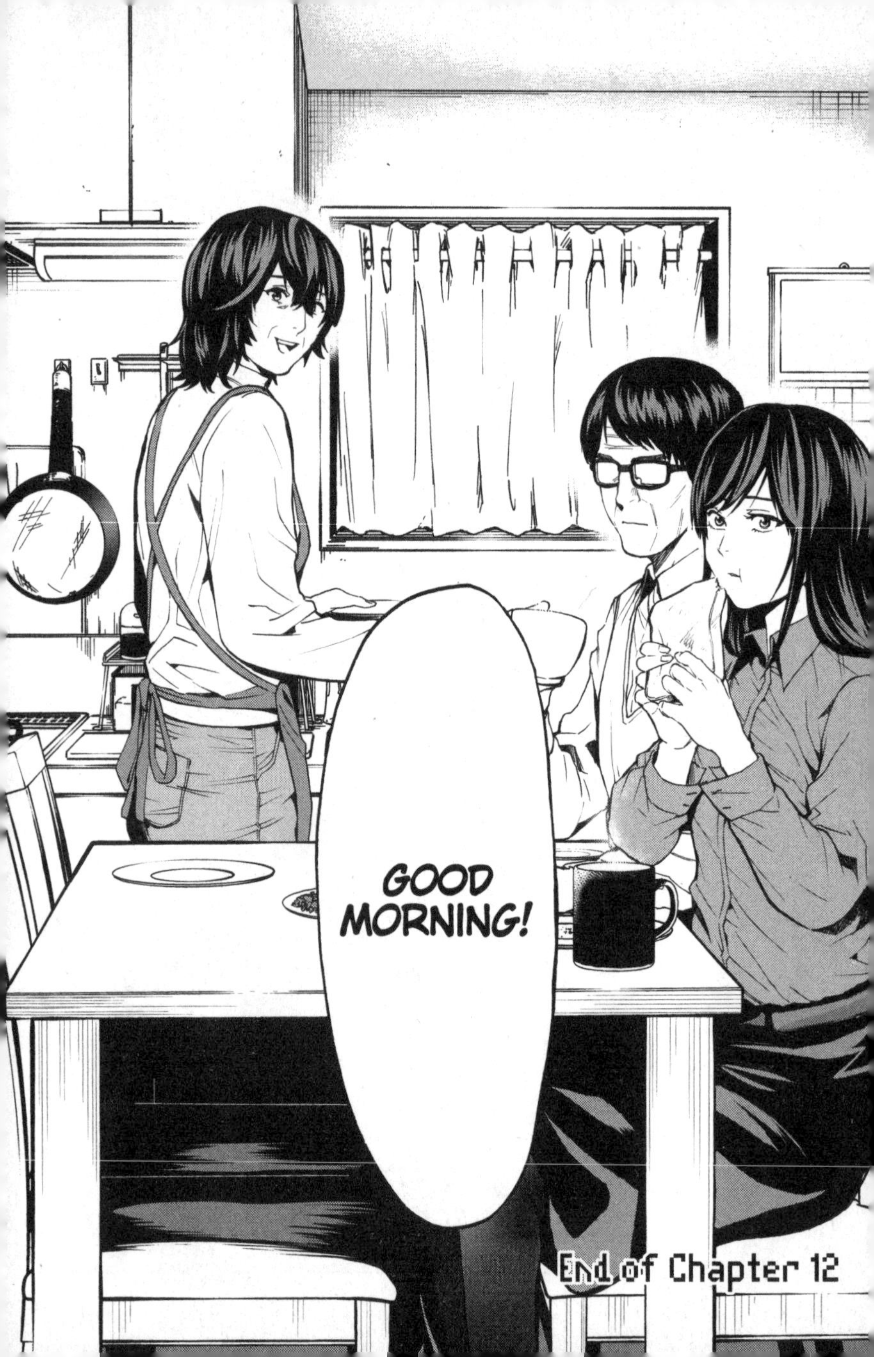
GOOD MORNING!
End of Chapter 12

Character

Yoshio's Dad (College Days)

▶ Gender: Male

Class: Playboy

E : Sunglasses

E : Fashionable cloth armor

E : Breezy attitude

THE NPCs IN THIS VILLAGE SIM GAME MUST BE REAL! ↵

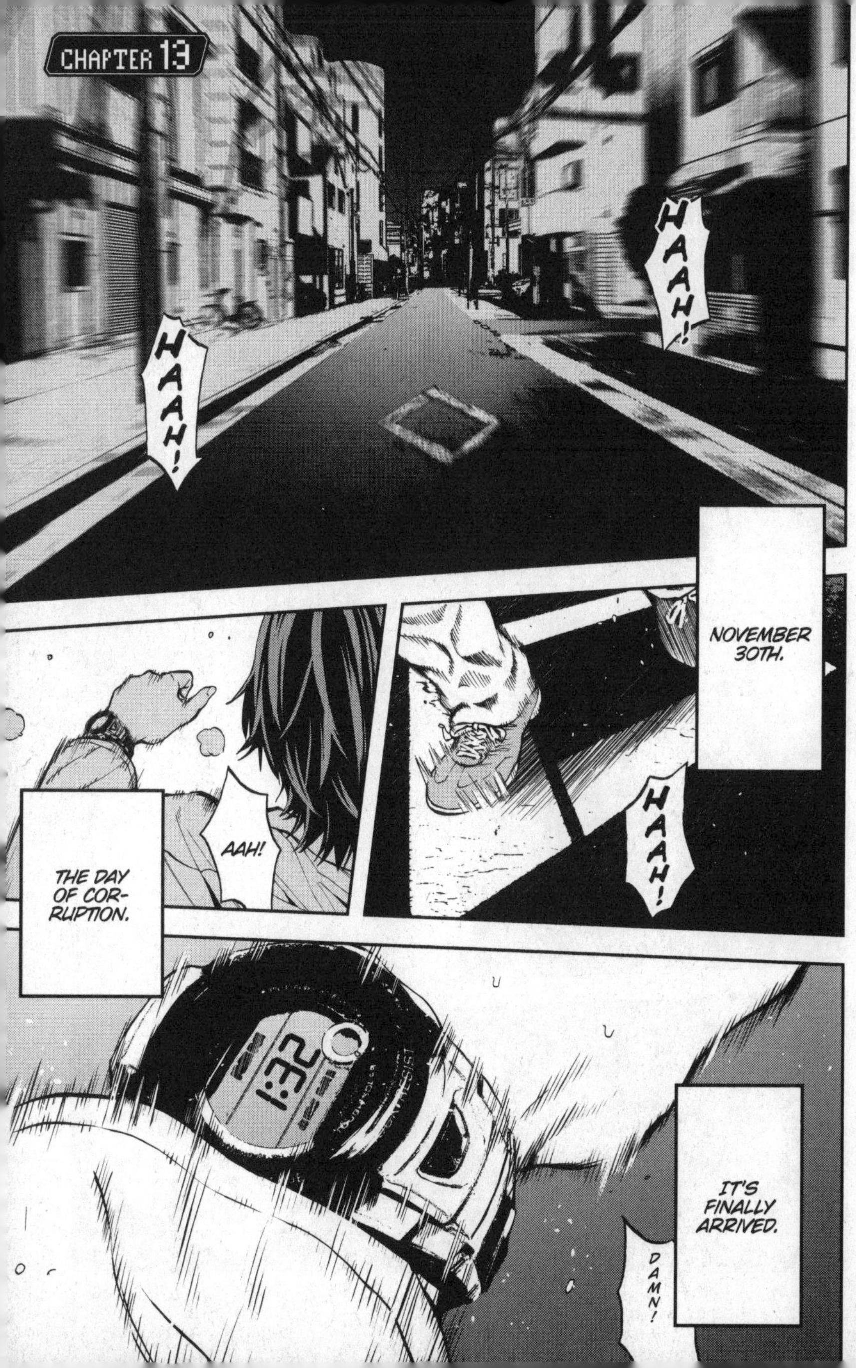
CHAPTER 13
HAAAH!
HAAAH!
NOVEMBER 30TH.
HAAAH!
AAH!
THE DAY OF COR-RUPTION.
IT'S FINALLY ARRIVED.
DAMN!

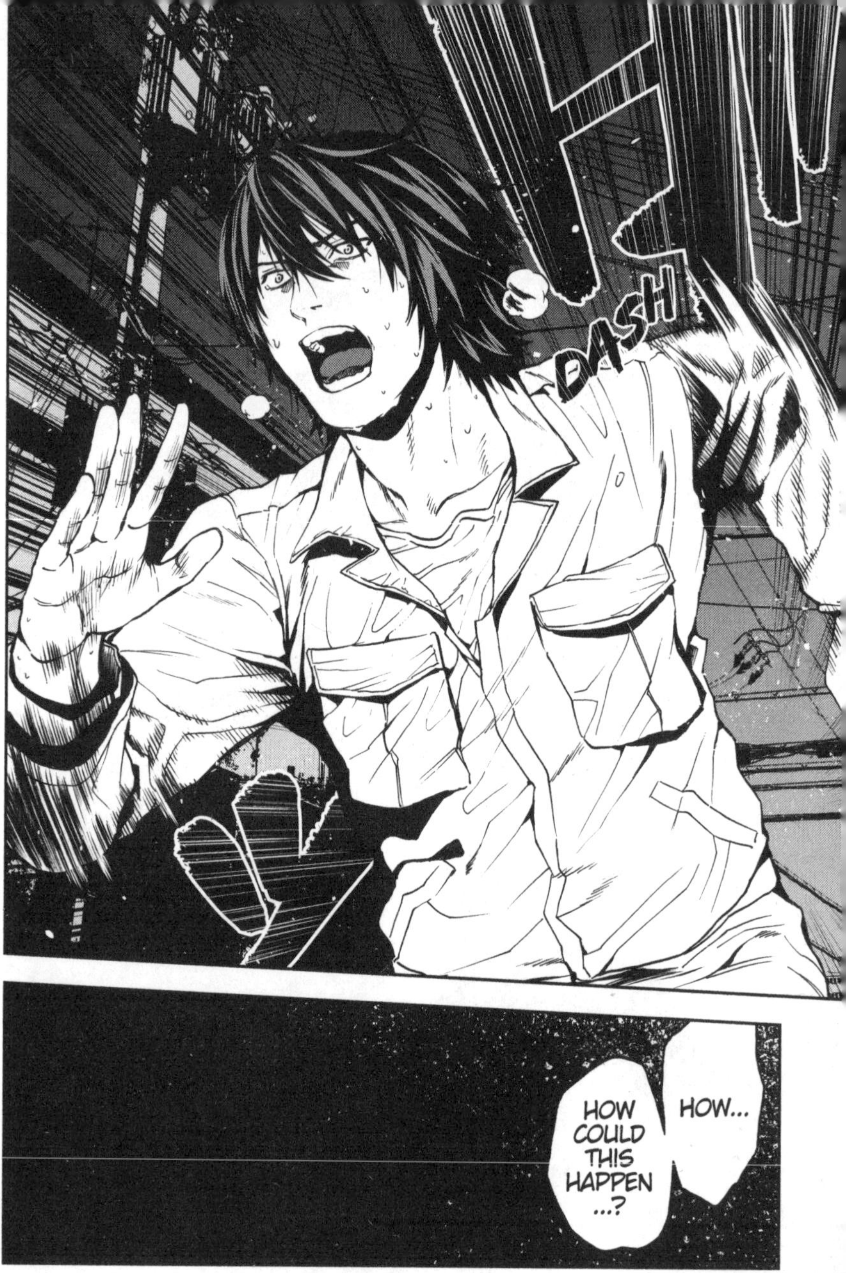
DASH
HOW...
HOW COULD THIS HAPPEN ...?

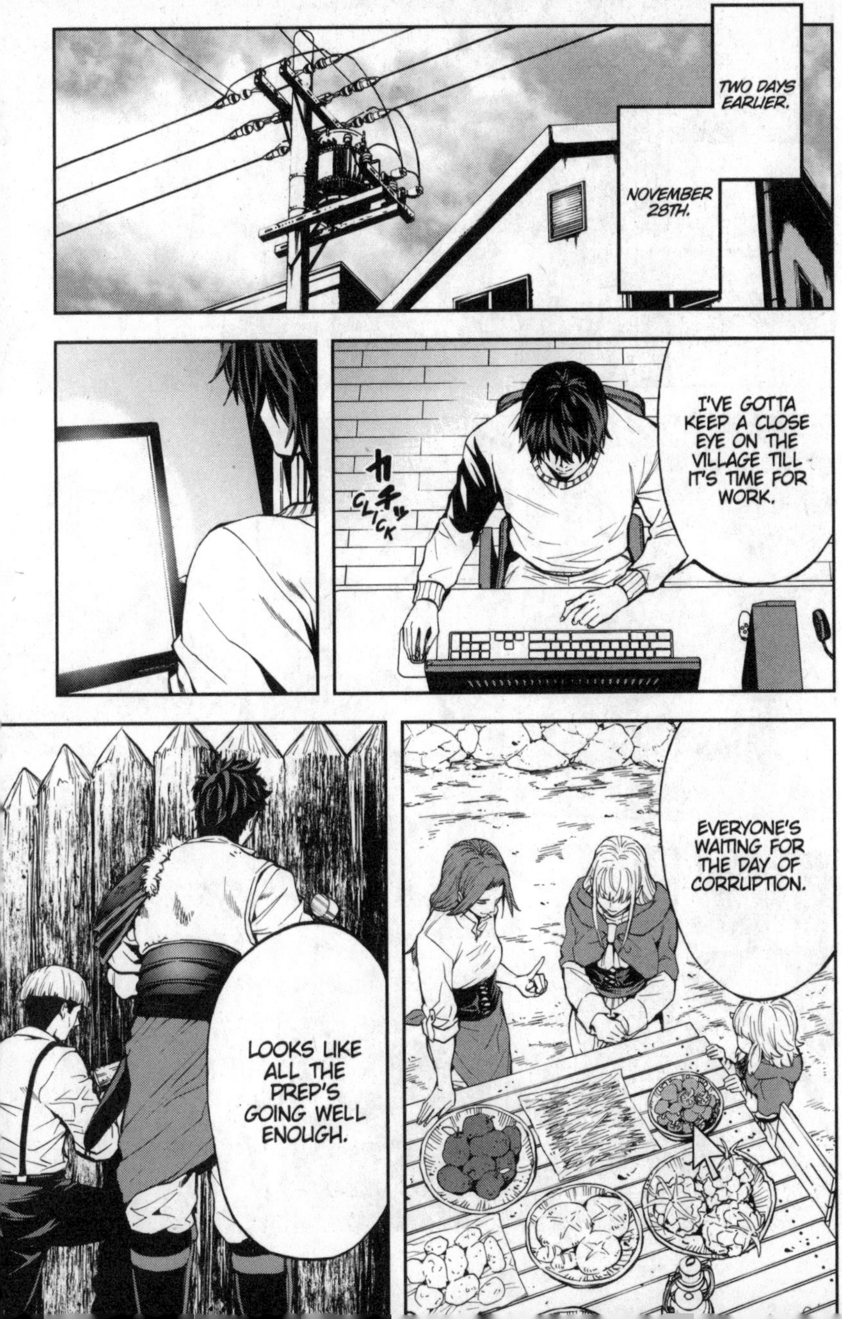
TWO DAYS EARLIER.
NOVEMBER 28TH.
I'VE GOTTA KEEP A CLOSE EYE ON THE VILLAGE TILL IT'S TIME FOR WORK.
カチッ CLICK
EVERYONE'S WAITING FOR THE DAY OF CORRUPTION.
LOOKS LIKE ALL THE PREP'S GOING WELL ENOUGH.

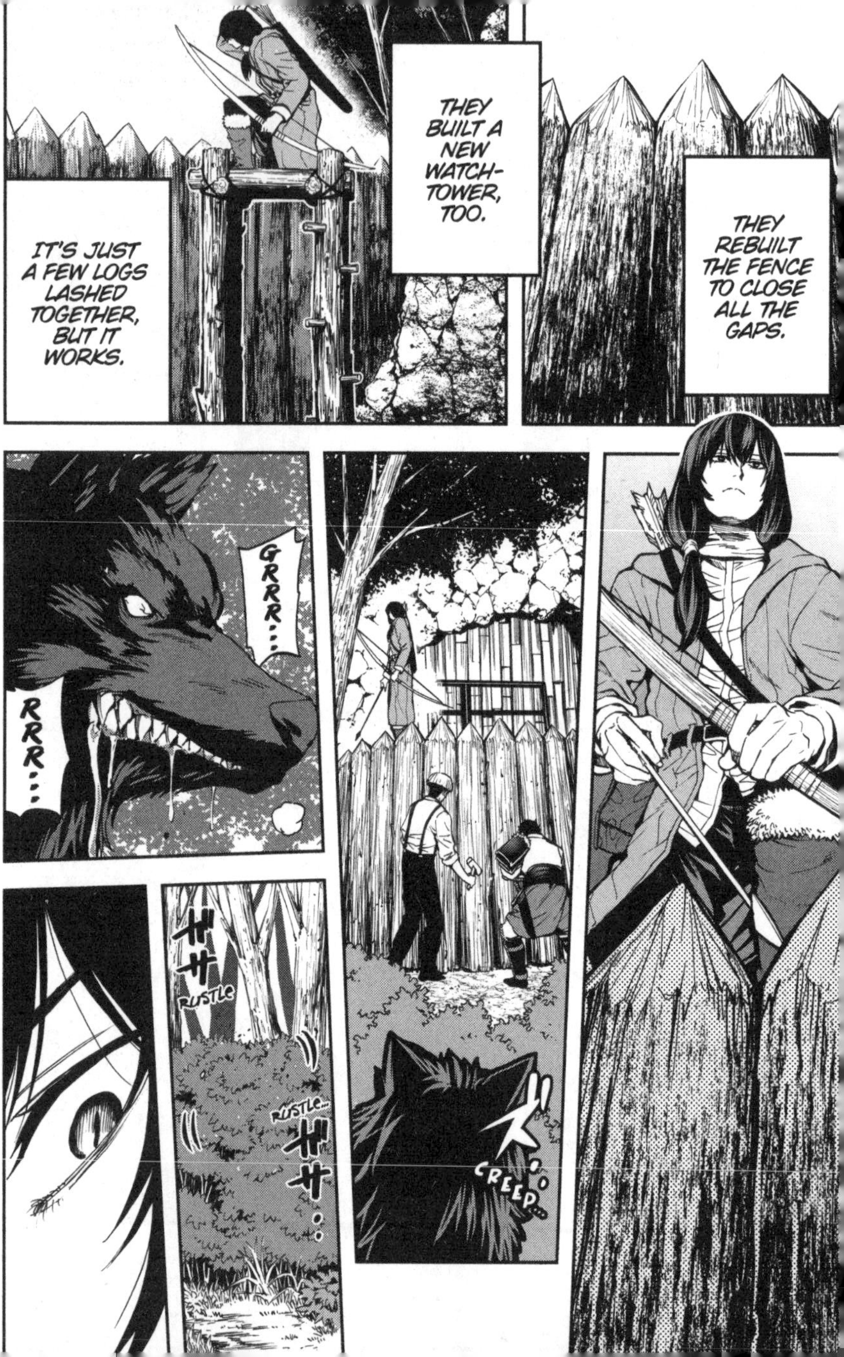
THEY REBUILT THE FENCE TO CLOSE ALL THE GAPS.
THEY BUILT A NEW WATCH-TOWER, TOO.
IT'S JUST A FEW LOGS LASHED TOGETHER, BUT IT WORKS.
GRRR...
RRR...
CREEP...
RUSTLE...
RUSTLE

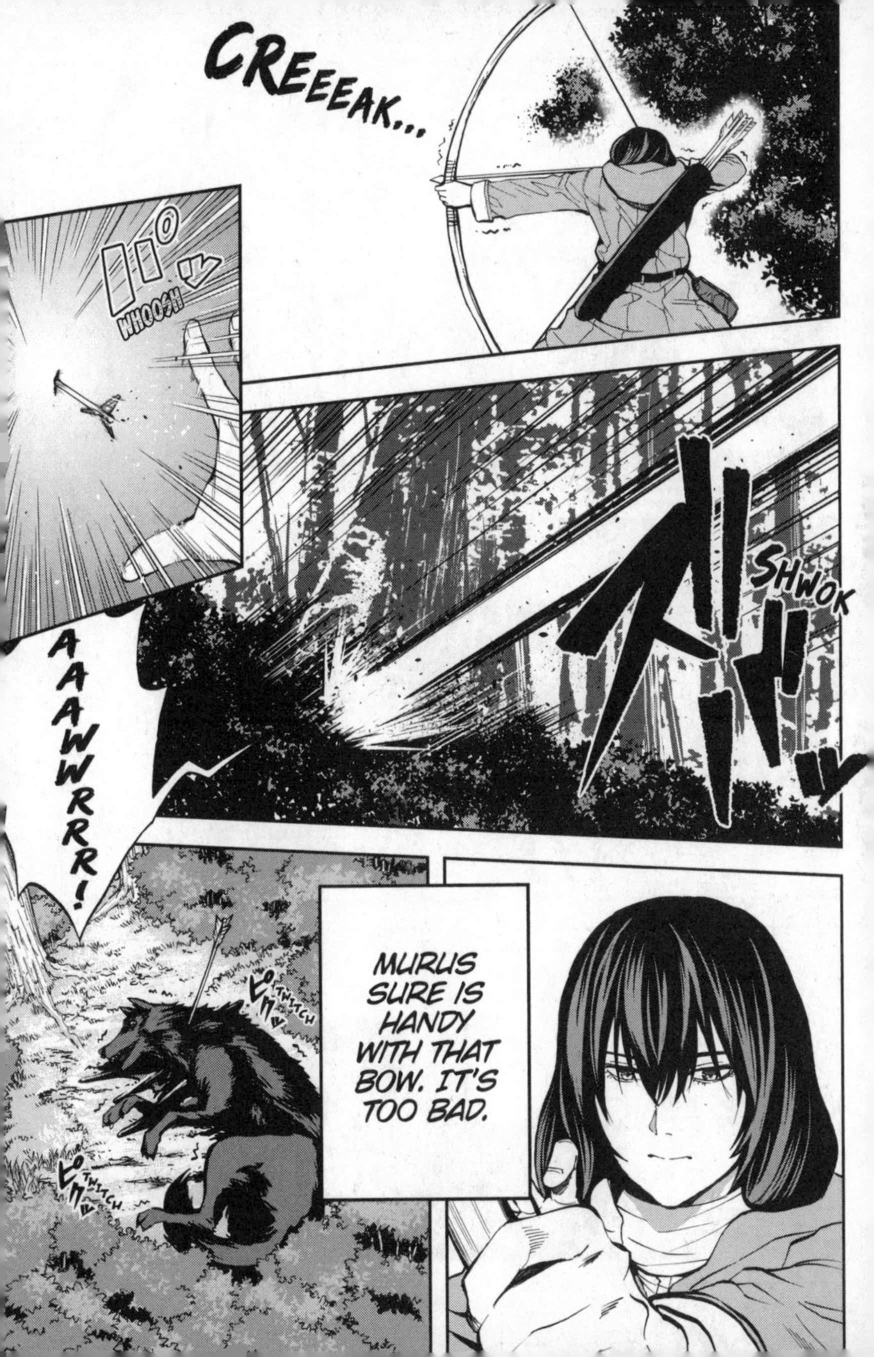
CREEEAK...
WHOOSH
SHWOK
AAAAWWRRR!
MURUS SURE IS HANDY WITH THAT BOW. IT'S TOO BAD.
TWITCH
TWITCH

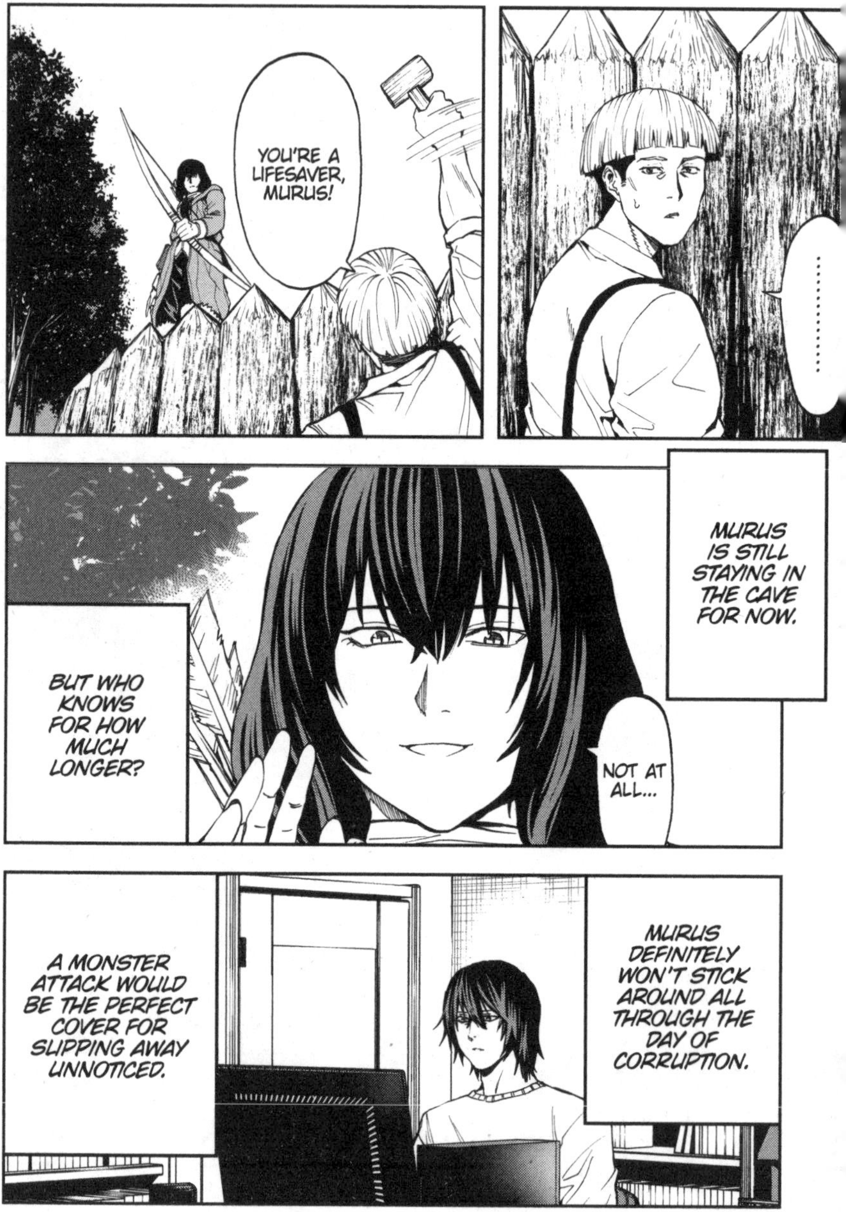
......
YOU'RE A LIFESAVER, MURUS!
MURUS IS STILL STAYING IN THE CAVE FOR NOW.
NOT AT ALL...
BUT WHO KNOWS FOR HOW MUCH LONGER?
MURUS DEFINITELY WON'T STICK AROUND ALL THROUGH THE DAY OF CORRUPTION.
A MONSTER ATTACK WOULD BE THE PERFECT COVER FOR SLIPPING AWAY UNNOTICED.

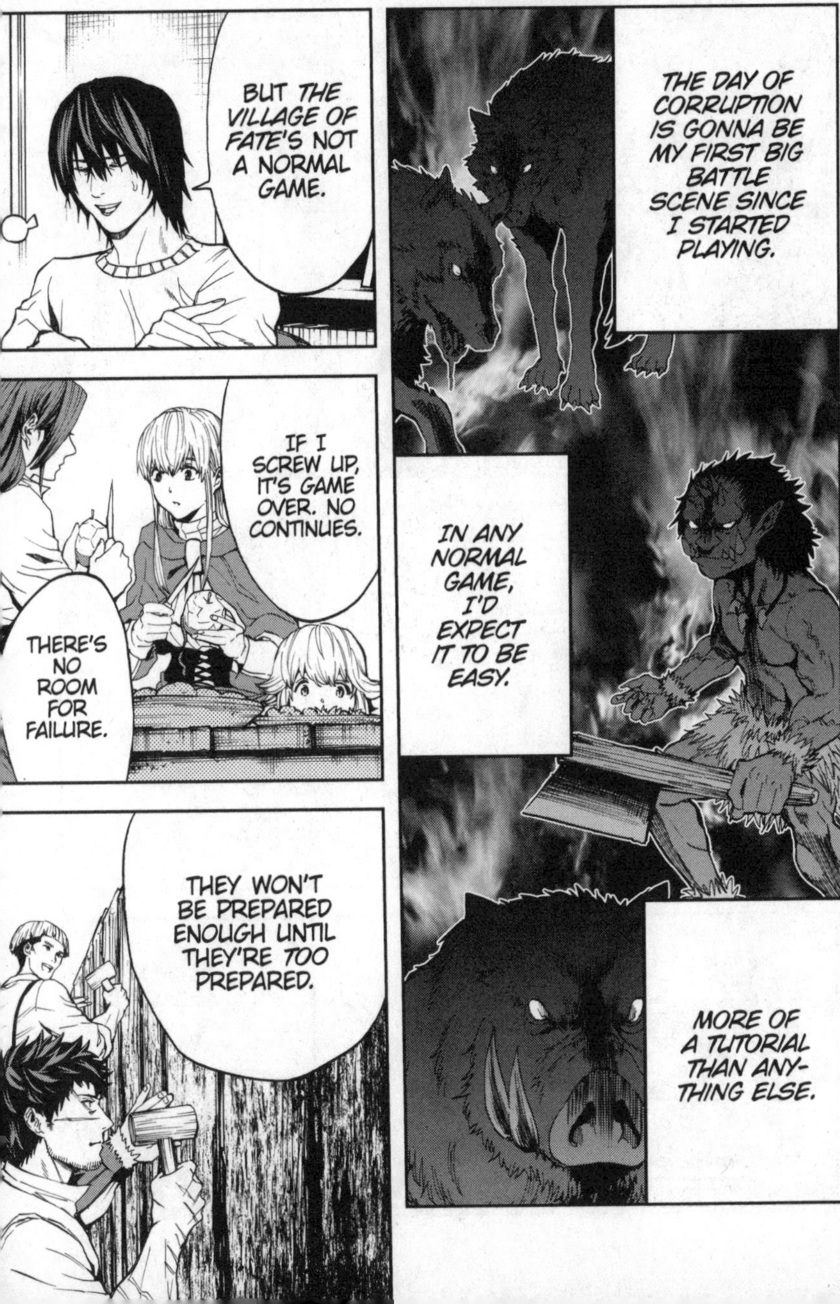
THE DAY OF CORRUPTION IS GONNA BE MY FIRST BIG BATTLE SCENE SINCE I STARTED PLAYING.
IN ANY NORMAL GAME, I'D EXPECT IT TO BE EASY.
MORE OF A TUTORIAL THAN ANY-THING ELSE.
BUT *THE VILLAGE OF FATE*'S NOT A NORMAL GAME.
IF I SCREW UP, IT'S GAME OVER. NO CONTINUES.
THERE'S NO ROOM FOR FAILURE.
THEY WON'T BE PREPARED ENOUGH UNTIL THEY'RE *TOO* PREPARED.

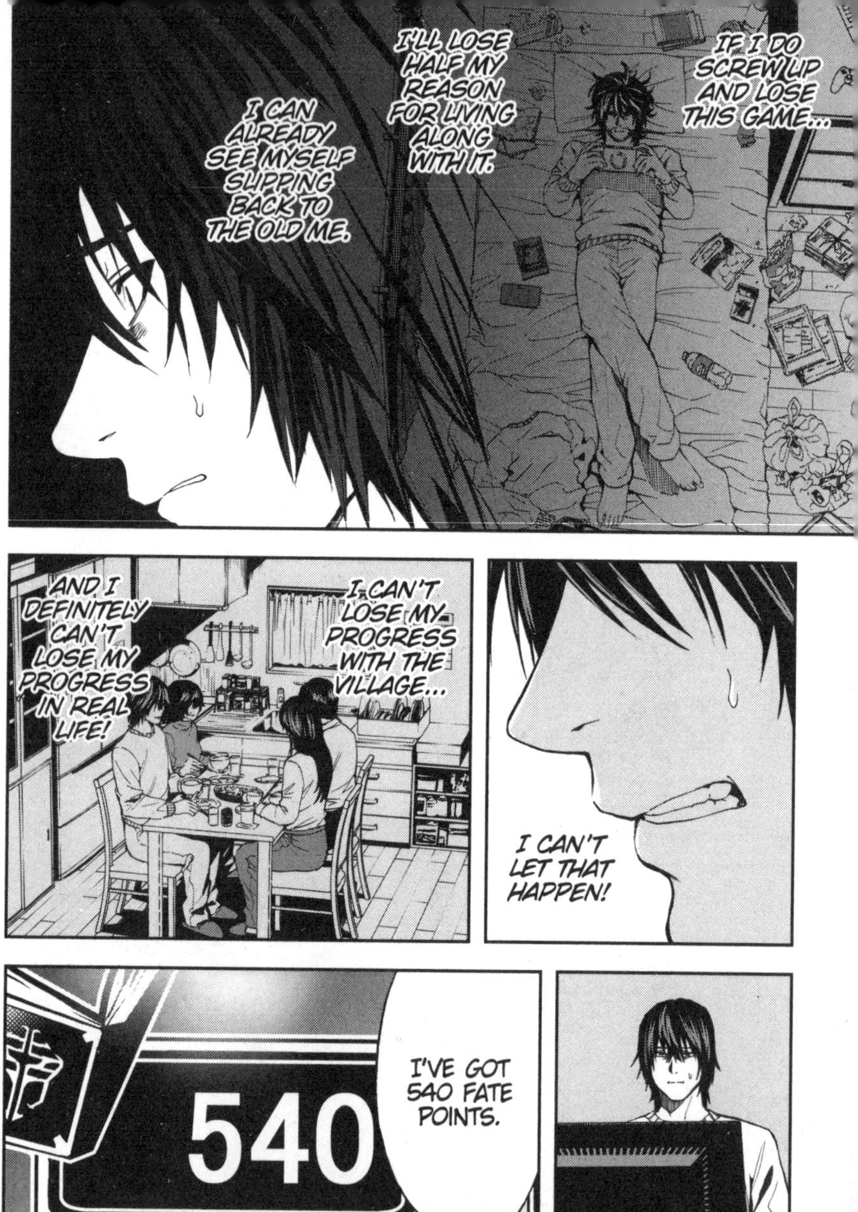
IF I DO SCREW UP AND LOSE THIS GAME...
I'LL LOSE HALF MY REASON FOR LIVING ALONG WITH IT.
I CAN ALREADY SEE MYSELF SLIPPING BACK TO THE OLD ME.
I CAN'T LET THAT HAPPEN!
I CAN'T LOSE MY PROGRESS WITH THE VILLAGE...
AND I DEFINITELY CAN'T LOSE MY PROGRESS IN REAL LIFE!
540
I'VE GOT 540 FATE POINTS.

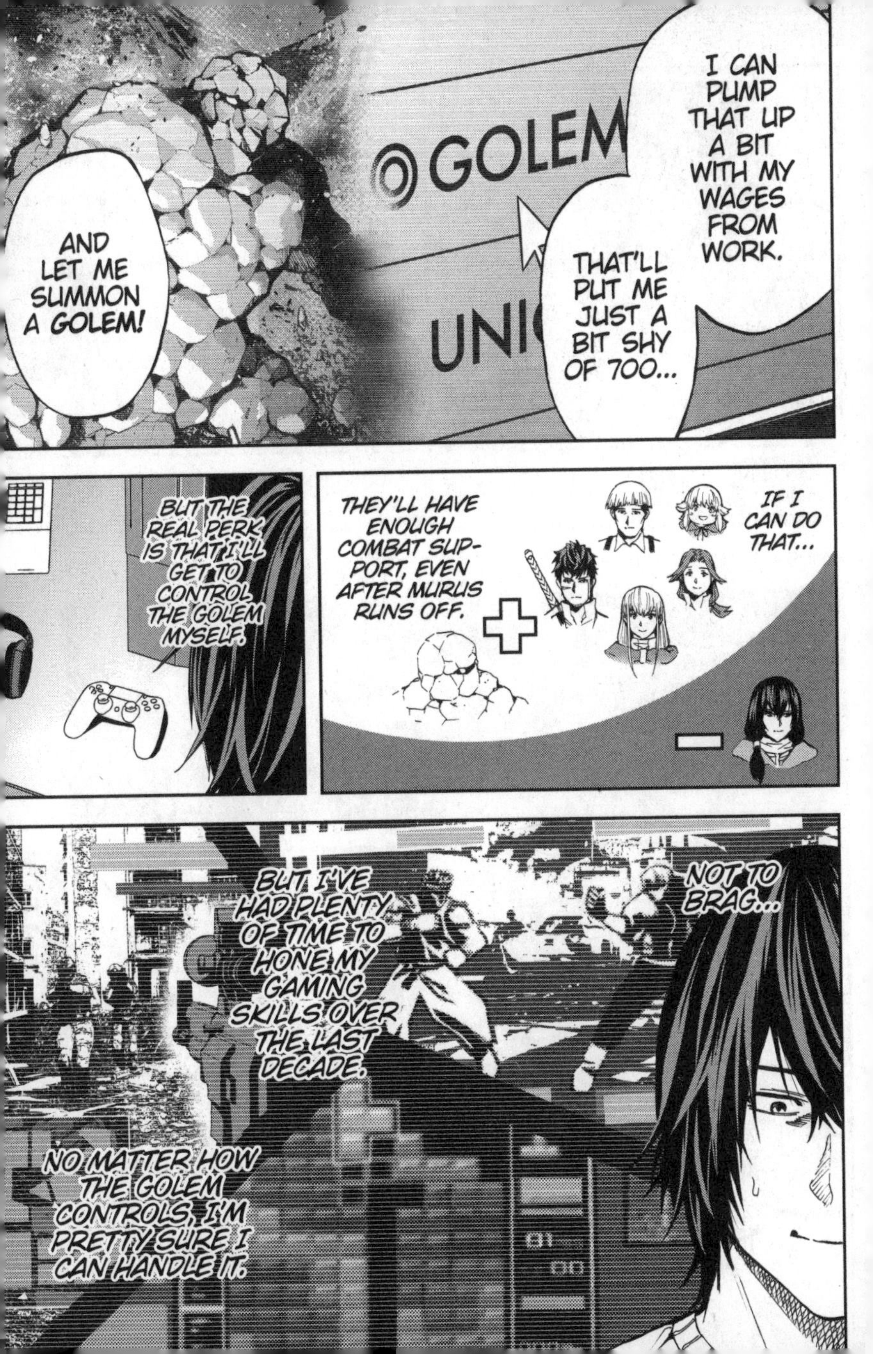
I CAN PUMP THAT UP A BIT WITH MY WAGES FROM WORK.
THAT'LL PUT ME JUST A BIT SHY OF 700...
GOLEM
AND LET ME SUMMON A GOLEM!
IF I CAN DO THAT...
THEY'LL HAVE ENOUGH COMBAT SUP-PORT, EVEN AFTER MURUS RUNS OFF.
BUT THE REAL PERK IS THAT I'LL GET TO CONTROL THE GOLEM MYSELF.
NOT TO BRAG...
BUT I'VE HAD PLENTY OF TIME TO HONE MY GAMING SKILLS OVER THE LAST DECADE.
NO MATTER HOW THE GOLEM CONTROLS, I'M PRETTY SURE I CAN HANDLE IT.

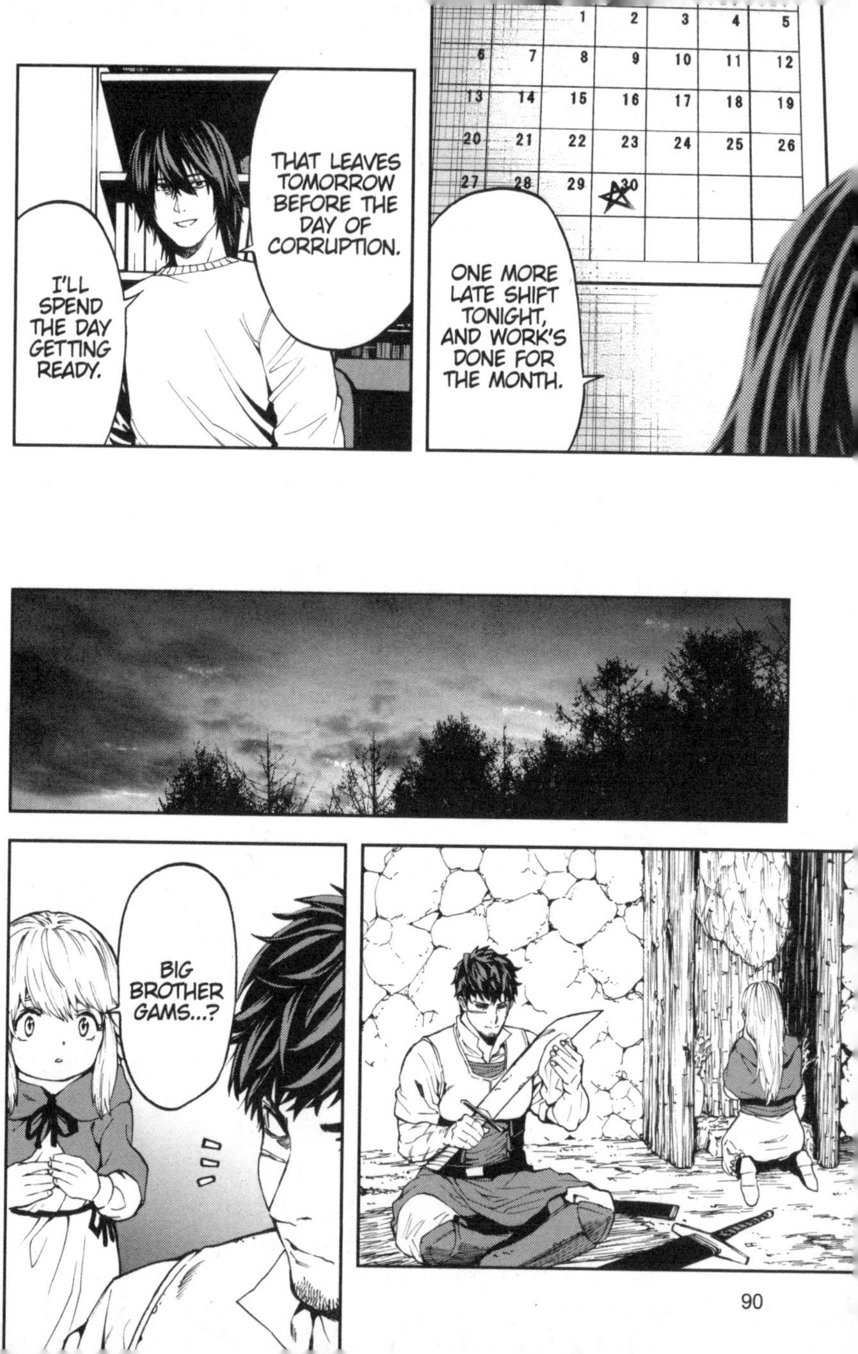
ONE MORE LATE SHIFT TONIGHT, AND WORK'S DONE FOR THE MONTH.
THAT LEAVES TOMORROW BEFORE THE DAY OF CORRUPTION.
I'LL SPEND THE DAY GETTING READY.
BIG BROTHER GAMS...?

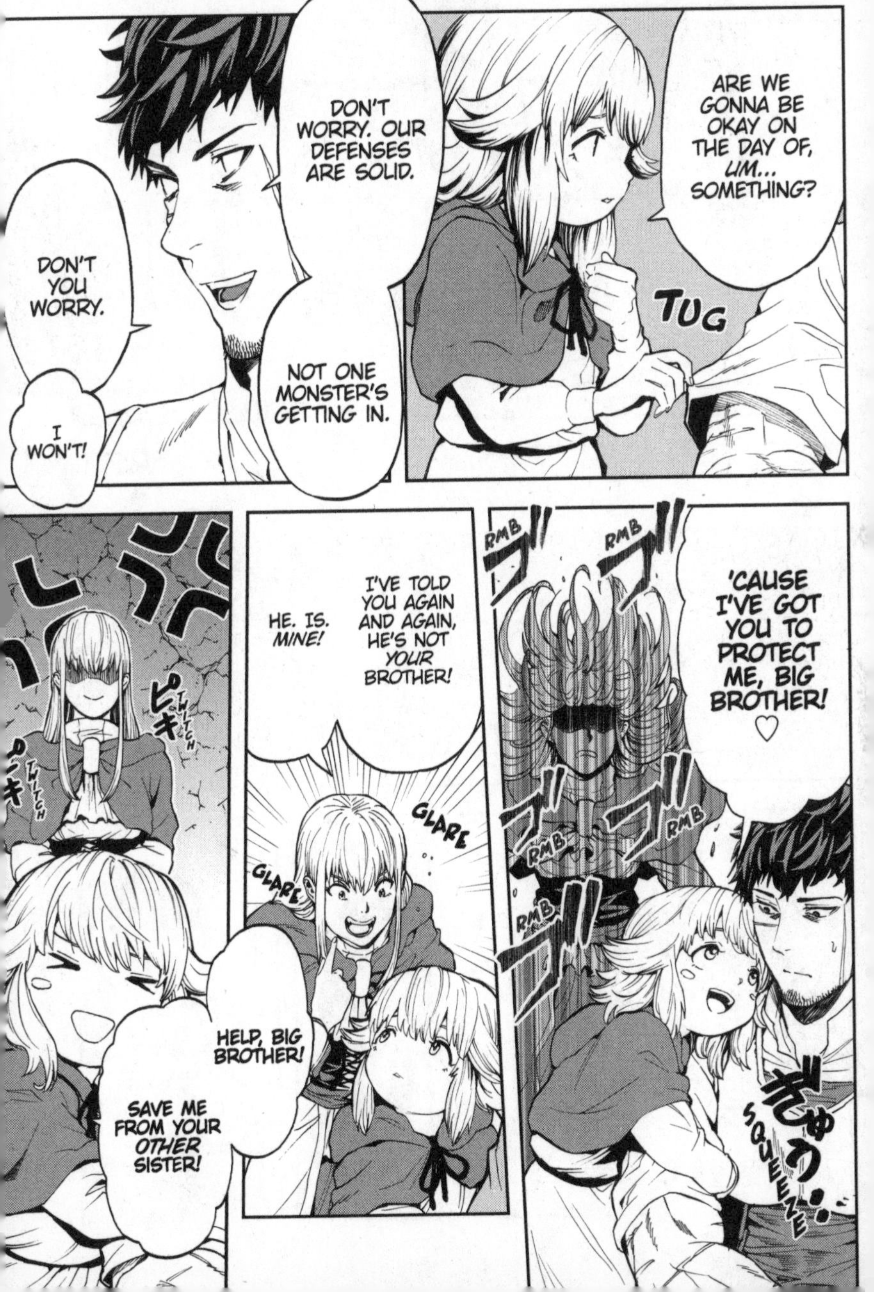
ARE WE GONNA BE OKAY ON THE DAY OF, *UM...* SOMETHING?
TUG
DON'T WORRY. OUR DEFENSES ARE SOLID.
NOT ONE MONSTER'S GETTING IN.
DON'T YOU WORRY.
I WON'T!
'CAUSE I'VE GOT YOU TO PROTECT ME, BIG BROTHER! ♡
RMB
RMB
RMB
RMB
RMB
SQUEEZE
I'VE TOLD YOU AGAIN AND AGAIN, HE'S NOT *YOUR* BROTHER!
HE. IS. *MINE!*
GLARE
GLARE
HELP, BIG BROTHER!
SAVE ME FROM YOUR *OTHER* SISTER!
TWITCH
TWITCH

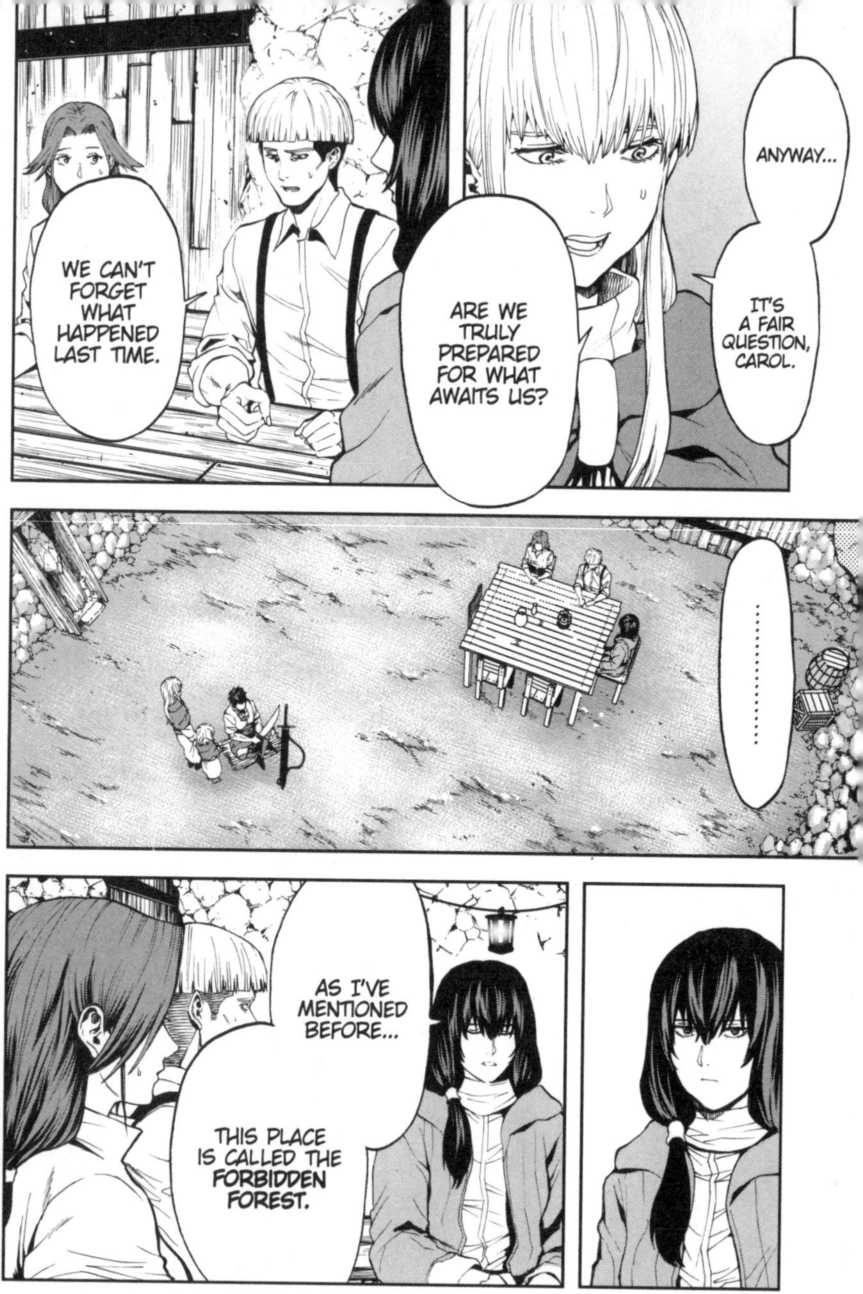
ANYWAY...
IT'S A FAIR QUESTION, CAROL.
ARE WE TRULY PREPARED FOR WHAT AWAITS US?
WE CAN'T FORGET WHAT HAPPENED LAST TIME.
......
AS I'VE MENTIONED BEFORE...
THIS PLACE IS CALLED THE **FORBIDDEN FOREST.**

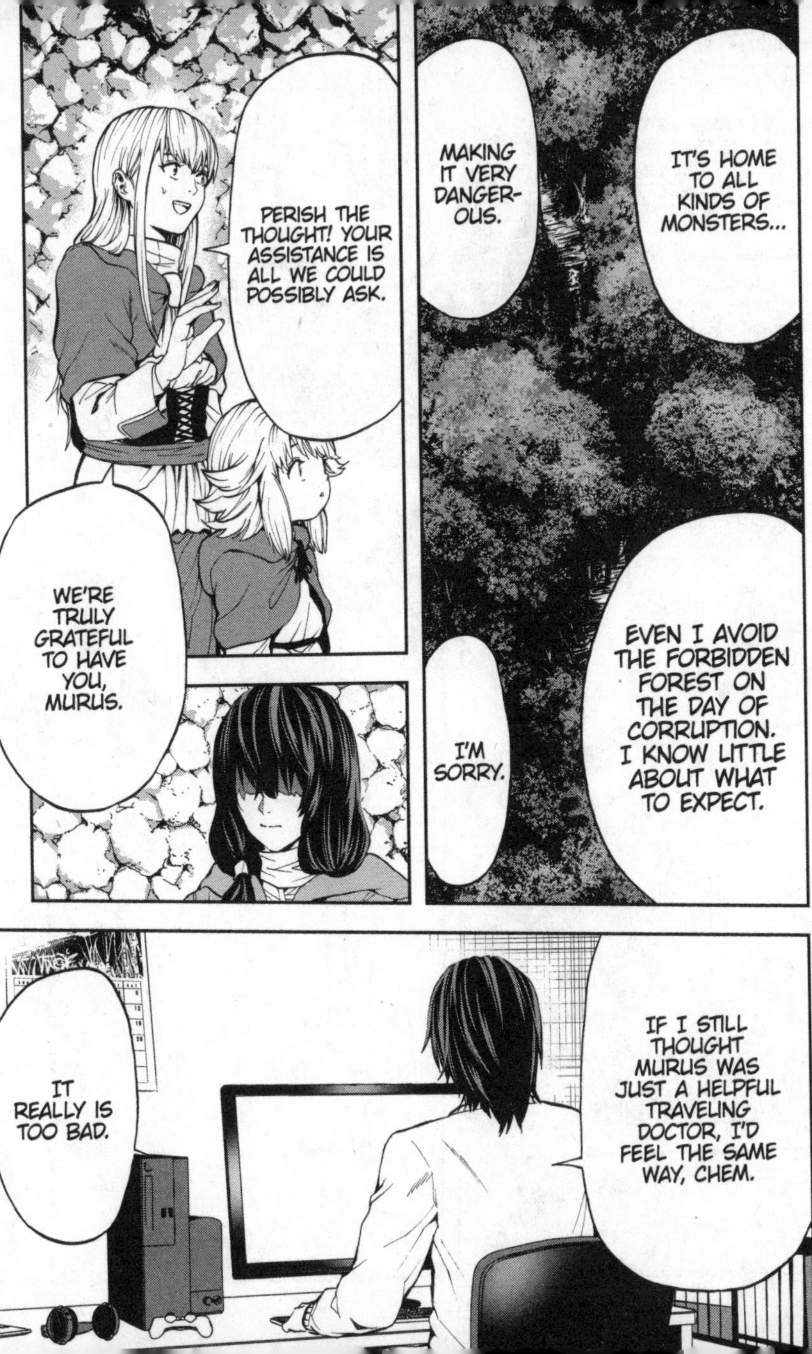
IT'S HOME TO ALL KINDS OF MONSTERS...
MAKING IT VERY DANGER-OUS.
EVEN I AVOID THE FORBIDDEN FOREST ON THE DAY OF CORRUPTION. I KNOW LITTLE ABOUT WHAT TO EXPECT.
I'M SORRY.
PERISH THE THOUGHT! YOUR ASSISTANCE IS ALL WE COULD POSSIBLY ASK.
WE'RE TRULY GRATEFUL TO HAVE YOU, MURUS.
IF I STILL THOUGHT MURUS WAS JUST A HELPFUL TRAVELING DOCTOR, I'D FEEL THE SAME WAY, CHEM.
IT REALLY IS TOO BAD.

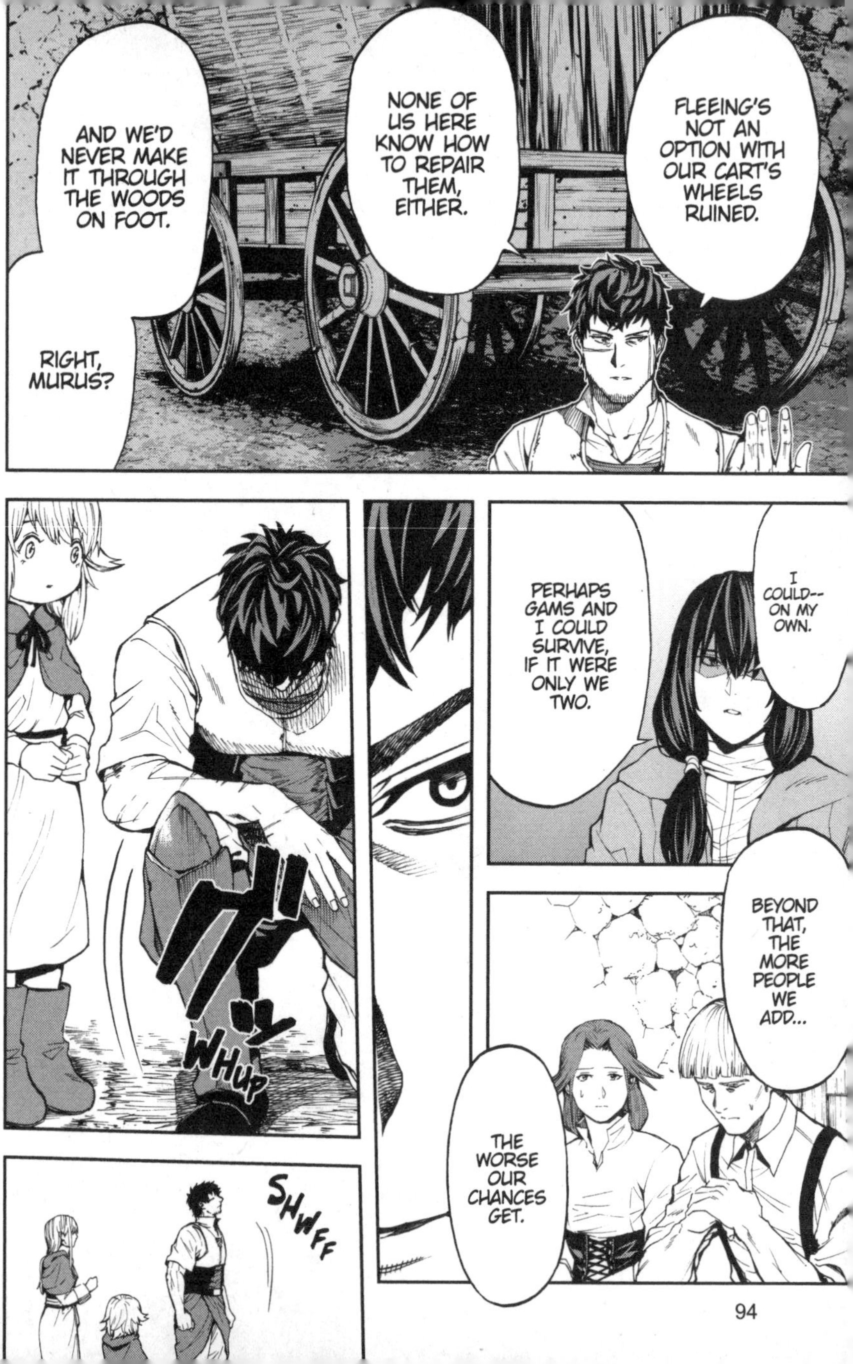
FLEEING'S NOT AN OPTION WITH OUR CART'S WHEELS RUINED.
NONE OF US HERE KNOW HOW TO REPAIR THEM, EITHER.
AND WE'D NEVER MAKE IT THROUGH THE WOODS ON FOOT.
RIGHT, MURUS?
I COULD-- ON MY OWN.
PERHAPS GAMS AND I COULD SURVIVE, IF IT WERE ONLY WE TWO.
BEYOND THAT, THE MORE PEOPLE WE ADD...
THE WORSE OUR CHANCES GET.
WHUP
SHWFF

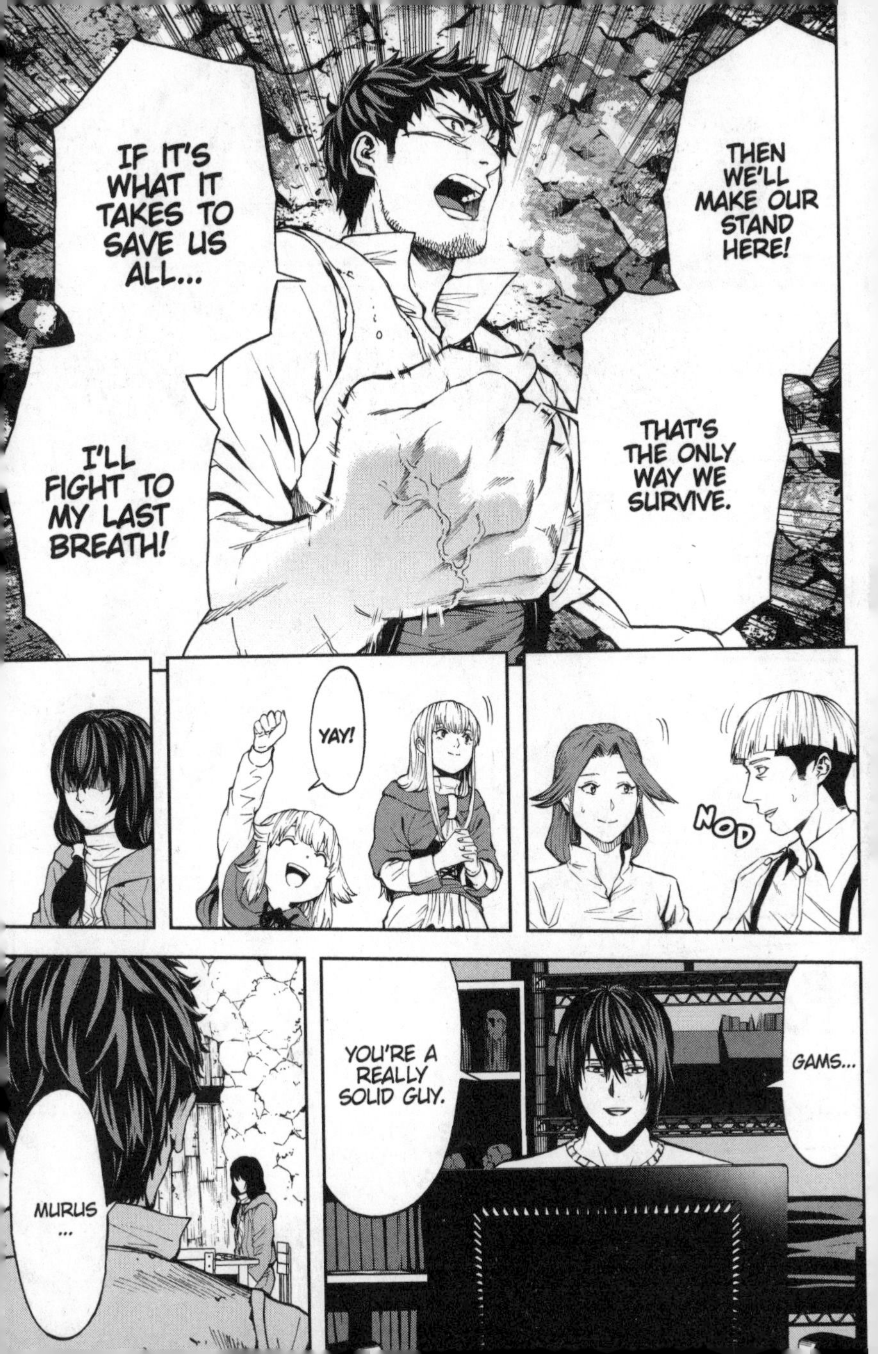
THEN WE'LL MAKE OUR STAND HERE!
THAT'S THE ONLY WAY WE SURVIVE.
IF IT'S WHAT IT TAKES TO SAVE US ALL...
I'LL FIGHT TO MY LAST BREATH!
NOD
YAY!
GAMS...
YOU'RE A REALLY SOLID GUY.
MURUS ...

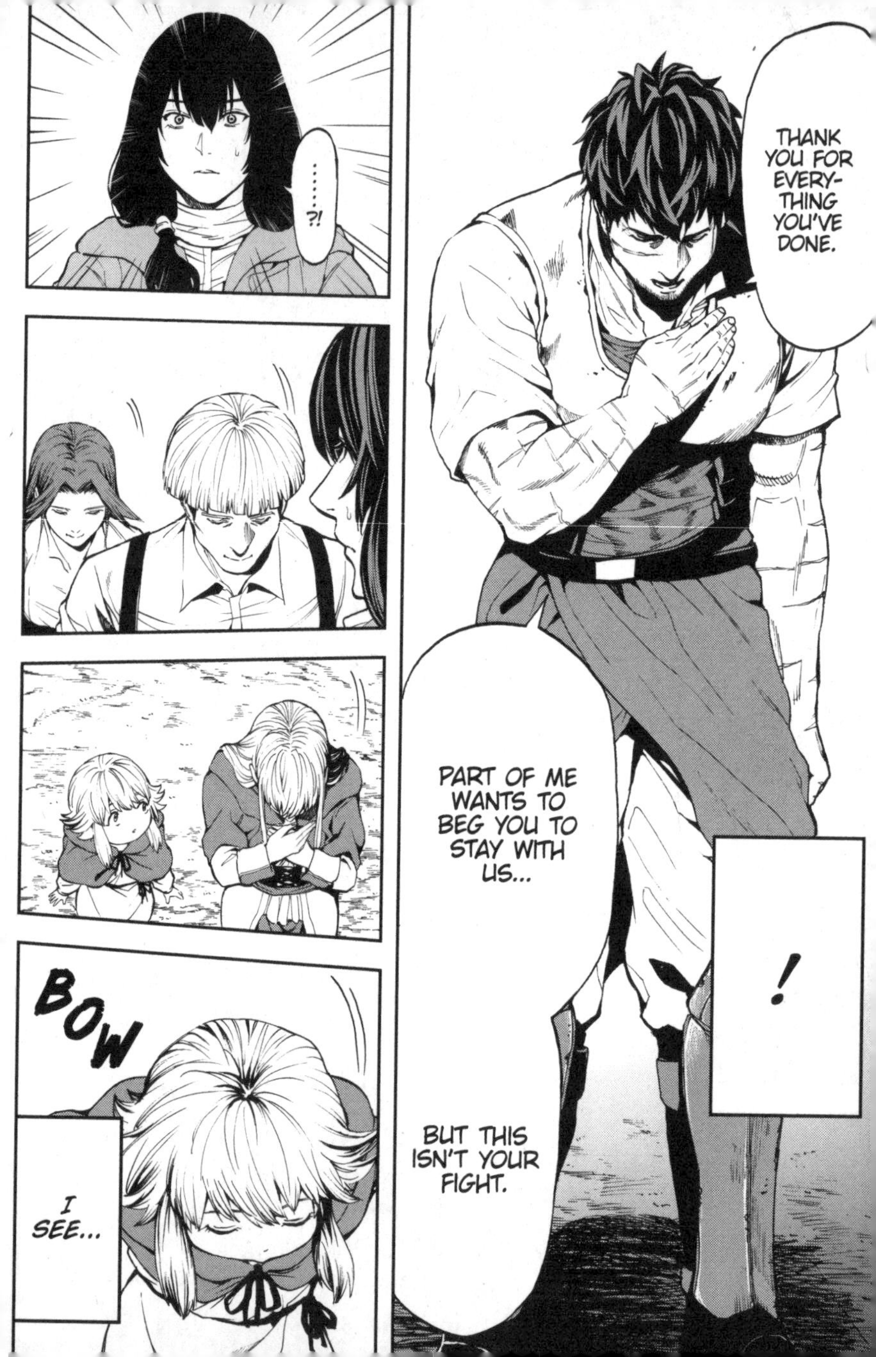
THANK YOU FOR EVERY-THING YOU'VE DONE.
PART OF ME WANTS TO BEG YOU TO STAY WITH US...
!
BUT THIS ISN'T YOUR FIGHT.
......?!
BOW
I SEE...

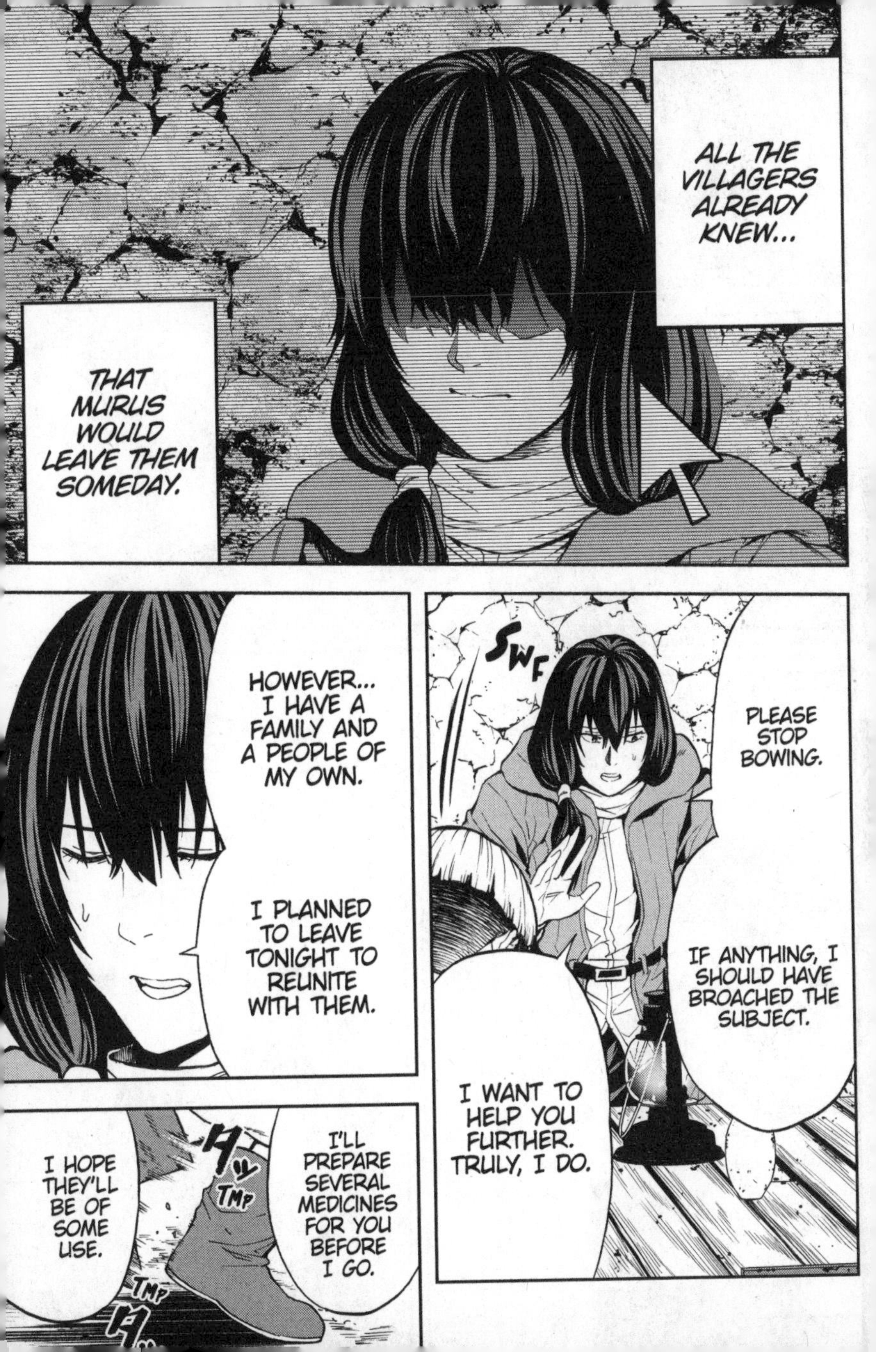
ALL THE VILLAGERS ALREADY KNEW...
THAT MURUS WOULD LEAVE THEM SOMEDAY.
SWF
PLEASE STOP BOWING.
IF ANYTHING, I SHOULD HAVE BROACHED THE SUBJECT.
I WANT TO HELP YOU FURTHER. TRULY, I DO.
HOWEVER... I HAVE A FAMILY AND A PEOPLE OF MY OWN.
I PLANNED TO LEAVE TONIGHT TO REUNITE WITH THEM.
TMP
I'LL PREPARE SEVERAL MEDICINES FOR YOU BEFORE I GO.
I HOPE THEY'LL BE OF SOME USE.
TMP

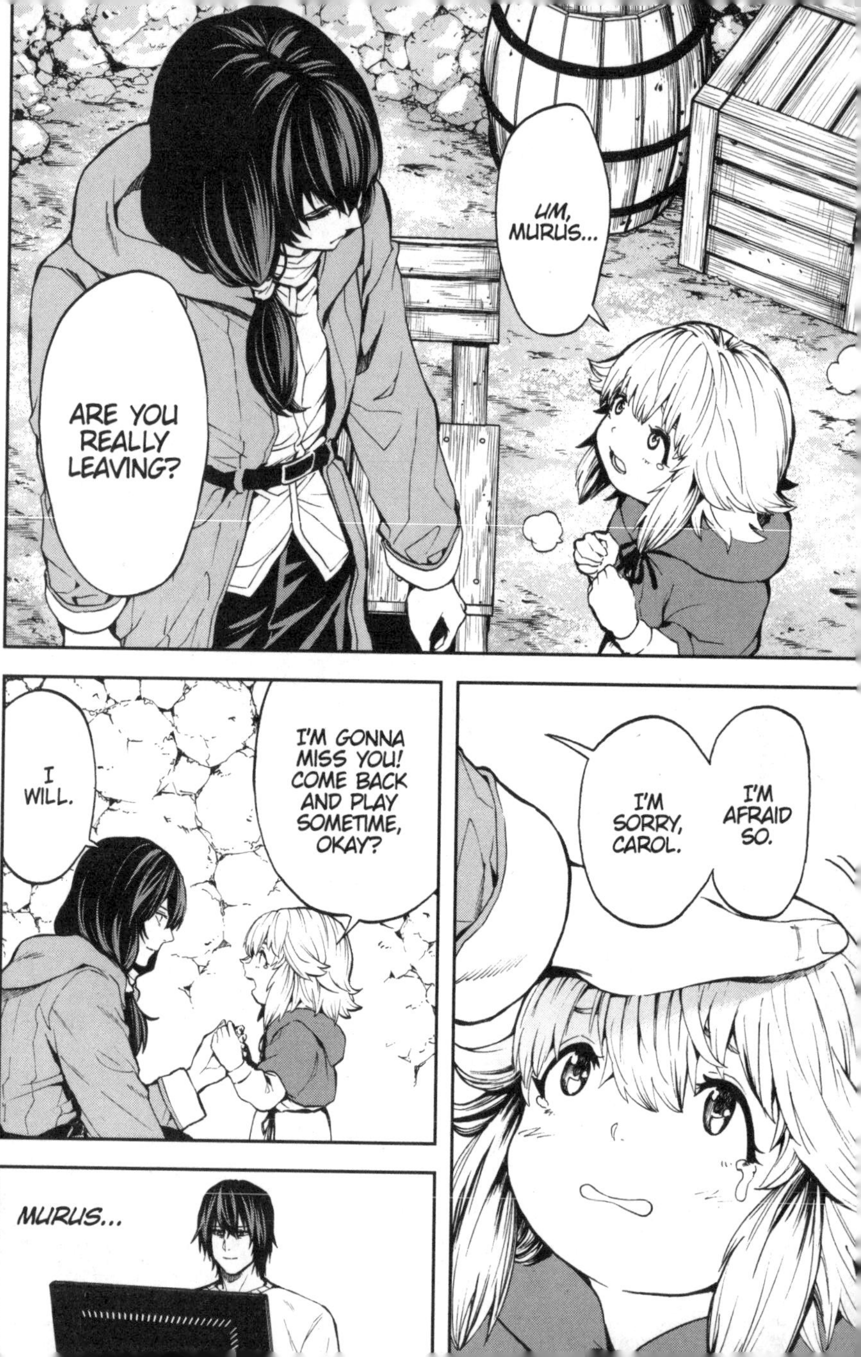
UM, MURUS...
ARE YOU REALLY LEAVING?
I'M AFRAID SO.
I'M SORRY, CAROL.
I'M GONNA MISS YOU! COME BACK AND PLAY SOMETIME, OKAY?
I WILL.
MURUS...

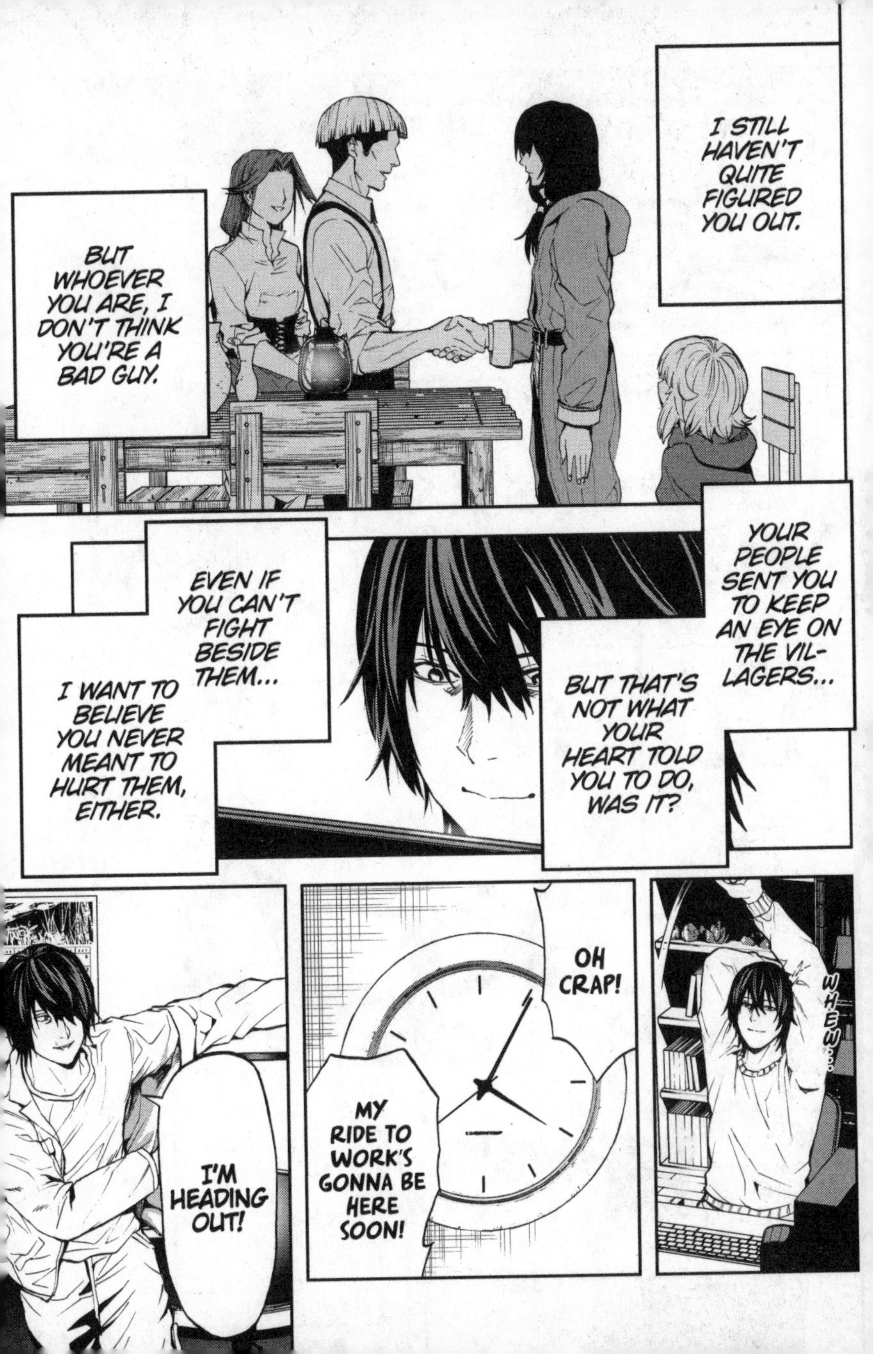
I STILL HAVEN'T QUITE FIGURED YOU OUT.
BUT WHOEVER YOU ARE, I DON'T THINK YOU'RE A BAD GUY.
YOUR PEOPLE SENT YOU TO KEEP AN EYE ON THE VIL-LAGERS...
BUT THAT'S NOT WHAT YOUR HEART TOLD YOU TO DO, WAS IT?
EVEN IF YOU CAN'T FIGHT BESIDE THEM...
I WANT TO BELIEVE YOU NEVER MEANT TO HURT THEM, EITHER.
WHEW...
OH CRAP!
MY RIDE TO WORK'S GONNA BE HERE SOON!
I'M HEADING OUT!

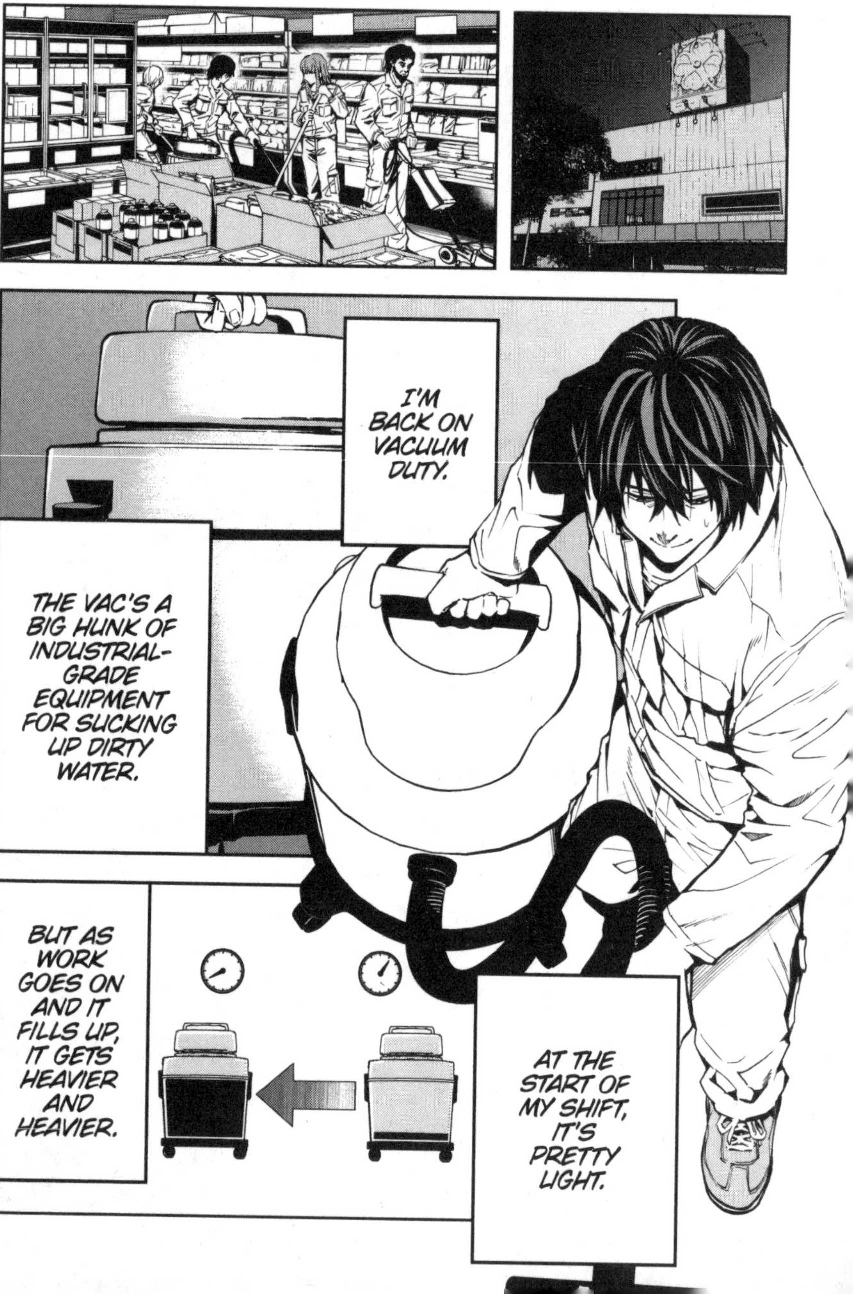
I'M BACK ON VACUUM DUTY.
THE VAC'S A BIG HUNK OF INDUSTRIAL-GRADE EQUIPMENT FOR SUCKING UP DIRTY WATER.
AT THE START OF MY SHIFT, IT'S PRETTY LIGHT.
BUT AS WORK GOES ON AND IT FILLS UP, IT GETS HEAVIER AND HEAVIER.

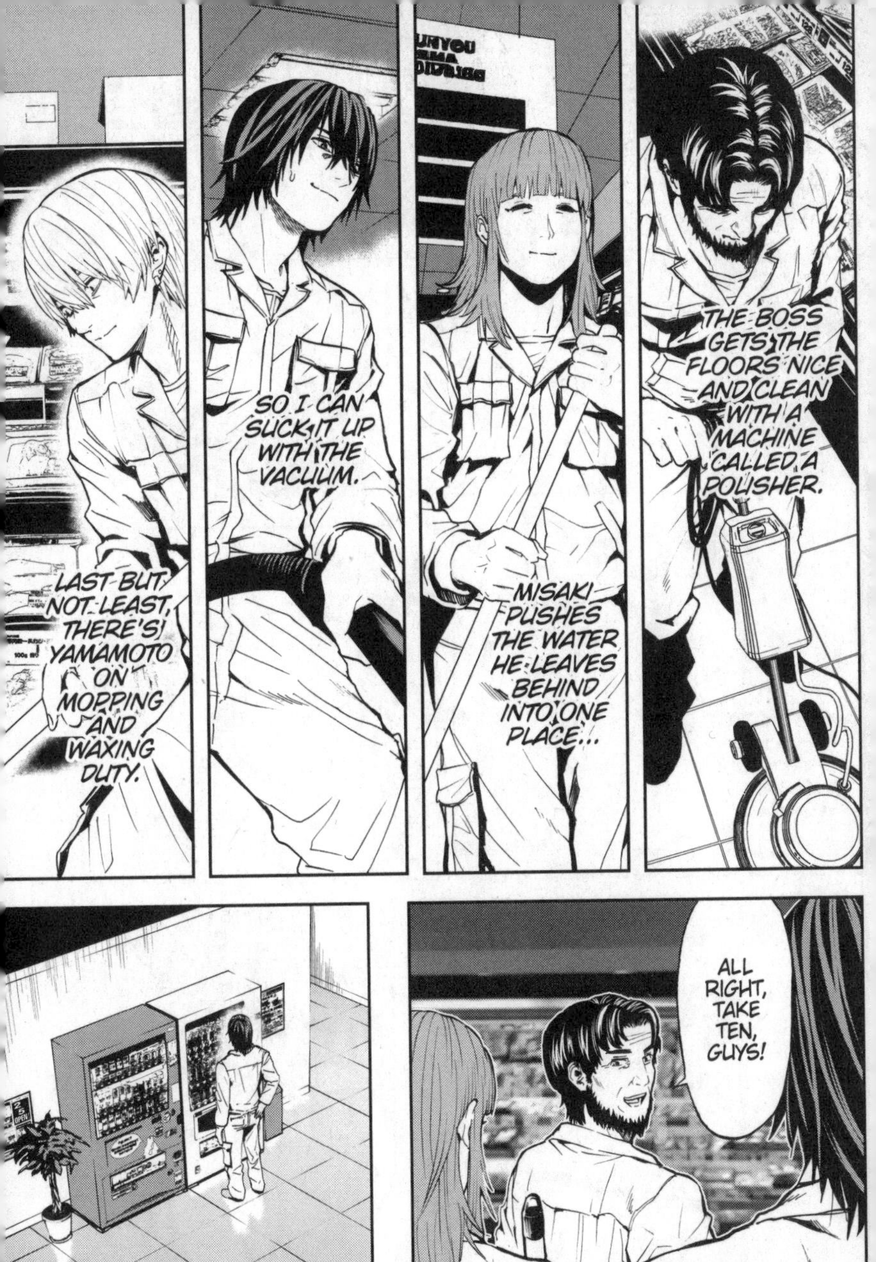
THE BOSS GETS THE FLOORS NICE AND CLEAN WITH A MACHINE CALLED A POLISHER.
MISAKI PUSHES THE WATER HE LEAVES BEHIND INTO ONE PLACE...
SO I CAN SUCK IT UP WITH THE VACUUM.
LAST BUT NOT LEAST, THERE'S YAMAMOTO ON MOPPING AND WAXING DUTY.
ALL RIGHT, TAKE TEN, GUYS!

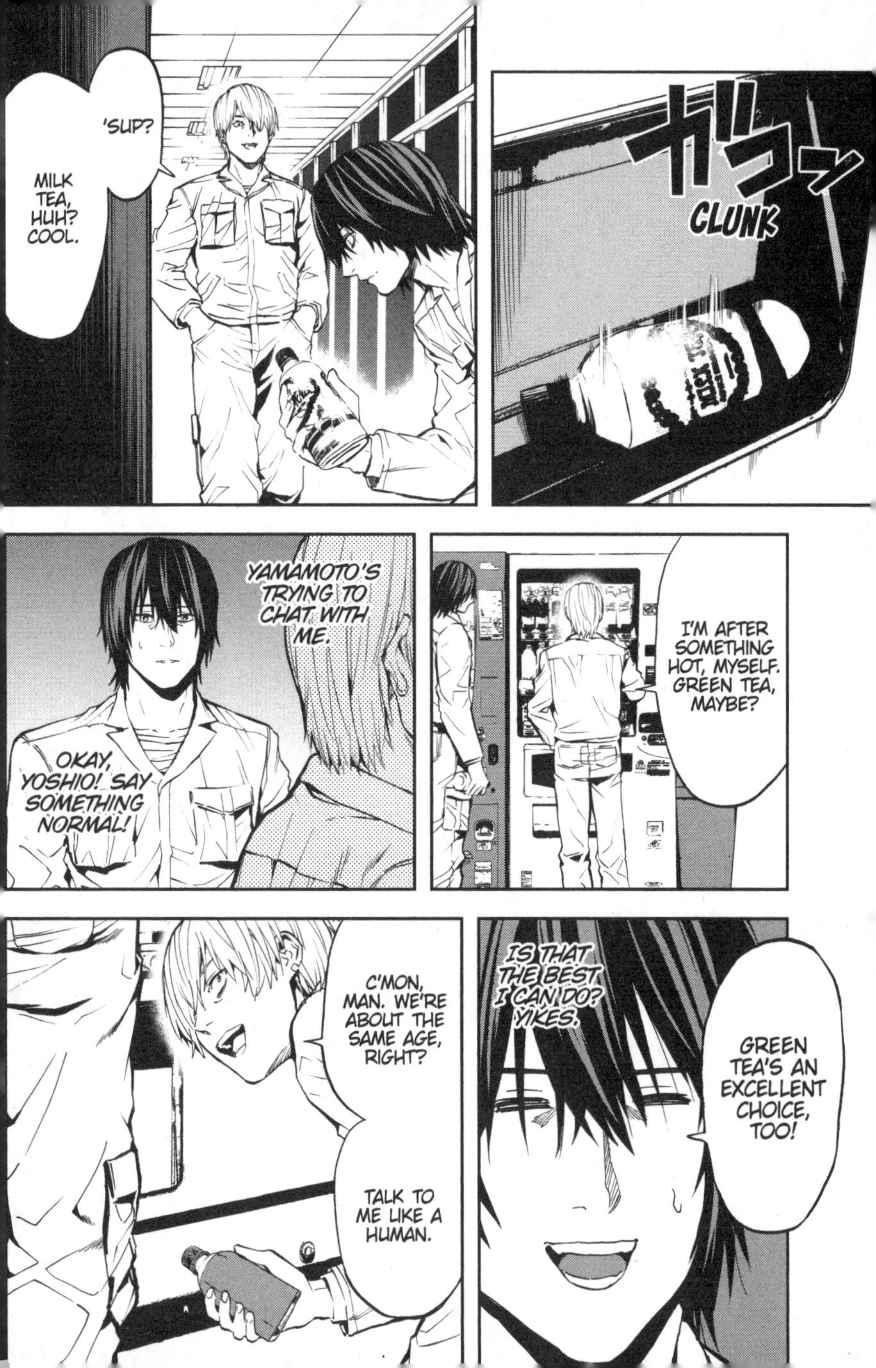
ガコッ
CLUNK
'SUP?
MILK TEA, HUH? COOL.
I'M AFTER SOMETHING HOT, MYSELF. GREEN TEA, MAYBE?
YAMAMOTO'S TRYING TO CHAT WITH ME.
OKAY, YOSHIO! SAY SOMETHING NORMAL!
GREEN TEA'S AN EXCELLENT CHOICE, TOO!
IS THAT THE BEST I CAN DO? YIKES.
C'MON, MAN. WE'RE ABOUT THE SAME AGE, RIGHT?
TALK TO ME LIKE A HUMAN.

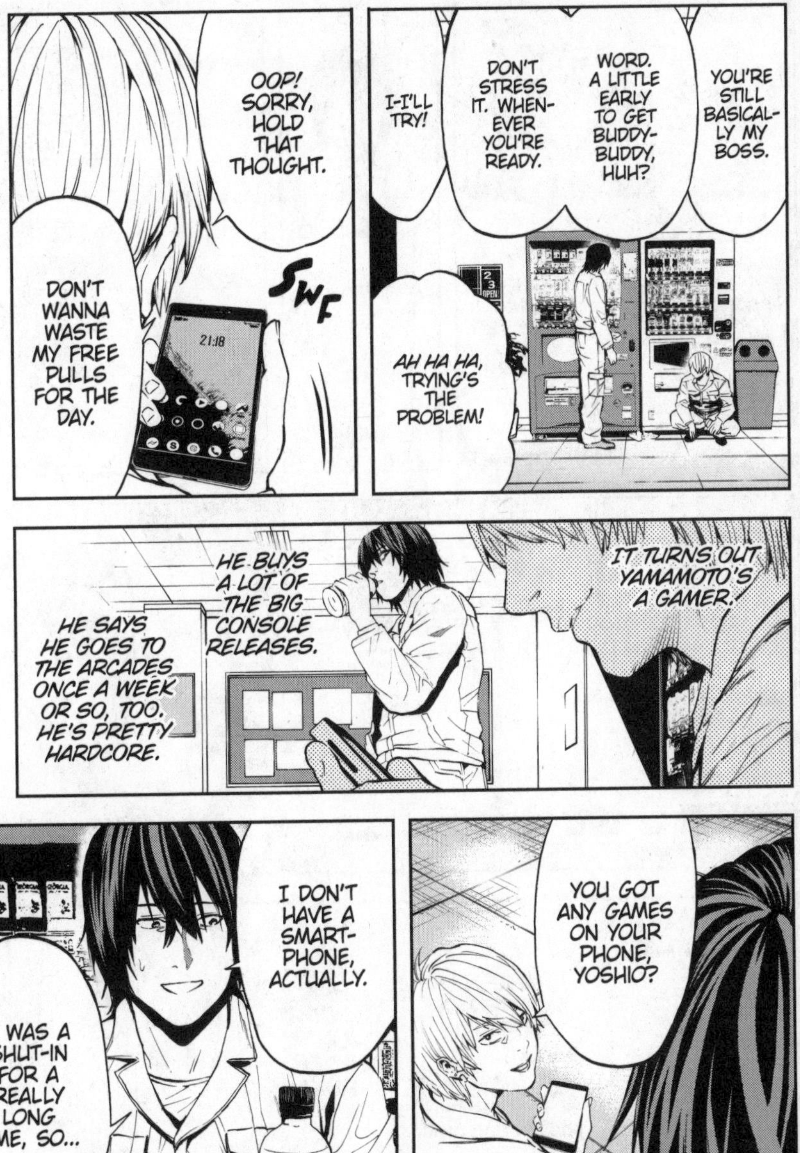
YOU'RE STILL BASICALLY MY BOSS.
WORD. A LITTLE EARLY TO GET BUDDY-BUDDY, HUH?
DON'T STRESS IT. WHENEVER YOU'RE READY.
I-I'LL TRY!
AH HA HA, TRYING'S THE PROBLEM!
OOP! SORRY, HOLD THAT THOUGHT.
SWF
21:18
DON'T WANNA WASTE MY FREE PULLS FOR THE DAY.
IT TURNS OUT YAMAMOTO'S A GAMER.
HE BUYS A LOT OF THE BIG CONSOLE RELEASES.
HE SAYS HE GOES TO THE ARCADES ONCE A WEEK OR SO, TOO. HE'S PRETTY HARDCORE.
YOU GOT ANY GAMES ON YOUR PHONE, YOSHIO?
I DON'T HAVE A SMARTPHONE, ACTUALLY.
I WAS A SHUT-IN FOR A REALLY LONG TIME, SO...

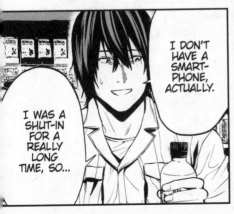

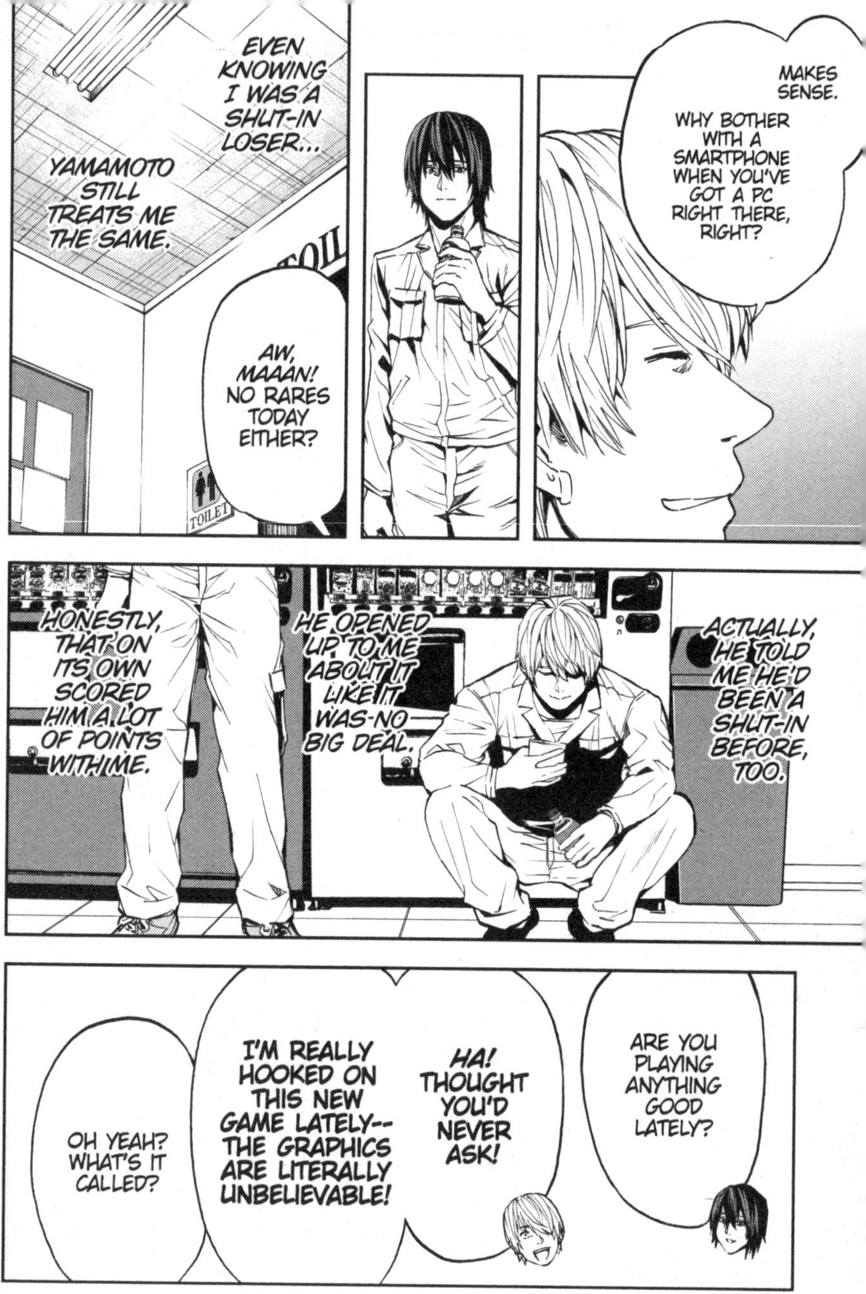
MAKES SENSE. WHY BOTHER WITH A SMARTPHONE WHEN YOU'VE GOT A PC RIGHT THERE, RIGHT?
EVEN KNOWING I WAS A SHUT-IN LOSER...
YAMAMOTO STILL TREATS ME THE SAME.
AW, MAAAN! NO RARES TODAY EITHER?
ACTUALLY, HE TOLD ME HE'D BEEN A SHUT-IN BEFORE, TOO.
HE OPENED UP TO ME ABOUT IT LIKE IT WAS NO BIG DEAL.
HONESTLY, THAT ON ITS OWN SCORED HIM A LOT OF POINTS WITH ME.
ARE YOU PLAYING ANYTHING GOOD LATELY?
HA! THOUGHT YOU'D NEVER ASK!
I'M REALLY HOOKED ON THIS NEW GAME LATELY-- THE GRAPHICS ARE LITERALLY UNBELIEVABLE!
OH YEAH? WHAT'S IT CALLED?

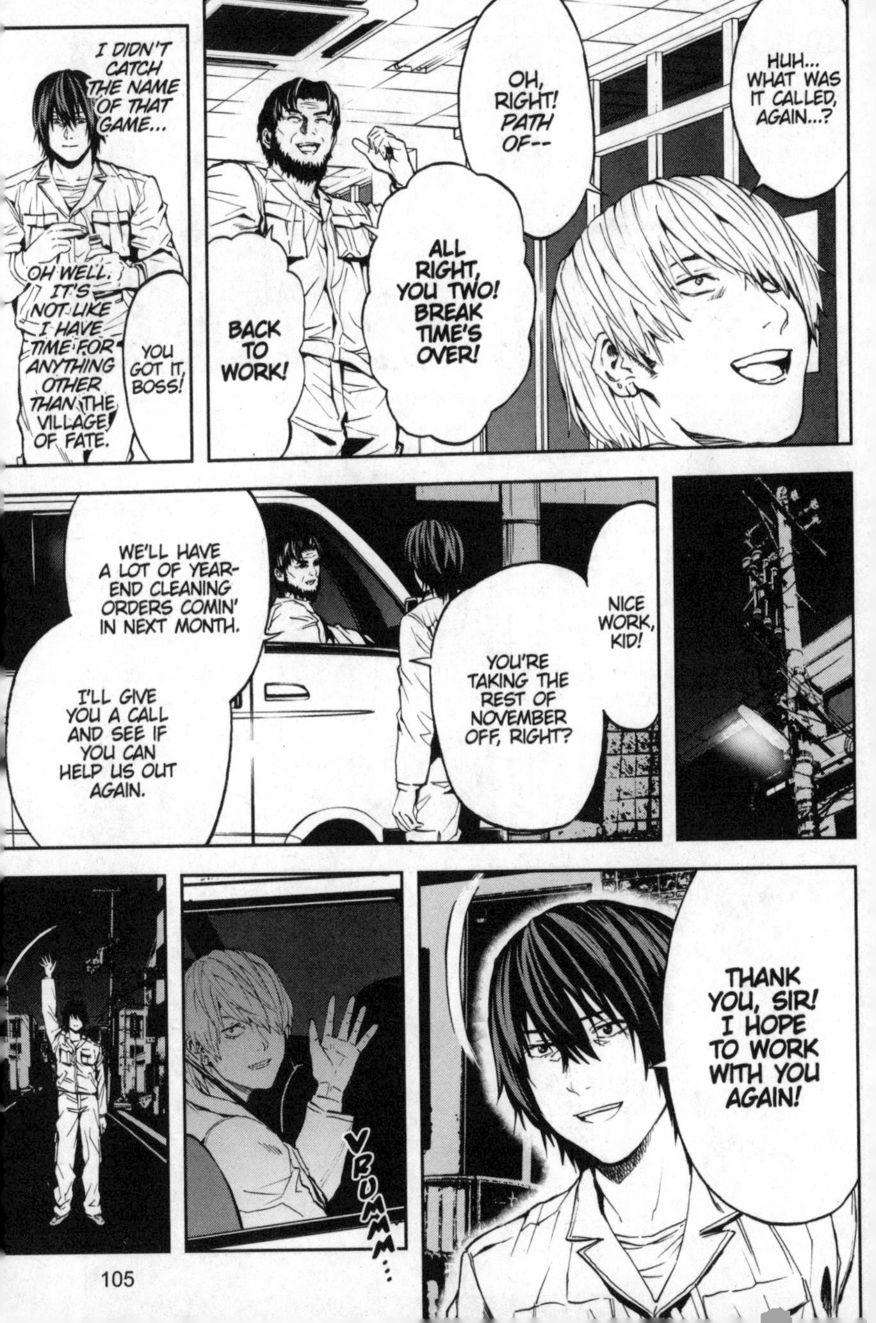
HUH... WHAT WAS IT CALLED, AGAIN...?
OH, RIGHT! PATH OF--
ALL RIGHT, YOU TWO! BREAK TIME'S OVER!
BACK TO WORK!
I DIDN'T CATCH THE NAME OF THAT GAME...
YOU GOT IT, BOSS!
OH WELL. IT'S NOT LIKE I HAVE TIME FOR ANYTHING OTHER THAN THE VILLAGE OF FATE.
NICE WORK, KID!
YOU'RE TAKING THE REST OF NOVEMBER OFF, RIGHT?
WE'LL HAVE A LOT OF YEAR-END CLEANING ORDERS COMIN' IN NEXT MONTH.
I'LL GIVE YOU A CALL AND SEE IF YOU CAN HELP US OUT AGAIN.
THANK YOU, SIR! I HOPE TO WORK WITH YOU AGAIN!
VRUMMM...

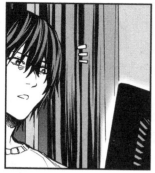

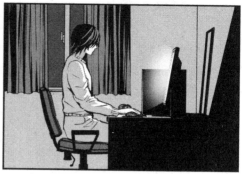

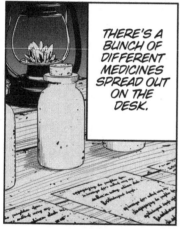

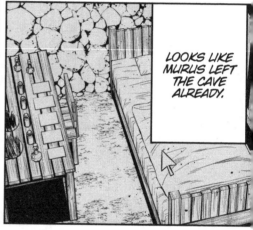

LOOKS LIKE MURUS LEFT THE CAVE ALREADY.
THERE'S A BUNCH OF DIFFERENT MEDICINES SPREAD OUT ON THE DESK.
EACH BOTTLE HAS A SHEET WITH IT...
DESCRIBING WHAT IT DOES, AND HOW MUCH TO TAKE. LOOKS PRETTY DETAILED.

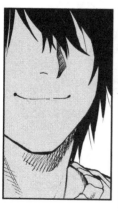

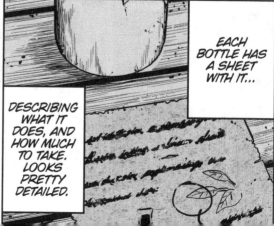

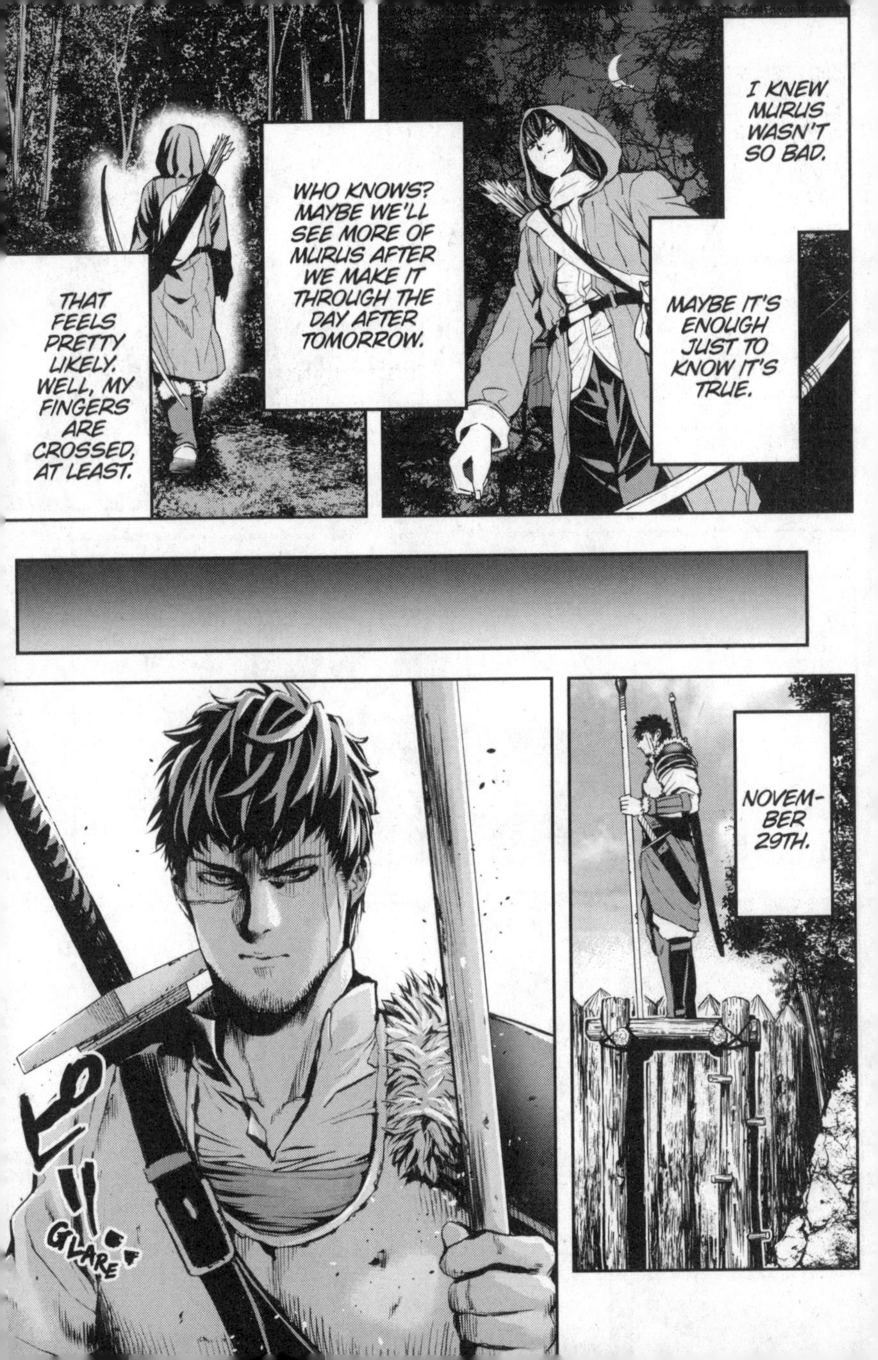
I KNEW MURUS WASN'T SO BAD.
MAYBE IT'S ENOUGH JUST TO KNOW IT'S TRUE.
WHO KNOWS? MAYBE WE'LL SEE MORE OF MURUS AFTER WE MAKE IT THROUGH THE DAY AFTER TOMORROW.
THAT FEELS PRETTY LIKELY. WELL, MY FINGERS ARE CROSSED, AT LEAST.
NOVEM-BER 29TH.
GLARE

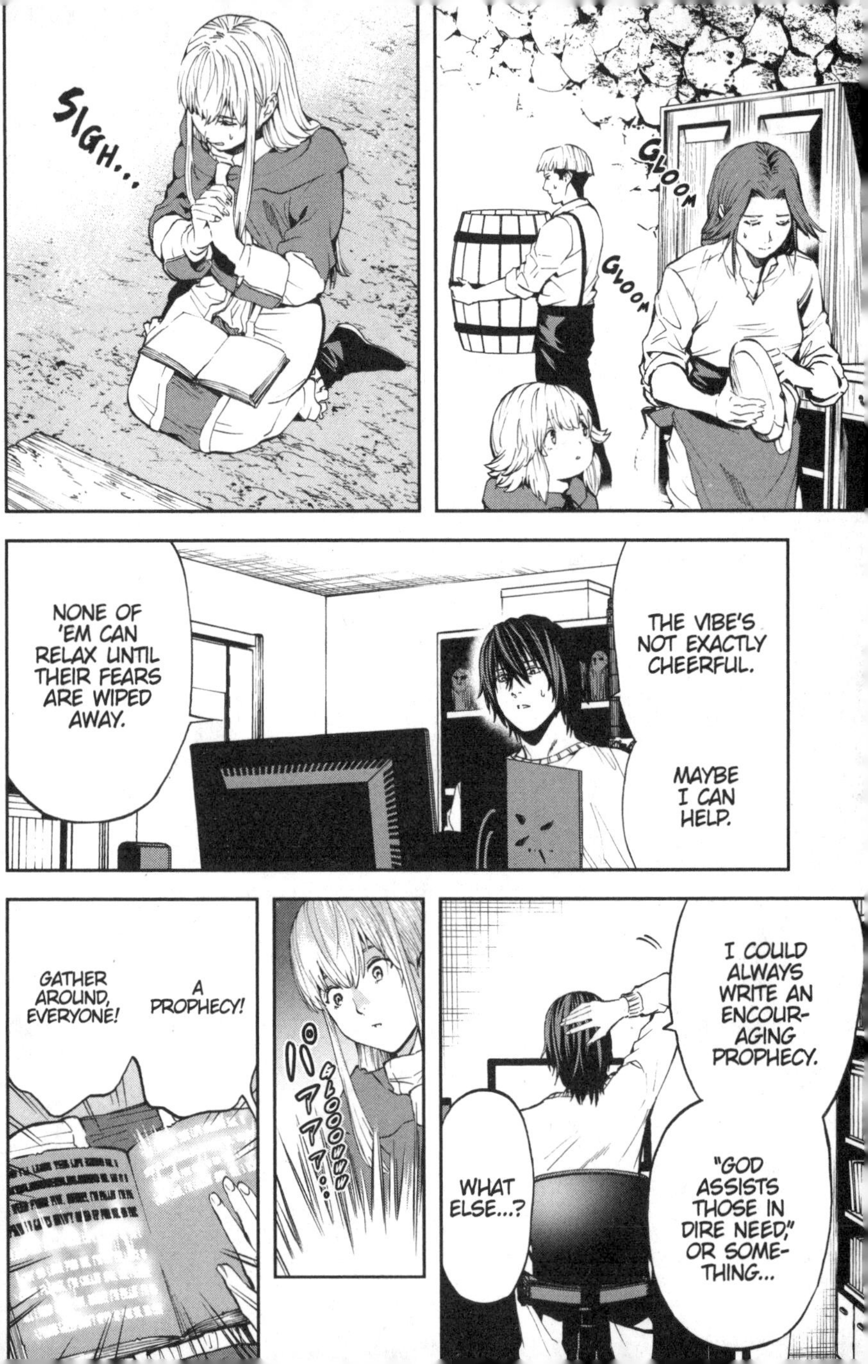
GLOOM
GLOOM
SIGH...
THE VIBE'S NOT EXACTLY CHEERFUL.
MAYBE I CAN HELP.
NONE OF 'EM CAN RELAX UNTIL THEIR FEARS ARE WIPED AWAY.
I COULD ALWAYS WRITE AN ENCOUR-AGING PROPHECY.
"GOD ASSISTS THOSE IN DIRE NEED," OR SOME-THING...
WHAT ELSE...?
A PROPHECY!
GATHER AROUND, EVERYONE!

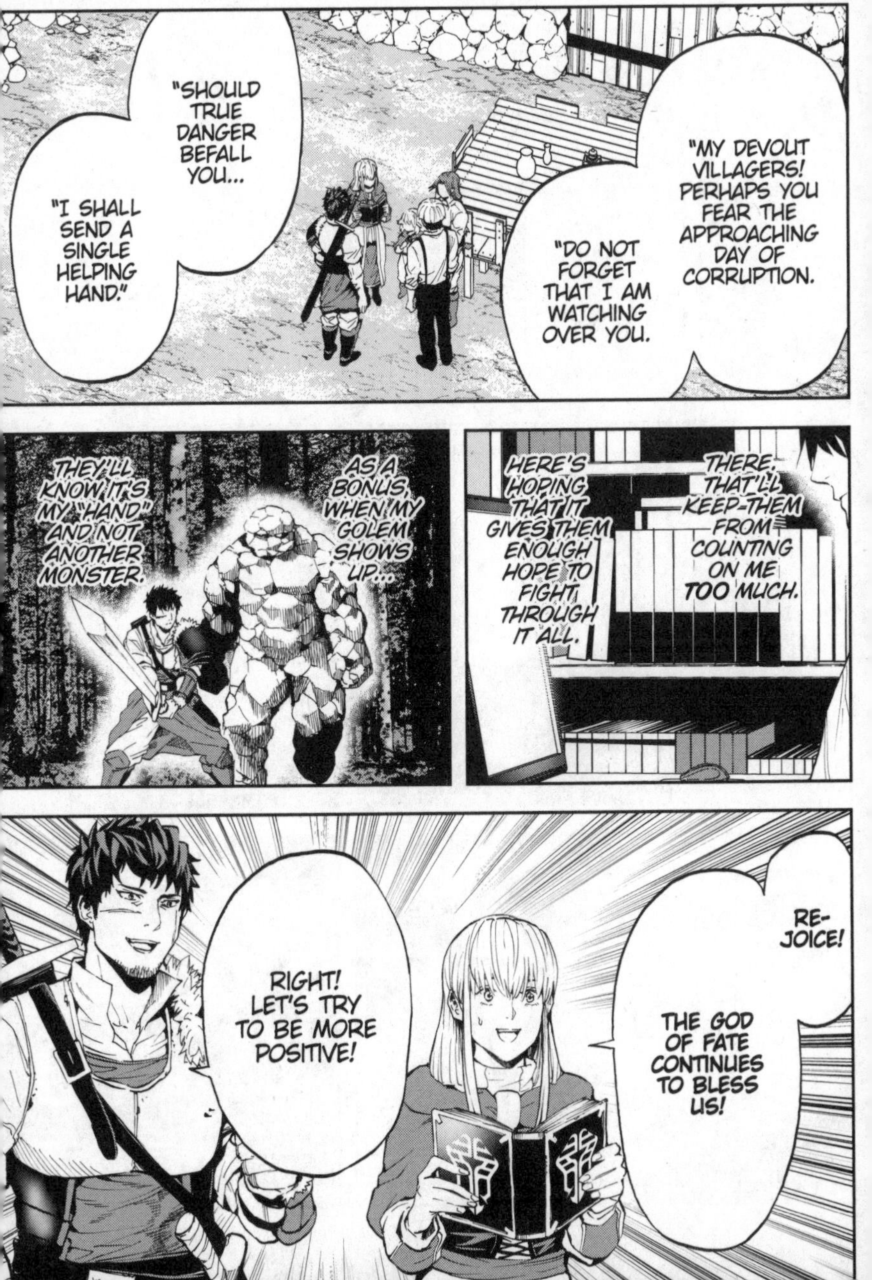
"MY DEVOUT VILLAGERS! PERHAPS YOU FEAR THE APPROACHING DAY OF CORRUPTION.
"DO NOT FORGET THAT I AM WATCHING OVER YOU.
"SHOULD TRUE DANGER BEFALL YOU...
"I SHALL SEND A SINGLE HELPING HAND."
THERE, THAT'LL KEEP THEM FROM COUNTING ON ME TOO MUCH.
HERE'S HOPING THAT IT GIVES THEM ENOUGH HOPE TO FIGHT THROUGH IT ALL.
AS A BONUS, WHEN MY GOLEM SHOWS UP...
THEY'LL KNOW IT'S MY "HAND" AND NOT ANOTHER MONSTER.
RE-JOICE!
THE GOD OF FATE CONTINUES TO BLESS US!
RIGHT! LET'S TRY TO BE MORE POSITIVE!

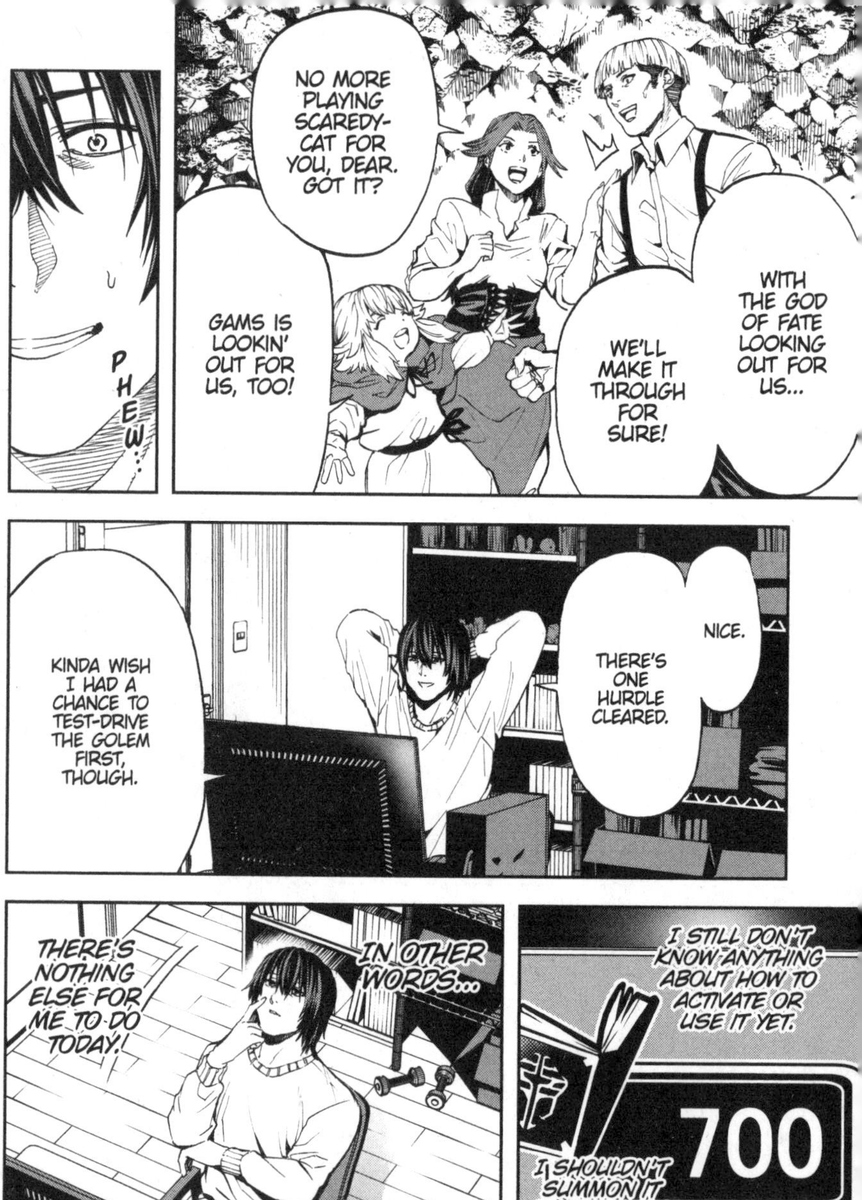
WITH THE GOD OF FATE LOOKING OUT FOR US...
WE'LL MAKE IT THROUGH FOR SURE!
NO MORE PLAYING SCAREDY-CAT FOR YOU, DEAR. GOT IT?
GAMS IS LOOKIN' OUT FOR US, TOO!
PHEW...
NICE.
THERE'S ONE HURDLE CLEARED.
KINDA WISH I HAD A CHANCE TO TEST-DRIVE THE GOLEM FIRST, THOUGH.
I STILL DON'T KNOW ANYTHING ABOUT HOW TO ACTIVATE OR USE IT YET.
700
I SHOULDN'T SUMMON IT UNTIL THINGS GET REALLY BAD.
IN OTHER WORDS...
THERE'S NOTHING ELSE FOR ME TO DO TODAY!

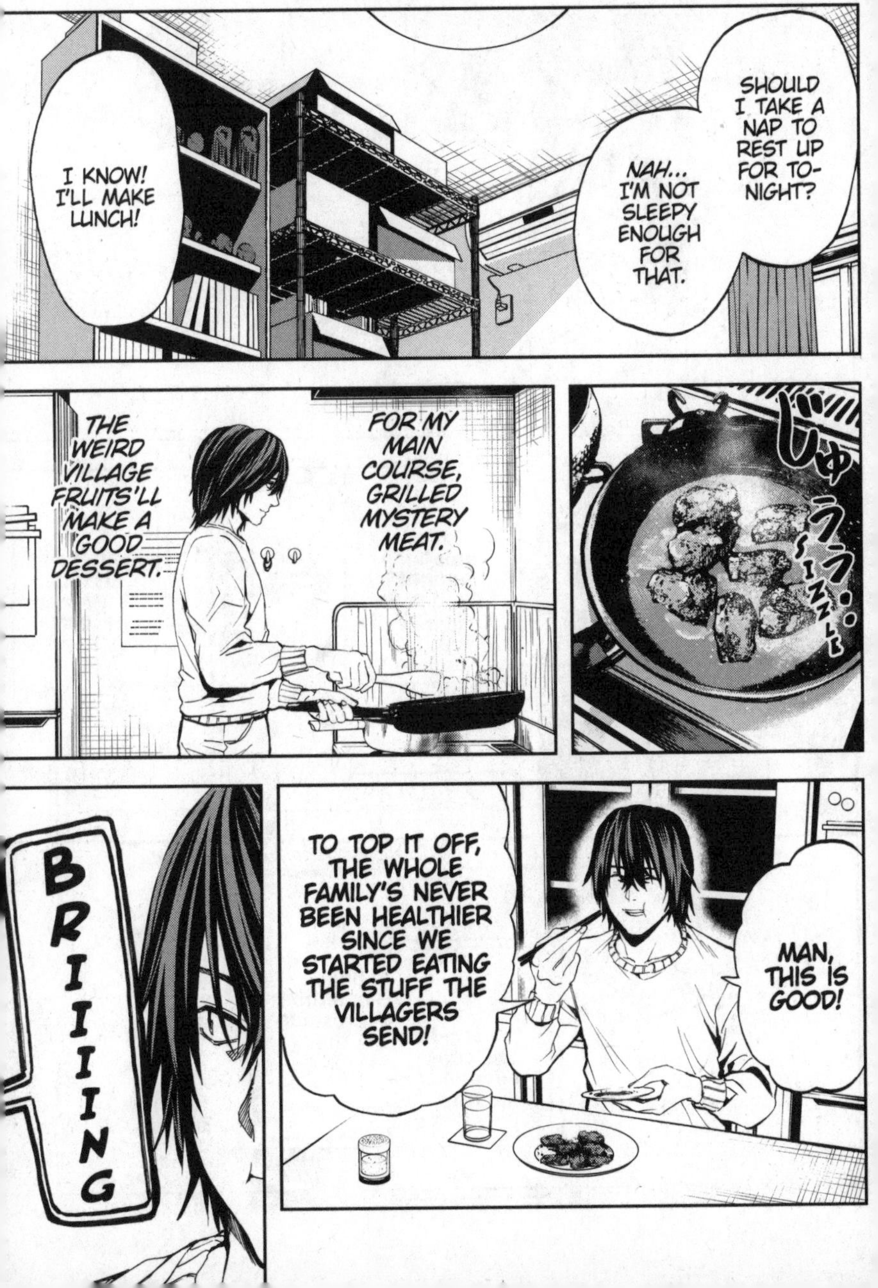
SHOULD I TAKE A NAP TO REST UP FOR TO-NIGHT?
NAH... I'M NOT SLEEPY ENOUGH FOR THAT.
I KNOW! I'LL MAKE LUNCH!
じゅうう
SIZZLE
FOR MY MAIN COURSE, GRILLED MYSTERY MEAT.
THE WEIRD VILLAGE FRUITS'LL MAKE A GOOD DESSERT.
MAN, THIS IS GOOD!
TO TOP IT OFF, THE WHOLE FAMILY'S NEVER BEEN HEALTHIER SINCE WE STARTED EATING THE STUFF THE VILLAGERS SEND!
BRIIIING

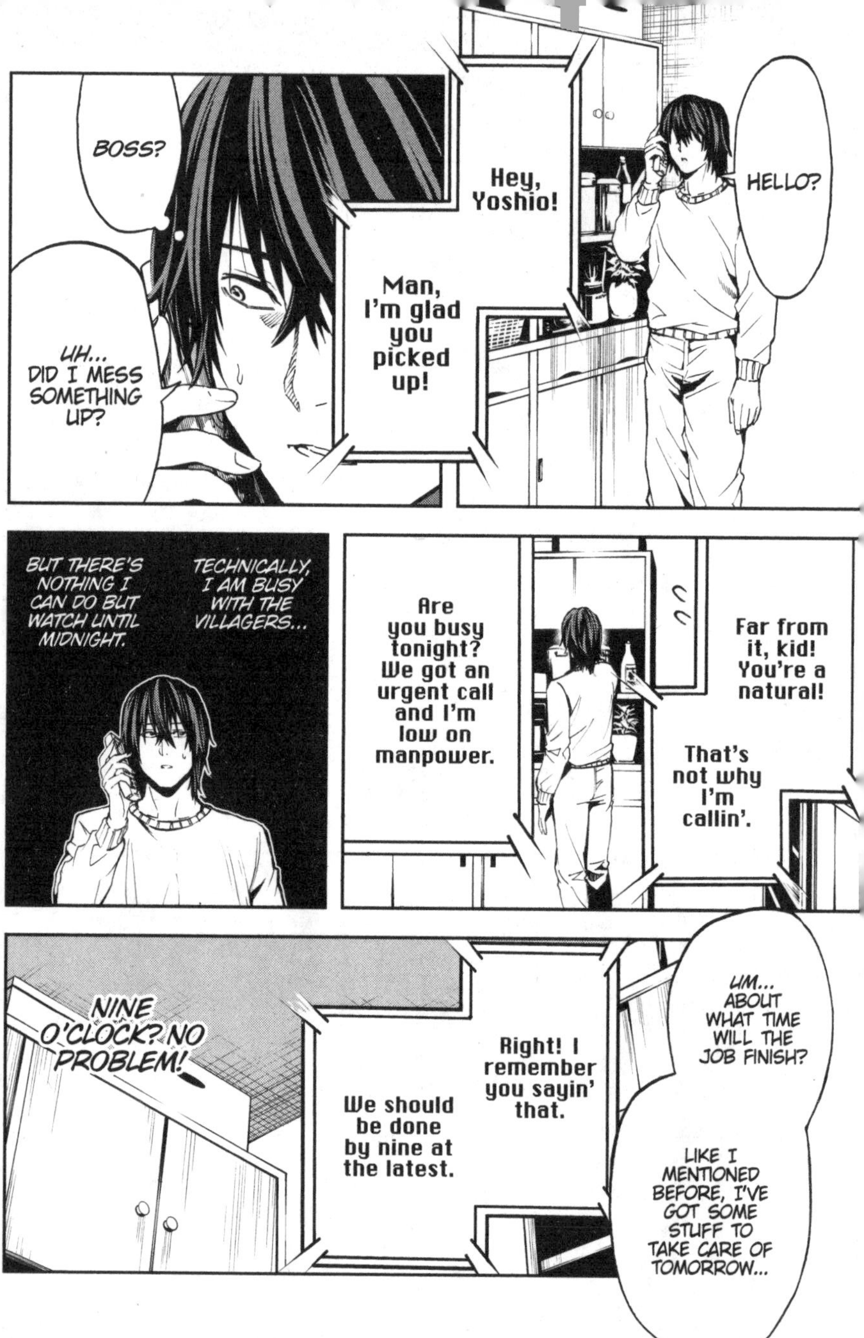
HELLO?
Hey, Yoshio!
Man, I'm glad you picked up!
BOSS?
UH... DID I MESS SOMETHING UP?
Far from it, kid! You're a natural!
That's not why I'm callin'.
Are you busy tonight? We got an urgent call and I'm low on manpower.
TECHNICALLY, I AM BUSY WITH THE VILLAGERS...
BUT THERE'S NOTHING I CAN DO BUT WATCH UNTIL MIDNIGHT.
UM... ABOUT WHAT TIME WILL THE JOB FINISH?
LIKE I MENTIONED BEFORE, I'VE GOT SOME STUFF TO TAKE CARE OF TOMORROW...
Right! I remember you sayin' that.
We should be done by nine at the latest.
NINE O'CLOCK? NO PROBLEM!

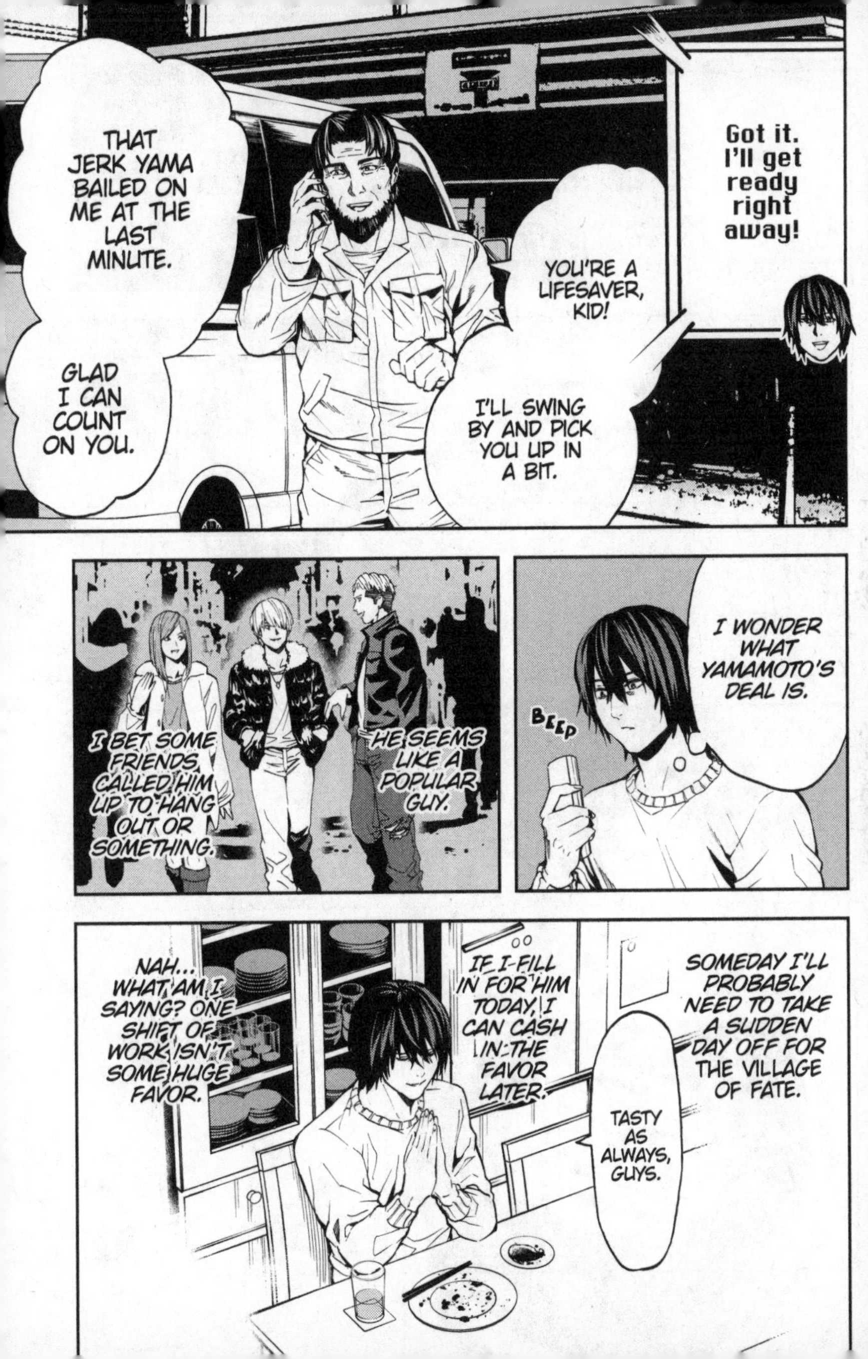
Got it. I'll get ready right away!
YOU'RE A LIFESAVER, KID!
THAT JERK YAMA BAILED ON ME AT THE LAST MINUTE.
I'LL SWING BY AND PICK YOU UP IN A BIT.
GLAD I CAN COUNT ON YOU.
I WONDER WHAT YAMAMOTO'S DEAL IS.
BEEP
HE SEEMS LIKE A POPULAR GUY.
I BET SOME FRIENDS CALLED HIM UP TO HANG OUT OR SOMETHING.
SOMEDAY I'LL PROBABLY NEED TO TAKE A SUDDEN DAY OFF FOR THE VILLAGE OF FATE.
TASTY AS ALWAYS, GUYS.
IF I FILL IN FOR HIM TODAY, I CAN CASH IN THE FAVOR LATER.
NAH... WHAT AM I SAYING? ONE SHIFT OF WORK ISN'T SOME HUGE FAVOR.

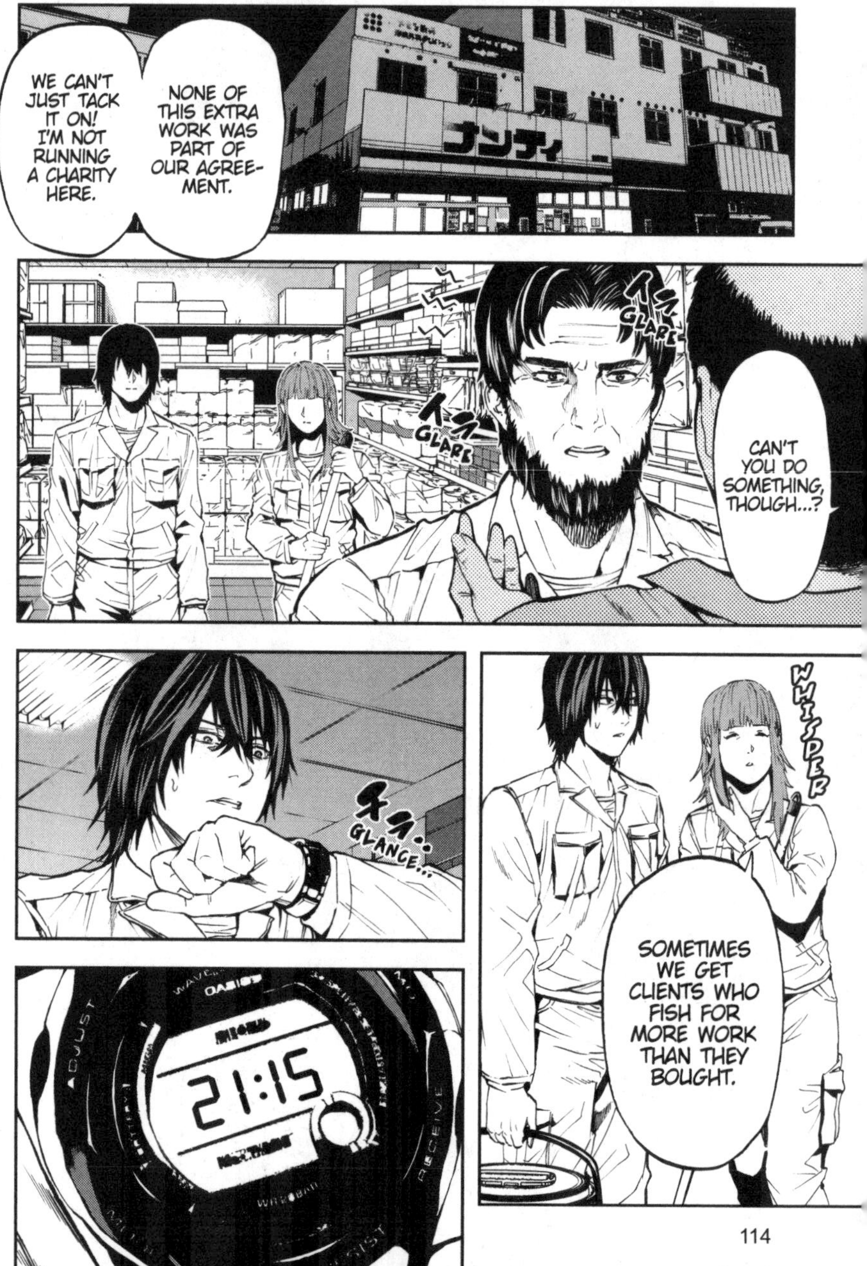
NONE OF THIS EXTRA WORK WAS PART OF OUR AGREEMENT.
WE CAN'T JUST TACK IT ON! I'M NOT RUNNING A CHARITY HERE.
ナンディ
GLARE
GLARE
CAN'T YOU DO SOMETHING, THOUGH...?
WHISPER
SOMETIMES WE GET CLIENTS WHO FISH FOR MORE WORK THAN THEY BOUGHT.
GLANCE...
21:15
ADJUST
RECEIVE

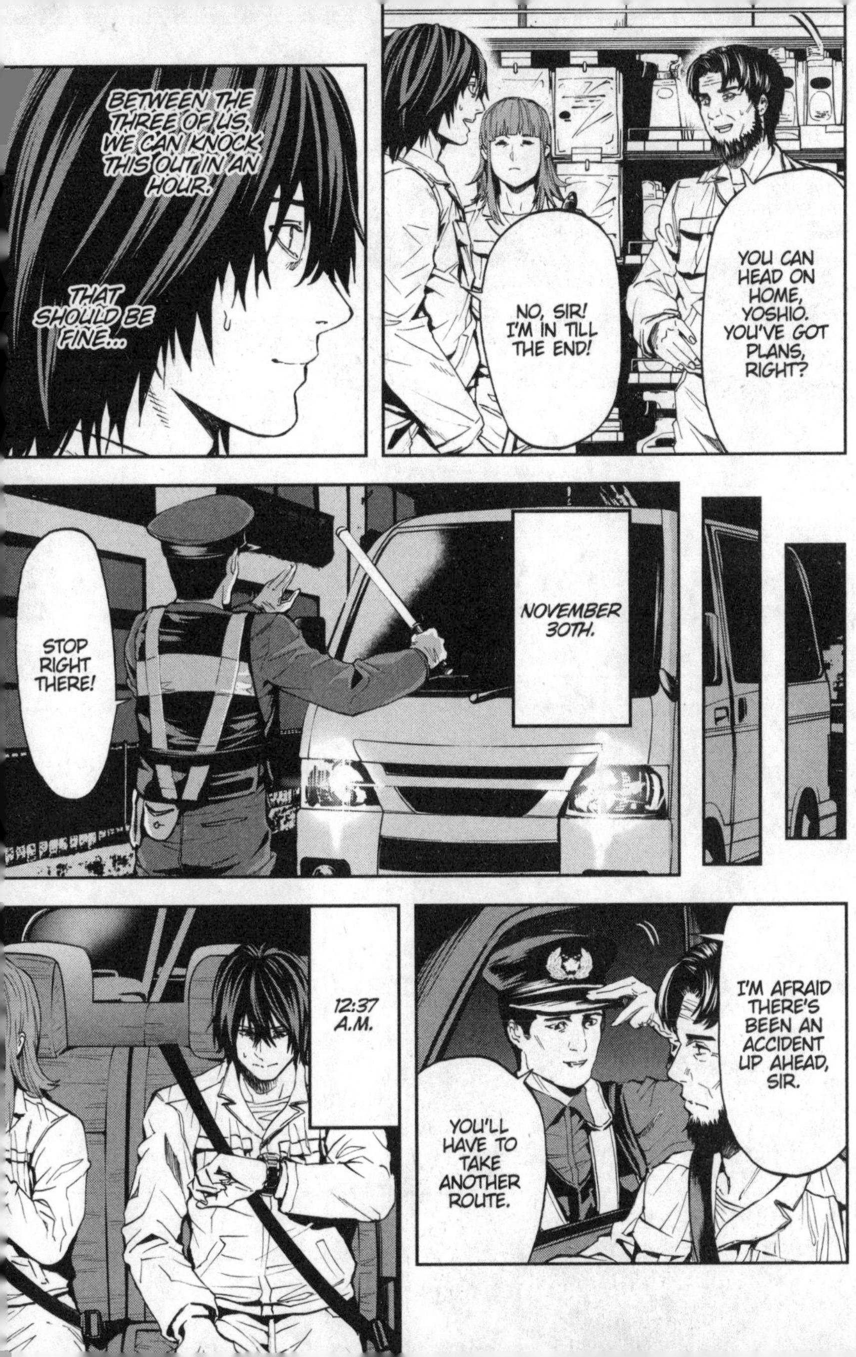
YOU CAN HEAD ON HOME, YOSHIO. YOU'VE GOT PLANS, RIGHT?
NO, SIR! I'M IN TILL THE END!
BETWEEN THE THREE OF US, WE CAN KNOCK THIS OUT IN AN HOUR.
THAT SHOULD BE FINE...
NOVEMBER 30TH.
STOP RIGHT THERE!
I'M AFRAID THERE'S BEEN AN ACCIDENT UP AHEAD, SIR.
YOU'LL HAVE TO TAKE ANOTHER ROUTE.
12:37 A.M.

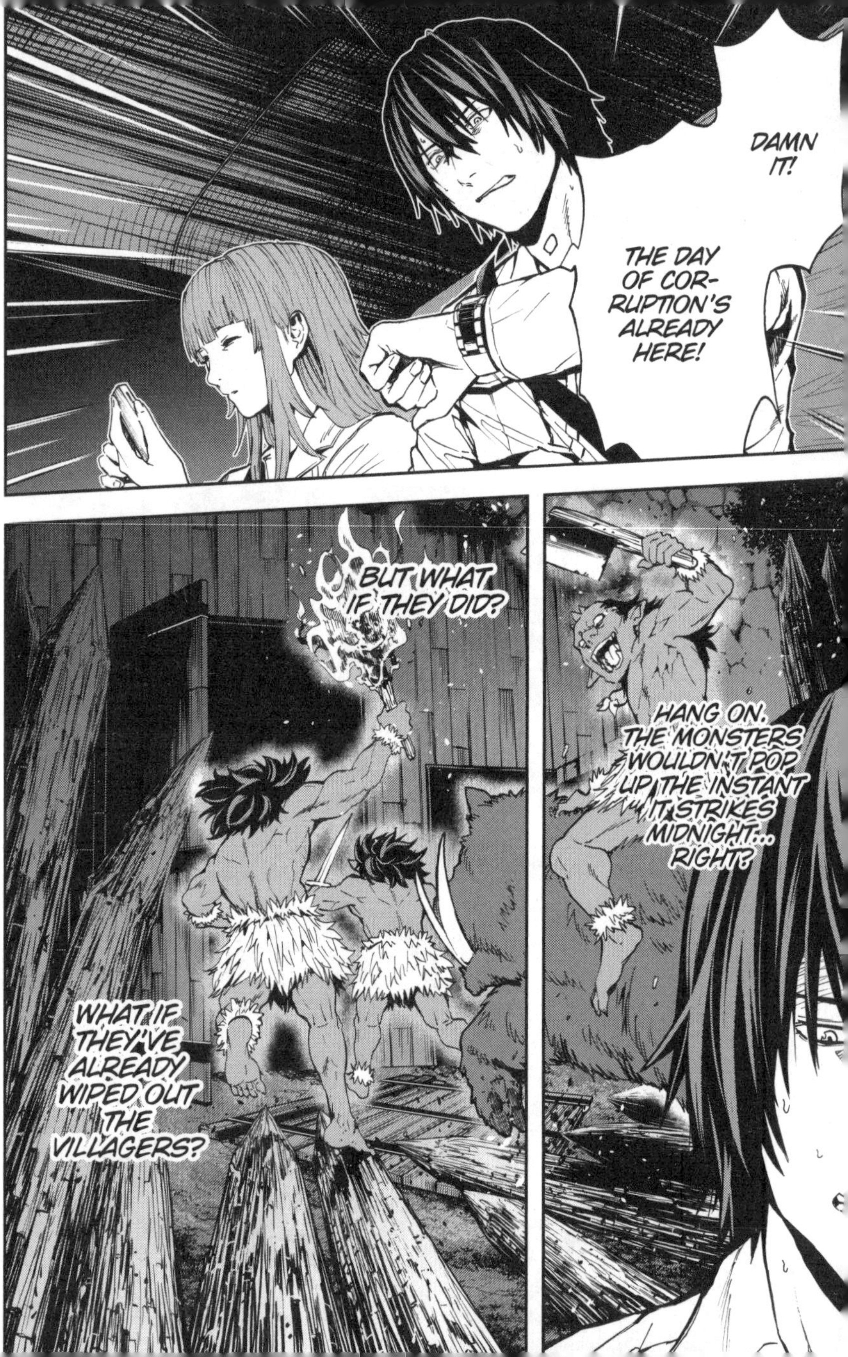
DAMN IT!
THE DAY OF COR-RUPTION'S ALREADY HERE!
HANG ON. THE MONSTERS WOULDN'T POP UP THE INSTANT IT STRIKES MIDNIGHT... RIGHT?
BUT WHAT IF THEY DID?
WHAT IF THEY'VE ALREADY WIPED OUT THE VILLAGERS?

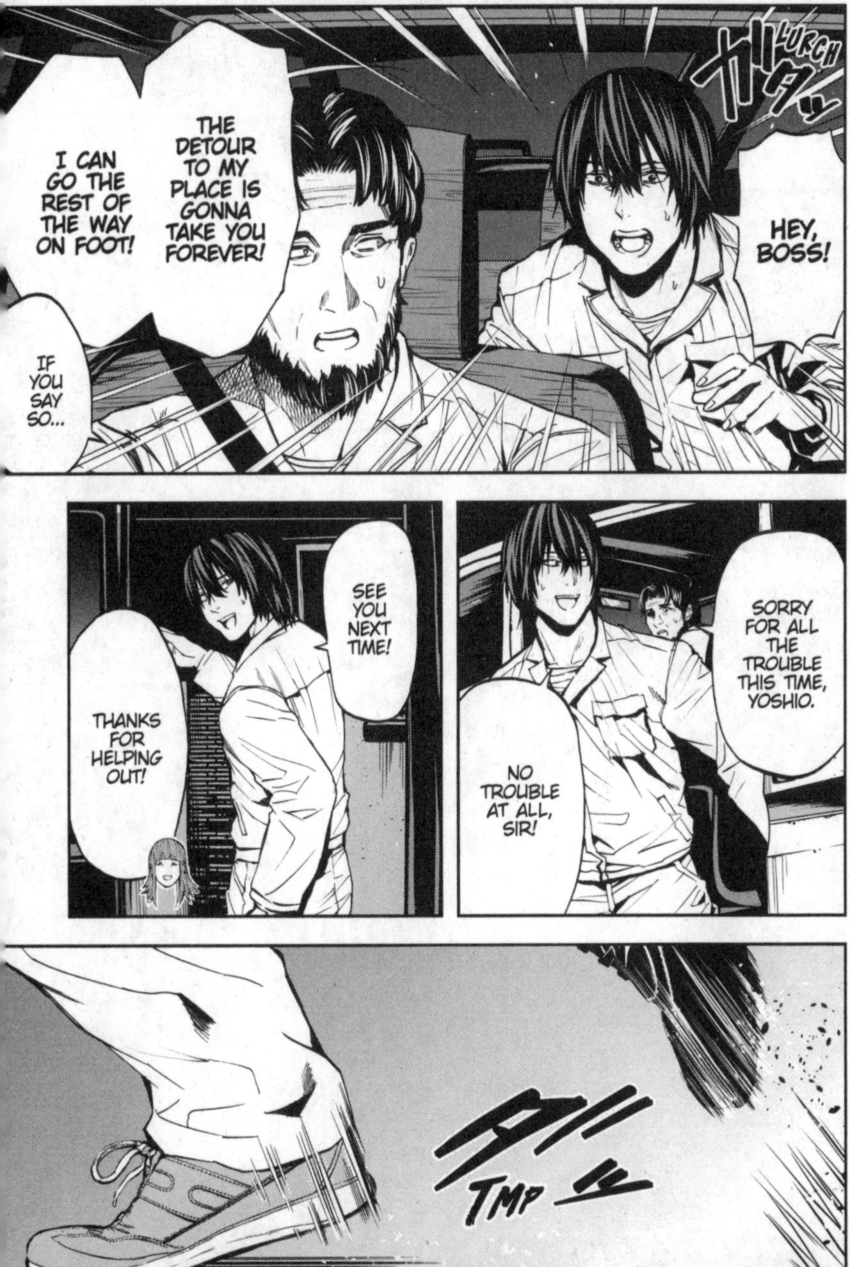
LURCH
HEY, BOSS!
THE DETOUR TO MY PLACE IS GONNA TAKE YOU FOREVER!
I CAN GO THE REST OF THE WAY ON FOOT!
IF YOU SAY SO...
SORRY FOR ALL THE TROUBLE THIS TIME, YOSHIO.
NO TROUBLE AT ALL, SIR!
SEE YOU NEXT TIME!
THANKS FOR HELPING OUT!
TMP

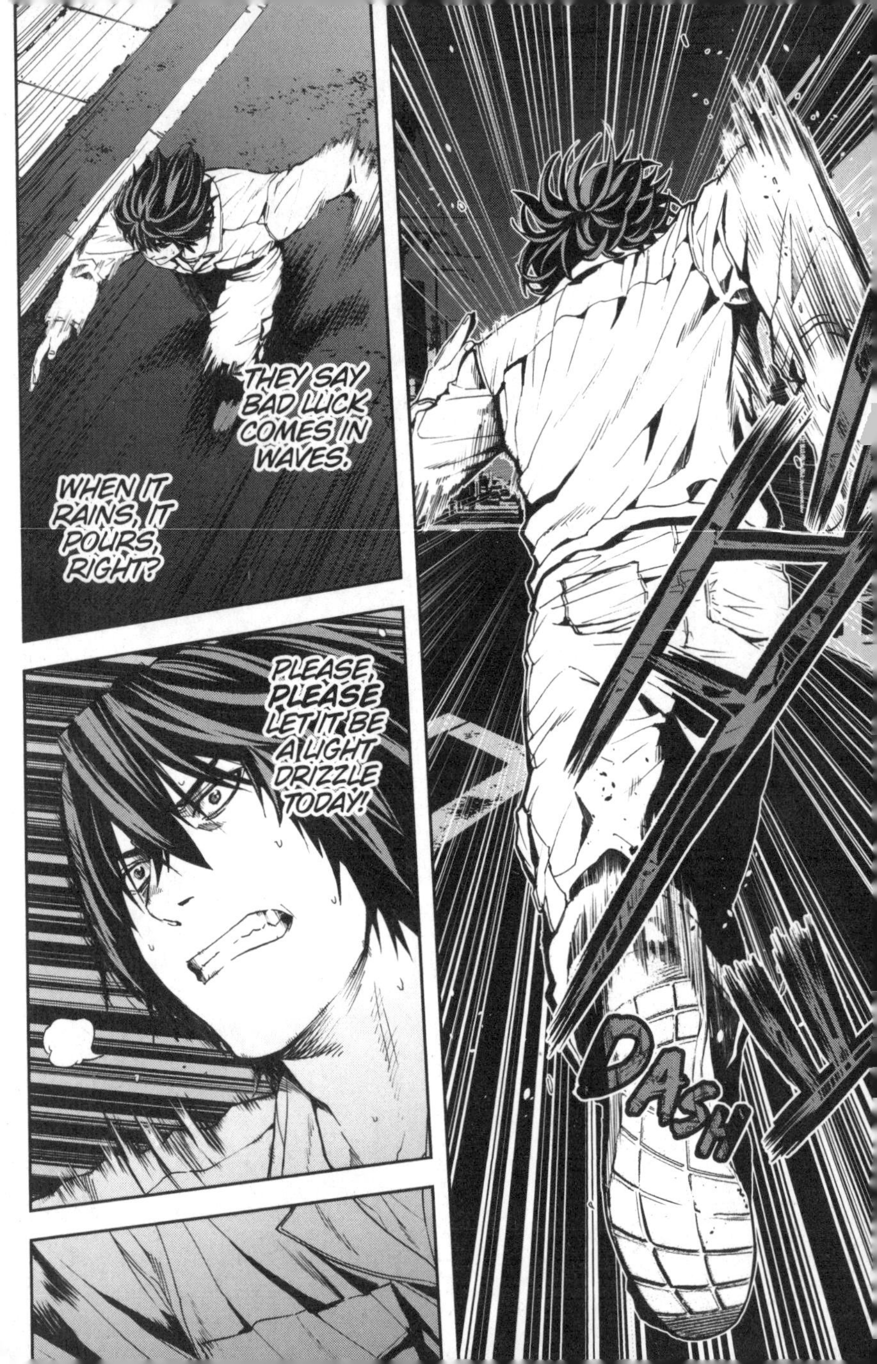
DASH
THEY SAY BAD LUCK COMES IN WAVES.
WHEN IT RAINS, IT POURS, RIGHT?
PLEASE, PLEASE LET IT BE A LIGHT DRIZZLE TODAY!

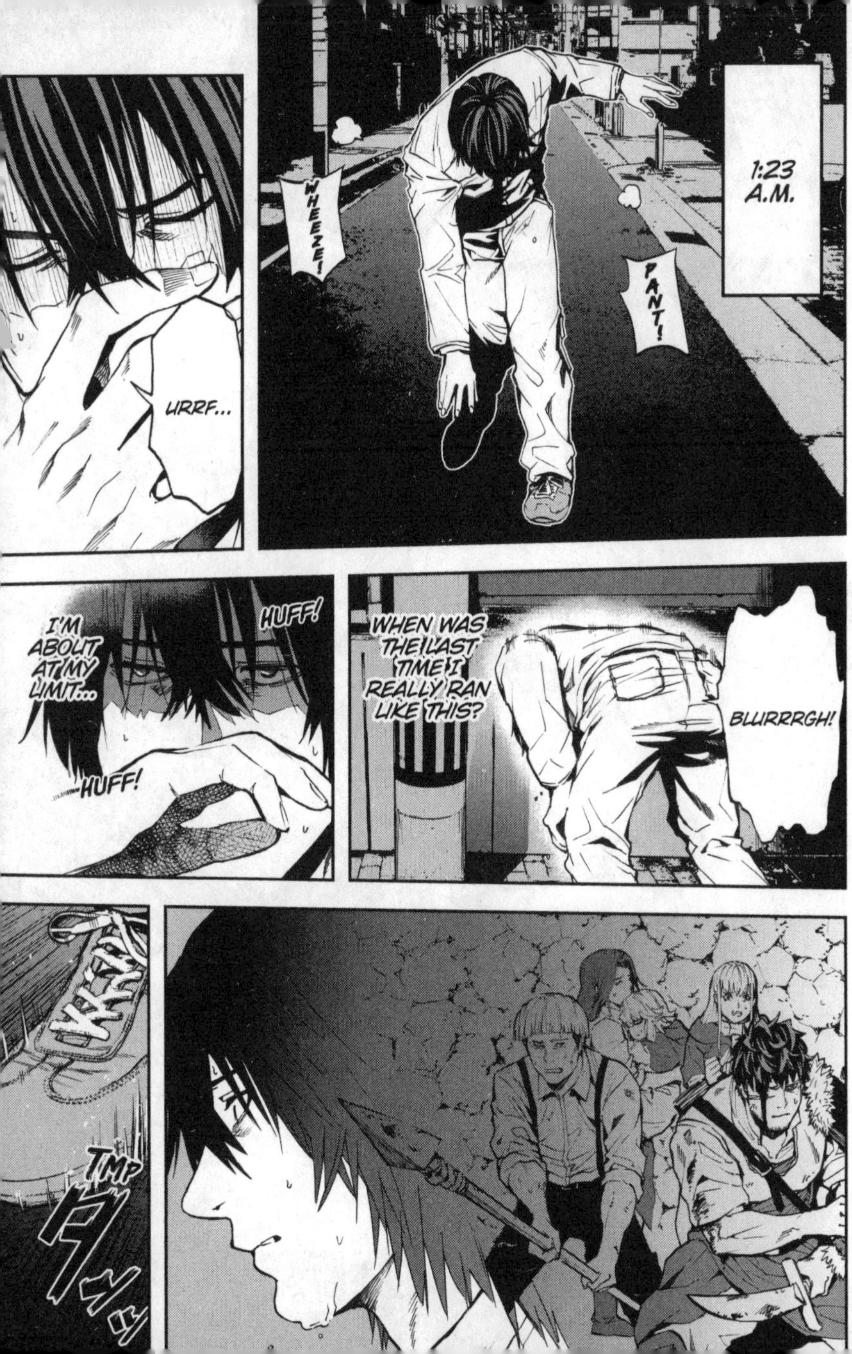
1:23 A.M.
PANT!
WHEEZE!
URRF...
BLURRRGH!
WHEN WAS THE LAST TIME I REALLY RAN LIKE THIS?
HUFF!
I'M ABOUT AT MY LIMIT...
HUFF!
TMP

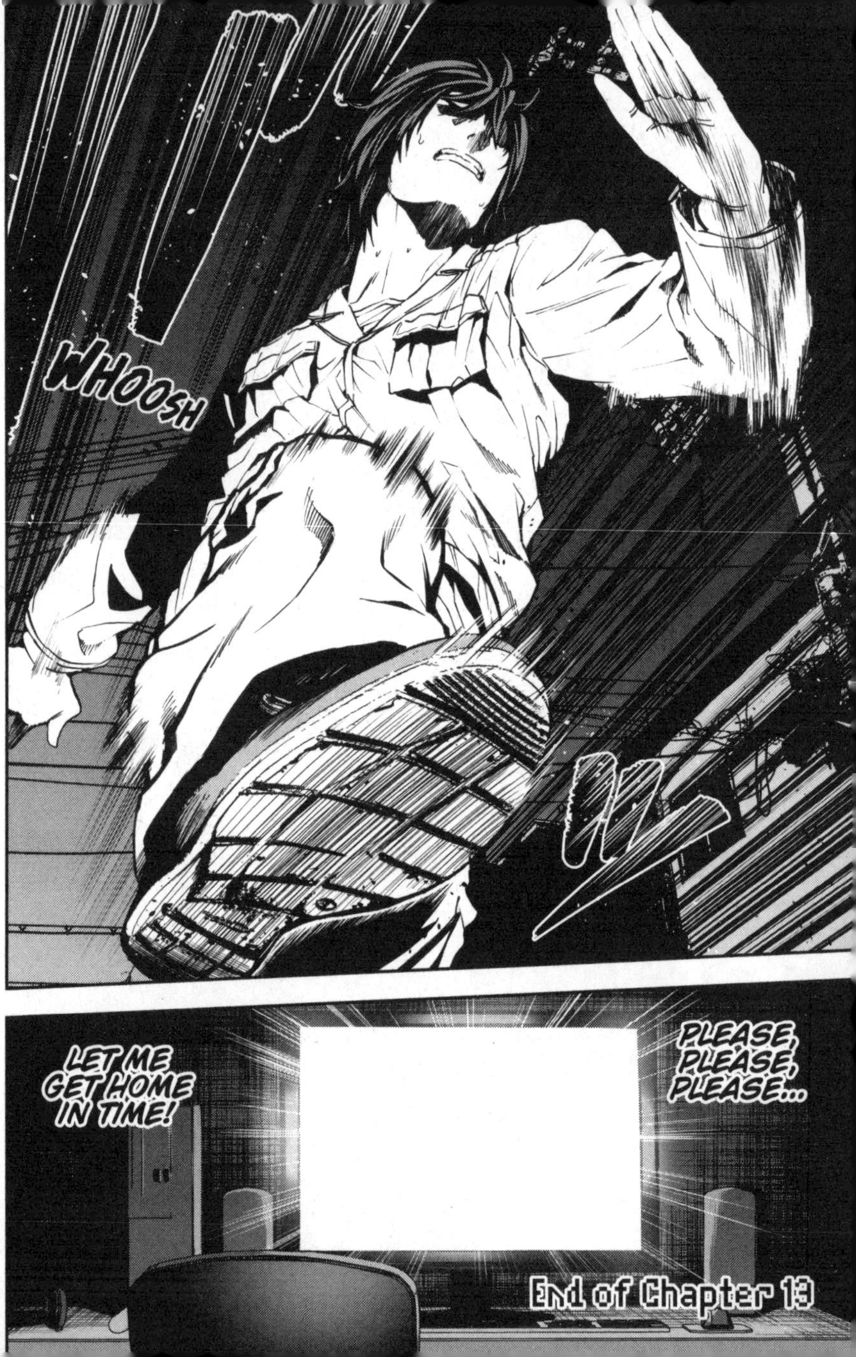
WHOOSH
PLEASE, PLEASE, PLEASE...
LET ME GET HOME IN TIME!
End of Chapter 13

Character

Yoshio

▶ Gender: Male

Class: God of Fate,
Part-Time Cleaner
(New!)

E : Cloth Armor (Work
Jumpsuit)

E : Industrial Vacuum

E : Work Ethic

**THE NPCs IN THIS
VILLAGE SIM GAME
MUST BE REAL!**

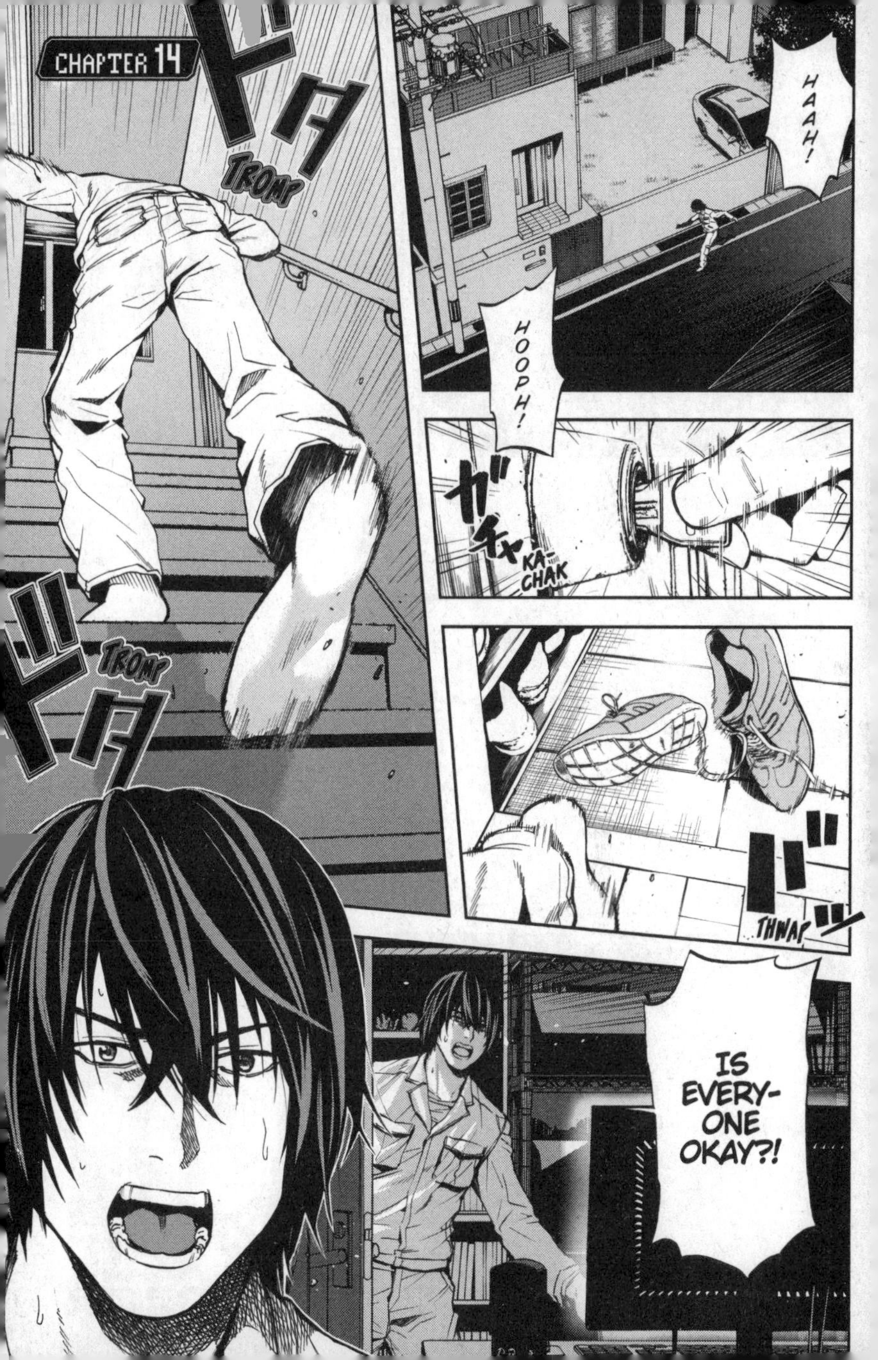
HAAAH!
HOOPH!
KA-CHAK
THWAP
CHAPTER 14
TROMP
TROMP
IS EVERY-ONE OKAY?!

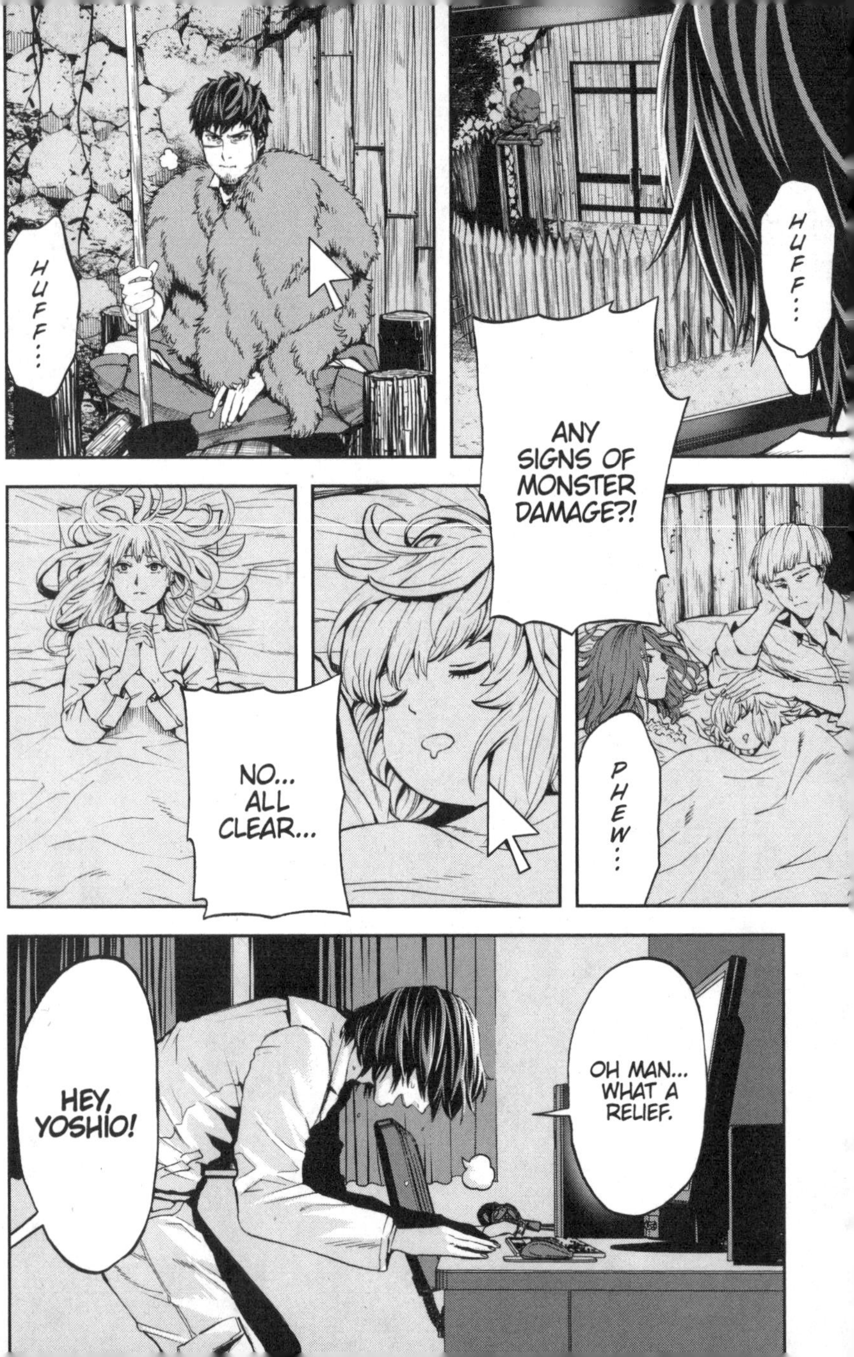
HUFF...
ANY SIGNS OF MONSTER DAMAGE?!
HUFF...
PHEW...
NO... ALL CLEAR...
OH MAN... WHAT A RELIEF.
HEY, YOSHIO!

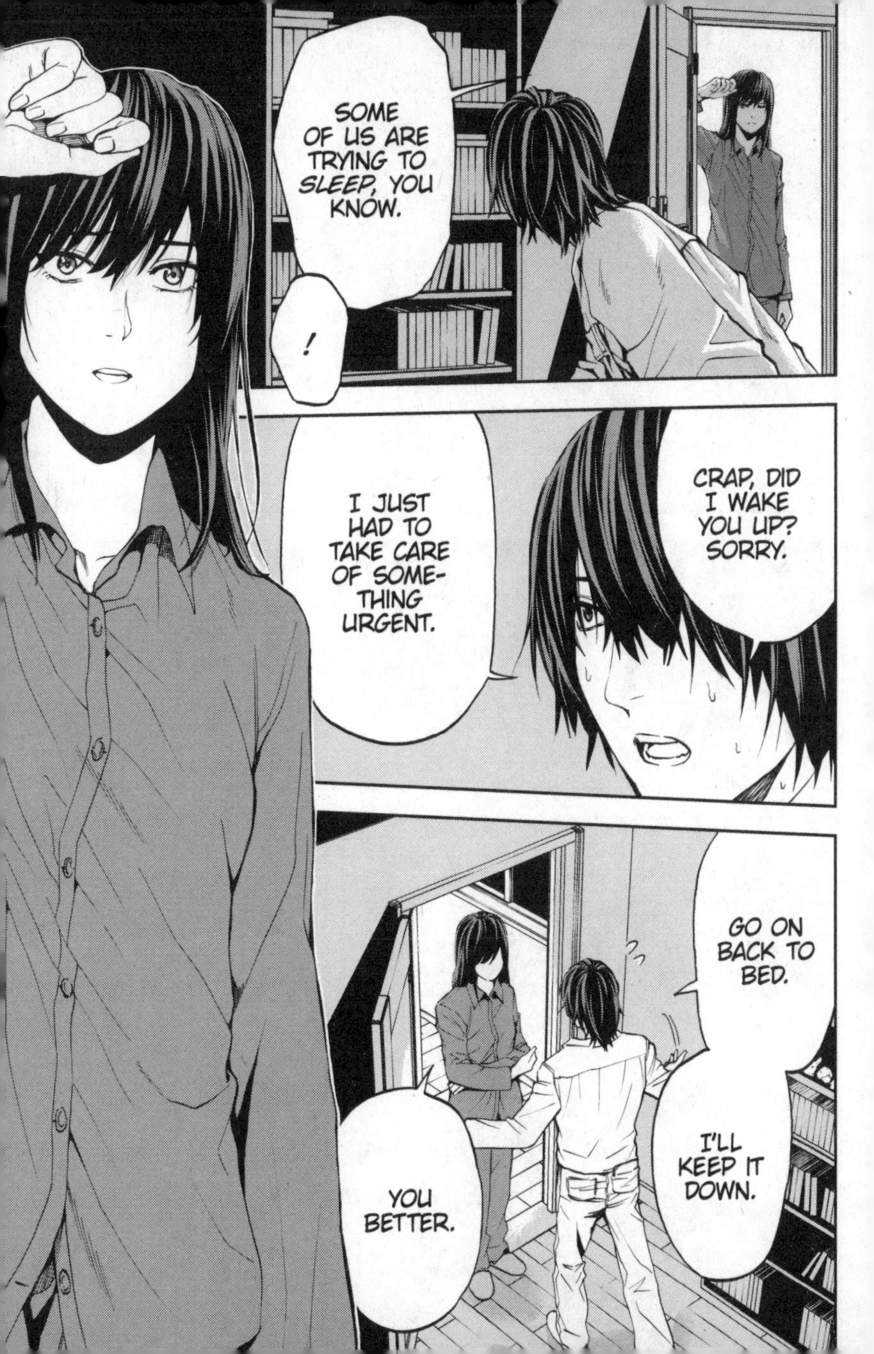
SOME OF US ARE TRYING TO *SLEEP*, YOU KNOW.
!
CRAP, DID I WAKE YOU UP? SORRY.
I JUST HAD TO TAKE CARE OF SOME-THING URGENT.
GO ON BACK TO BED.
I'LL KEEP IT DOWN.
YOU BETTER.

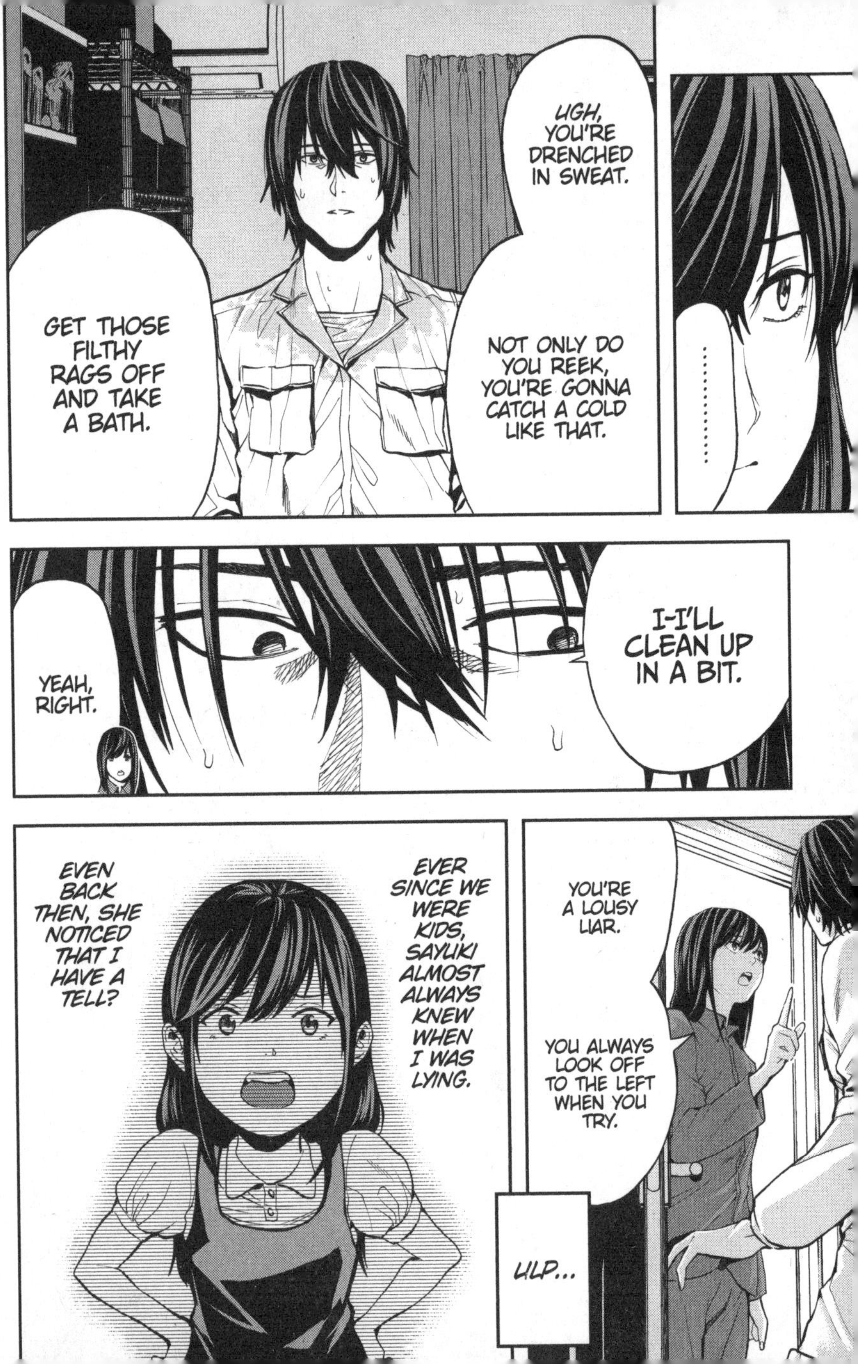
......
UGH, YOU'RE DRENCHED IN SWEAT.
NOT ONLY DO YOU REEK, YOU'RE GONNA CATCH A COLD LIKE THAT.
GET THOSE FILTHY RAGS OFF AND TAKE A BATH.
I-I'LL CLEAN UP IN A BIT.
YEAH, RIGHT.
YOU'RE A LOUSY LIAR.
YOU ALWAYS LOOK OFF TO THE LEFT WHEN YOU TRY.
ULP...
EVER SINCE WE WERE KIDS, SAYUKI ALMOST ALWAYS KNEW WHEN I WAS LYING.
EVEN BACK THEN, SHE NOTICED THAT I HAVE A TELL?

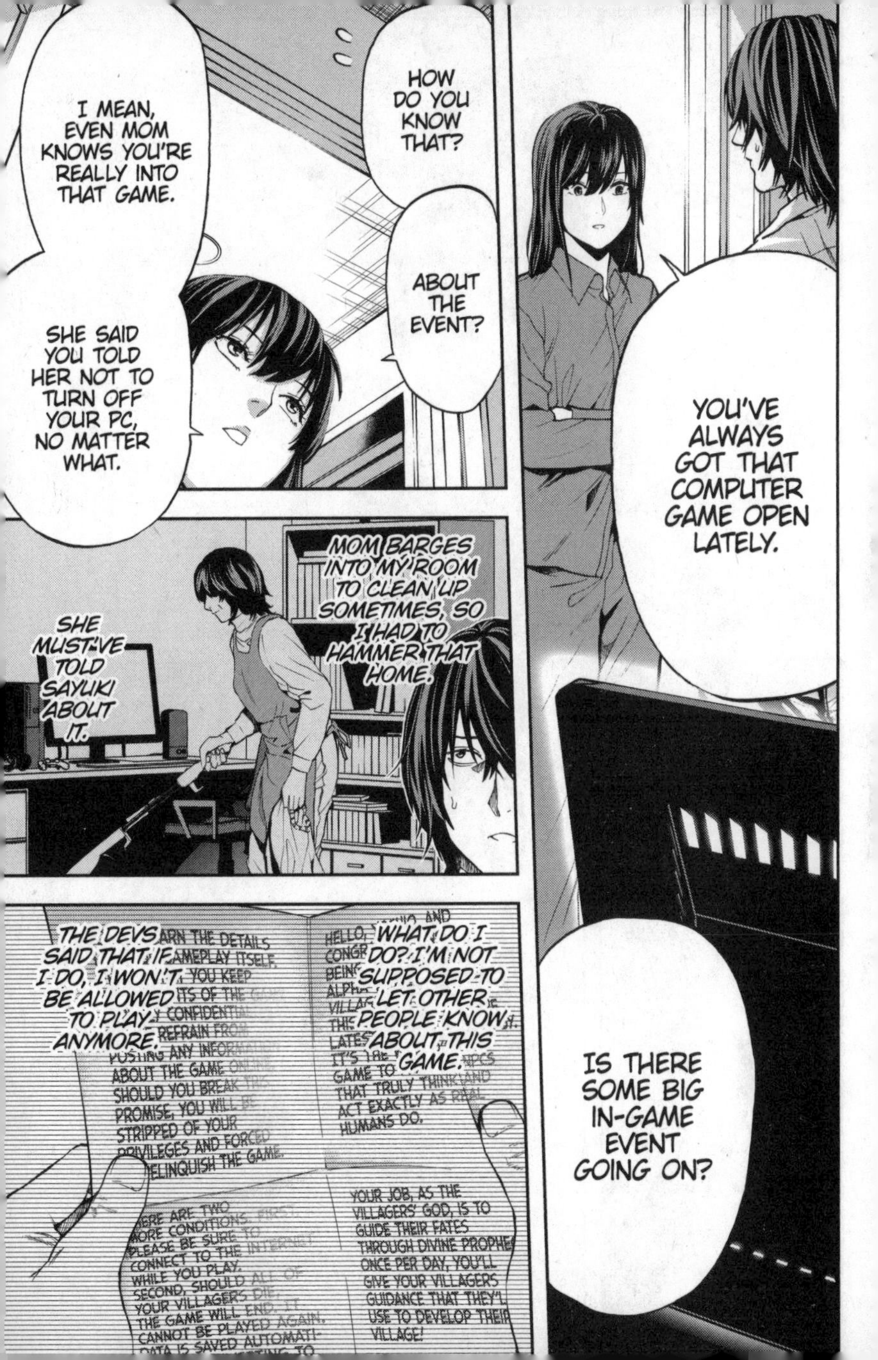
YOU'VE ALWAYS GOT THAT COMPUTER GAME OPEN LATELY.
IS THERE SOME BIG IN-GAME EVENT GOING ON?
HOW DO YOU KNOW THAT?
ABOUT THE EVENT?
I MEAN, EVEN MOM KNOWS YOU'RE REALLY INTO THAT GAME.
SHE SAID YOU TOLD HER NOT TO TURN OFF YOUR PC, NO MATTER WHAT.
MOM BARGES INTO MY ROOM TO CLEAN UP SOMETIMES, SO I HAD TO HAMMER THAT HOME.
SHE MUST'VE TOLD SAYUKI ABOUT IT.
WHAT DO I DO? I'M NOT SUPPOSED TO LET OTHER PEOPLE KNOW ABOUT THIS GAME.
THE DEVS SAID THAT IF I DO, I WON'T BE ALLOWED TO PLAY ANYMORE.

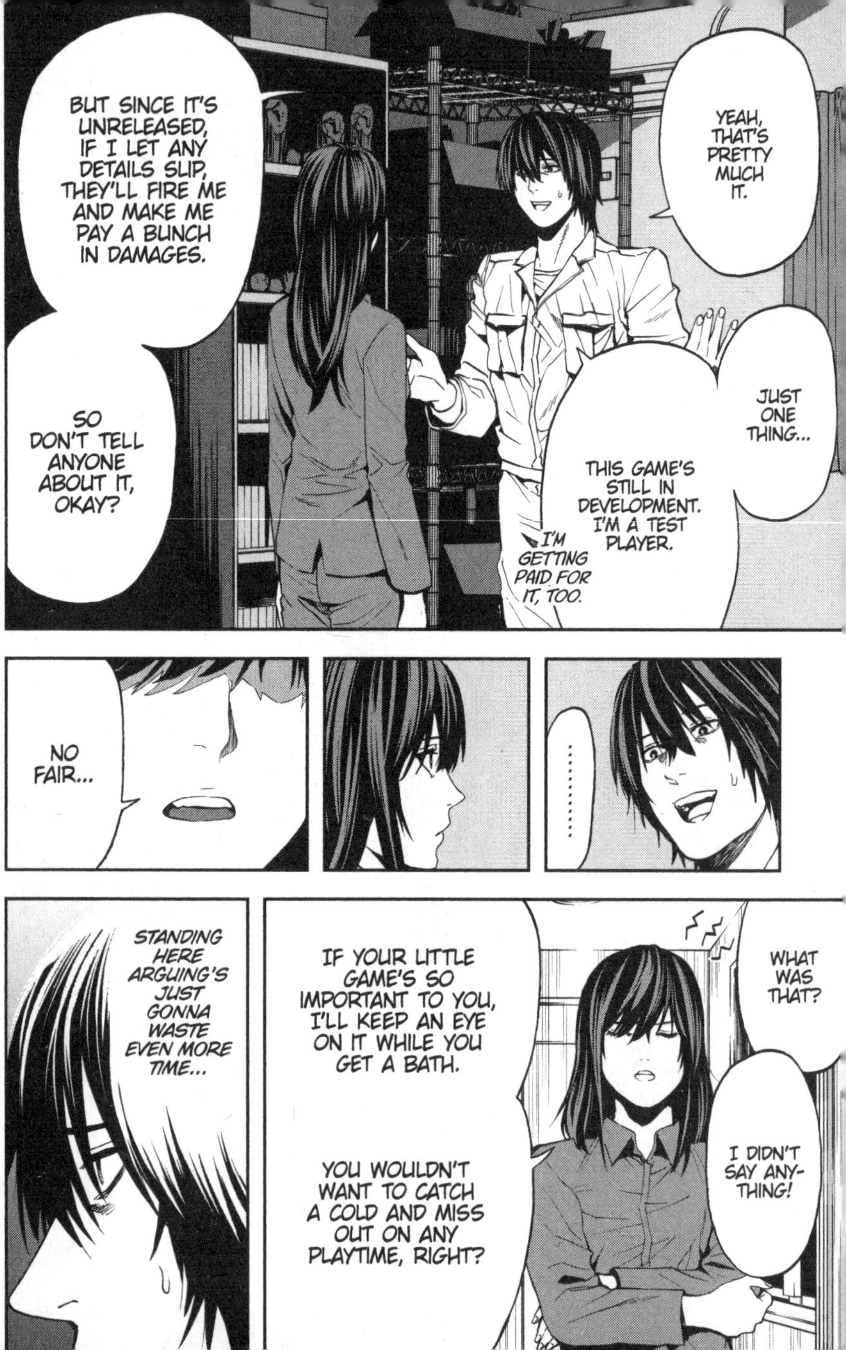
YEAH, THAT'S PRETTY MUCH IT.
JUST ONE THING...
THIS GAME'S STILL IN DEVELOPMENT. I'M A TEST PLAYER.
I'M GETTING PAID FOR IT, TOO.
BUT SINCE IT'S UNRELEASED, IF I LET ANY DETAILS SLIP, THEY'LL FIRE ME AND MAKE ME PAY A BUNCH IN DAMAGES.
SO DON'T TELL ANYONE ABOUT IT, OKAY?
......
NO FAIR...
WHAT WAS THAT?
IF YOUR LITTLE GAME'S SO IMPORTANT TO YOU, I'LL KEEP AN EYE ON IT WHILE YOU GET A BATH.
I DIDN'T SAY ANY-THING!
YOU WOULDN'T WANT TO CATCH A COLD AND MISS OUT ON ANY PLAYTIME, RIGHT?
STANDING HERE ARGUING'S JUST GONNA WASTE EVEN MORE TIME...

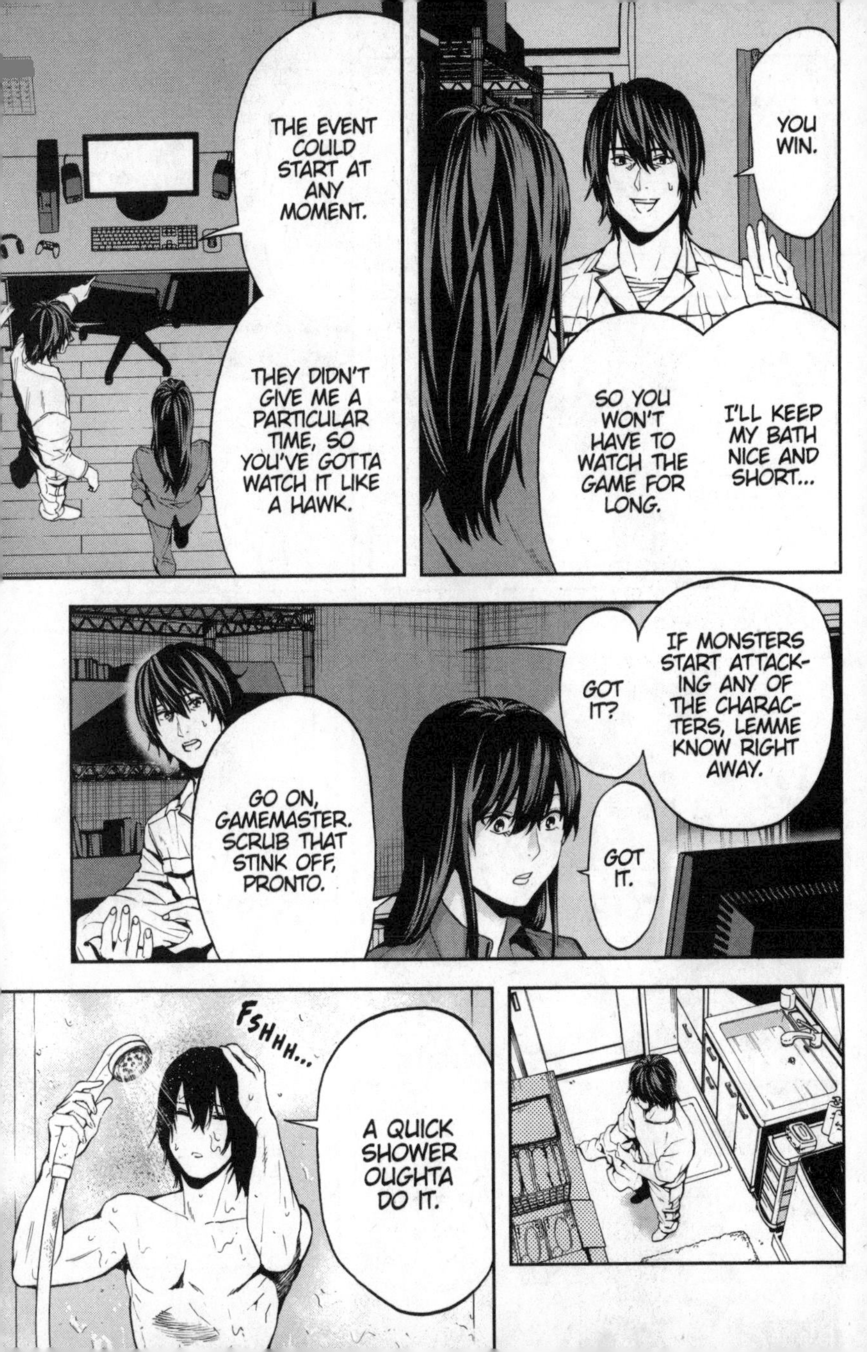
YOU WIN.
I'LL KEEP MY BATH NICE AND SHORT...
SO YOU WON'T HAVE TO WATCH THE GAME FOR LONG.
THE EVENT COULD START AT ANY MOMENT.
THEY DIDN'T GIVE ME A PARTICULAR TIME, SO YOU'VE GOTTA WATCH IT LIKE A HAWK.
IF MONSTERS START ATTACKING ANY OF THE CHARACTERS, LEMME KNOW RIGHT AWAY.
GOT IT?
GOT IT.
GO ON, GAMEMASTER. SCRUB THAT STINK OFF, PRONTO.
FSHHH...
A QUICK SHOWER OUGHTA DO IT.

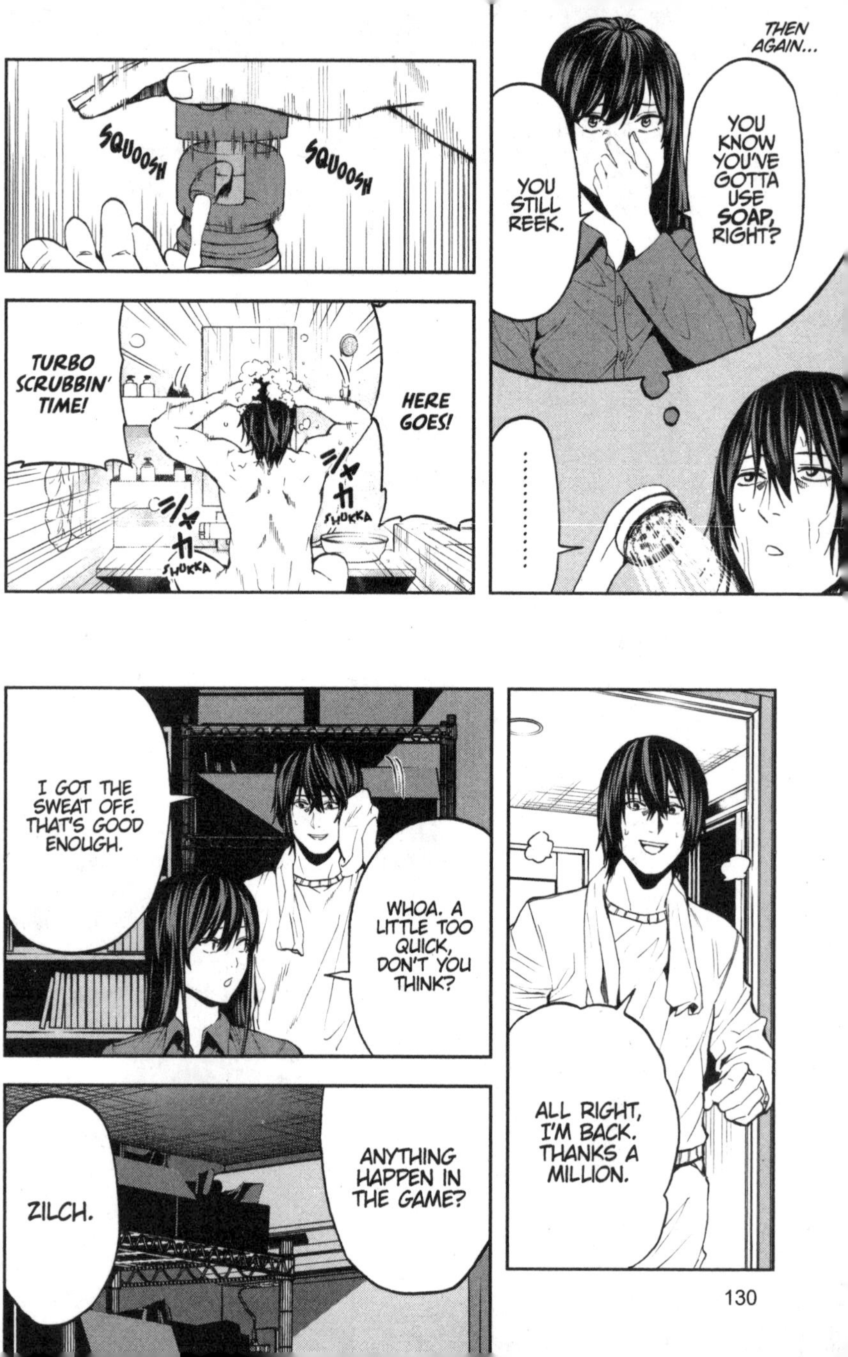
THEN AGAIN...
YOU KNOW YOU'VE GOTTA USE SOAP, RIGHT?
YOU STILL REEK.
......
SQUOOSH
SQUOOSH
HERE GOES!
TURBO SCRUBBIN' TIME!
SHUKKA
SHUKKA
ALL RIGHT, I'M BACK. THANKS A MILLION.
WHOA. A LITTLE TOO QUICK, DON'T YOU THINK?
I GOT THE SWEAT OFF. THAT'S GOOD ENOUGH.
ANYTHING HAPPEN IN THE GAME?
ZILCH.

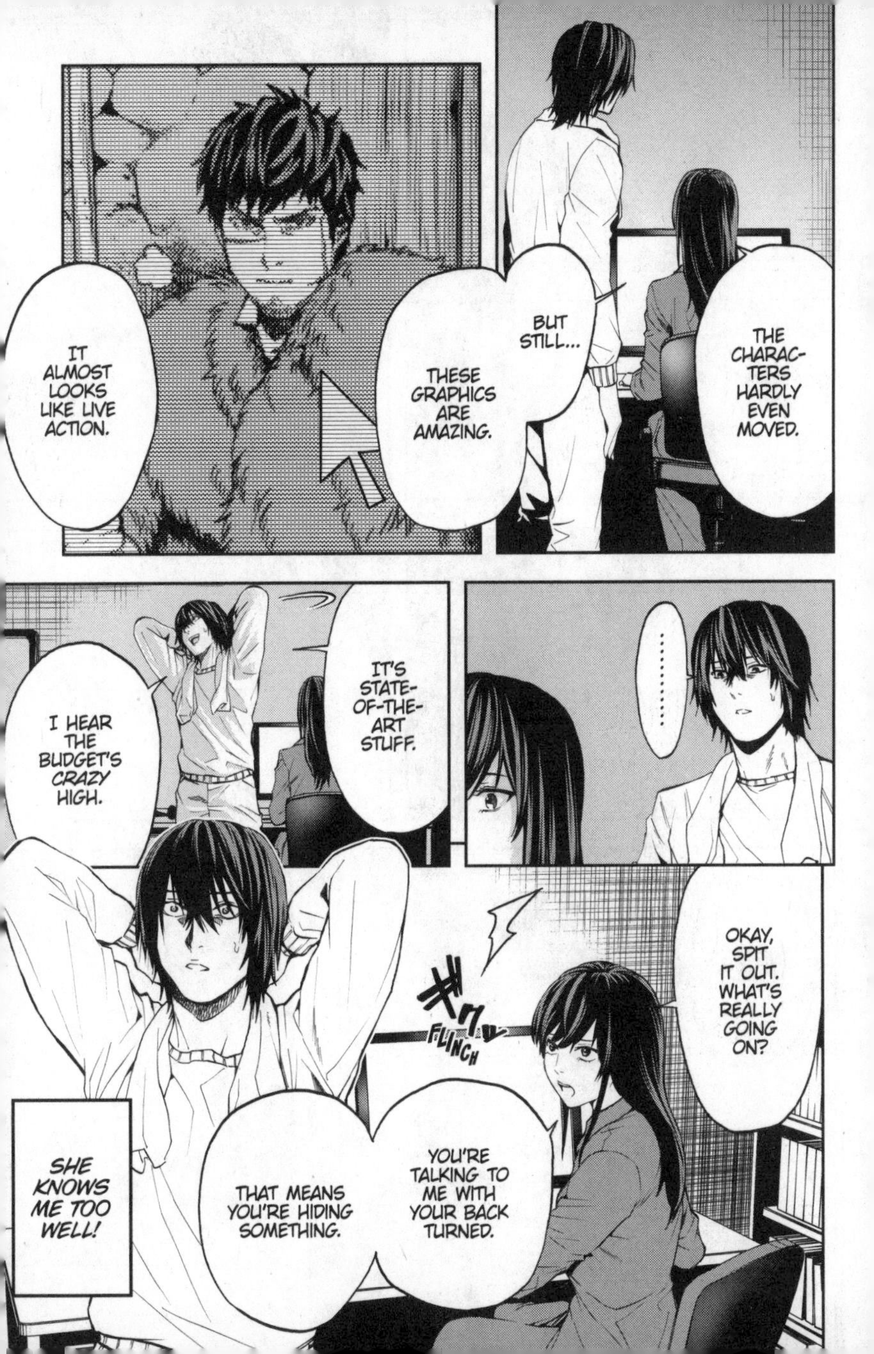
THE CHARACTERS HARDLY EVEN MOVED.
BUT STILL...
THESE GRAPHICS ARE AMAZING.
IT ALMOST LOOKS LIKE LIVE ACTION.
......
IT'S STATE-OF-THE-ART STUFF.
I HEAR THE BUDGET'S CRAZY HIGH.
OKAY, SPIT IT OUT. WHAT'S REALLY GOING ON?
FLINCH
YOU'RE TALKING TO ME WITH YOUR BACK TURNED.
THAT MEANS YOU'RE HIDING SOMETHING.
SHE KNOWS ME TOO WELL!

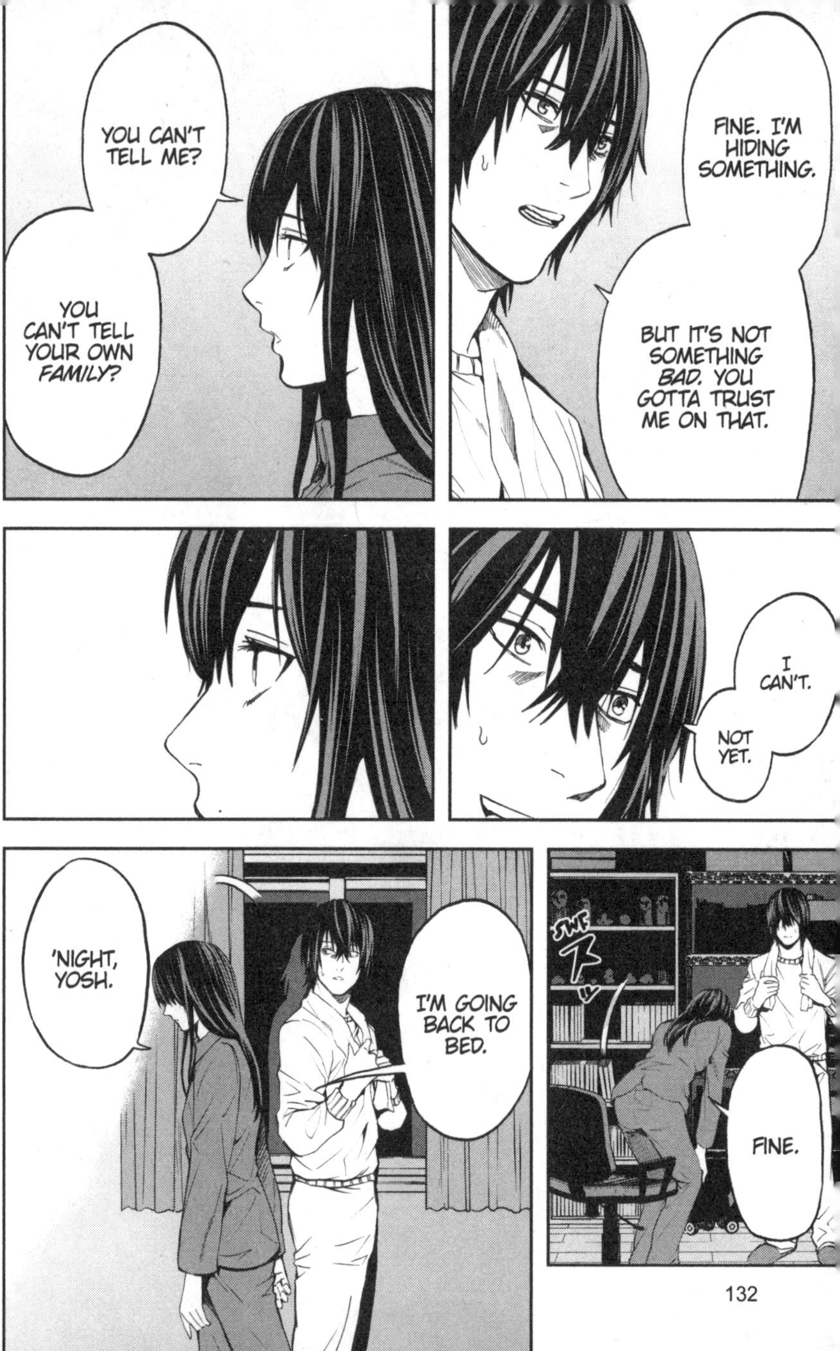
FINE. I'M HIDING SOMETHING.
BUT IT'S NOT SOMETHING *BAD.* YOU GOTTA TRUST ME ON THAT.
YOU CAN'T TELL ME?
YOU CAN'T TELL YOUR OWN *FAMILY?*
I CAN'T.
NOT YET.
SWF
FINE.
I'M GOING BACK TO BED.
'NIGHT, YOSH.

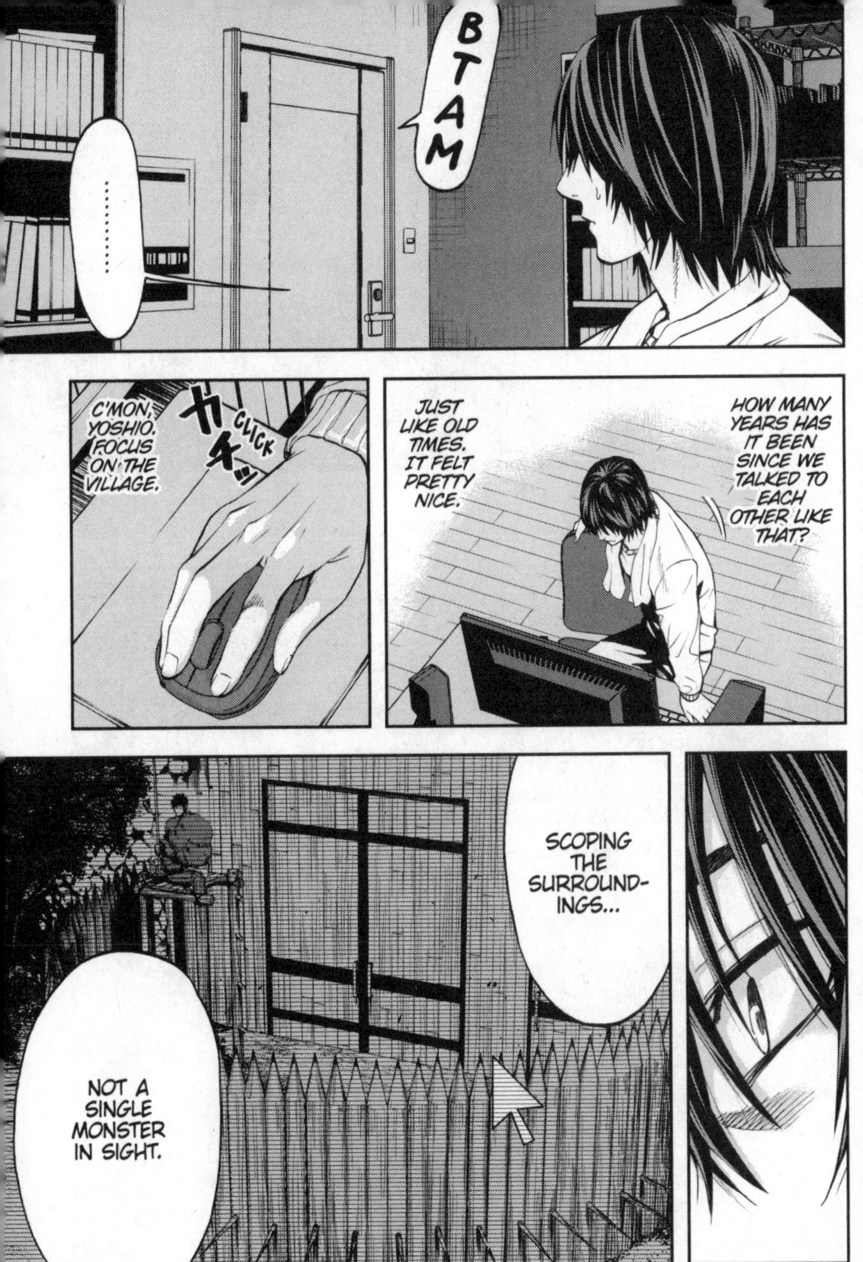
BTAM
......
HOW MANY YEARS HAS IT BEEN SINCE WE TALKED TO EACH OTHER LIKE THAT?
JUST LIKE OLD TIMES. IT FELT PRETTY NICE.
CLICK
C'MON, YOSHIO. FOCUS ON THE VILLAGE.
SCOPING THE SURROUND-INGS...
NOT A SINGLE MONSTER IN SIGHT.

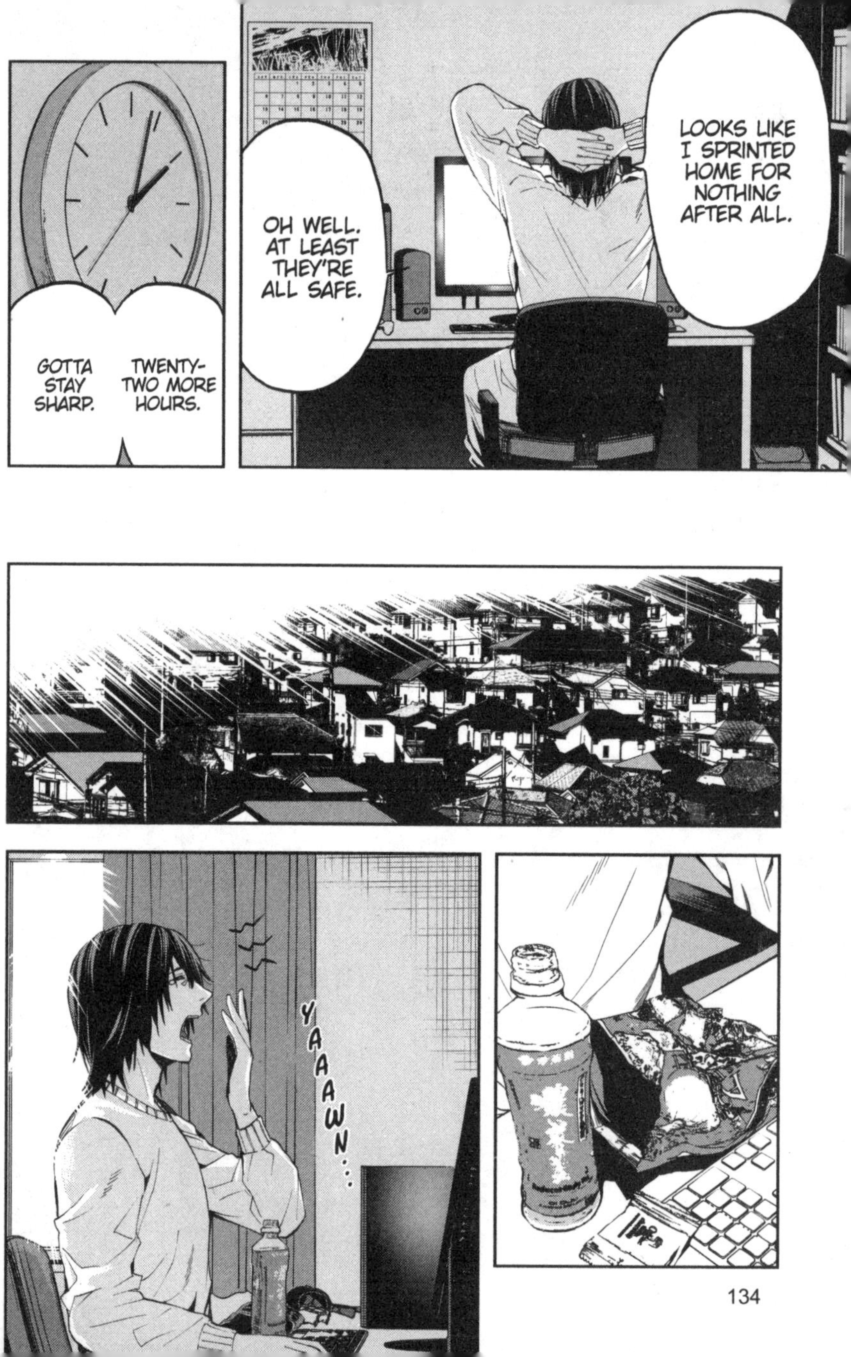
LOOKS LIKE I SPRINTED HOME FOR NOTHING AFTER ALL.
OH WELL. AT LEAST THEY'RE ALL SAFE.
TWENTY-TWO MORE HOURS.
GOTTA STAY SHARP.
YAAAWN...

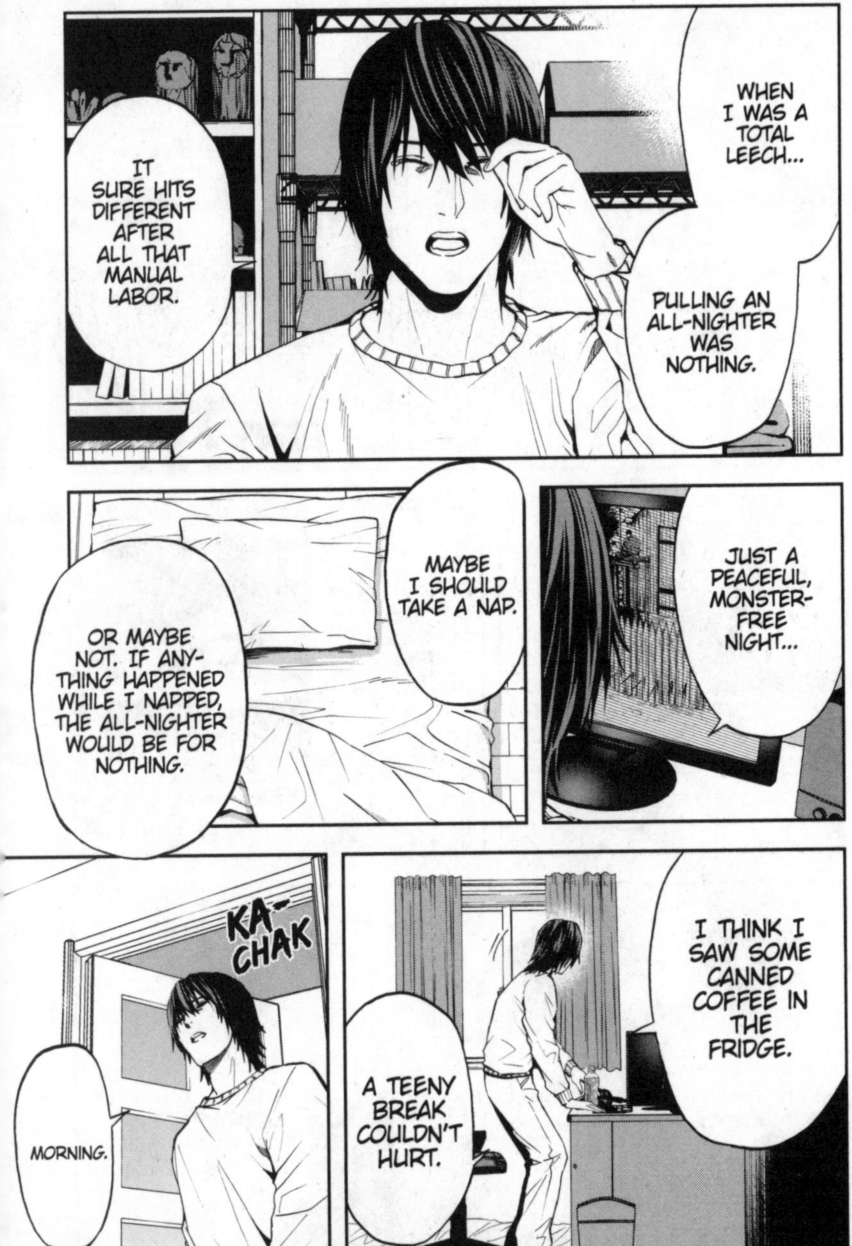
WHEN I WAS A TOTAL LEECH...
PULLING AN ALL-NIGHTER WAS NOTHING.
IT SURE HITS DIFFERENT AFTER ALL THAT MANUAL LABOR.
JUST A PEACEFUL, MONSTER-FREE NIGHT...
MAYBE I SHOULD TAKE A NAP.
OR MAYBE NOT. IF ANYTHING HAPPENED WHILE I NAPPED, THE ALL-NIGHTER WOULD BE FOR NOTHING.
I THINK I SAW SOME CANNED COFFEE IN THE FRIDGE.
A TEENY BREAK COULDN'T HURT.
KA-CHAK
MORNING.

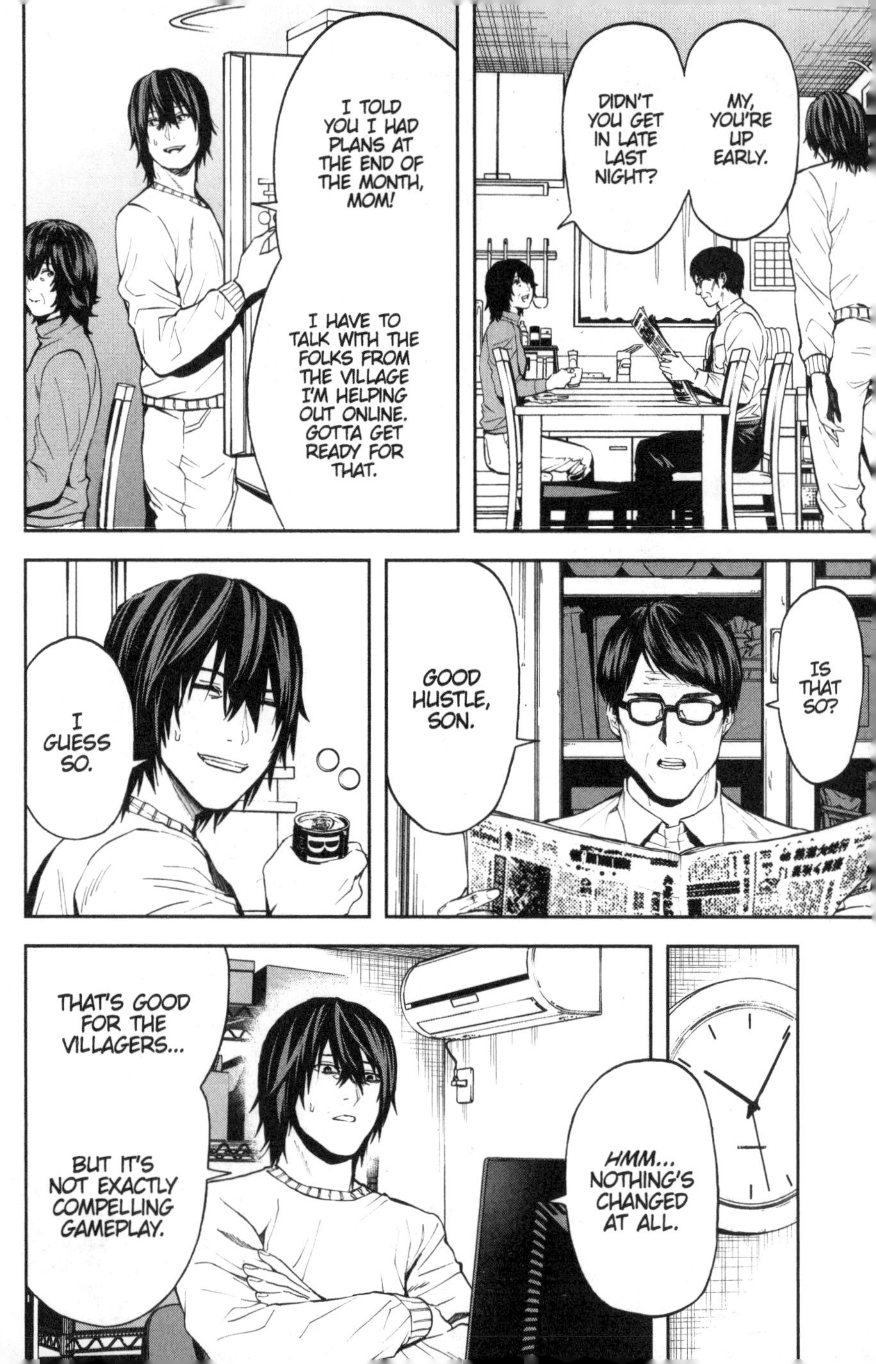
MY, YOU'RE UP EARLY.
DIDN'T YOU GET IN LATE LAST NIGHT?
I TOLD YOU I HAD PLANS AT THE END OF THE MONTH, MOM!
I HAVE TO TALK WITH THE FOLKS FROM THE VILLAGE I'M HELPING OUT ONLINE. GOTTA GET READY FOR THAT.
IS THAT SO?
GOOD HUSTLE, SON.
I GUESS SO.
HMM... NOTHING'S CHANGED AT ALL.
THAT'S GOOD FOR THE VILLAGERS...
BUT IT'S NOT EXACTLY COMPELLING GAMEPLAY.

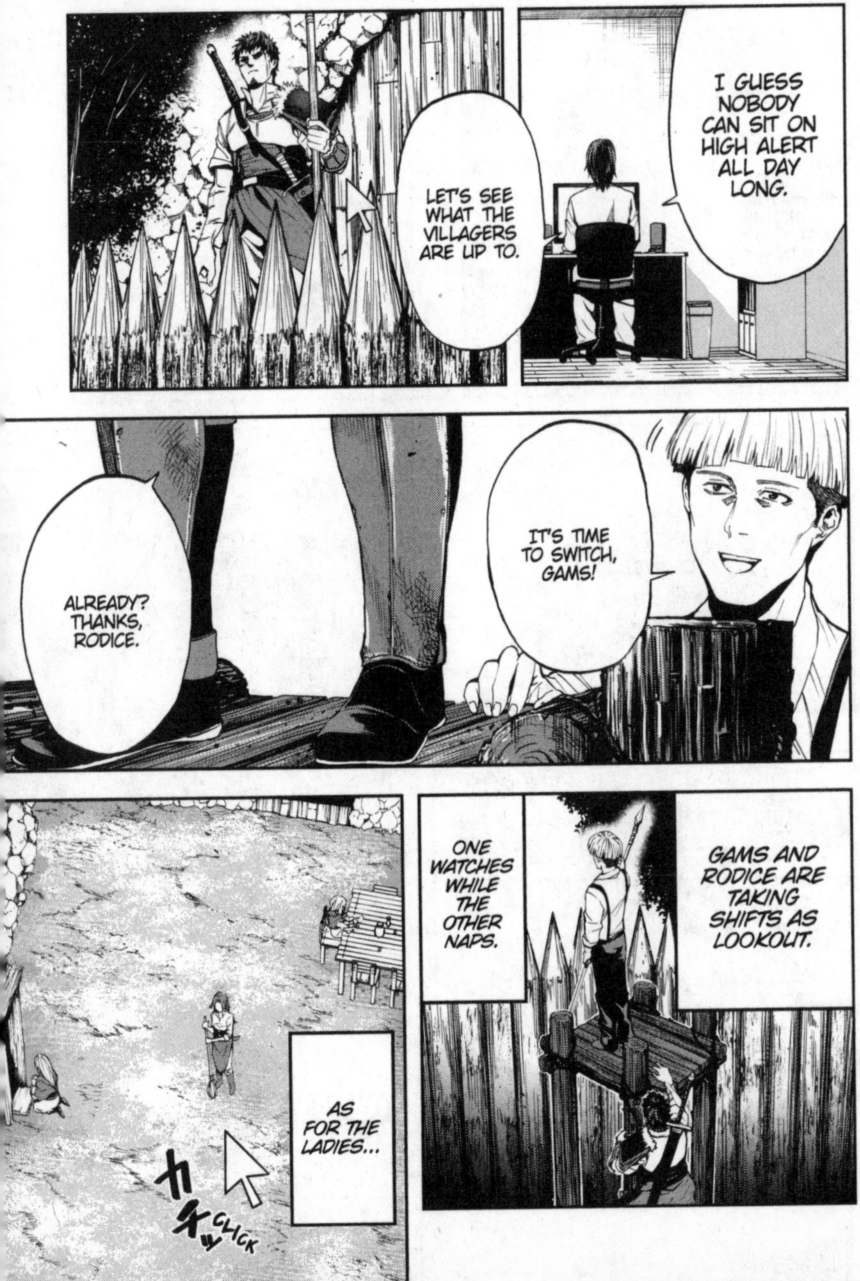
I GUESS NOBODY CAN SIT ON HIGH ALERT ALL DAY LONG.
LET'S SEE WHAT THE VILLAGERS ARE UP TO.
IT'S TIME TO SWITCH, GAMS!
ALREADY? THANKS, RODICE.
GAMS AND RODICE ARE TAKING SHIFTS AS LOOKOUT.
ONE WATCHES WHILE THE OTHER NAPS.
AS FOR THE LADIES...
カチッ
CLICK

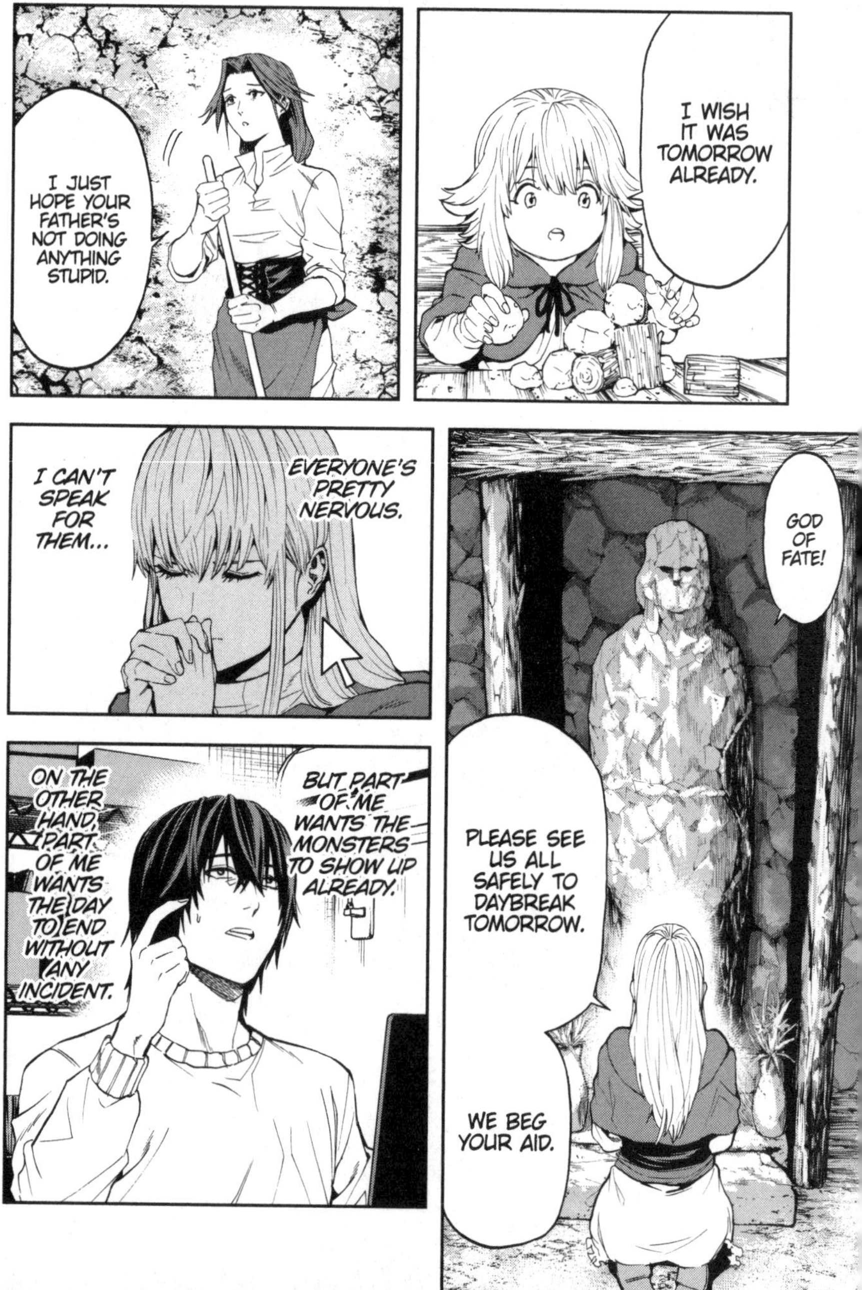
I WISH IT WAS TOMORROW ALREADY.
I JUST HOPE YOUR FATHER'S NOT DOING ANYTHING STUPID.
GOD OF FATE!
PLEASE SEE US ALL SAFELY TO DAYBREAK TOMORROW.
WE BEG YOUR AID.
EVERYONE'S PRETTY NERVOUS.
I CAN'T SPEAK FOR THEM...
BUT PART OF ME WANTS THE MONSTERS TO SHOW UP ALREADY.
ON THE OTHER HAND, PART OF ME WANTS THE DAY TO END WITHOUT ANY INCIDENT.

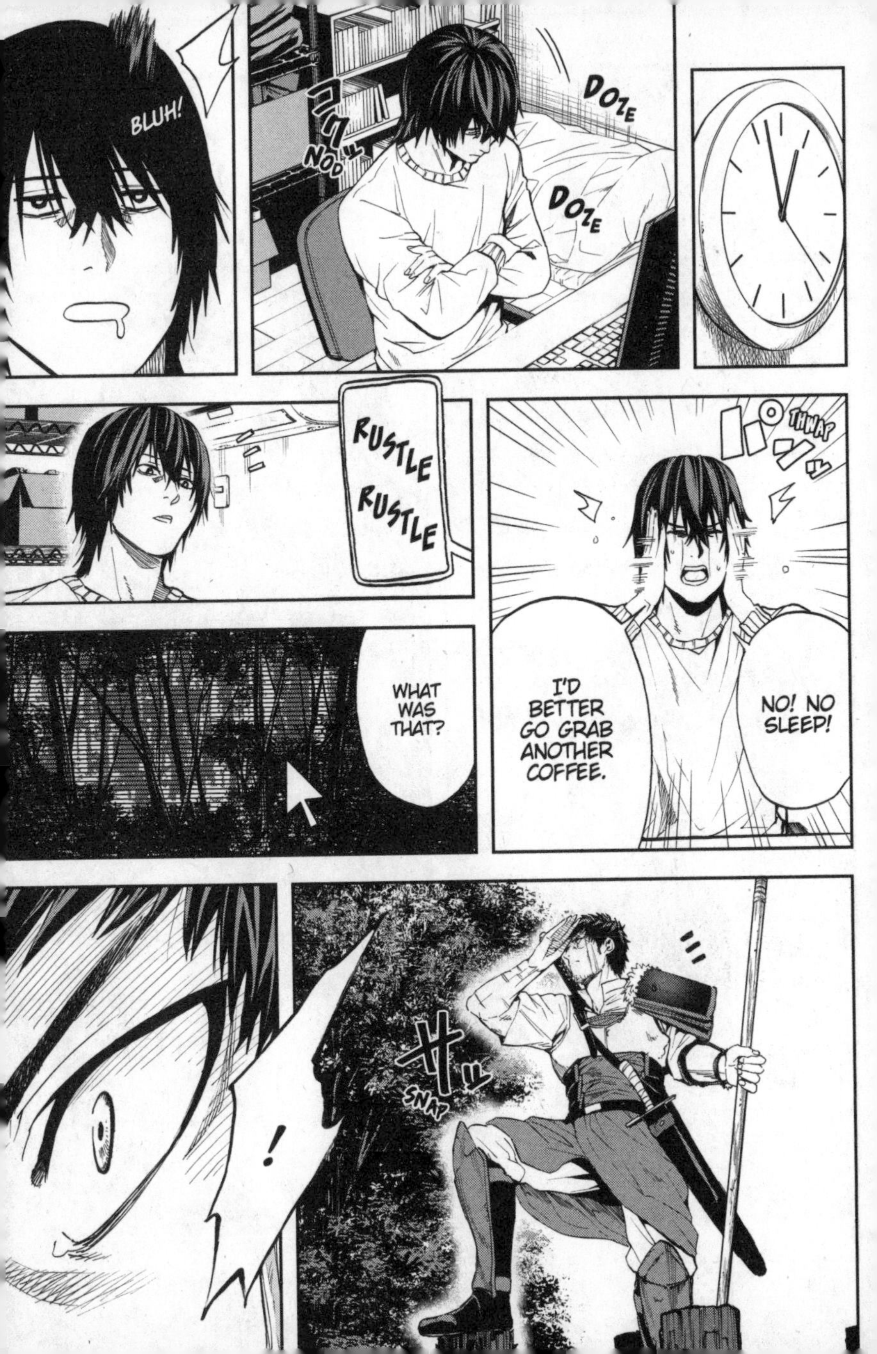
DOZE
DOZE
NOD
BLUH!
THWAP
RUSTLE
RUSTLE
NO! NO SLEEP!
I'D BETTER GO GRAB ANOTHER COFFEE.
WHAT WAS THAT?
SNAP
!

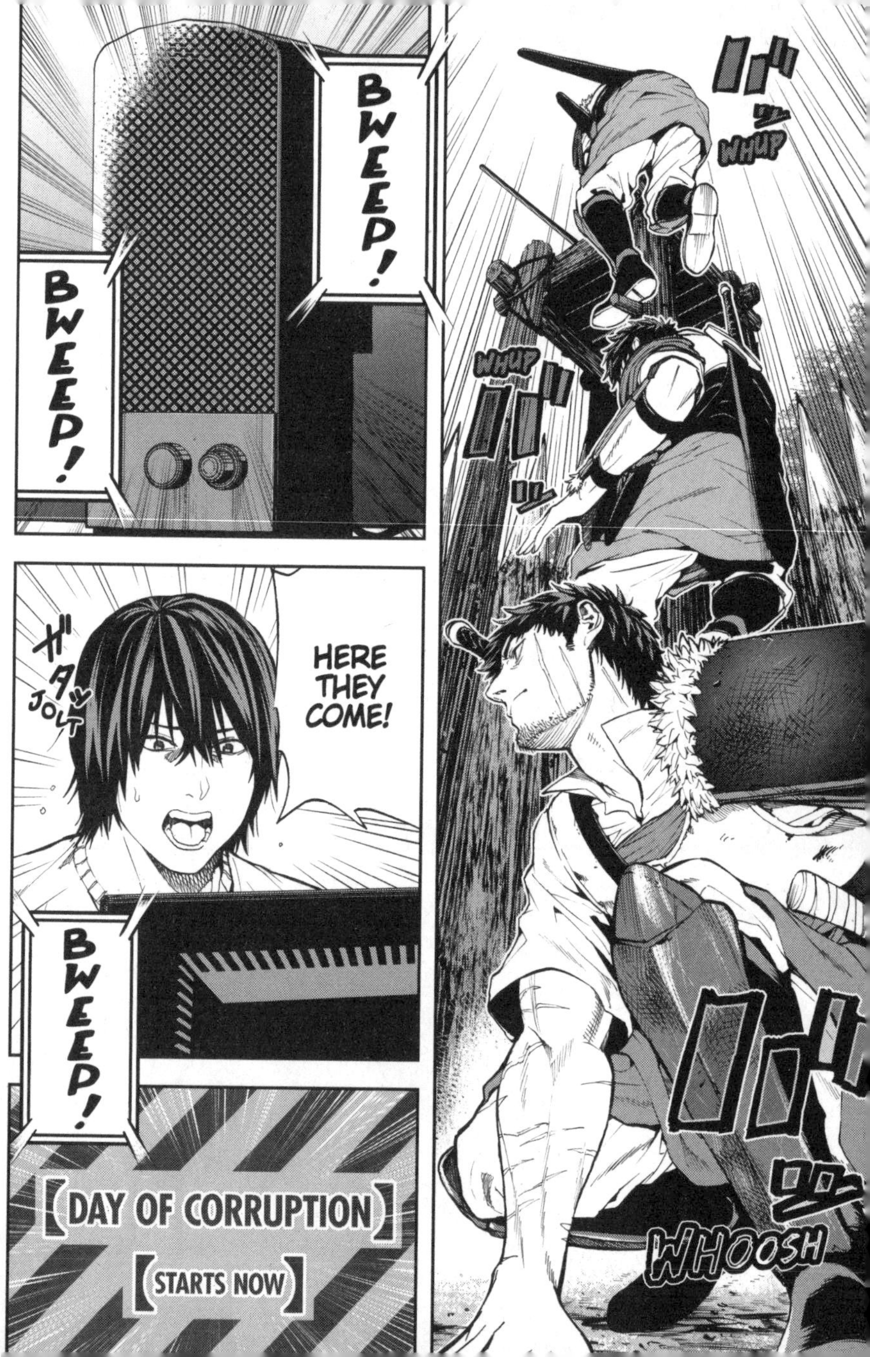
WHUP
WHUP
WHOOSH
BWEEP!
BWEEP!
HERE THEY COME!
JOLT
BWEEP!
【DAY OF CORRUPTION】
【STARTS NOW】

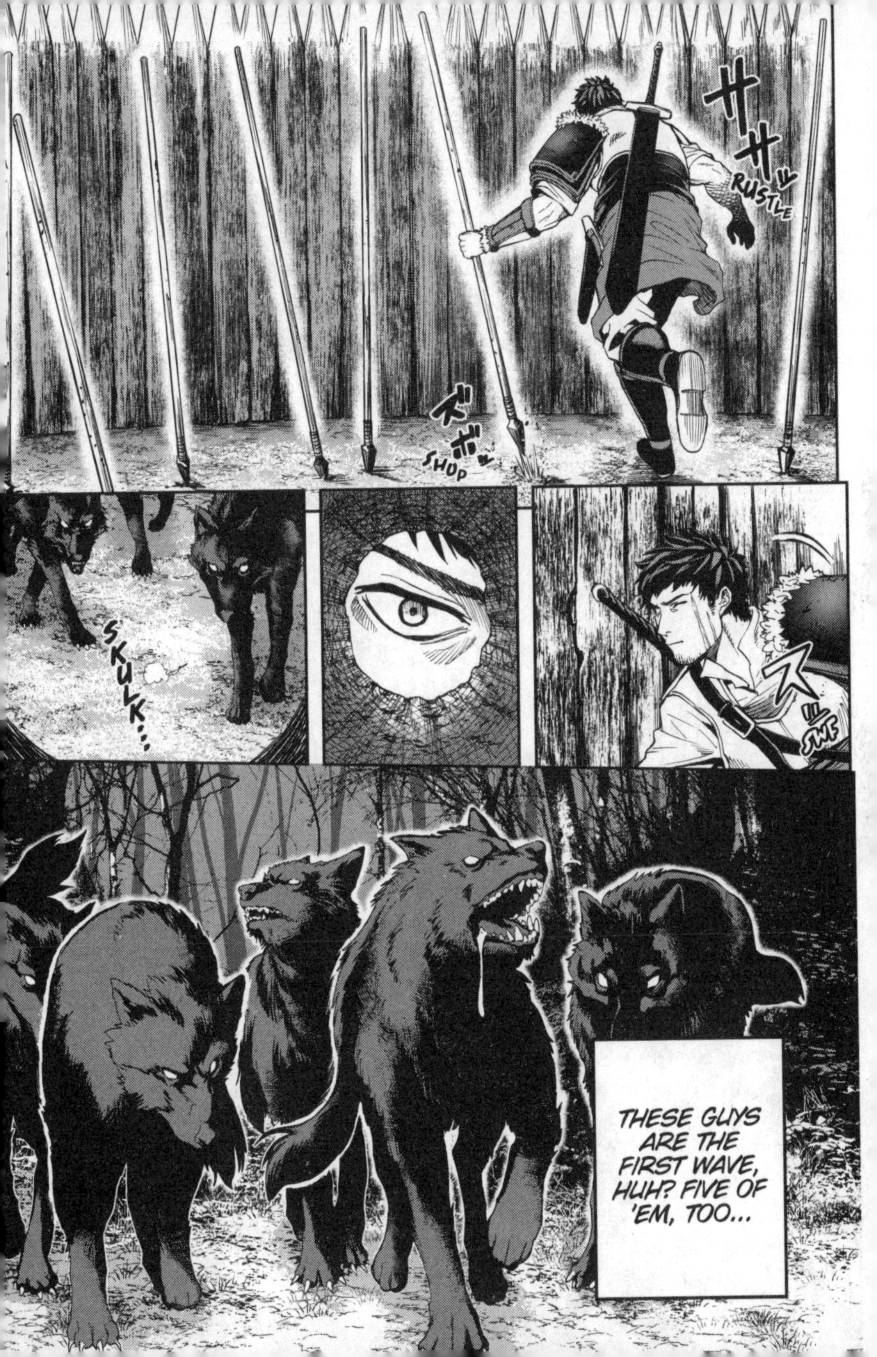
RUSTLE
SHUP
SWF
SKULK...
THESE GUYS ARE THE FIRST WAVE, HUH? FIVE OF 'EM, TOO...

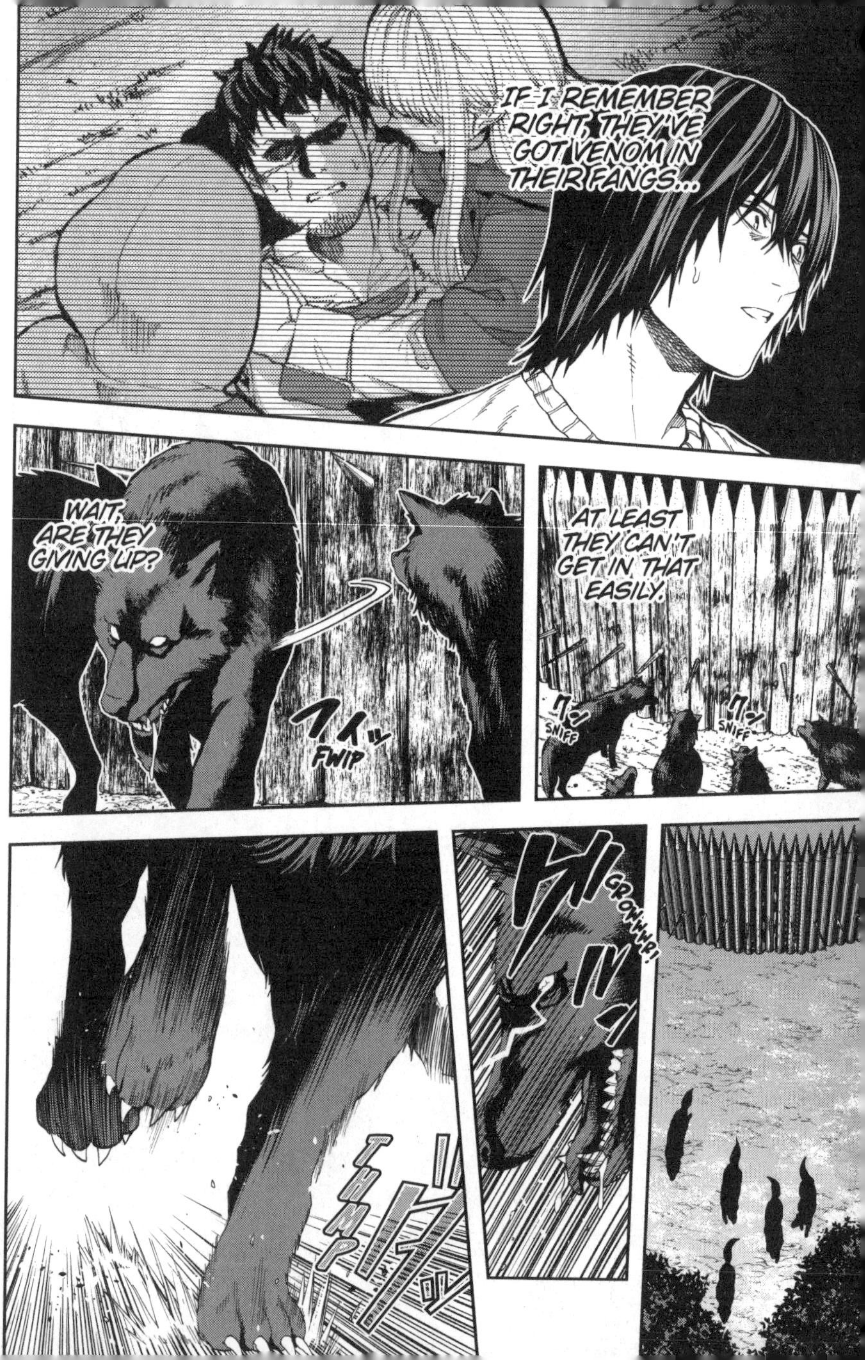
IF I REMEMBER RIGHT, THEY'VE GOT VENOM IN THEIR FANGS...
AT LEAST THEY CAN'T GET IN THAT EASILY.
SNIFF
SNIFF
WAIT, ARE THEY GIVING UP?
FWIP
GROWWWR!
THMP

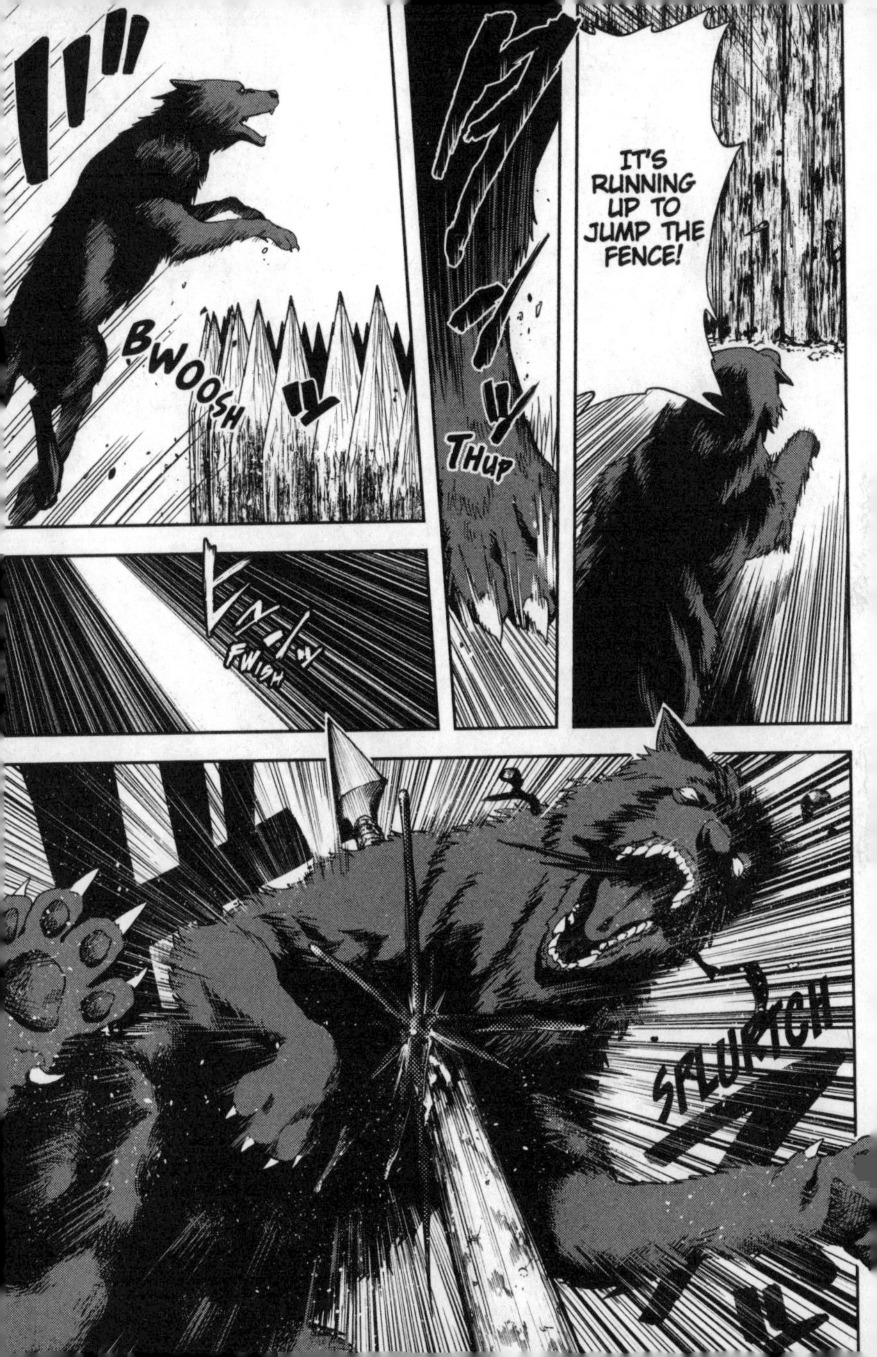
IT'S RUNNING UP TO JUMP THE FENCE!
THUP
BWOOSH
FWISH
SPLURTCH

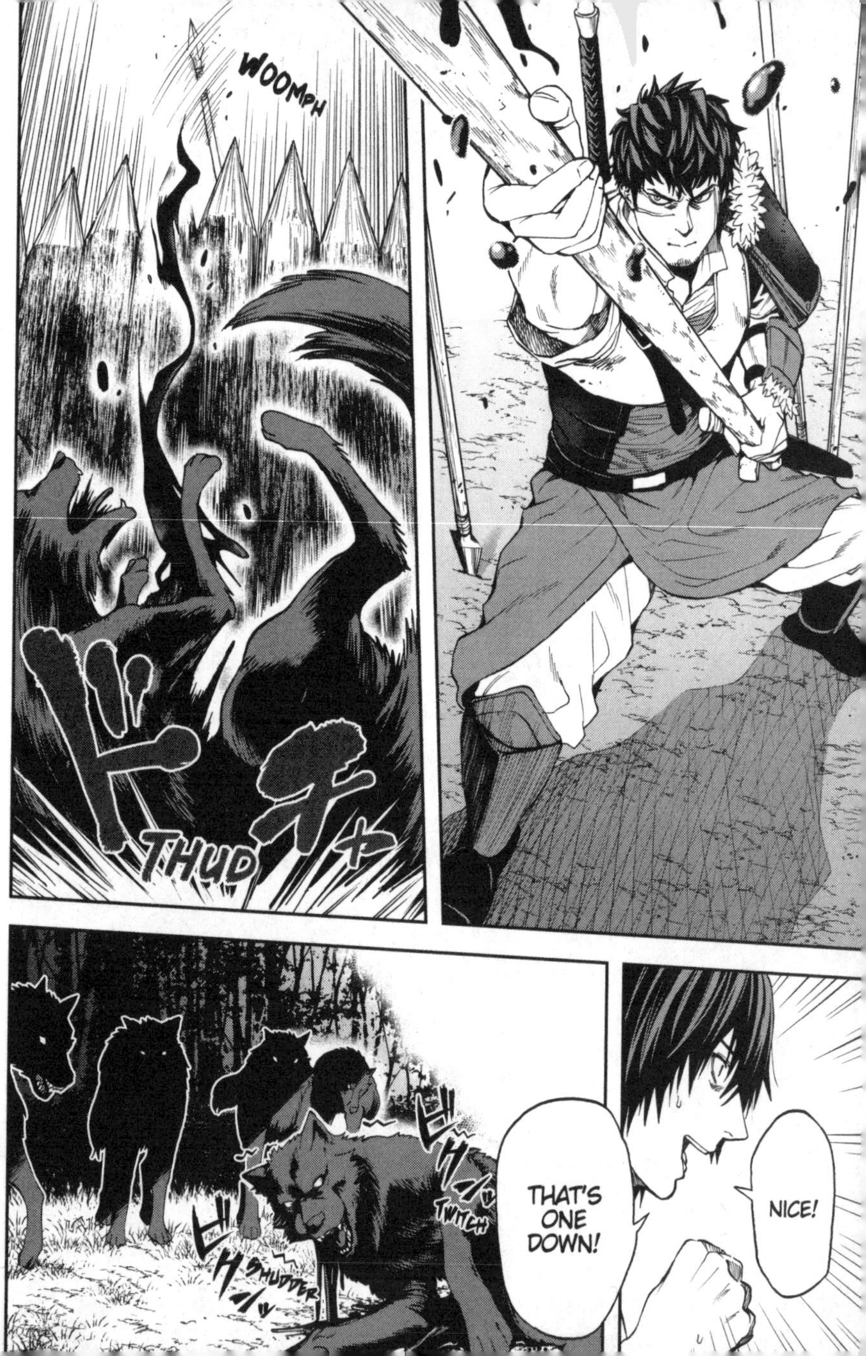
WOOMPH
ドチャ
THUD
NICE!
THAT'S ONE DOWN!
TWITCH
SHUDDER

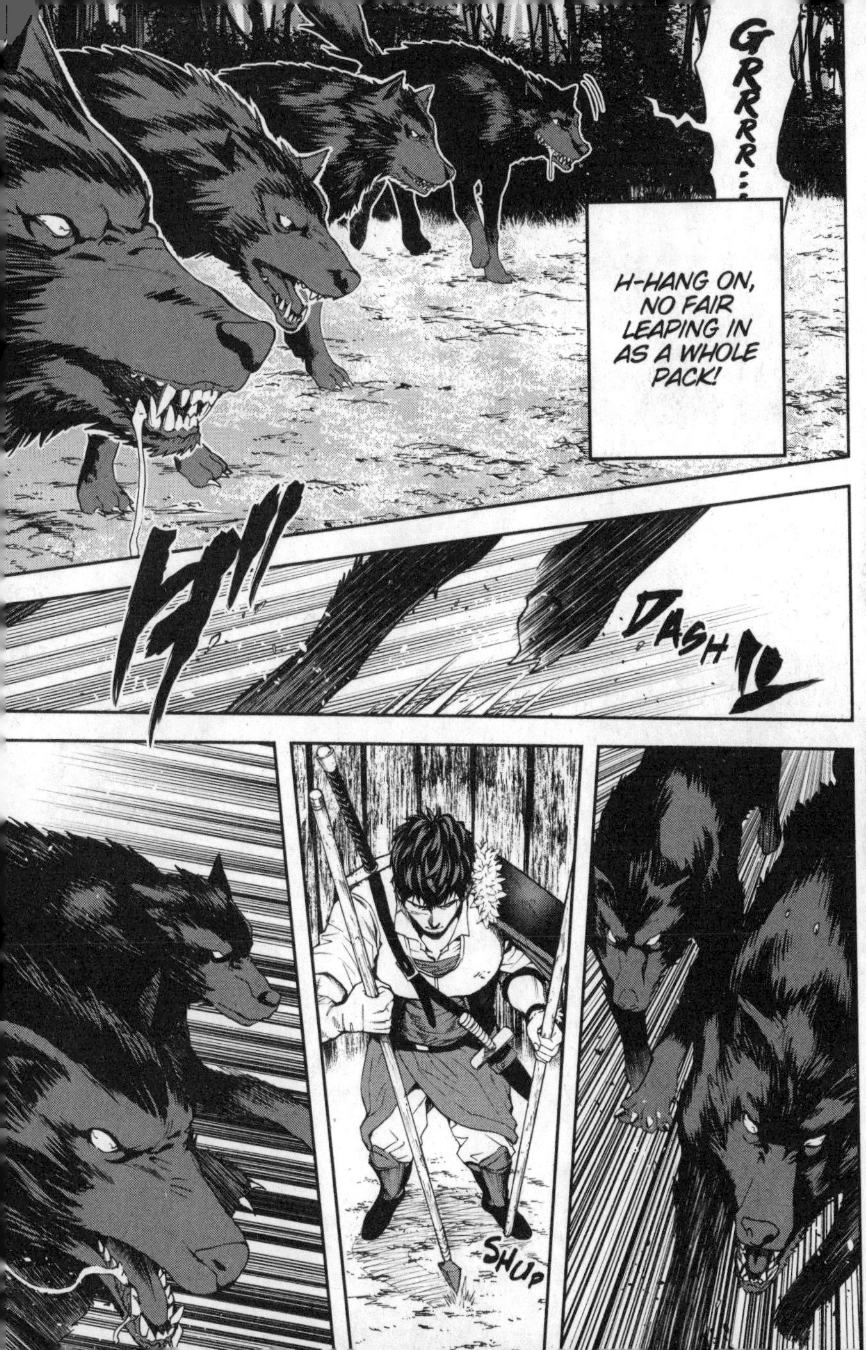
GRRRR...
H-HANG ON, NO FAIR LEAPING IN AS A WHOLE PACK!
DASH
SHUP

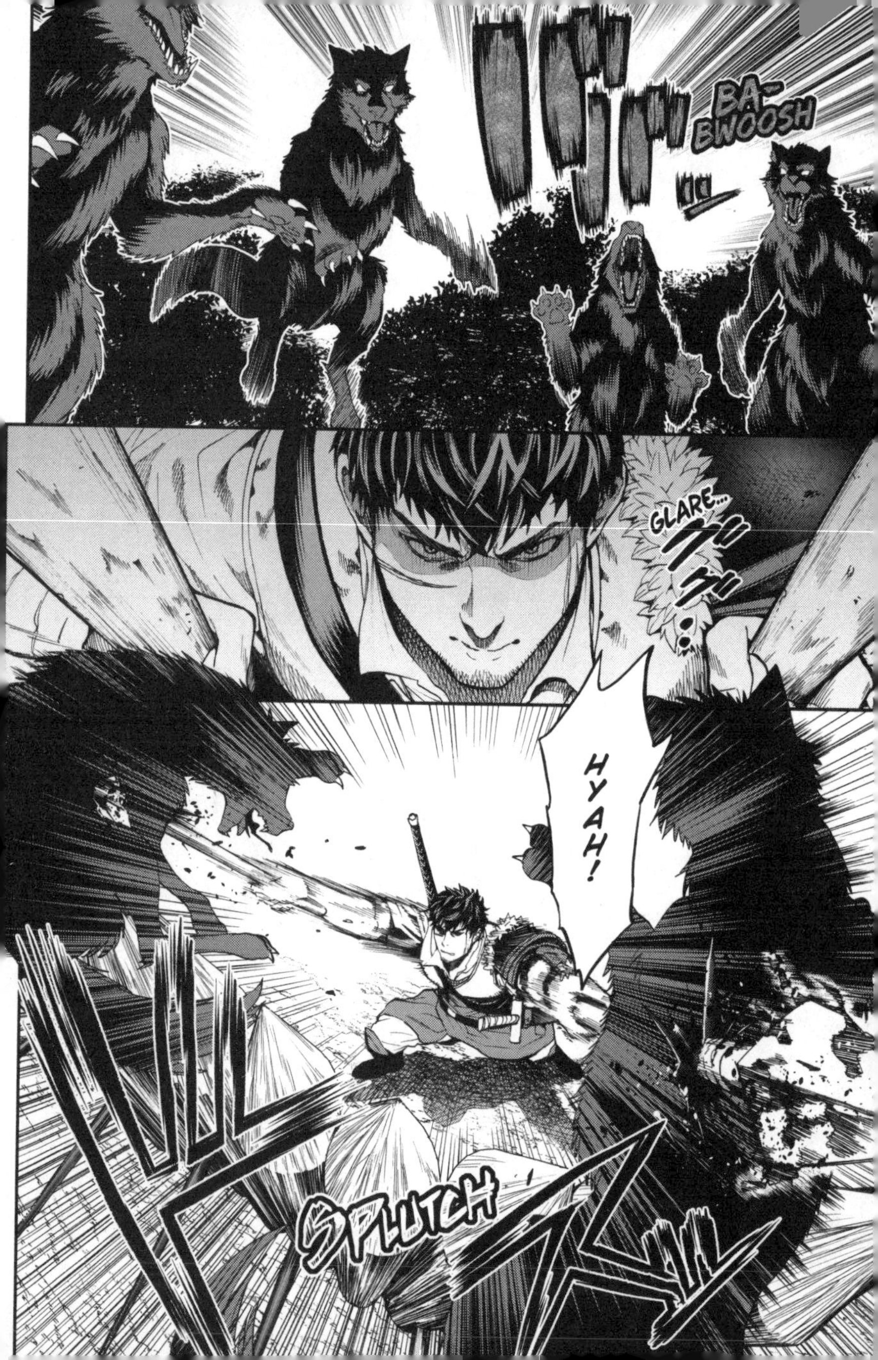
BA-BWOOSH
GLARE...
HYAH!
SPLUTCH

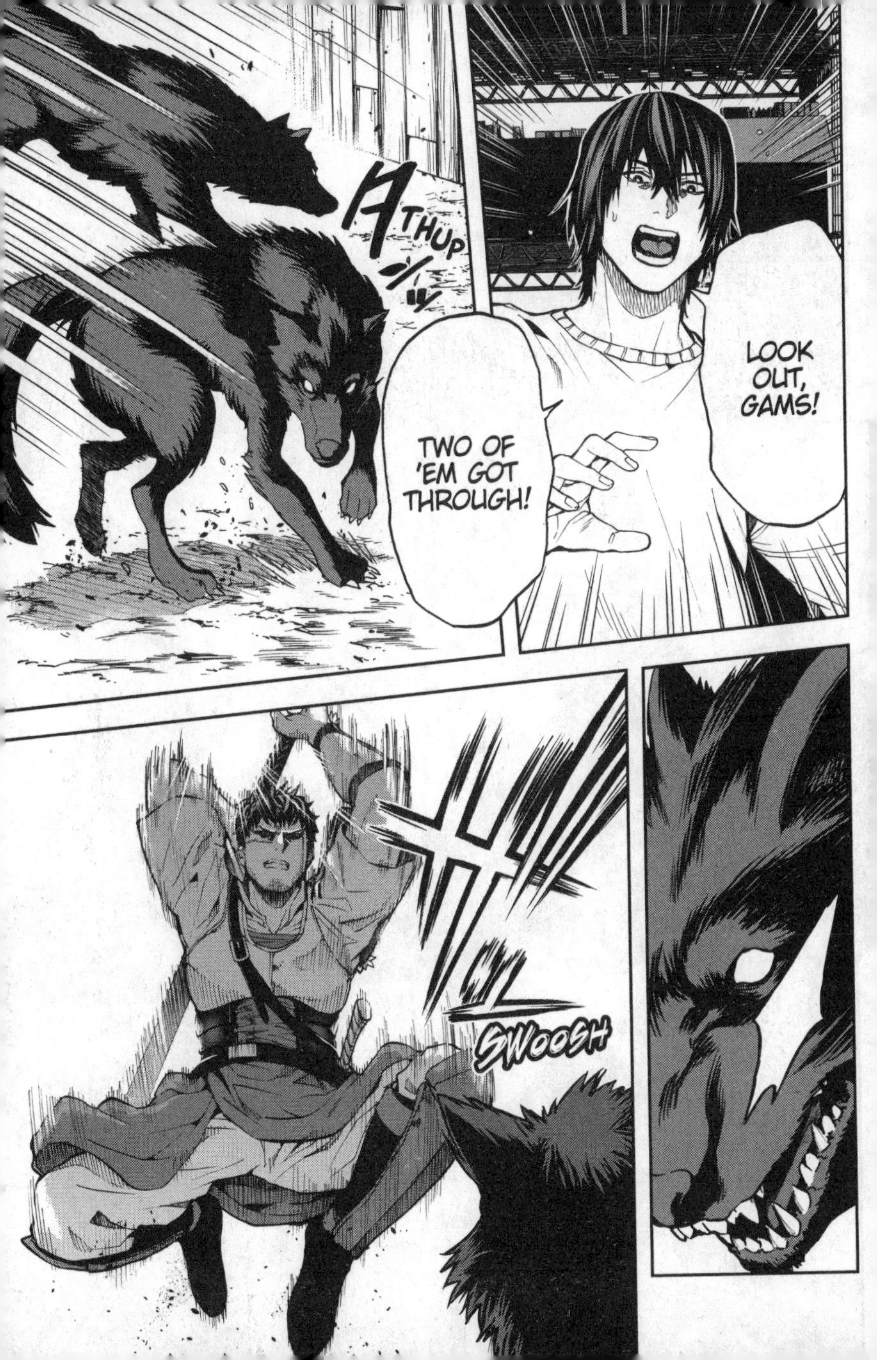
LOOK OUT, GAMS!
TWO OF 'EM GOT THROUGH!
THUP
SWOOSH

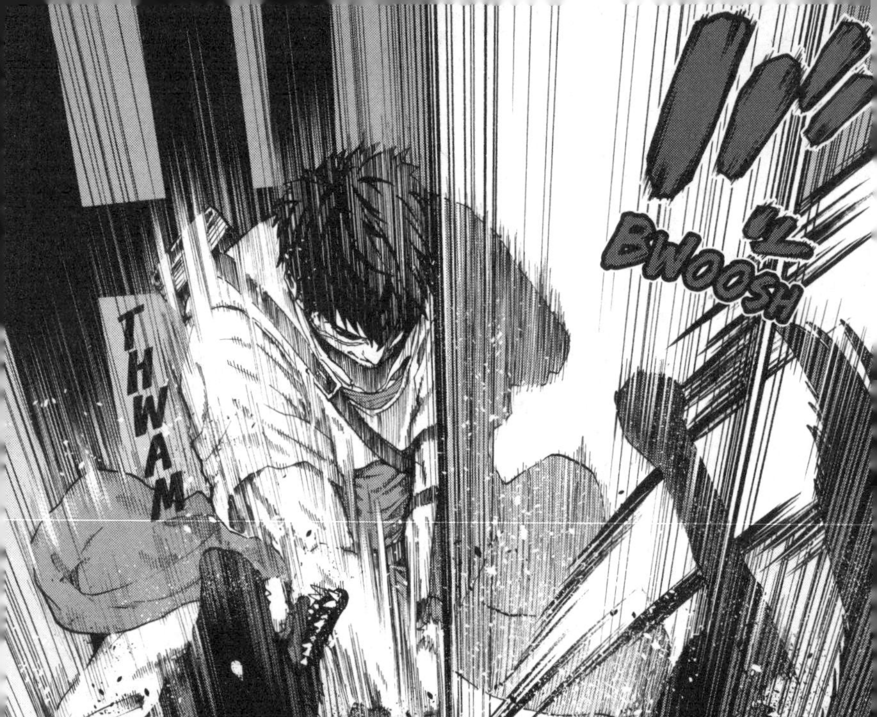
BWOOSH
THWAM
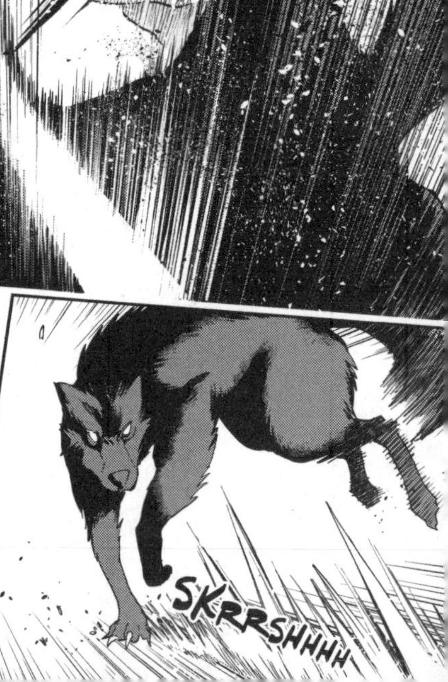
SKRRSHHHH
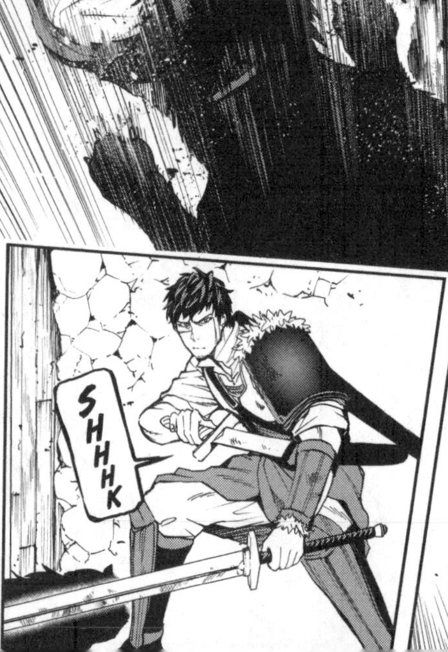
SHHHK

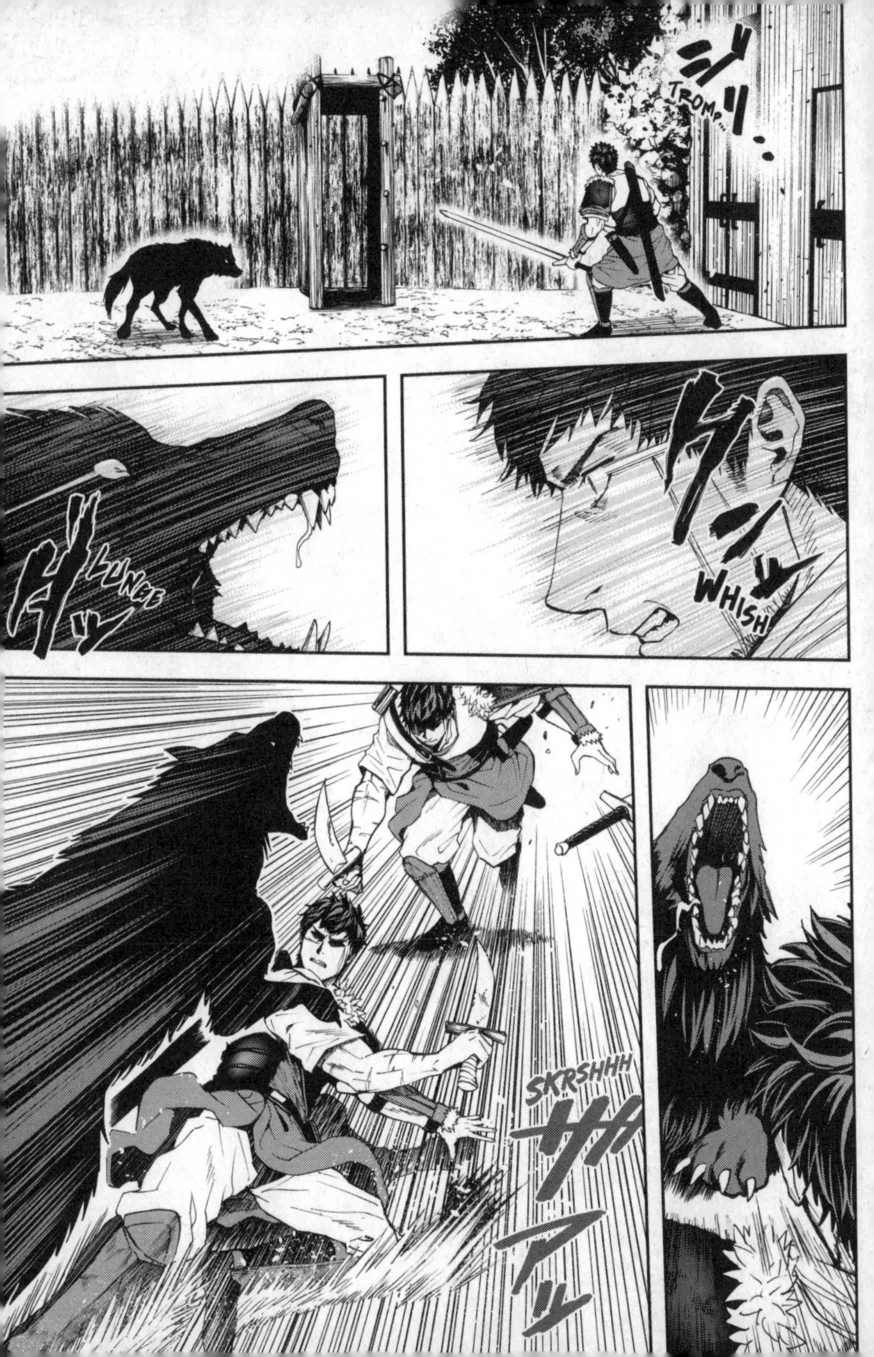
TROMP...
WHISH
LUNGE
SKRSHHH

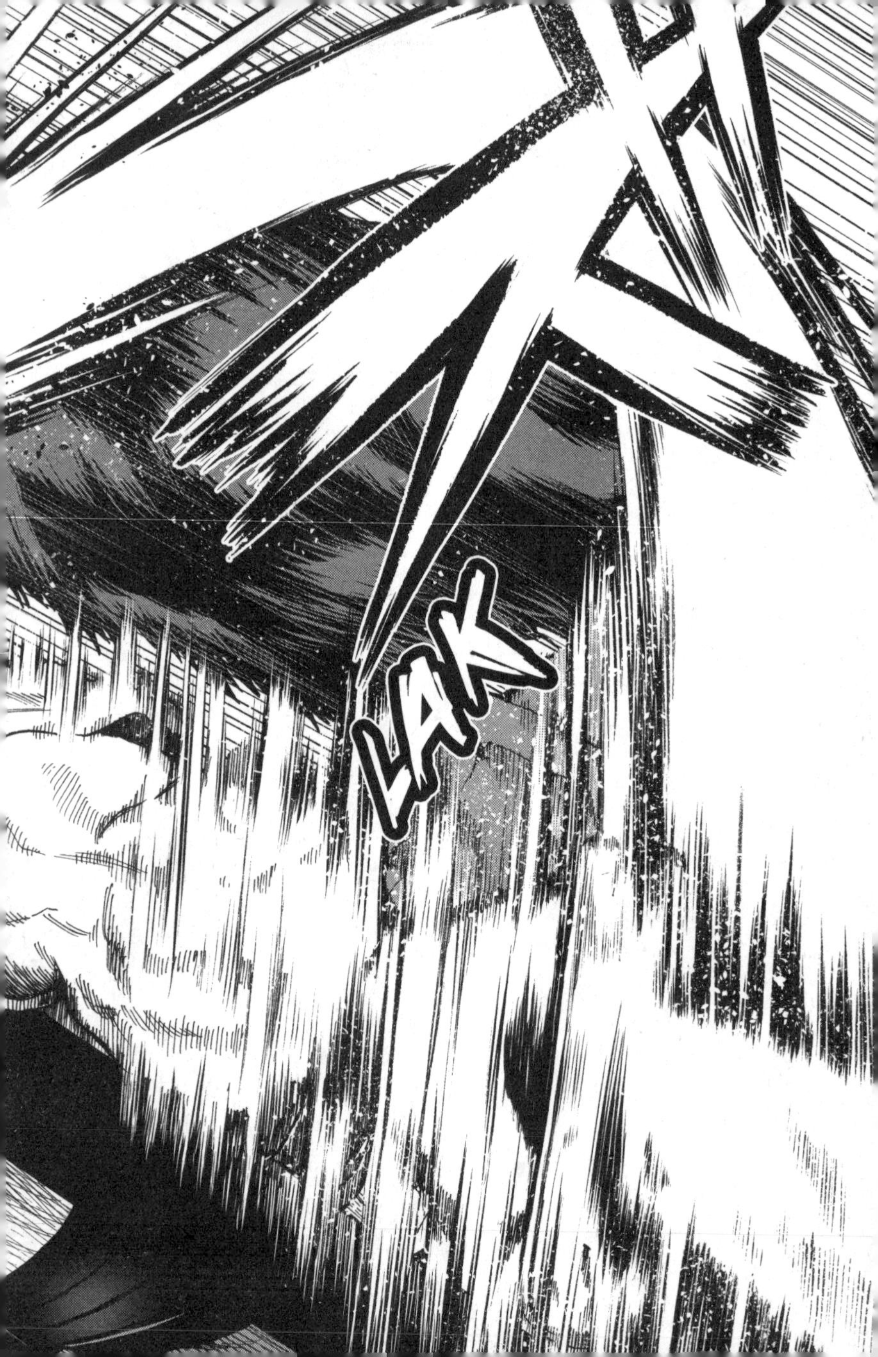
LAK

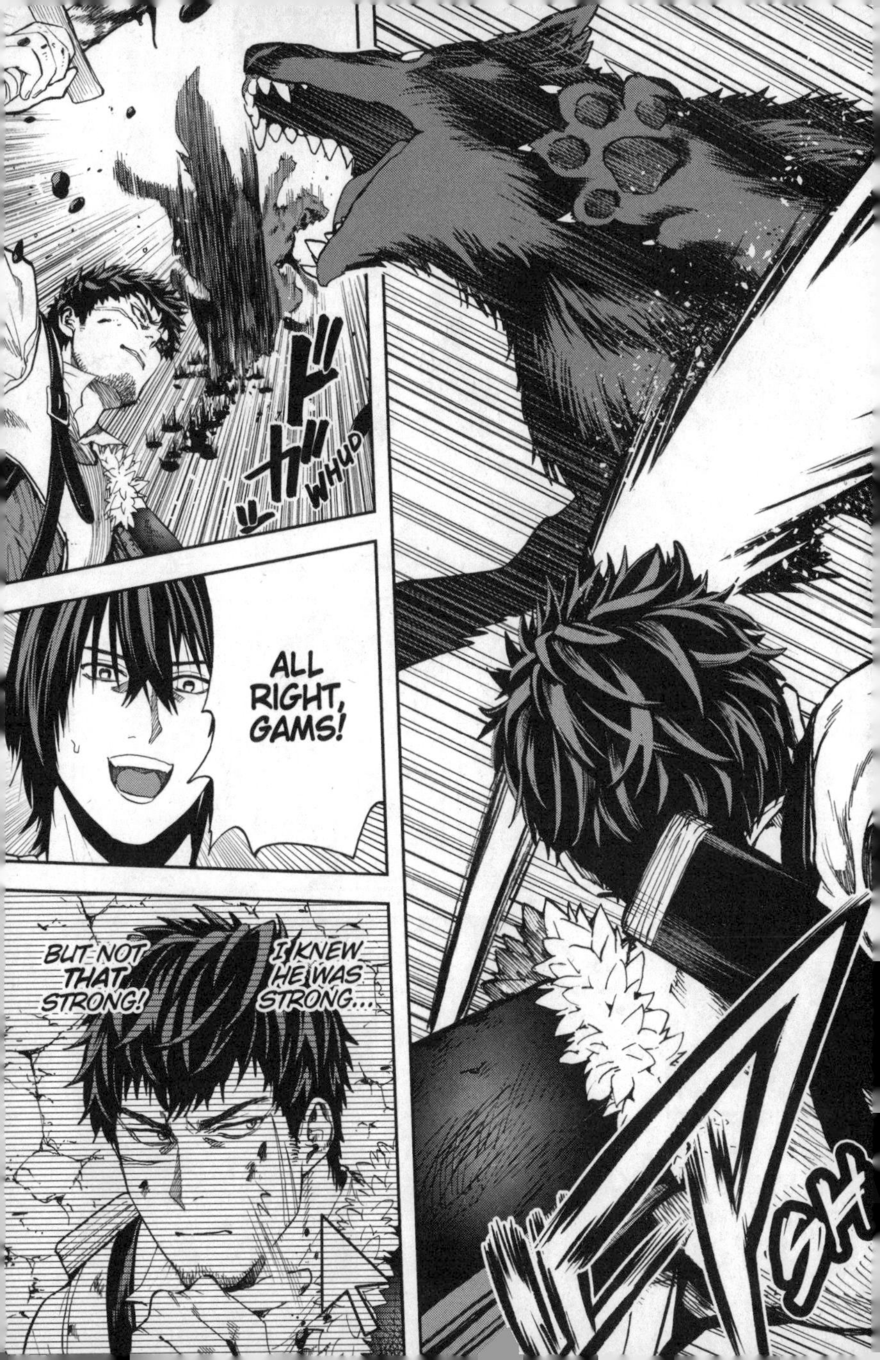
SH
ドガッ
WHUD
ALL RIGHT, GAMS!
I KNEW HE WAS STRONG...
BUT NOT THAT STRONG!

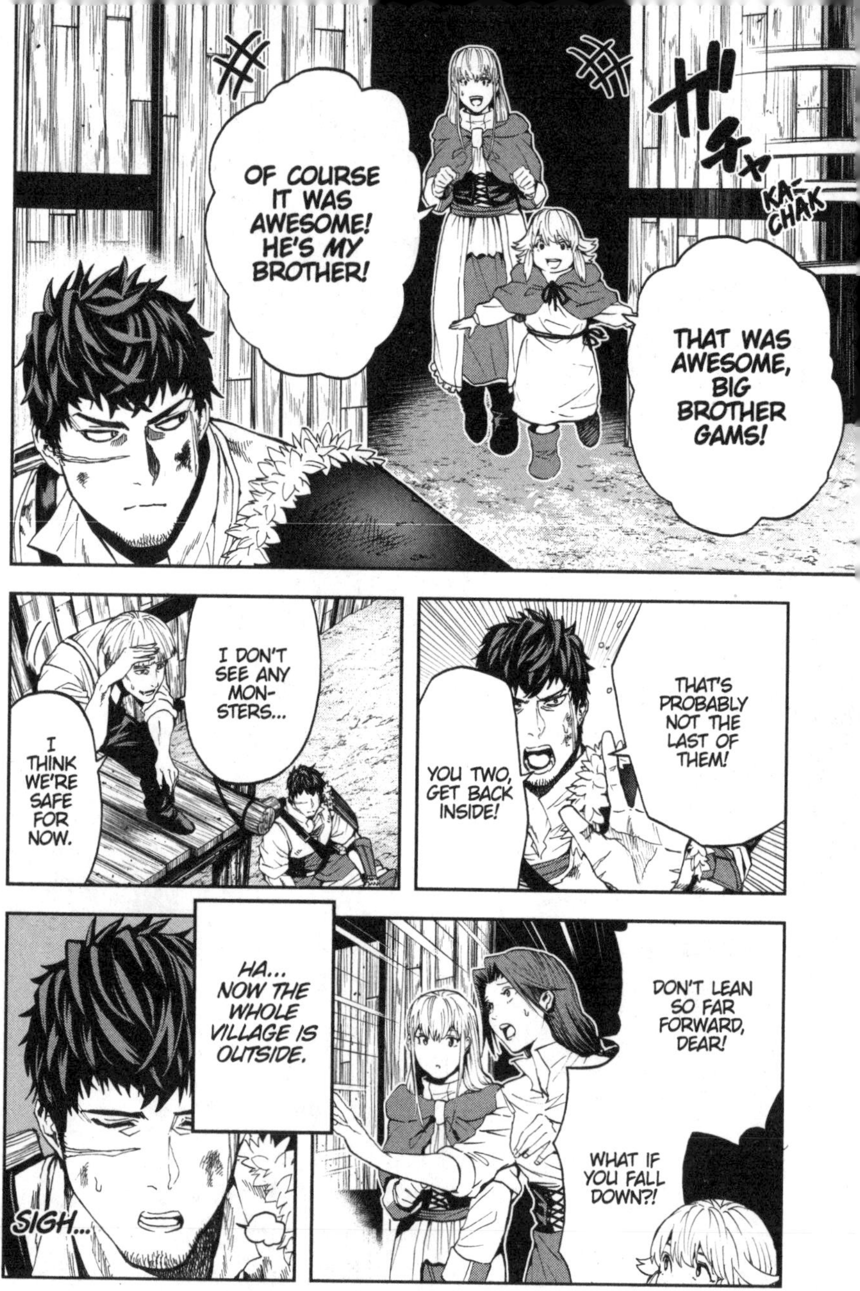
KA-CHAK
THAT WAS AWESOME, BIG BROTHER GAMS!
OF COURSE IT WAS AWESOME! HE'S MY BROTHER!
THAT'S PROBABLY NOT THE LAST OF THEM!
YOU TWO, GET BACK INSIDE!
I DON'T SEE ANY MON-STERS...
I THINK WE'RE SAFE FOR NOW.
DON'T LEAN SO FAR FORWARD, DEAR!
WHAT IF YOU FALL DOWN?!
HA... NOW THE WHOLE VILLAGE IS OUTSIDE.
SIGH...

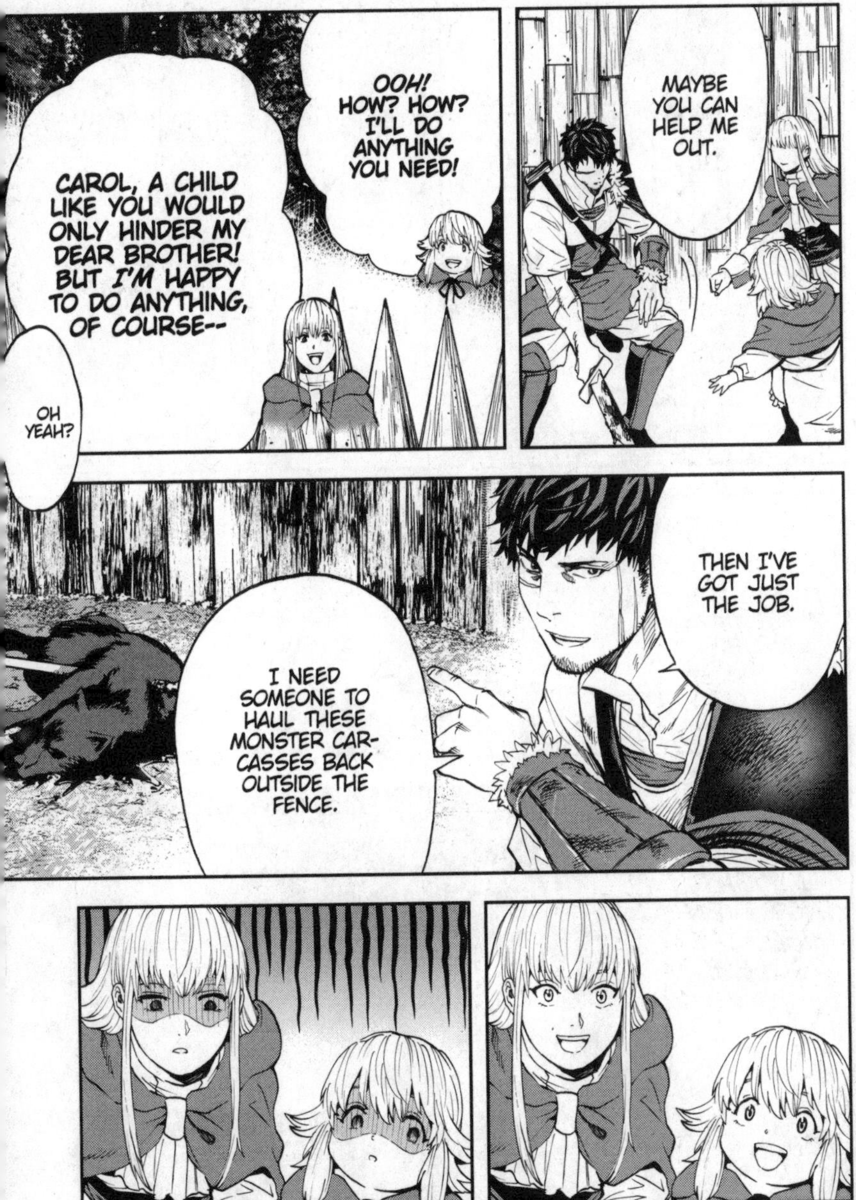
MAYBE YOU CAN HELP ME OUT.
OOH! HOW? HOW? I'LL DO ANYTHING YOU NEED!
CAROL, A CHILD LIKE YOU WOULD ONLY HINDER MY DEAR BROTHER! BUT *I'M* HAPPY TO DO ANYTHING, OF COURSE--
OH YEAH?
THEN I'VE GOT JUST THE JOB.
I NEED SOMEONE TO HAUL THESE MONSTER CAR-CASSES BACK OUTSIDE THE FENCE.

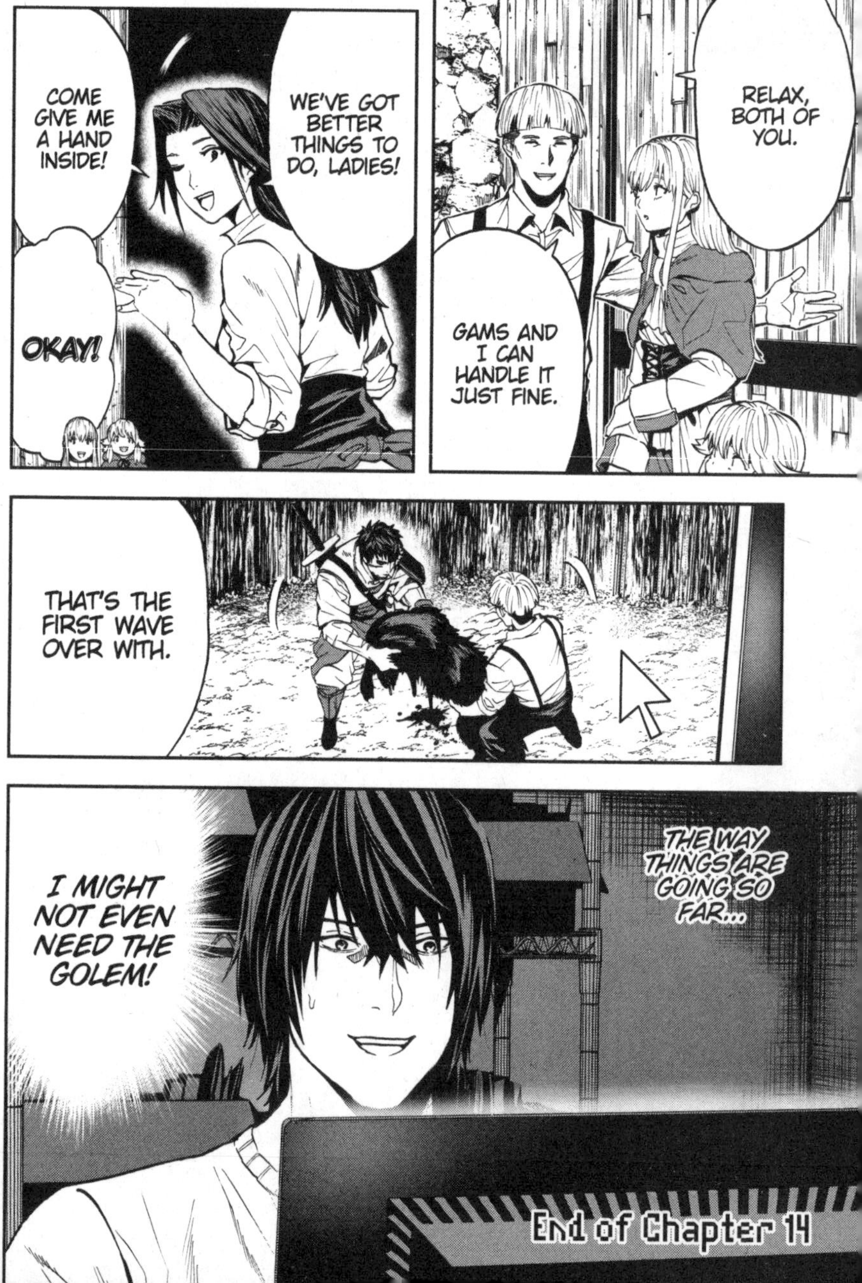
RELAX, BOTH OF YOU.
GAMS AND I CAN HANDLE IT JUST FINE.
WE'VE GOT BETTER THINGS TO DO, LADIES!
COME GIVE ME A HAND INSIDE!
OKAY!
THAT'S THE FIRST WAVE OVER WITH.
THE WAY THINGS ARE GOING SO FAR...
I MIGHT NOT EVEN NEED THE GOLEM!
End of Chapter 14

Character

Sayuki

▶ Gender: Female

Class: Office Worker

E : Cloth armor (Pajama top)

E : Cloth armor (Pajama bottoms)

E : Complicated feelings about her brother

THE NPCs IN THIS VILLAGE SIM GAME MUST BE REAL!↵

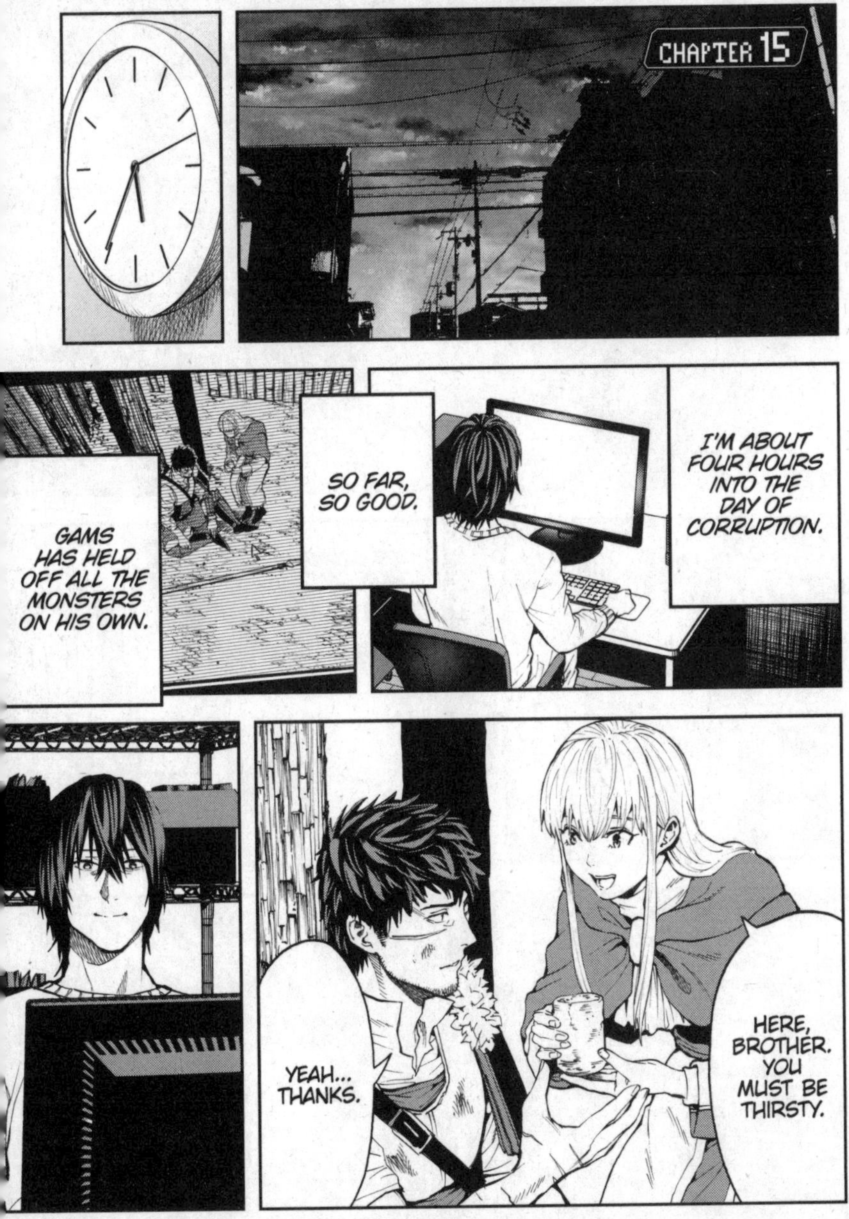
CHAPTER 15
I'M ABOUT FOUR HOURS INTO THE DAY OF CORRUPTION.
SO FAR, SO GOOD.
GAMS HAS HELD OFF ALL THE MONSTERS ON HIS OWN.
HERE, BROTHER. YOU MUST BE THIRSTY.
YEAH... THANKS.

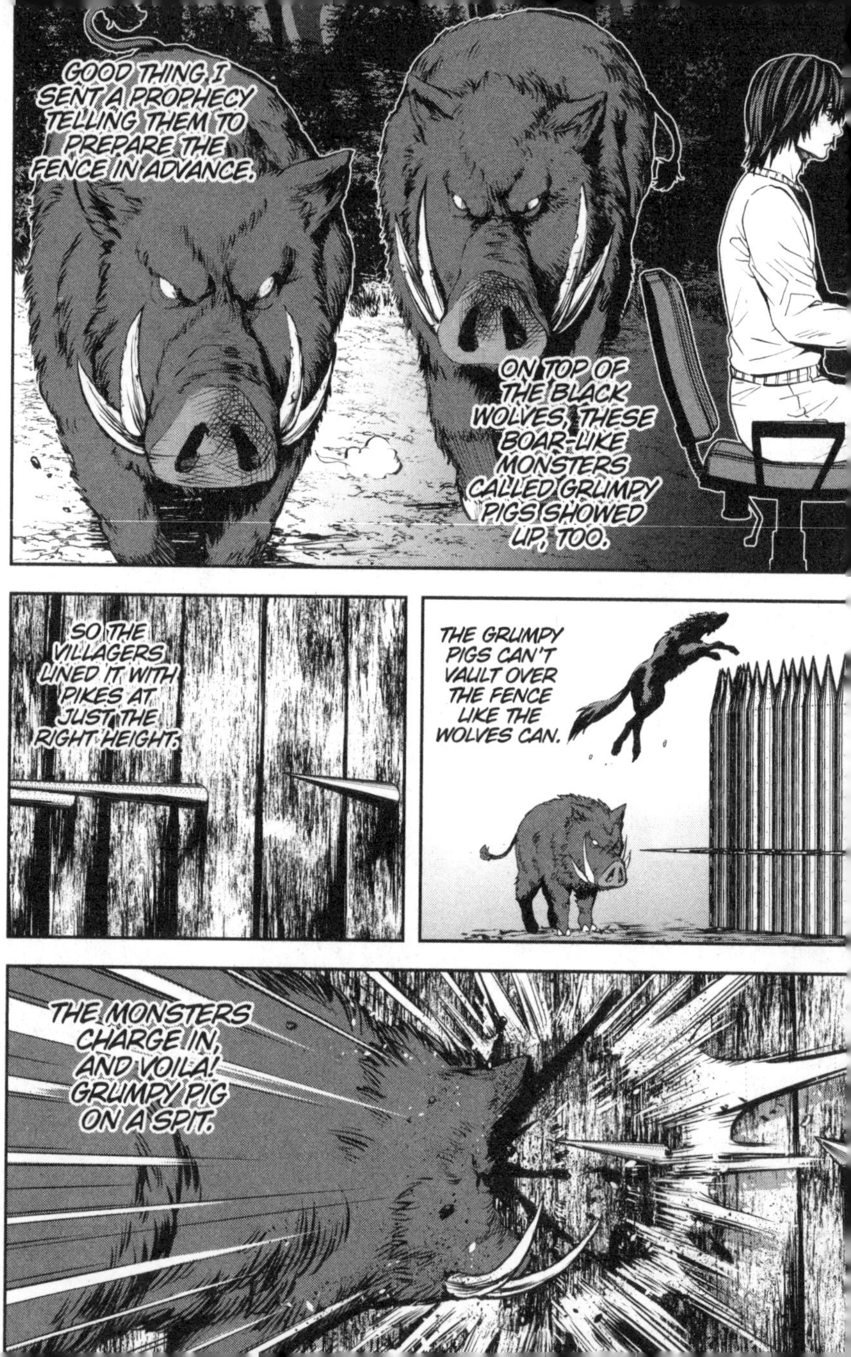
ON TOP OF THE BLACK WOLVES, THESE BOAR-LIKE MONSTERS CALLED GRUMPY PIGS SHOWED UP, TOO.
GOOD THING I SENT A PROPHECY TELLING THEM TO PREPARE THE FENCE IN ADVANCE.
THE GRUMPY PIGS CAN'T VAULT OVER THE FENCE LIKE THE WOLVES CAN.
SO THE VILLAGERS LINED IT WITH PIKES AT JUST THE RIGHT HEIGHT.
THE MONSTERS CHARGE IN, AND VOILA! GRUMPY PIG ON A SPIT.

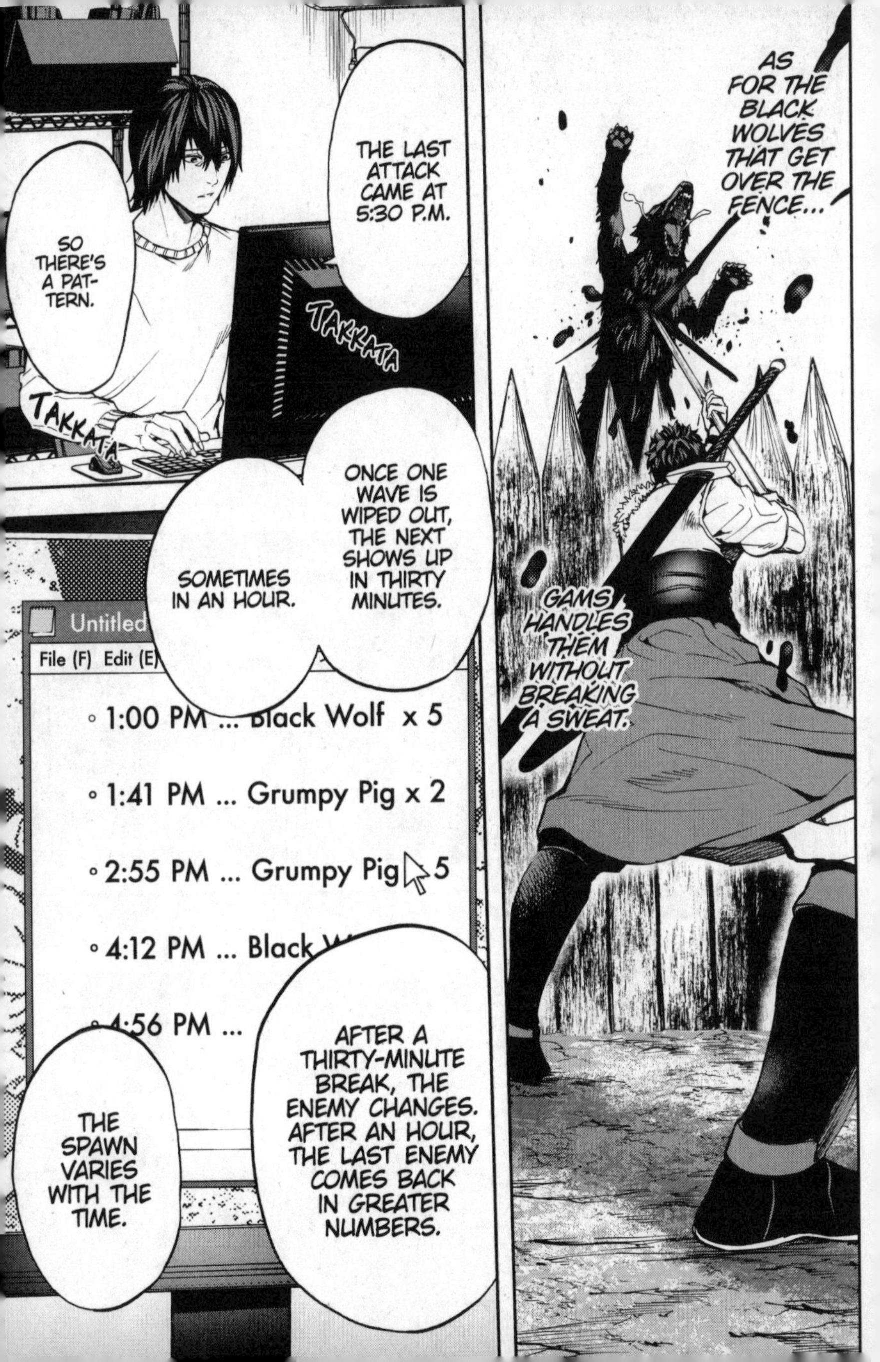
AS FOR THE BLACK WOLVES THAT GET OVER THE FENCE...
GAMS HANDLES THEM WITHOUT BREAKING A SWEAT.
THE LAST ATTACK CAME AT 5:30 P.M.
SO THERE'S A PATTERN.
TAKKATA
TAKKATA
ONCE ONE WAVE IS WIPED OUT, THE NEXT SHOWS UP IN THIRTY MINUTES.
SOMETIMES IN AN HOUR.
Untitled
File (F) Edit (E)
◦ 1:00 PM ... Black Wolf x 5
◦ 1:41 PM ... Grumpy Pig x 2
◦ 2:55 PM ... Grumpy Pig 5
◦ 4:12 PM ... Black
◦ 4:56 PM ...
AFTER A THIRTY-MINUTE BREAK, THE ENEMY CHANGES. AFTER AN HOUR, THE LAST ENEMY COMES BACK IN GREATER NUMBERS.
THE SPAWN VARIES WITH THE TIME.

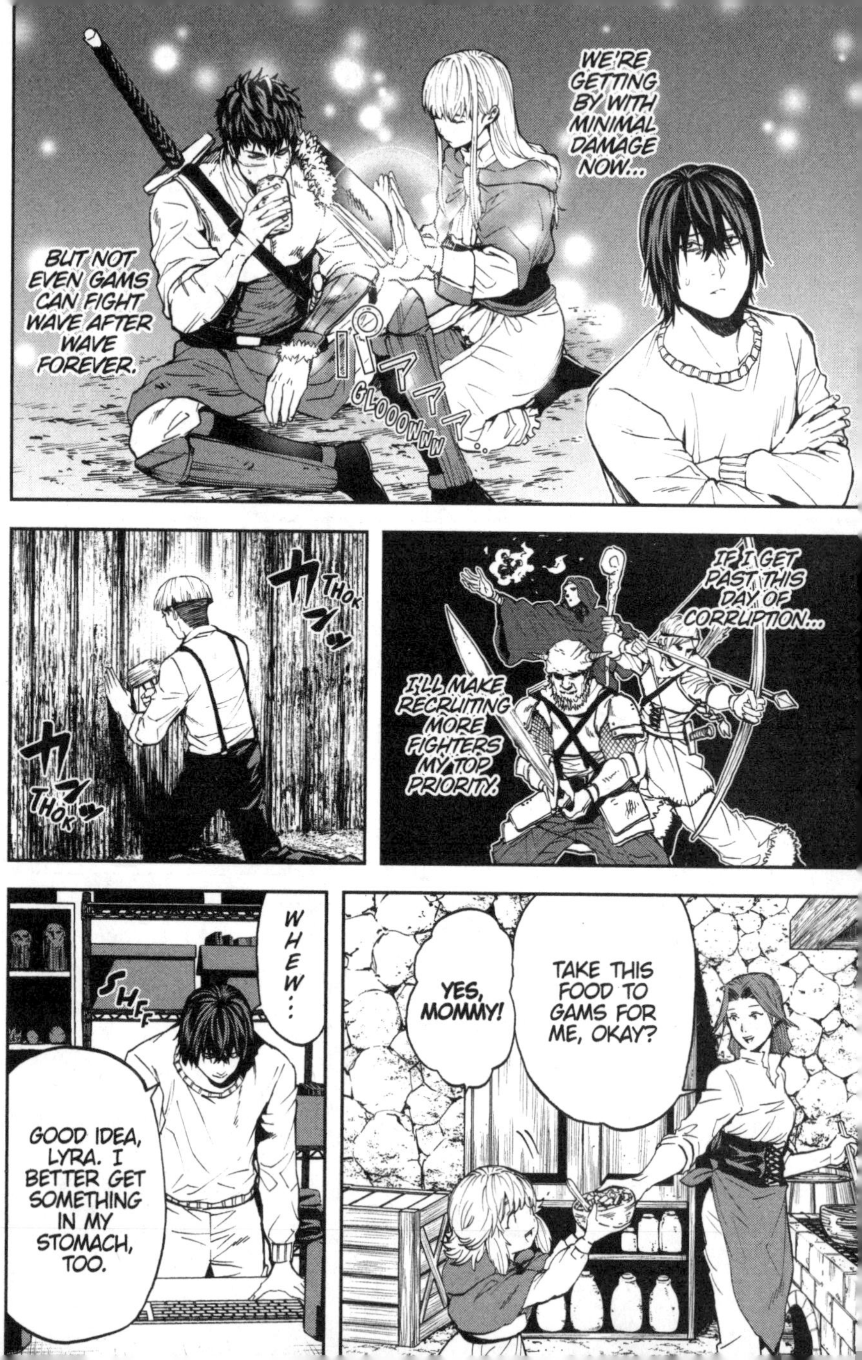
WE'RE GETTING BY WITH MINIMAL DAMAGE NOW...
BUT NOT EVEN GAMS CAN FIGHT WAVE AFTER WAVE FOREVER.
GLOOOWWW
IF I GET PAST THIS DAY OF CORRUPTION...
I'LL MAKE RECRUITING MORE FIGHTERS MY TOP PRIORITY.
THOK
THOK
TAKE THIS FOOD TO GAMS FOR ME, OKAY?
YES, MOMMY!
WHEW...
SHFF
GOOD IDEA, LYRA. I BETTER GET SOMETHING IN MY STOMACH, TOO.

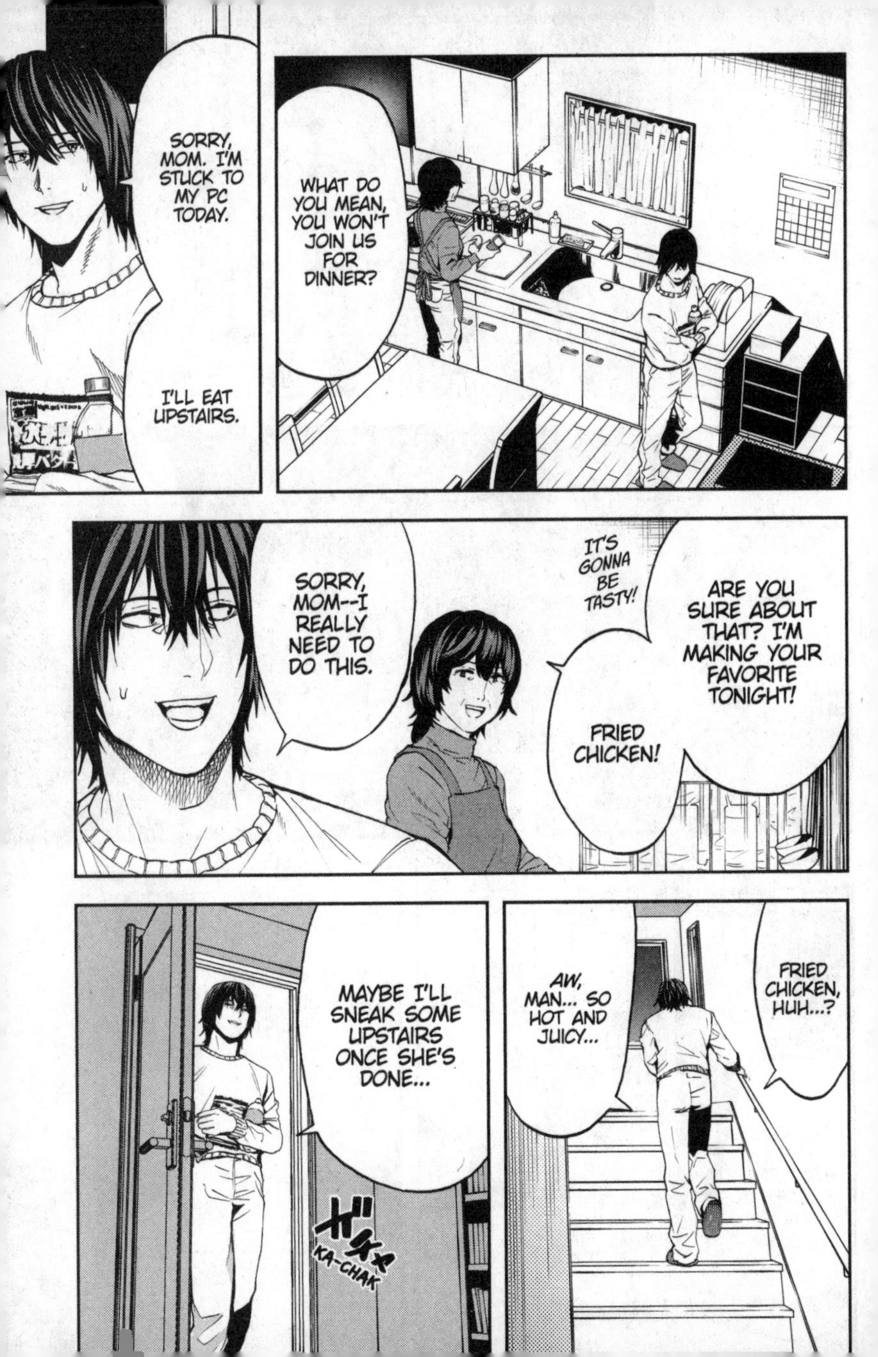
WHAT DO YOU MEAN, YOU WON'T JOIN US FOR DINNER?
SORRY, MOM. I'M STUCK TO MY PC TODAY.
I'LL EAT UPSTAIRS.
ARE YOU SURE ABOUT THAT? I'M MAKING YOUR FAVORITE TONIGHT!
IT'S GONNA BE TASTY!
FRIED CHICKEN!
SORRY, MOM--I REALLY NEED TO DO THIS.
FRIED CHICKEN, HUH...?
AW, MAN... SO HOT AND JUICY...
MAYBE I'LL SNEAK SOME UPSTAIRS ONCE SHE'S DONE...
KA-CHAK

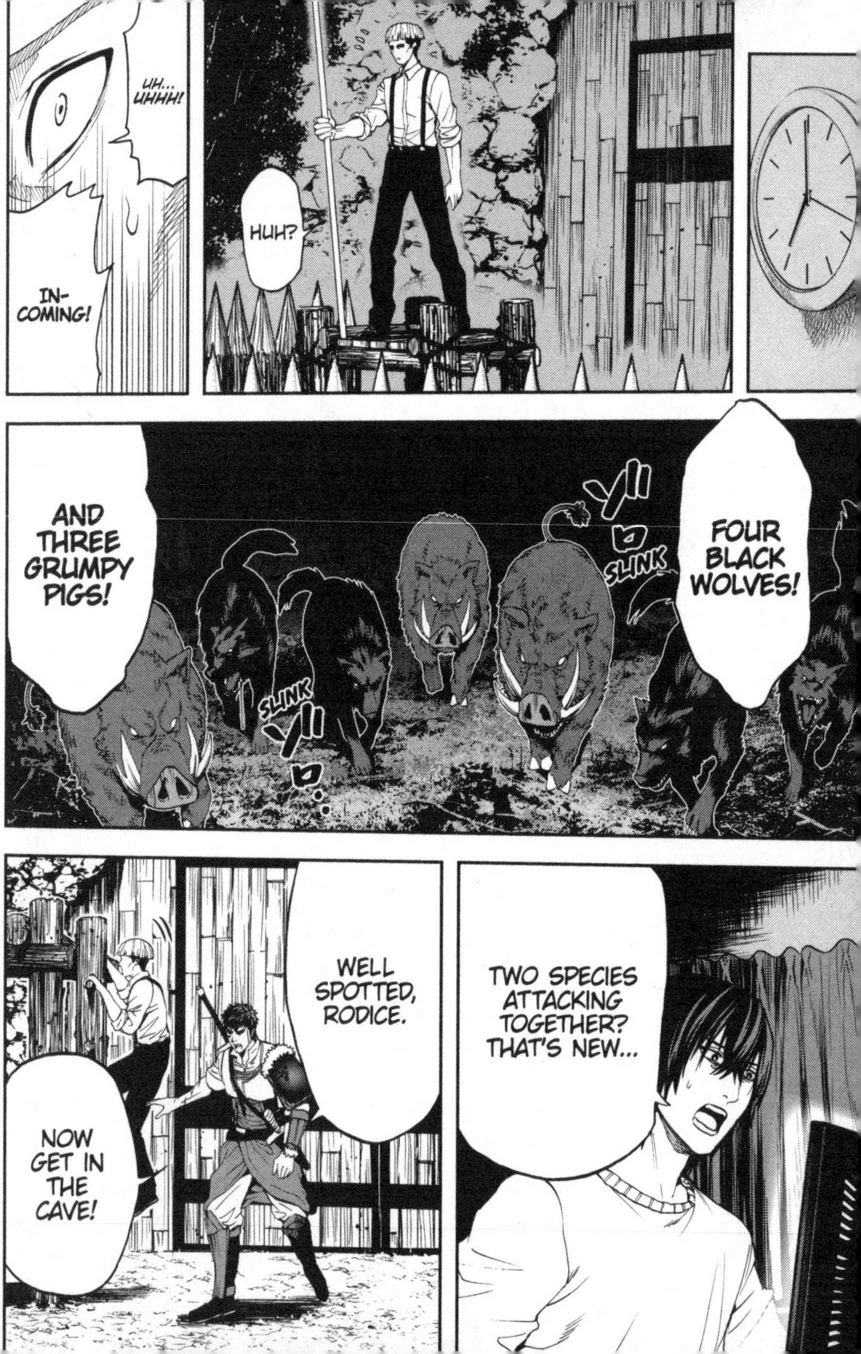
HUH?
UH... UHHH!
IN-COMING!
FOUR BLACK WOLVES!
SLINK
SLINK
AND THREE GRUMPY PIGS!
TWO SPECIES ATTACKING TOGETHER? THAT'S NEW...
WELL SPOTTED, RODICE.
NOW GET IN THE CAVE!

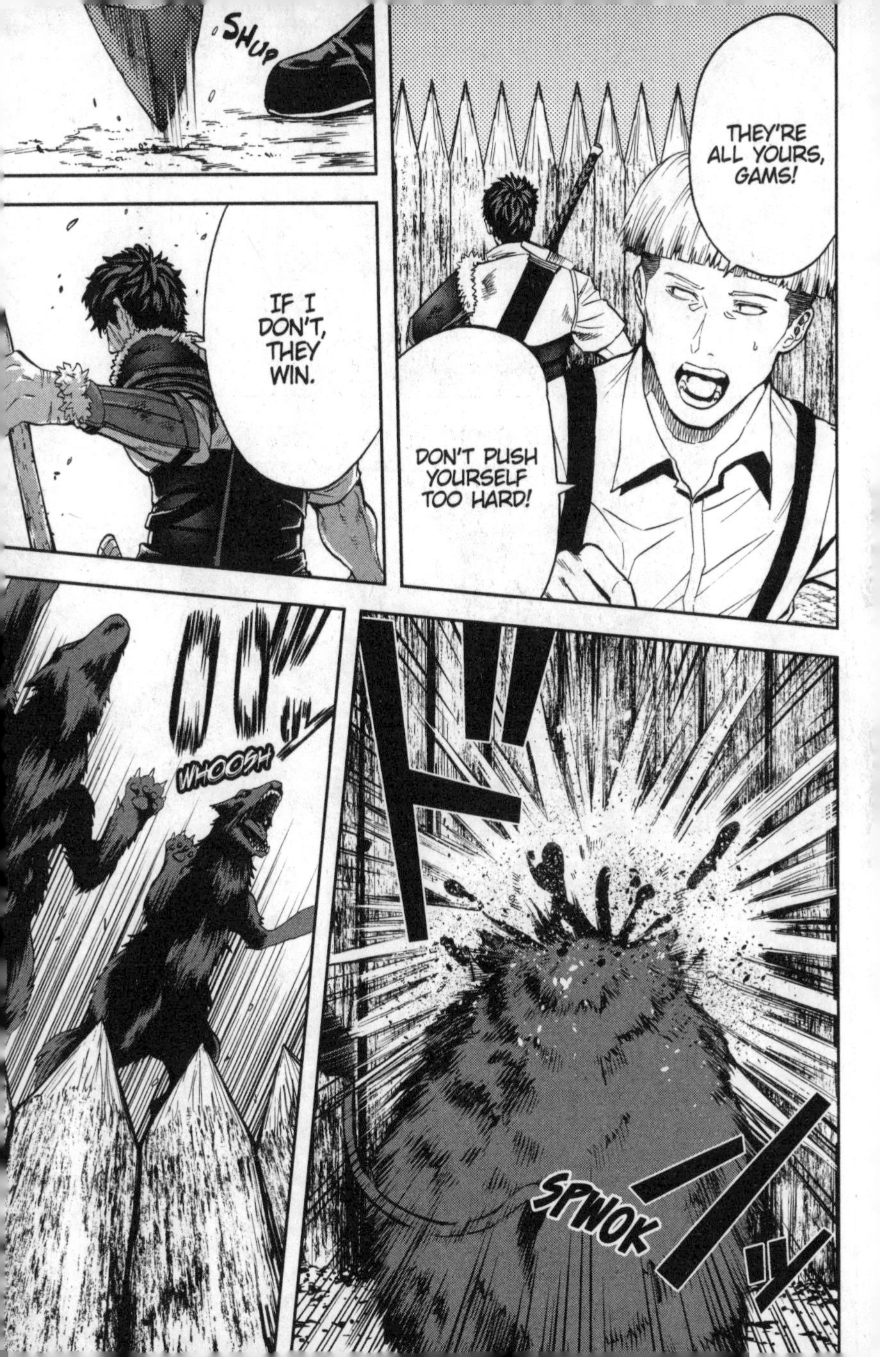
THEY'RE ALL YOURS, GAMS!
DON'T PUSH YOURSELF TOO HARD!
SHUP
IF I DON'T, THEY WIN.
SPWOK
WHOOSH

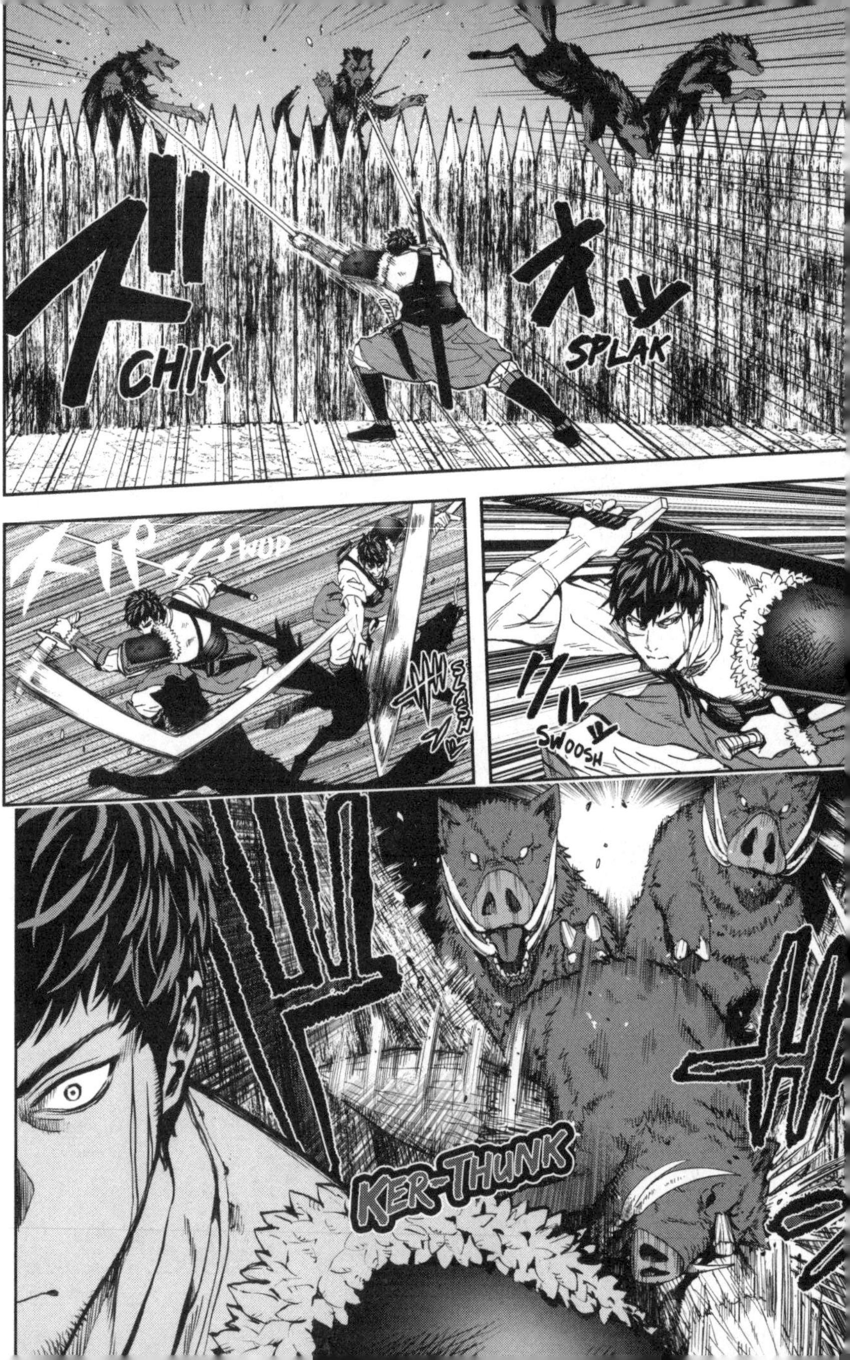
SPLAK
CHIK
SWOOSH
SLASH
SWOP
KER-THUNK

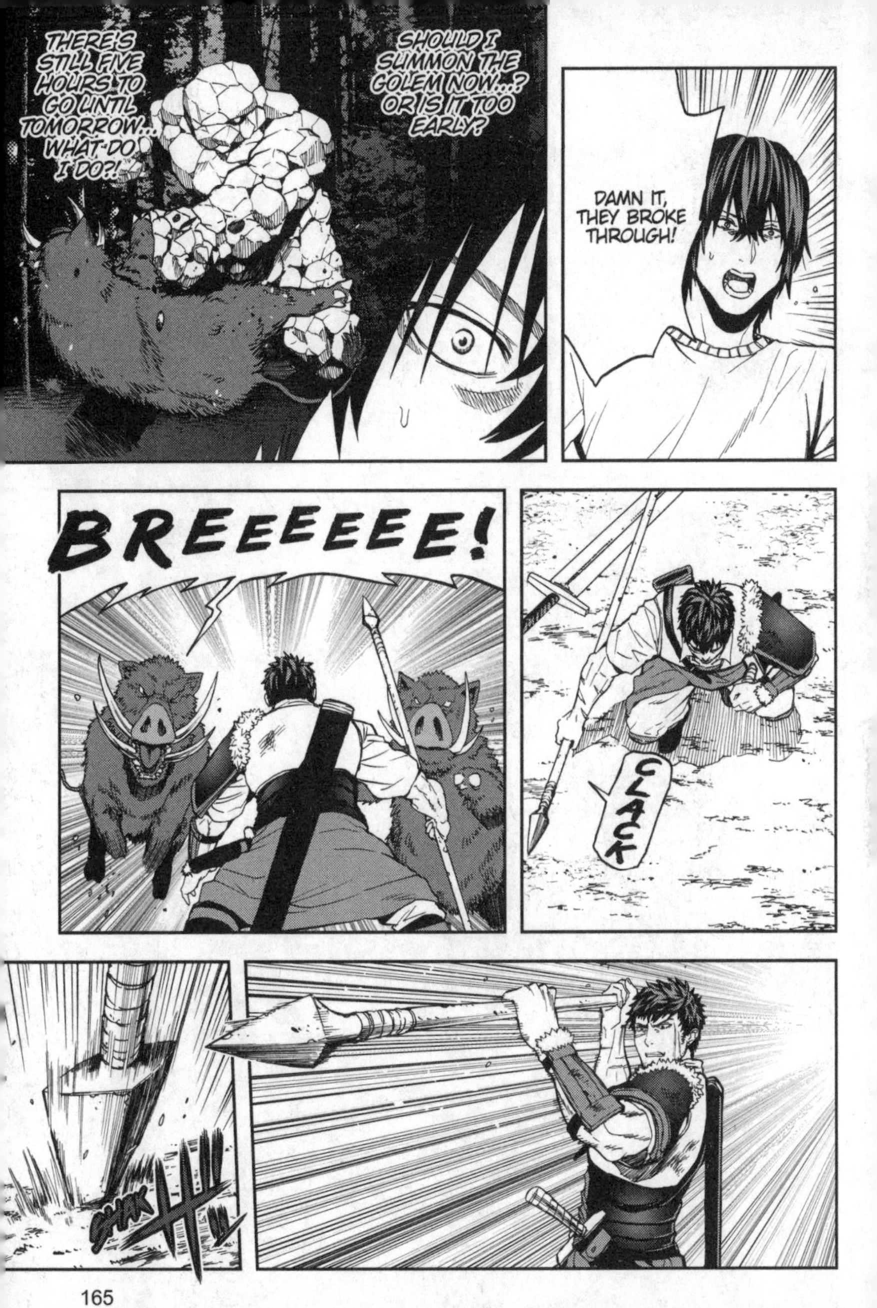
DAMN IT, THEY BROKE THROUGH!
SHOULD I SUMMON THE GOLEM NOW...? OR IS IT TOO EARLY?
THERE'S STILL FIVE HOURS TO GO UNTIL TOMORROW... WHAT DO I DO?!
CLACK
BREEEEEEE!
SHAK

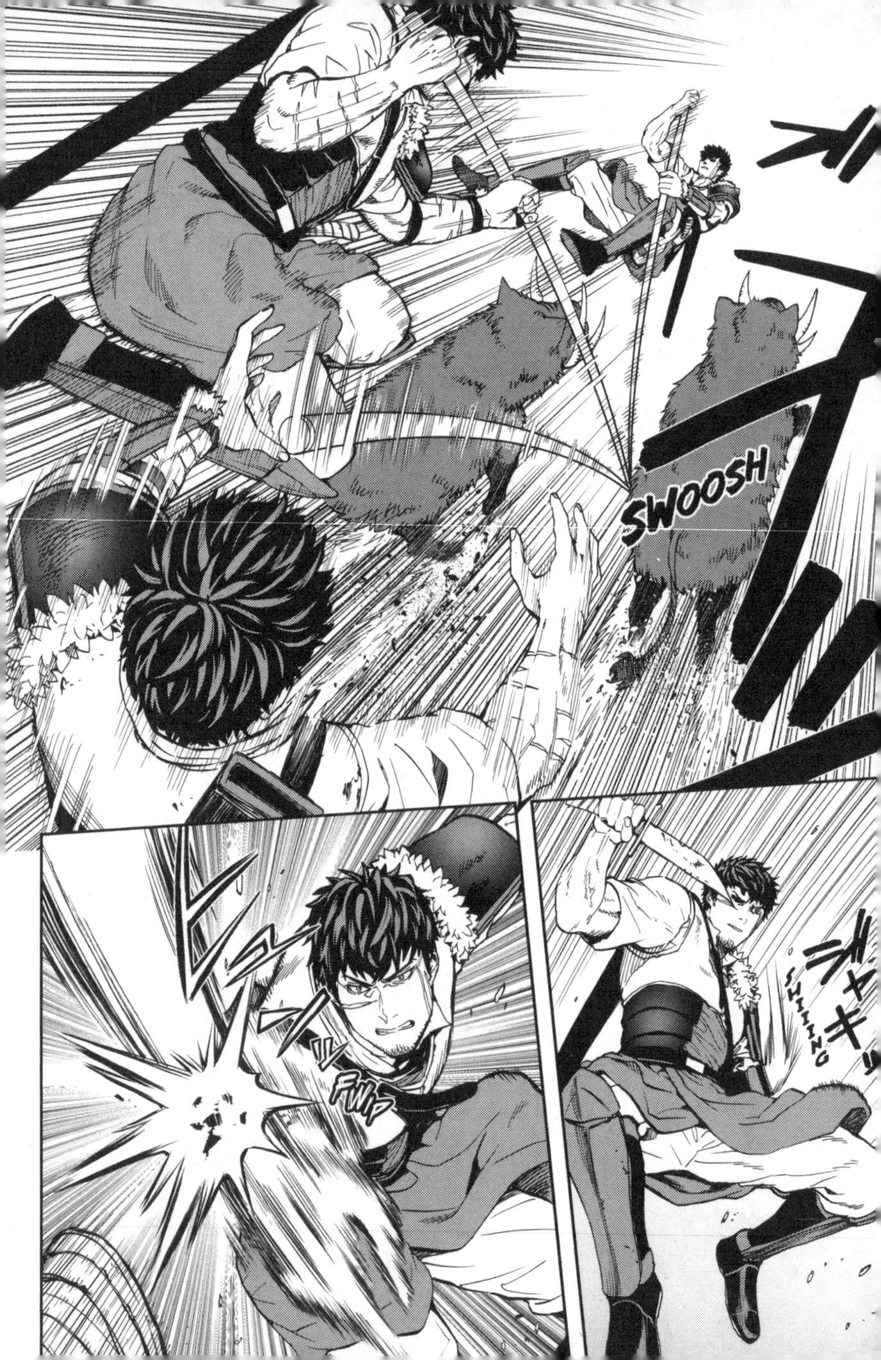
SWOOSH
SHIIING
FWIP

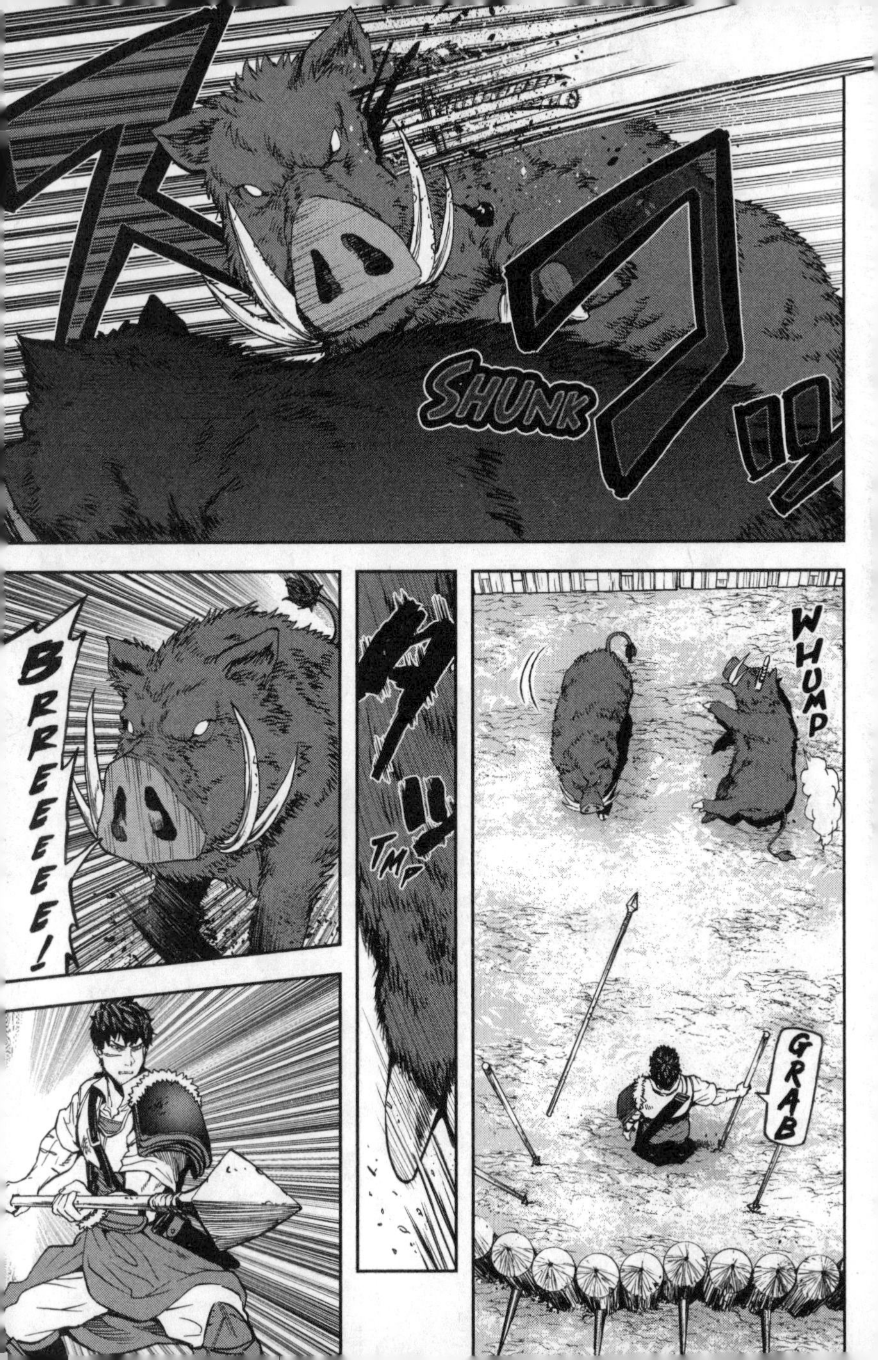
SHUNK
WHUMP
GRAB
TMP
BRREEEEEE!

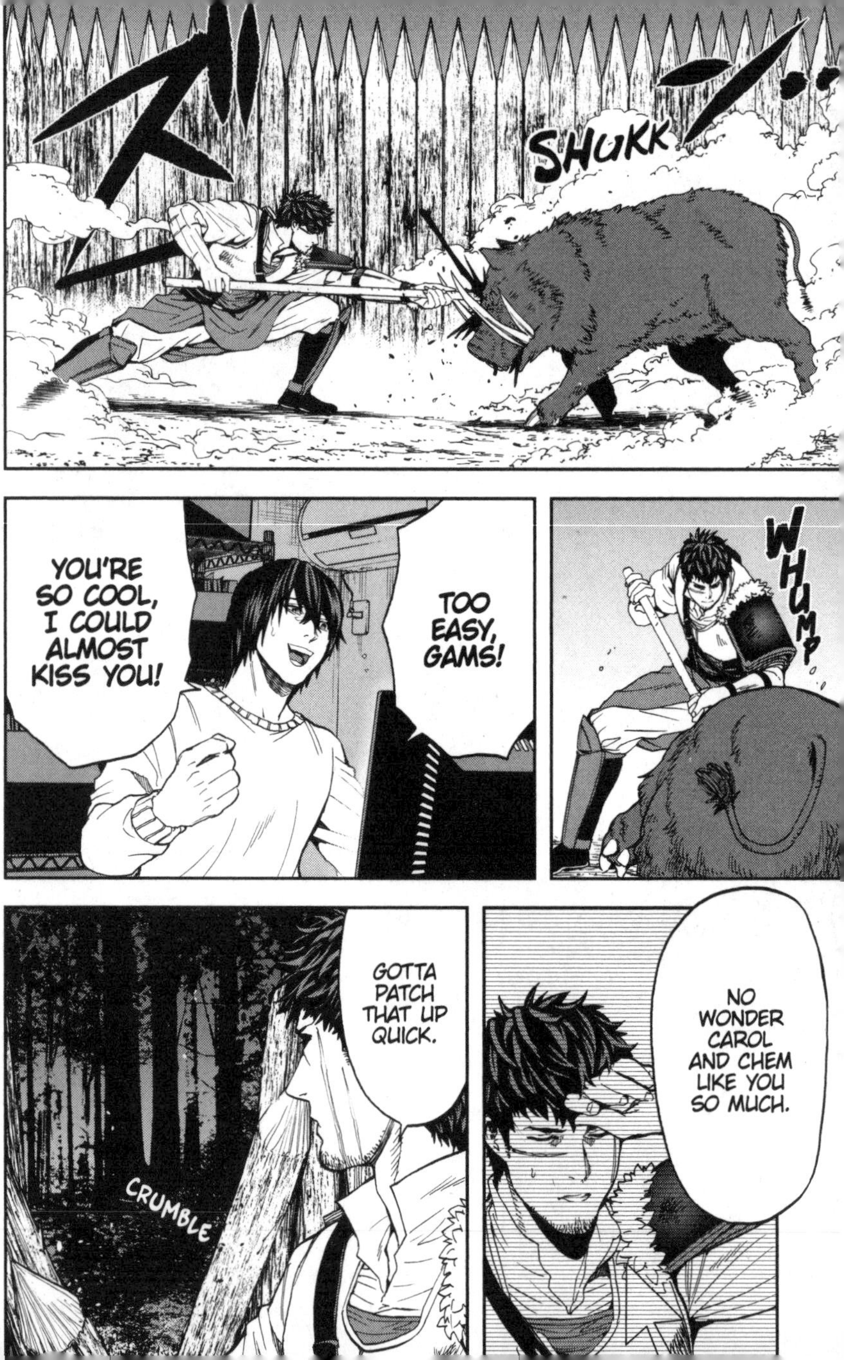
SHUKK
WHUMP
TOO EASY, GAMS!
YOU'RE SO COOL, I COULD ALMOST KISS YOU!
NO WONDER CAROL AND CHEM LIKE YOU SO MUCH.
GOTTA PATCH THAT UP QUICK.
CRUMBLE

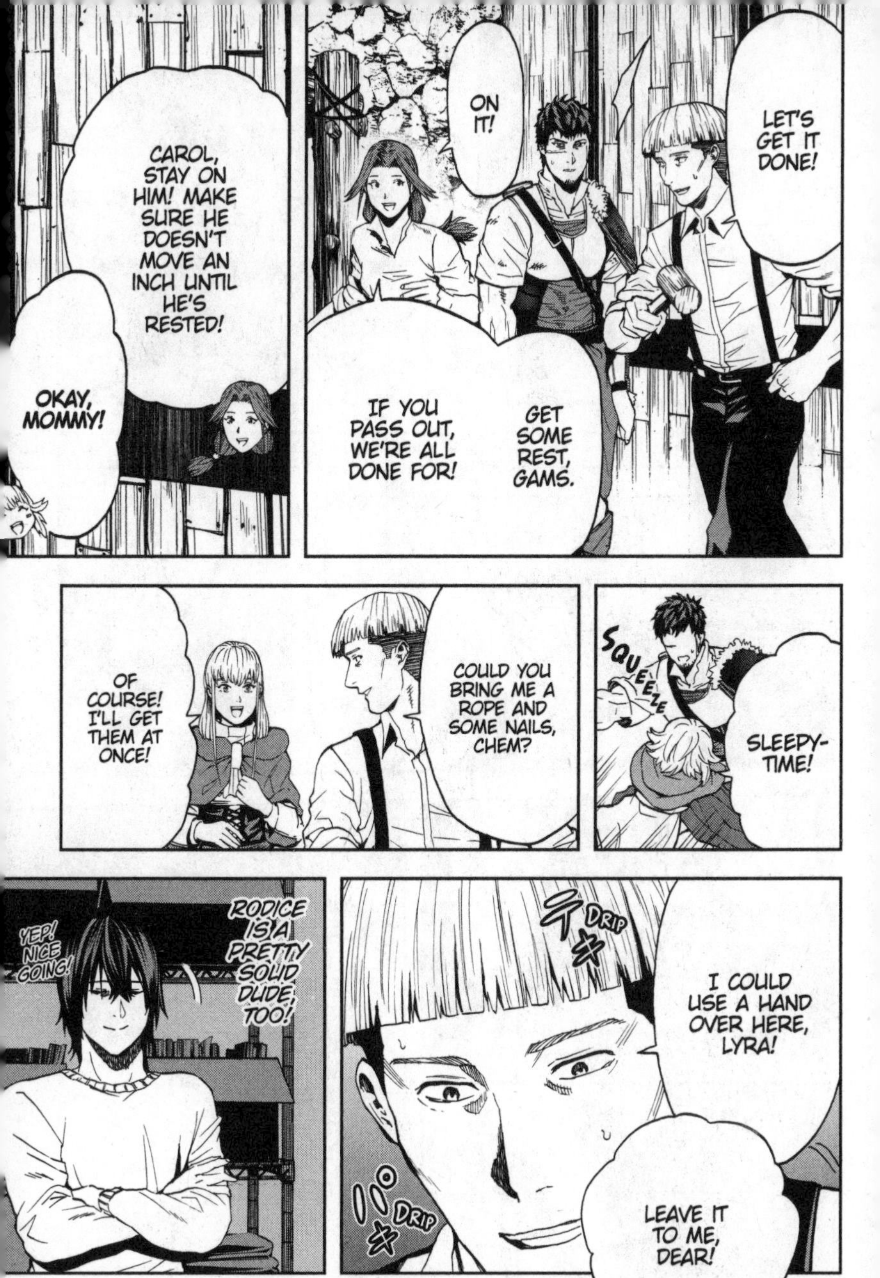
LET'S GET IT DONE!
ON IT!
GET SOME REST, GAMS.
IF YOU PASS OUT, WE'RE ALL DONE FOR!
CAROL, STAY ON HIM! MAKE SURE HE DOESN'T MOVE AN INCH UNTIL HE'S RESTED!
OKAY, MOMMY!
SQUEEZE
SLEEPY-TIME!
COULD YOU BRING ME A ROPE AND SOME NAILS, CHEM?
OF COURSE! I'LL GET THEM AT ONCE!
テキ DRIP
I COULD USE A HAND OVER HERE, LYRA!
LEAVE IT TO ME, DEAR!
パキ DRIP
RODICE IS A PRETTY SOLID DUDE, TOO!
YEP! NICE GOING!

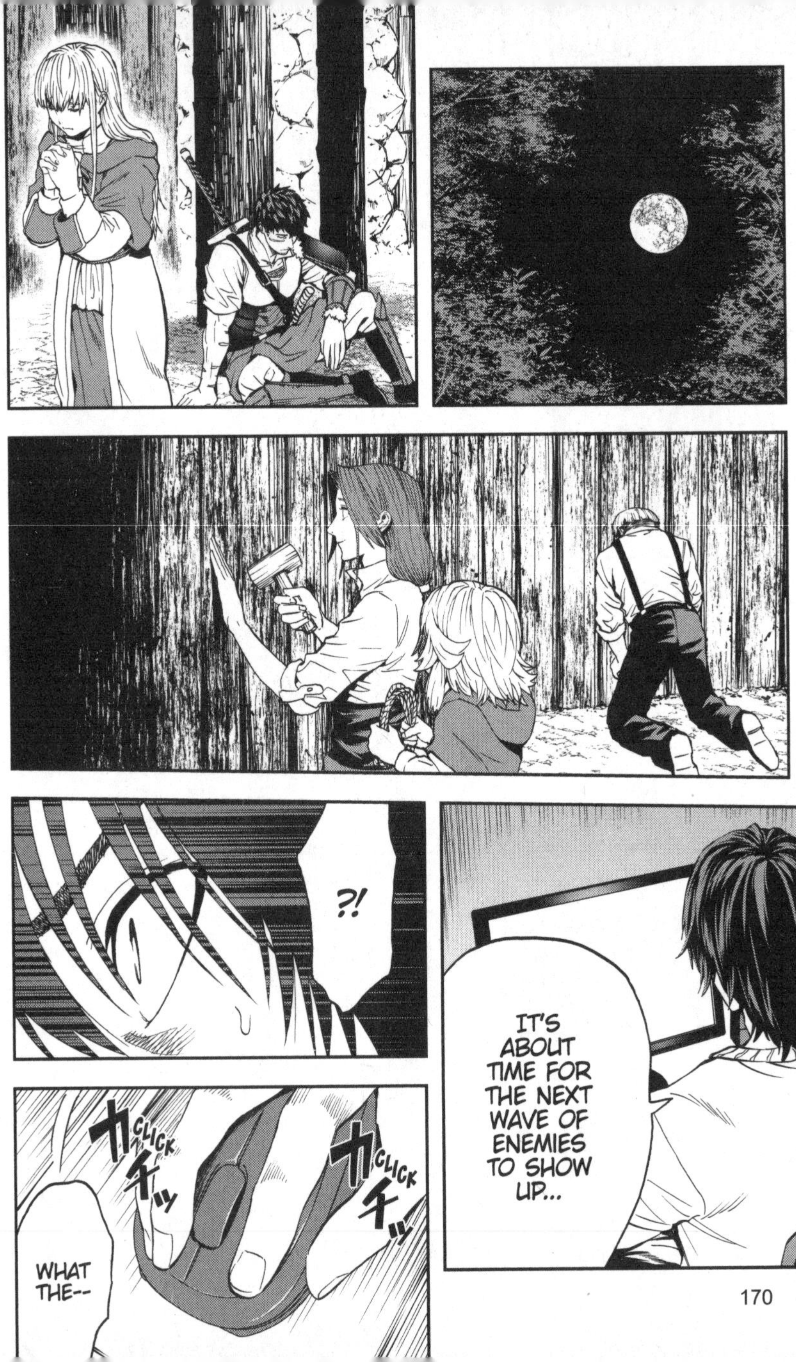
IT'S ABOUT TIME FOR THE NEXT WAVE OF ENEMIES TO SHOW UP...
?!
カチッ CLICK
カチッ CLICK
WHAT THE--

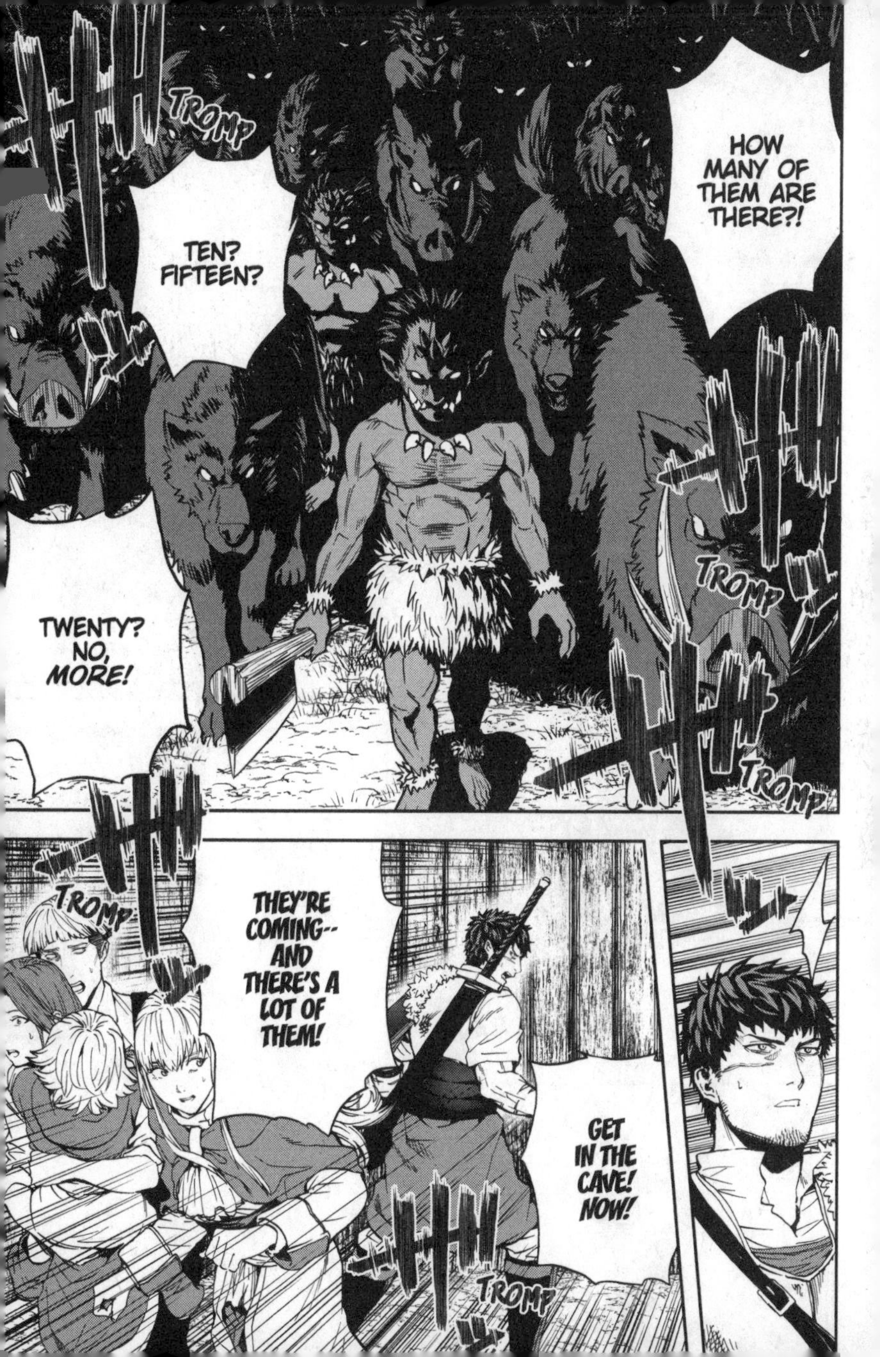
HOW MANY OF THEM ARE THERE?!
TROMP
TROMP
TEN? FIFTEEN?
TWENTY? NO, MORE!
TROMP
GET IN THE CAVE! NOW!
THEY'RE COMING-- AND THERE'S A LOT OF THEM!
TROMP
TROMP

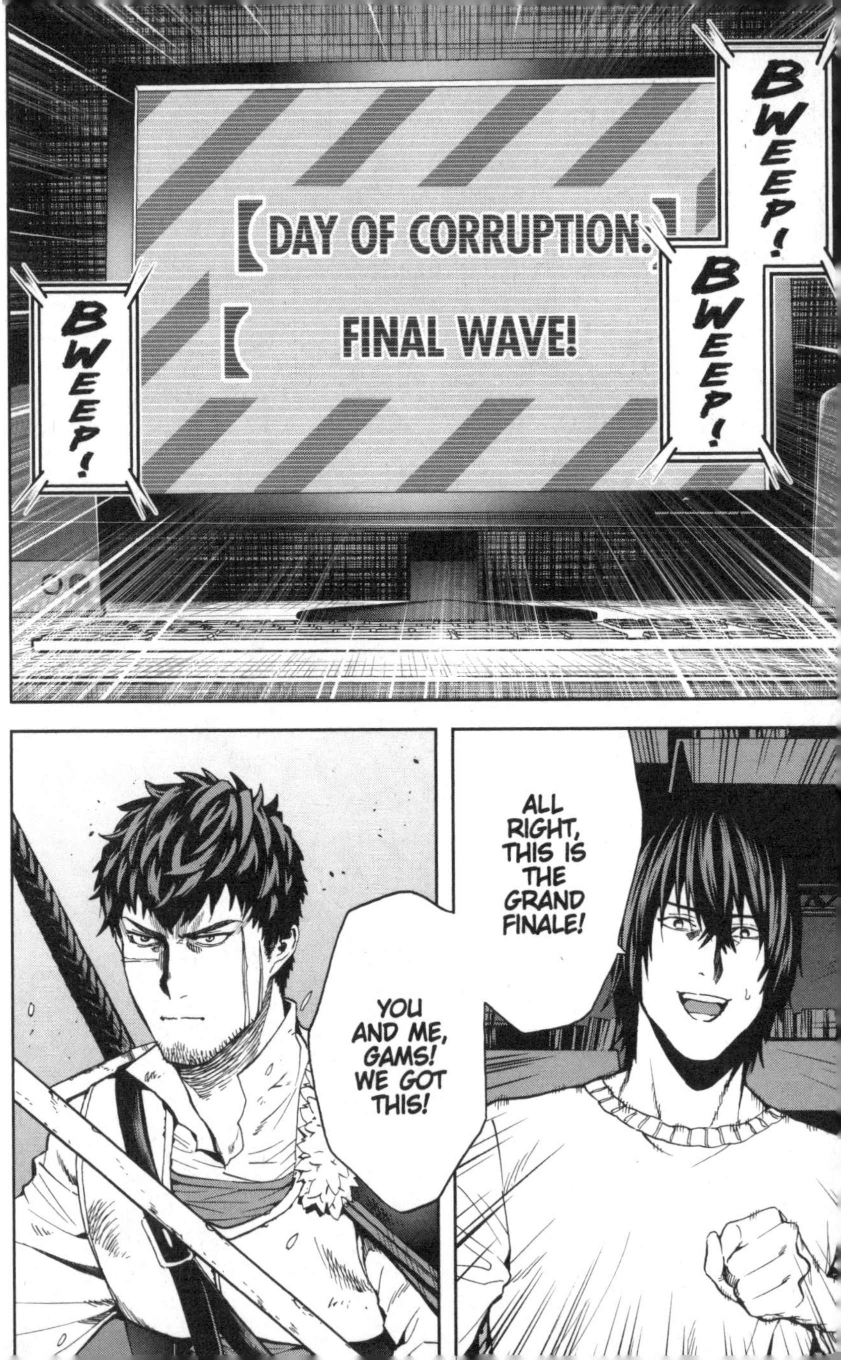
BWEEP!
BWEEP!
【DAY OF CORRUPTION.】
【FINAL WAVE!
BWEEP!
ALL RIGHT, THIS IS THE GRAND FINALE!
YOU AND ME, GAMS! WE GOT THIS!

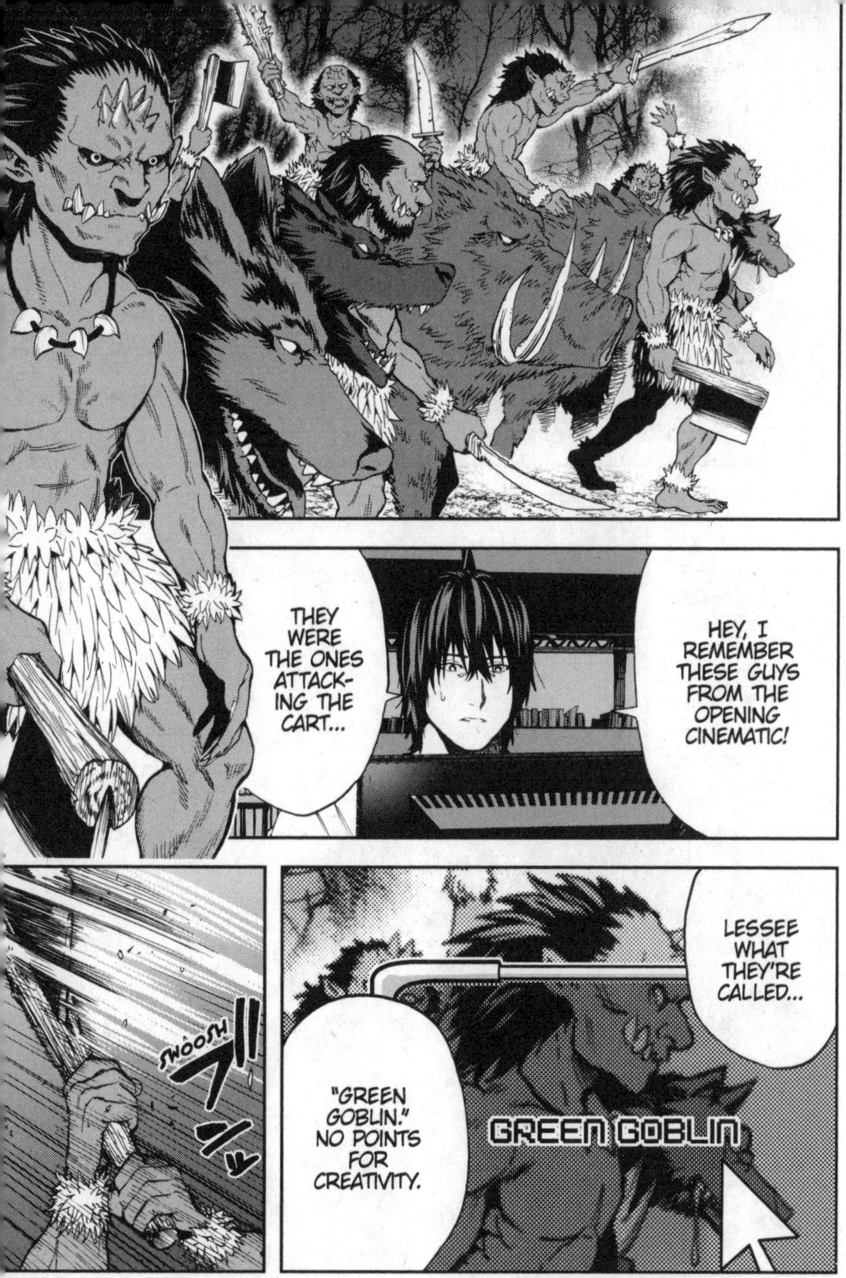
HEY, I REMEMBER THESE GUYS FROM THE OPENING CINEMATIC!
THEY WERE THE ONES ATTACKING THE CART...
LESSEE WHAT THEY'RE CALLED...
GREEN GOBLIN
"GREEN GOBLIN." NO POINTS FOR CREATIVITY.
SWOOSH

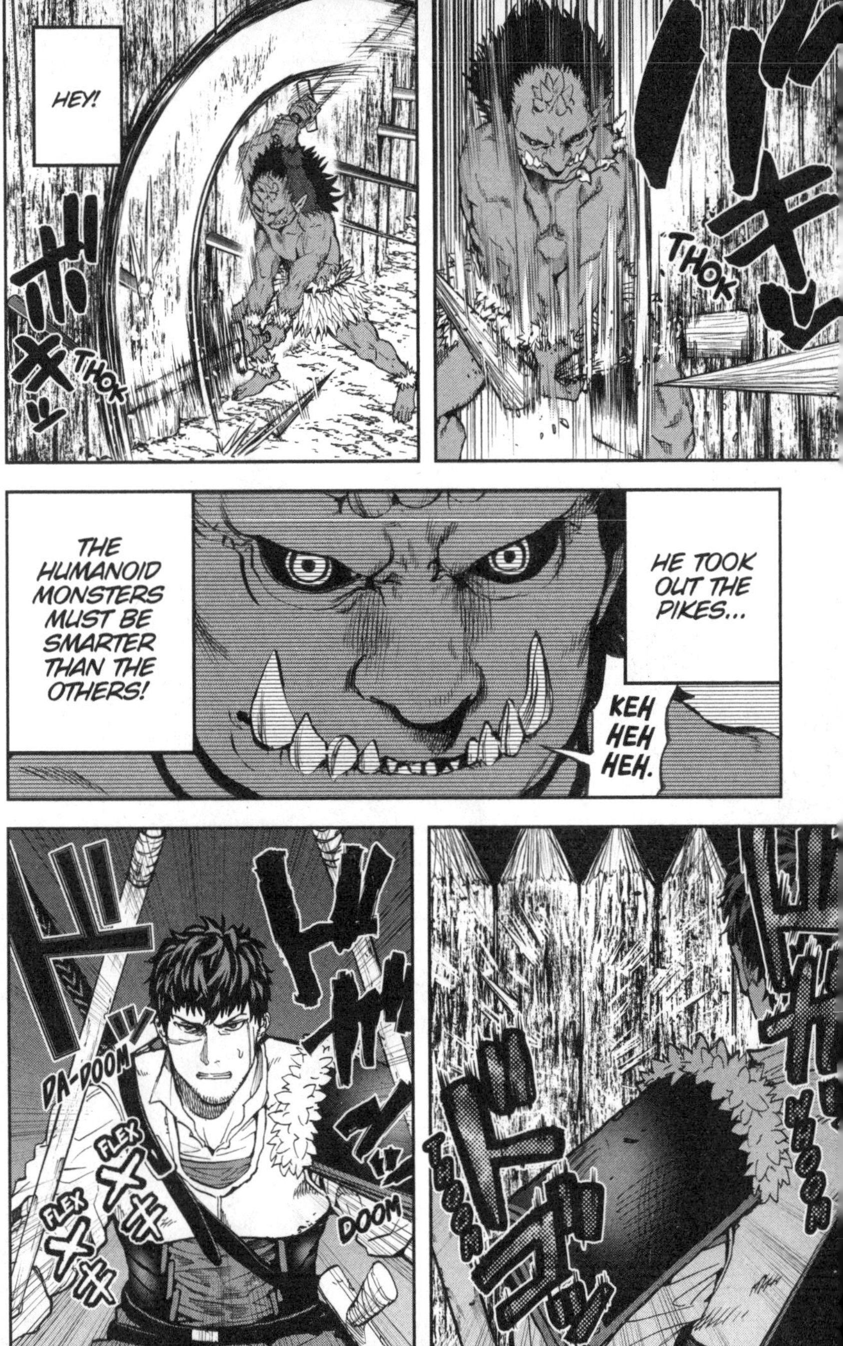
THOK
HEY!
THOK
HE TOOK OUT THE PIKES...
THE HUMANOID MONSTERS MUST BE SMARTER THAN THE OTHERS!
KEH HEH HEH.
DA-DOOM
DOOM
FLEX
FLEX

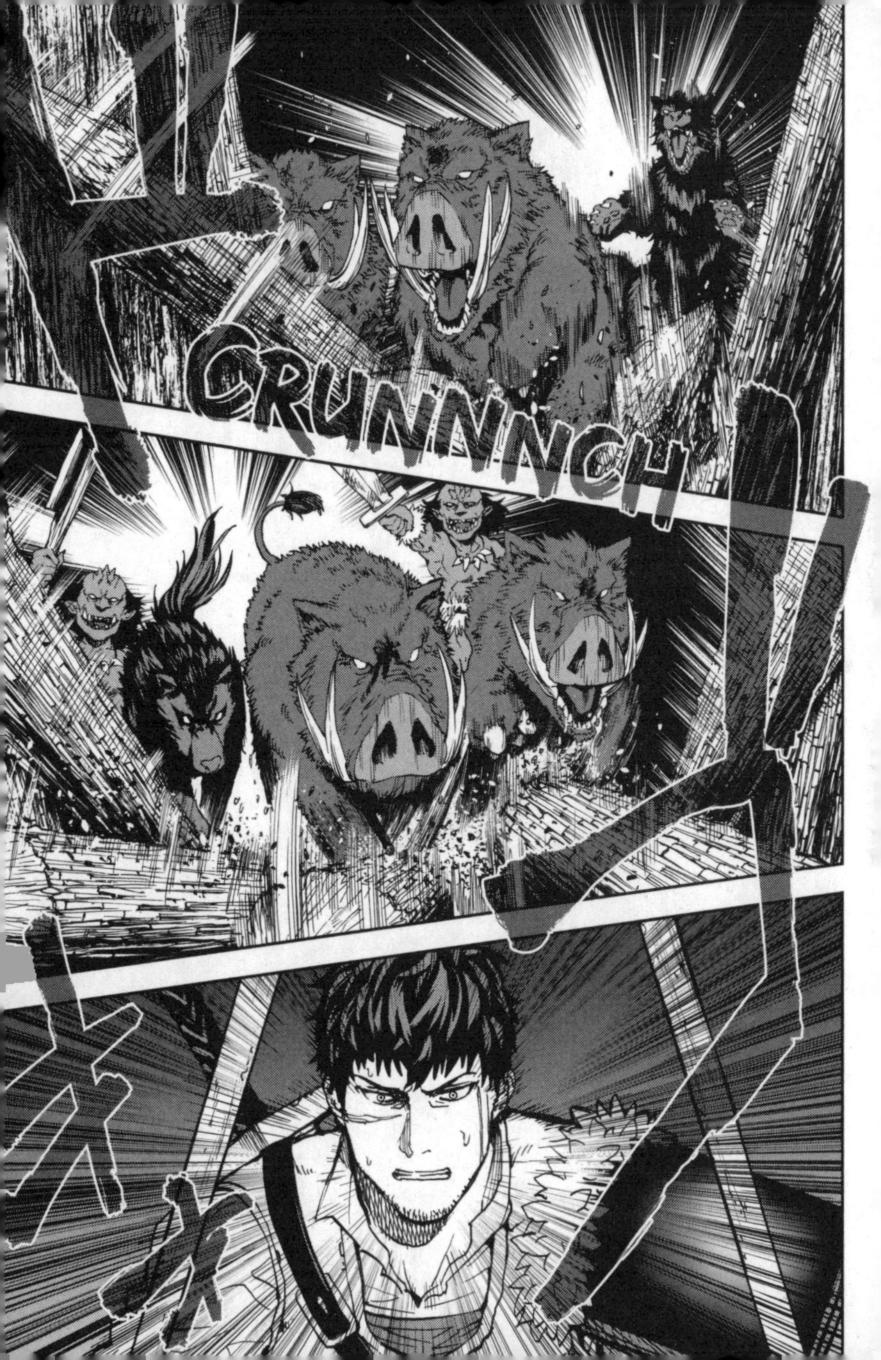
CRUNNNCH

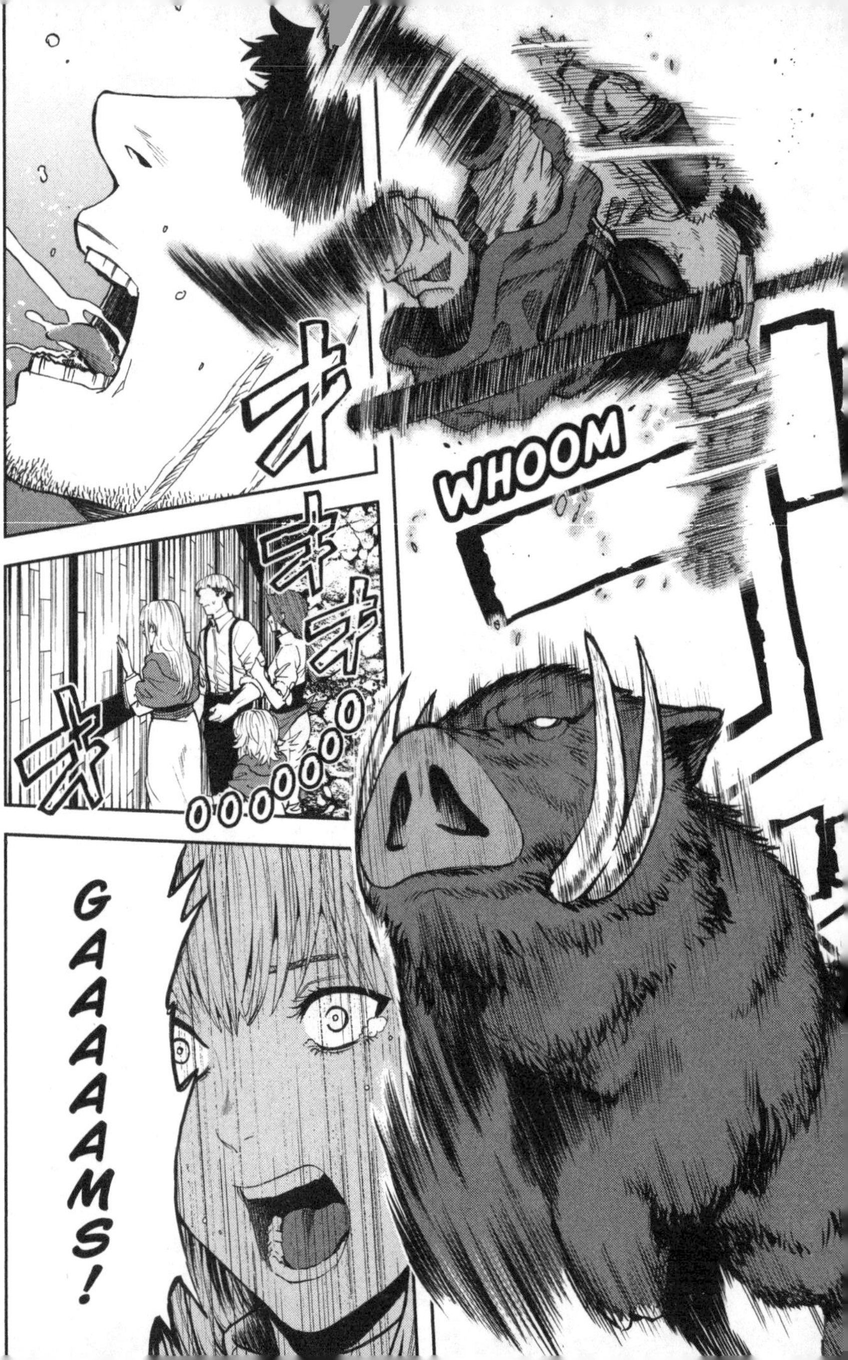
WHOOM
オオオオ
OOOOOOO
GAAAAAMS!

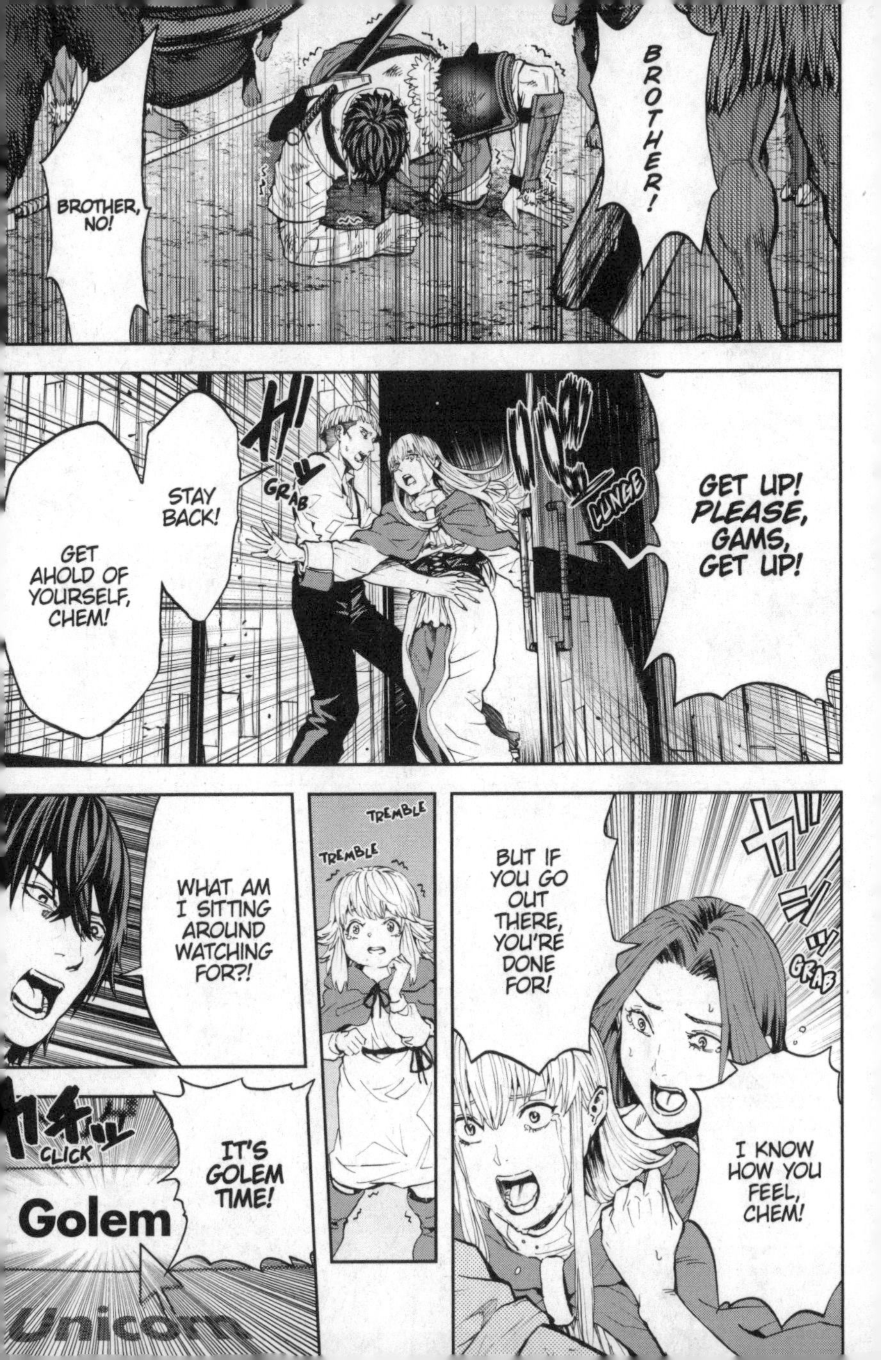
BROTHER!
BROTHER, NO!
LUNGE
GET UP! PLEASE, GAMS, GET UP!
GRAB
STAY BACK!
GET AHOLD OF YOURSELF, CHEM!
GRAB
I KNOW HOW YOU FEEL, CHEM!
BUT IF YOU GO OUT THERE, YOU'RE DONE FOR!
TREMBLE
TREMBLE
WHAT AM I SITTING AROUND WATCHING FOR?!
CLICK
IT'S GOLEM TIME!
Golem
Unicorn

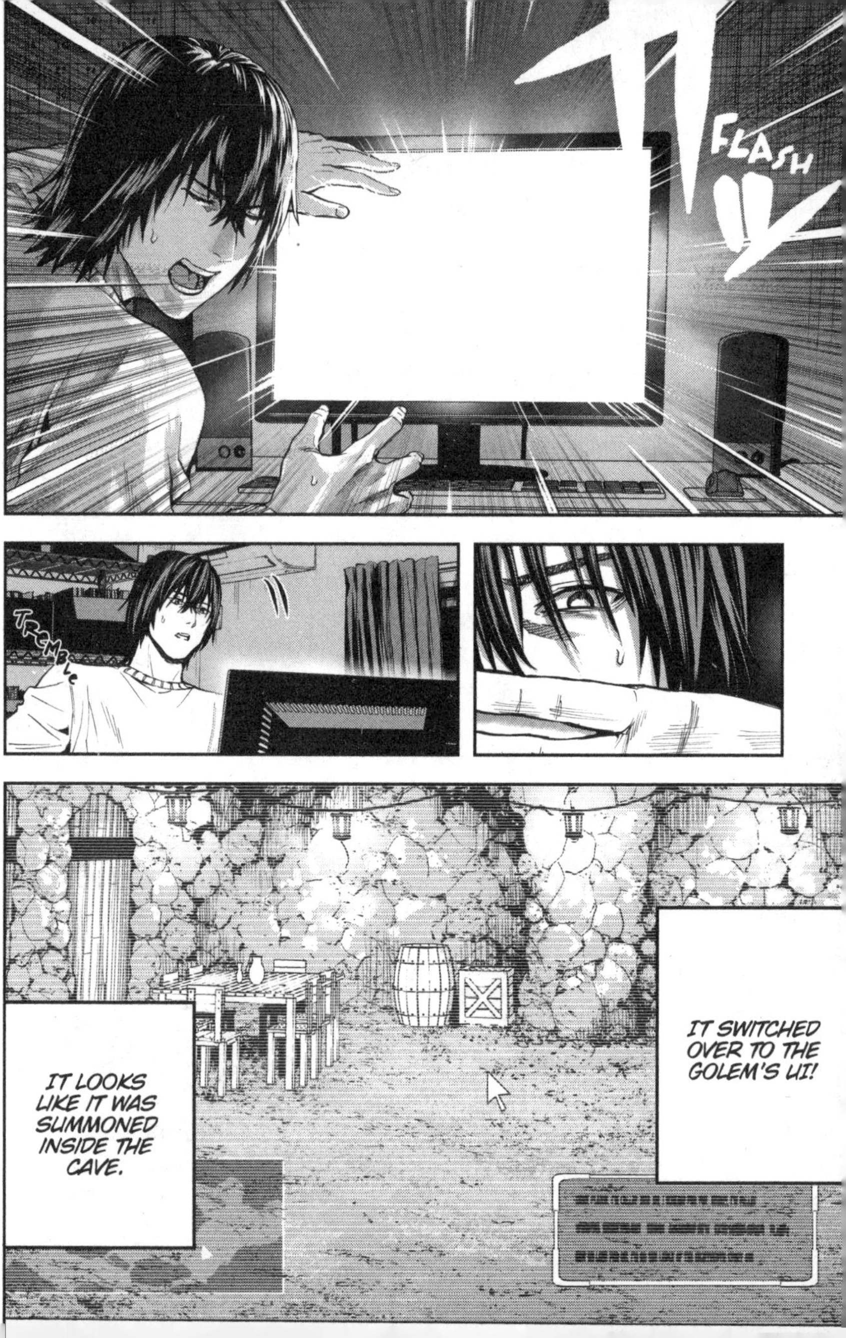
FLASH
TREMBLE
IT SWITCHED OVER TO THE GOLEM'S UI!
IT LOOKS LIKE IT WAS SUMMONED INSIDE THE CAVE.

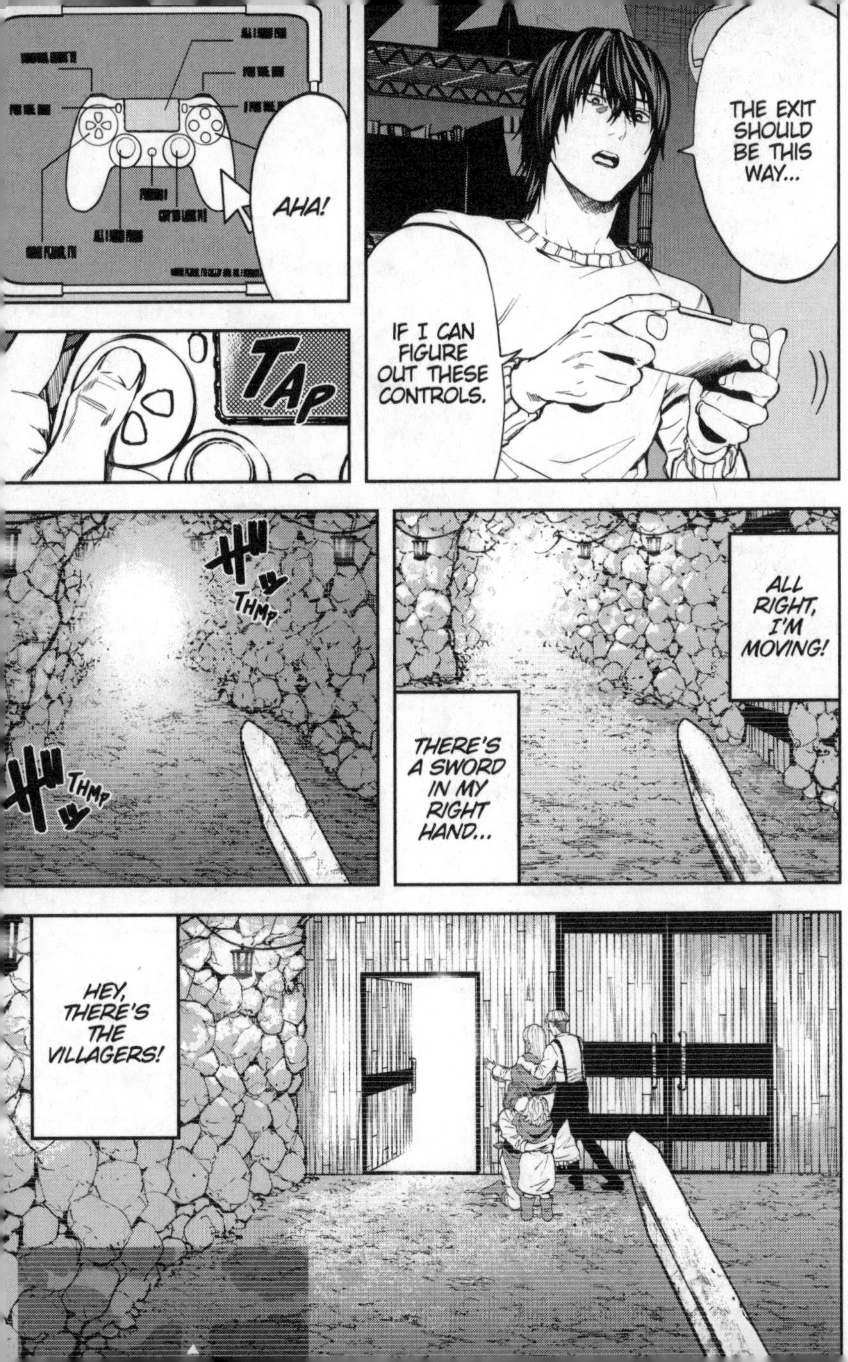
THE EXIT SHOULD BE THIS WAY...
IF I CAN FIGURE OUT THESE CONTROLS.
AHA!
TAP
ALL RIGHT, I'M MOVING!
THERE'S A SWORD IN MY RIGHT HAND...
THMP
THMP
HEY, THERE'S THE VILLAGERS!

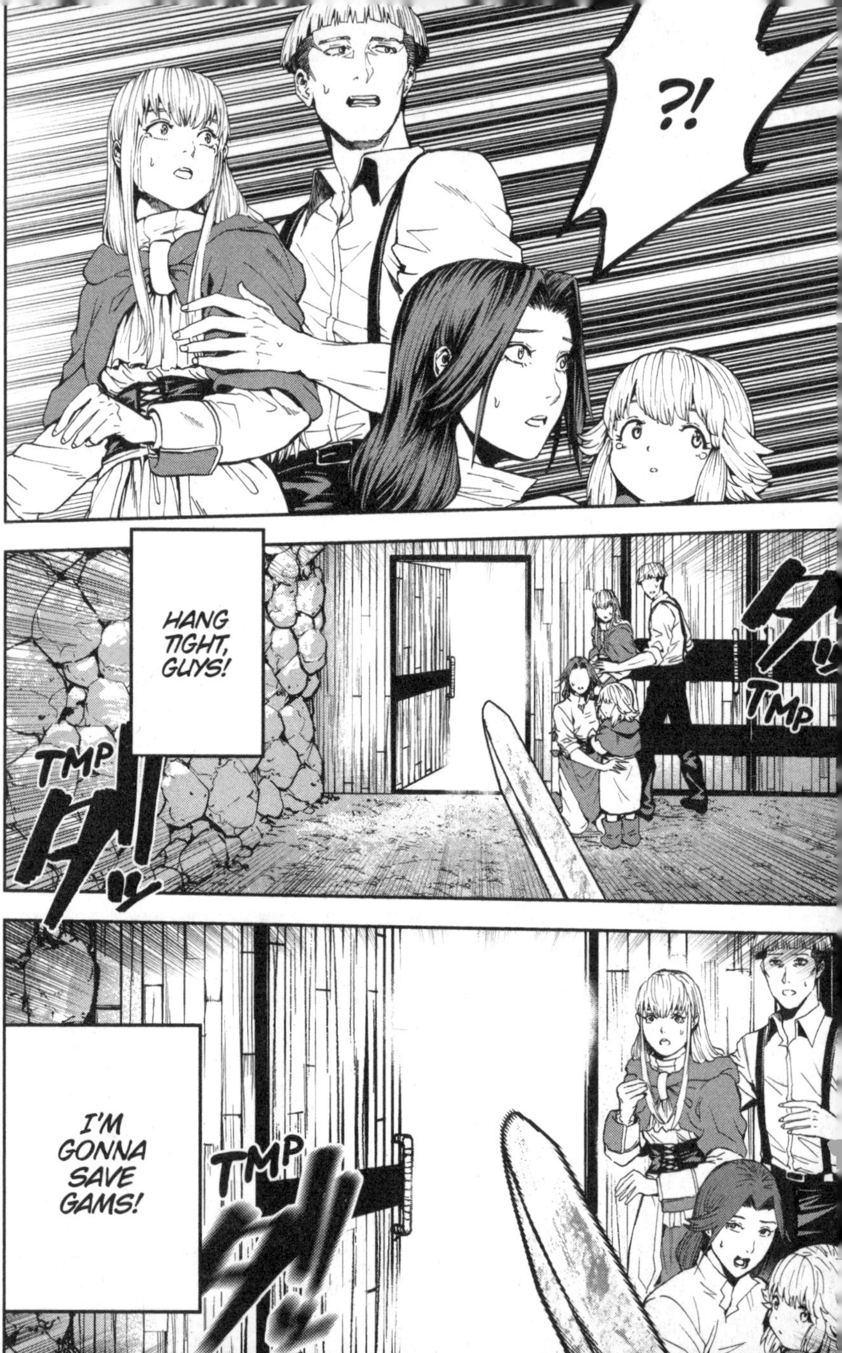
?!
TMP
HANG TIGHT, GUYS!
TMP
I'M GONNA SAVE GAMS!
TMP

BWOOSH

G-GOD
OF
FATE...

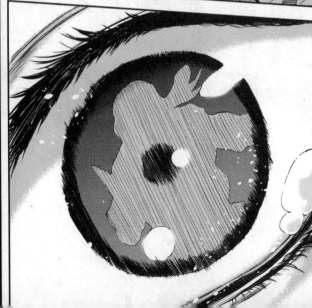

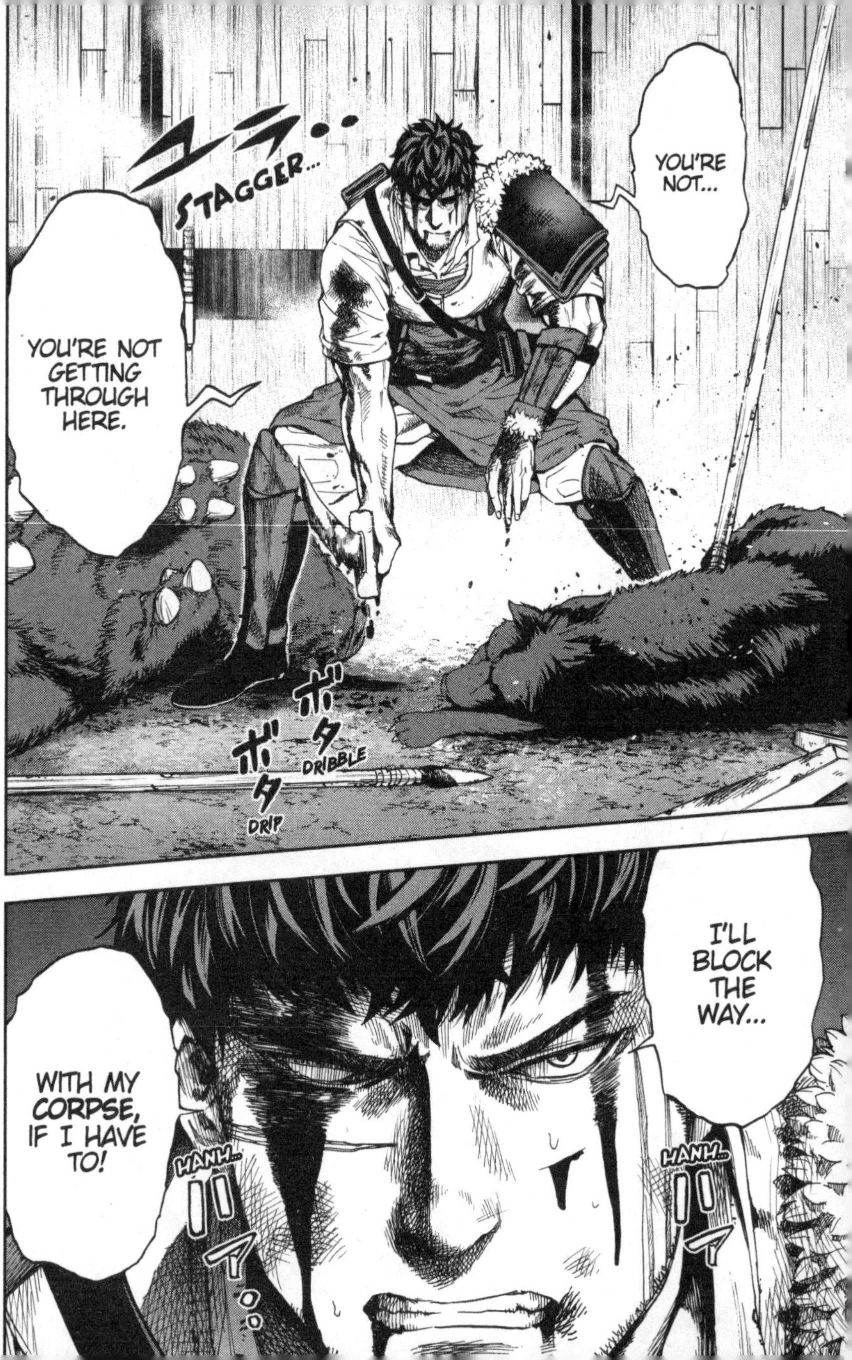
YOU'RE NOT...
STAGGER...
YOU'RE NOT GETTING THROUGH HERE.
ボタ
DRIBBLE
ボタ
DRIP
I'LL BLOCK THE WAY...
HANH...
WITH MY CORPSE, IF I HAVE TO!
HANH...

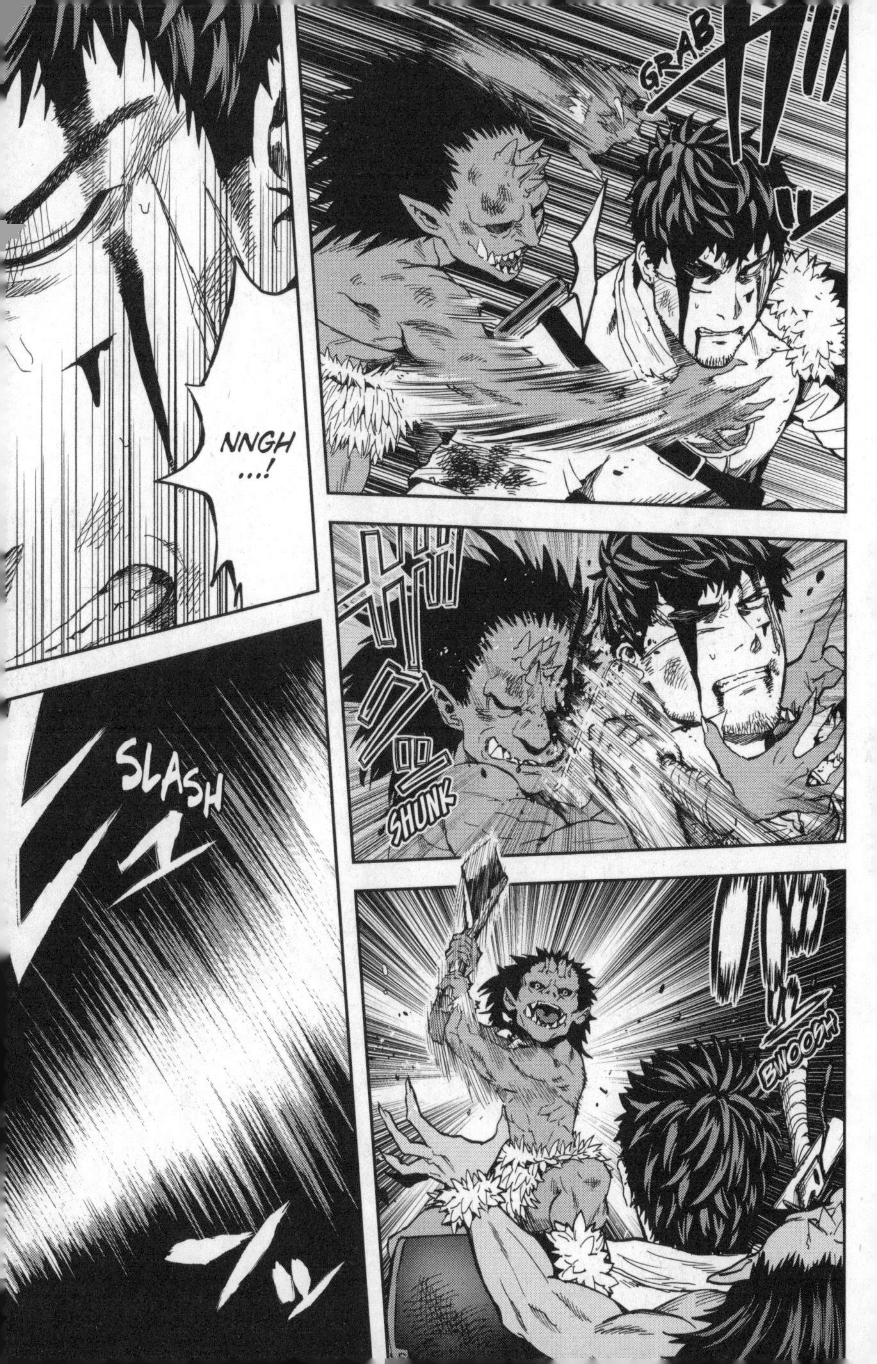
GRAB
NNGH
...!
SHUNK
BWOOSH
SLASH

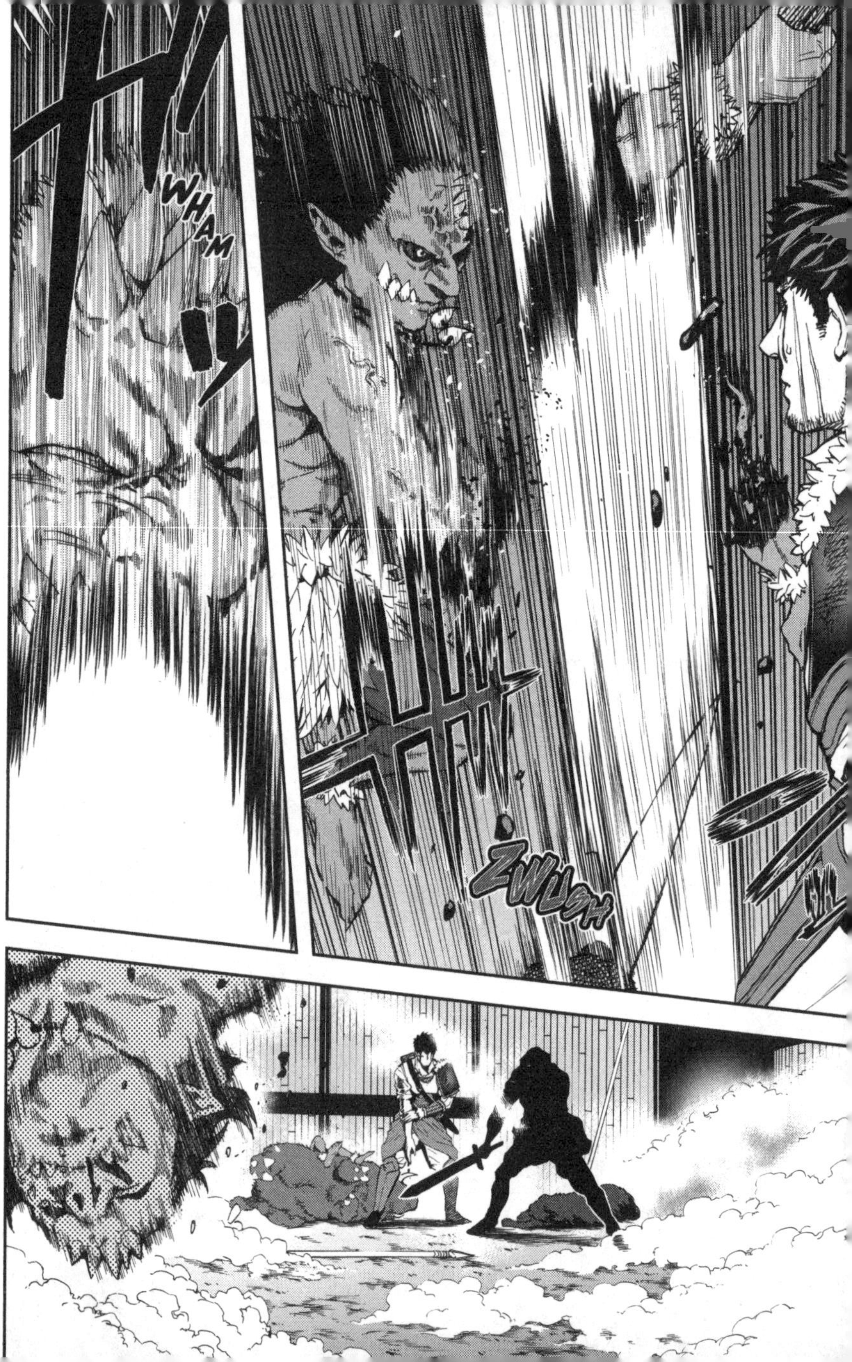
ZWUSH
WHAM

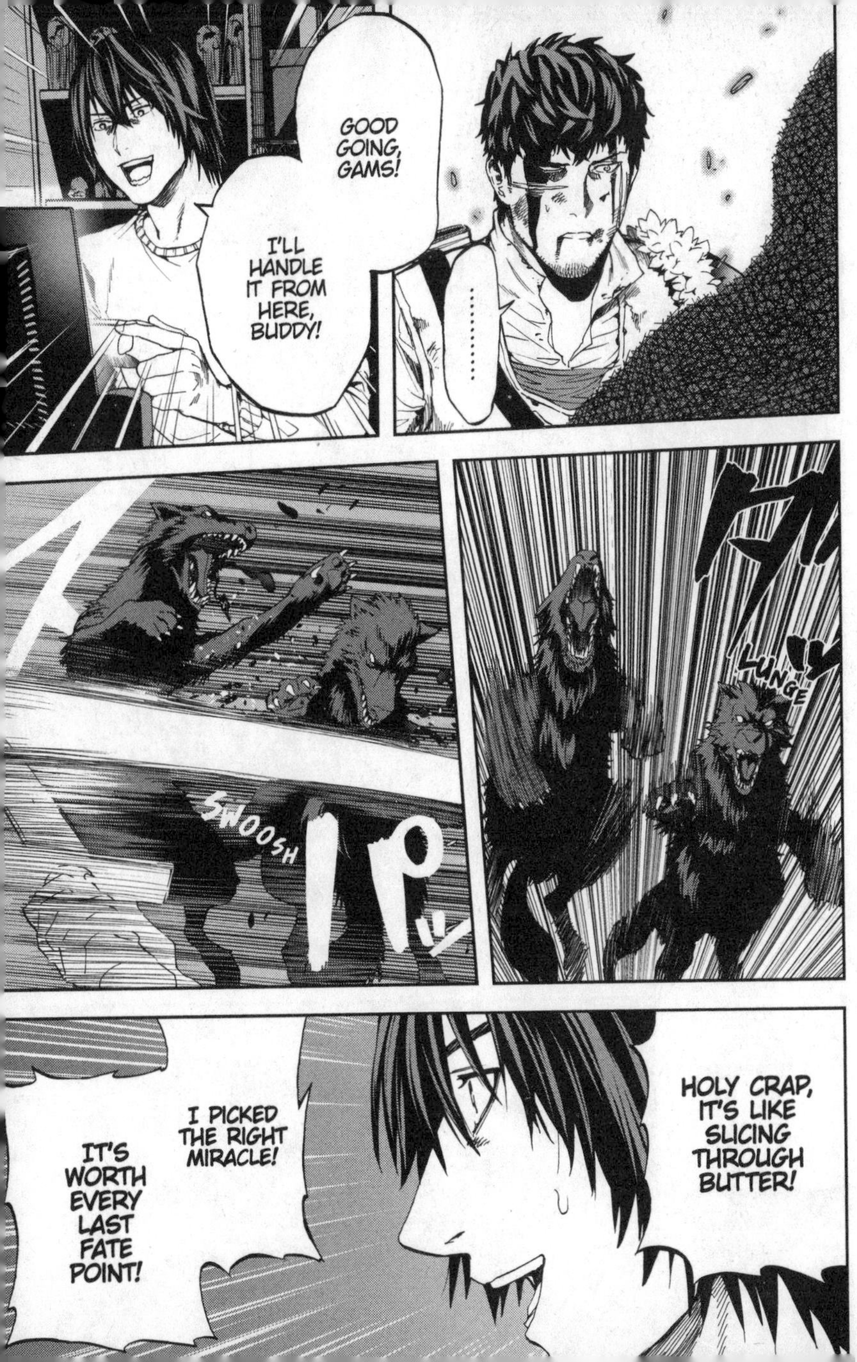
......
GOOD GOING, GAMS!
I'LL HANDLE IT FROM HERE, BUDDY!
LUNGE
SWOOSH
HOLY CRAP, IT'S LIKE SLICING THROUGH BUTTER!
I PICKED THE RIGHT MIRACLE!
IT'S WORTH EVERY LAST FATE POINT!

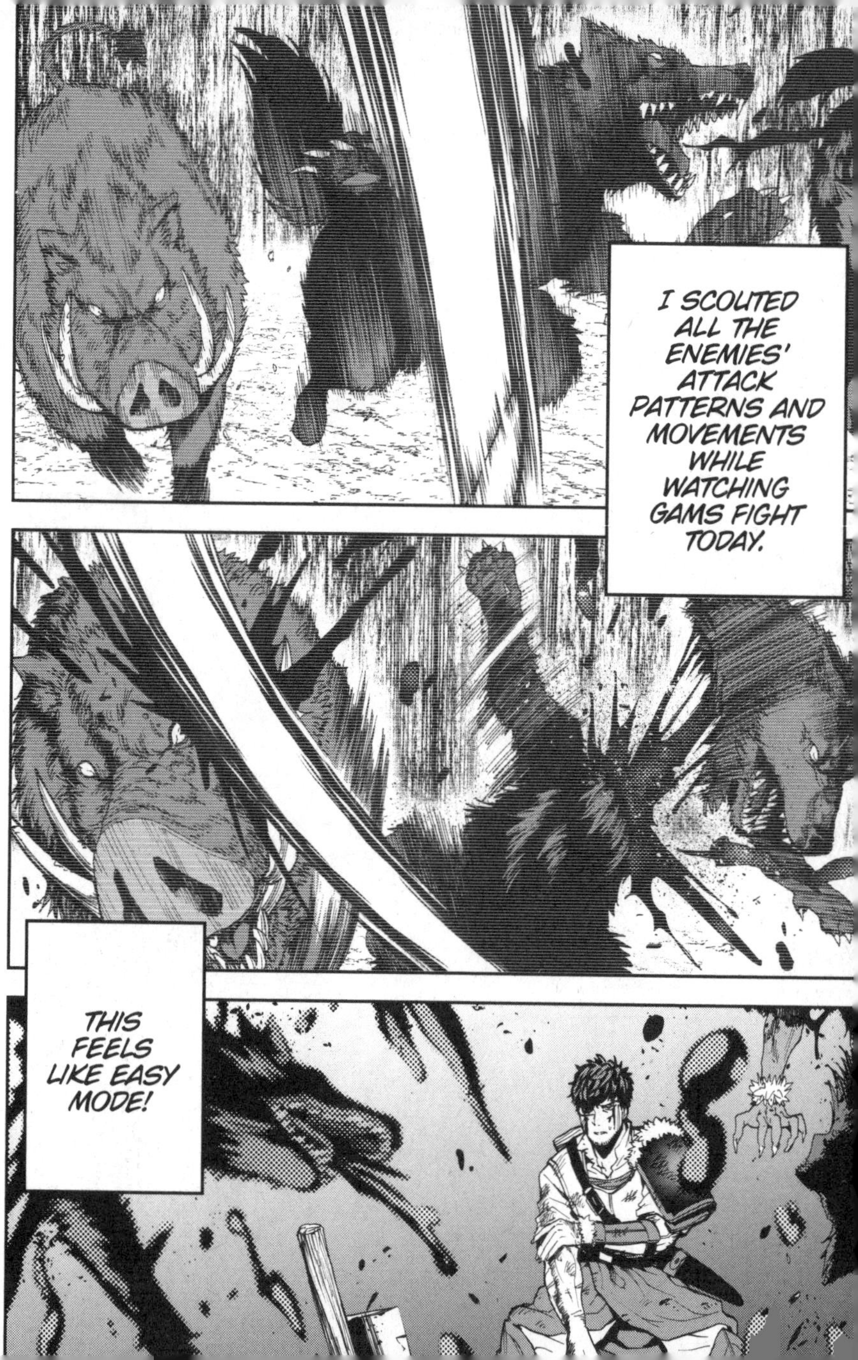
I SCOUTED ALL THE ENEMIES' ATTACK PATTERNS AND MOVEMENTS WHILE WATCHING GAMS FIGHT TODAY.
THIS FEELS LIKE EASY MODE!

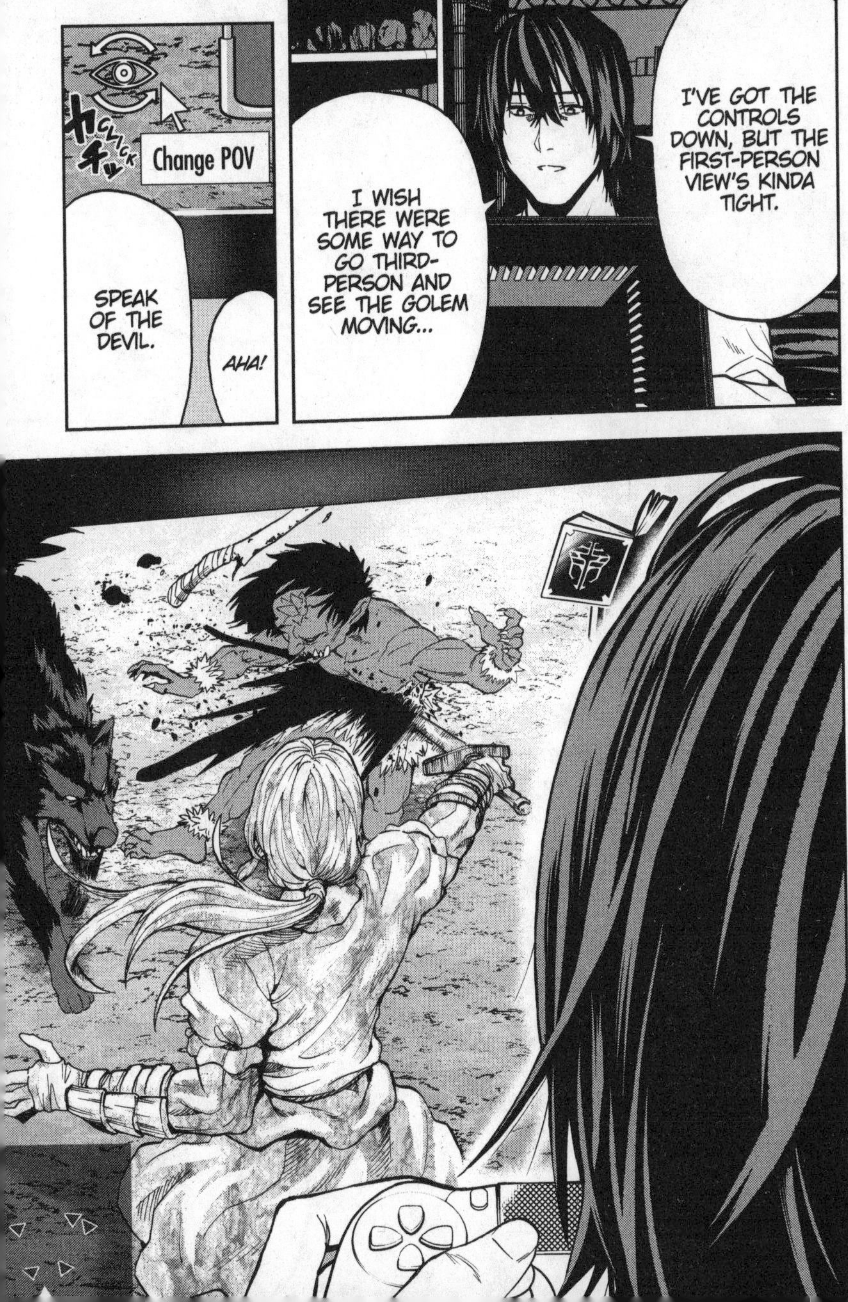
I'VE GOT THE CONTROLS DOWN, BUT THE FIRST-PERSON VIEW'S KINDA TIGHT.
I WISH THERE WERE SOME WAY TO GO THIRD-PERSON AND SEE THE GOLEM MOVING...
Change POV
CLICK
AHA!
SPEAK OF THE DEVIL.

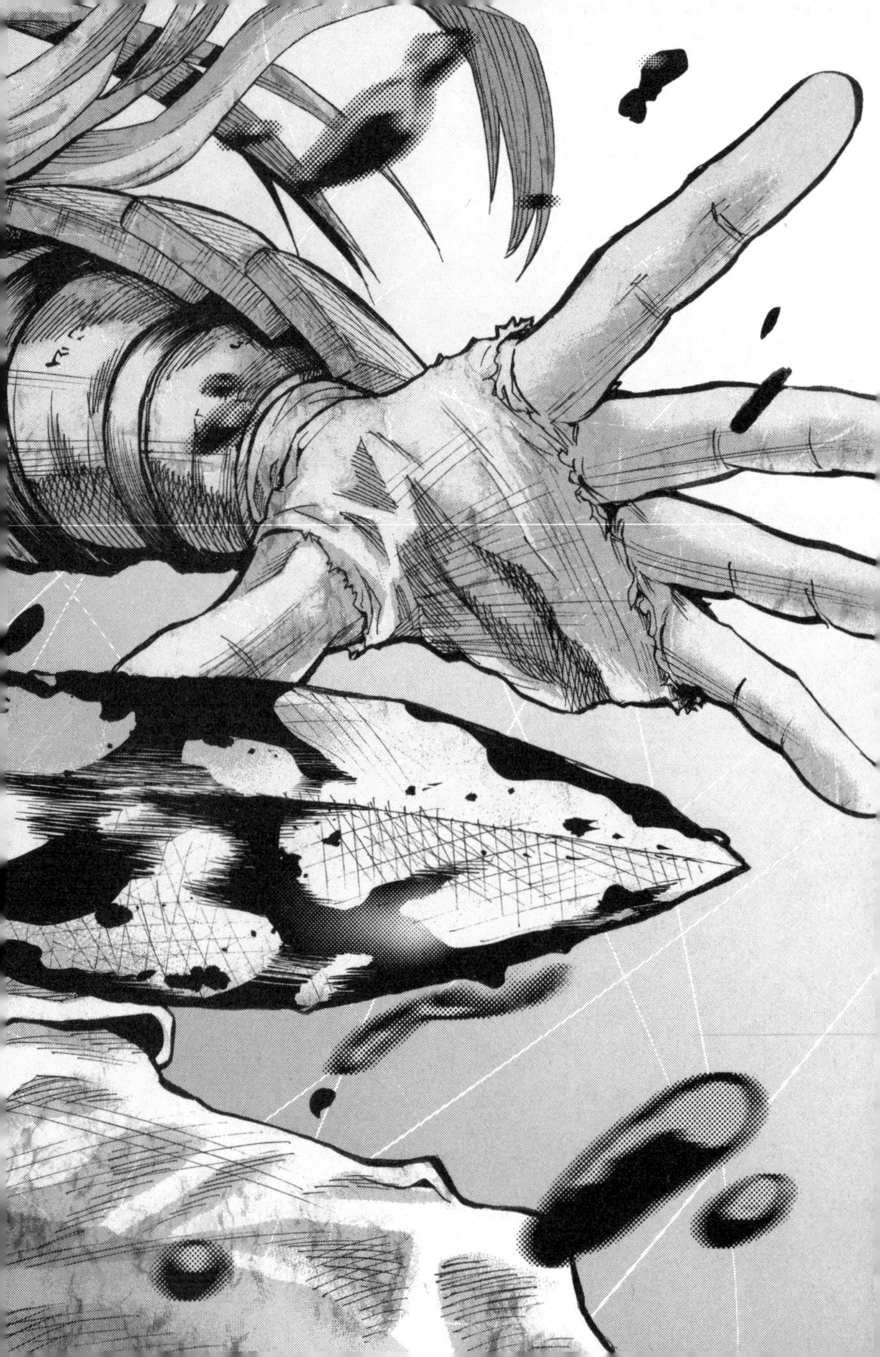

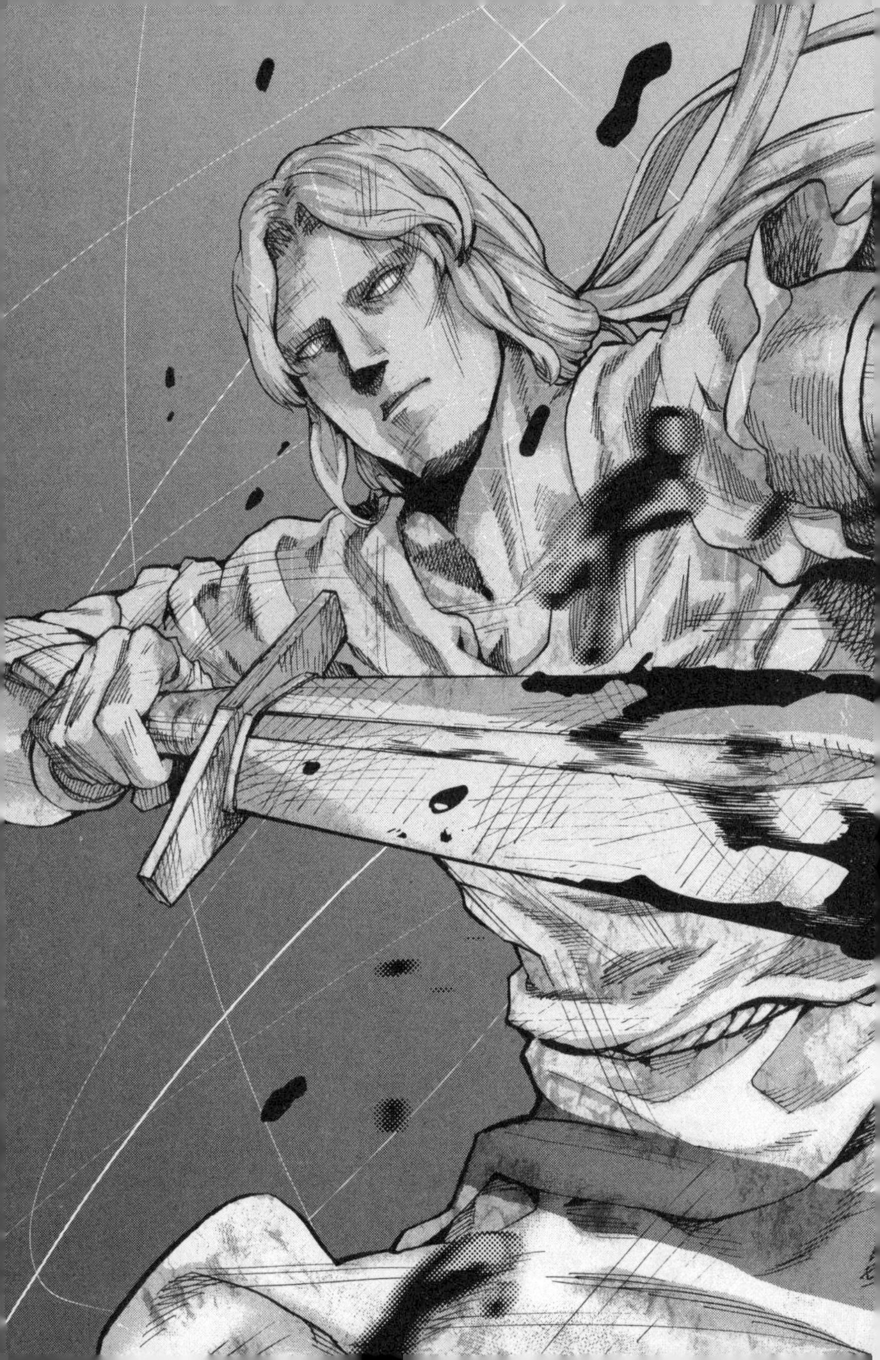

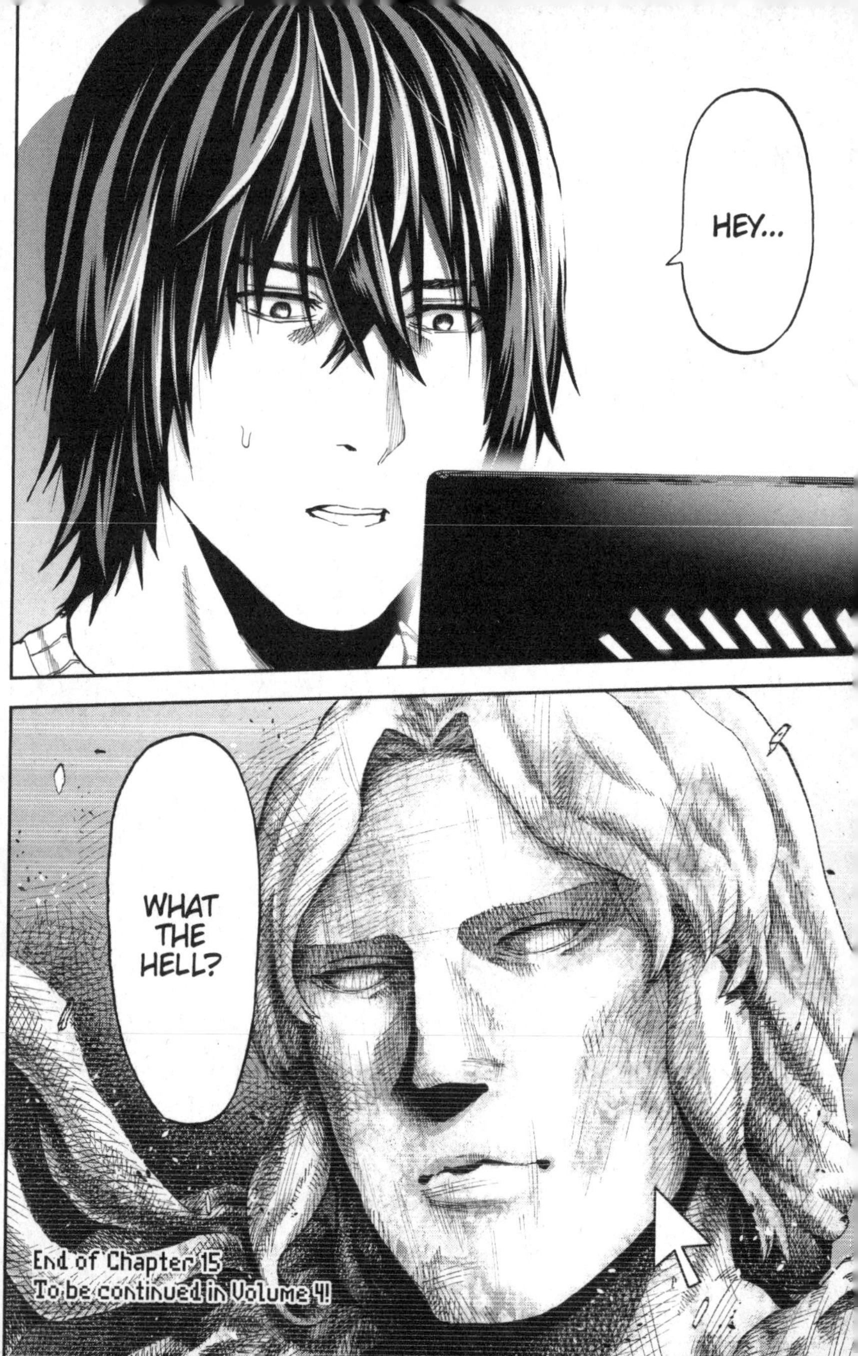
HEY...
WHAT THE HELL?
End of Chapter 15
To be continued in Volume 4!

THE NPCs IN THIS VILLAGE SIM GAME MUST BE REAL!↵

THE NPCs IN THIS VILLAGE SIM GAME MUST BE REAL! ↵

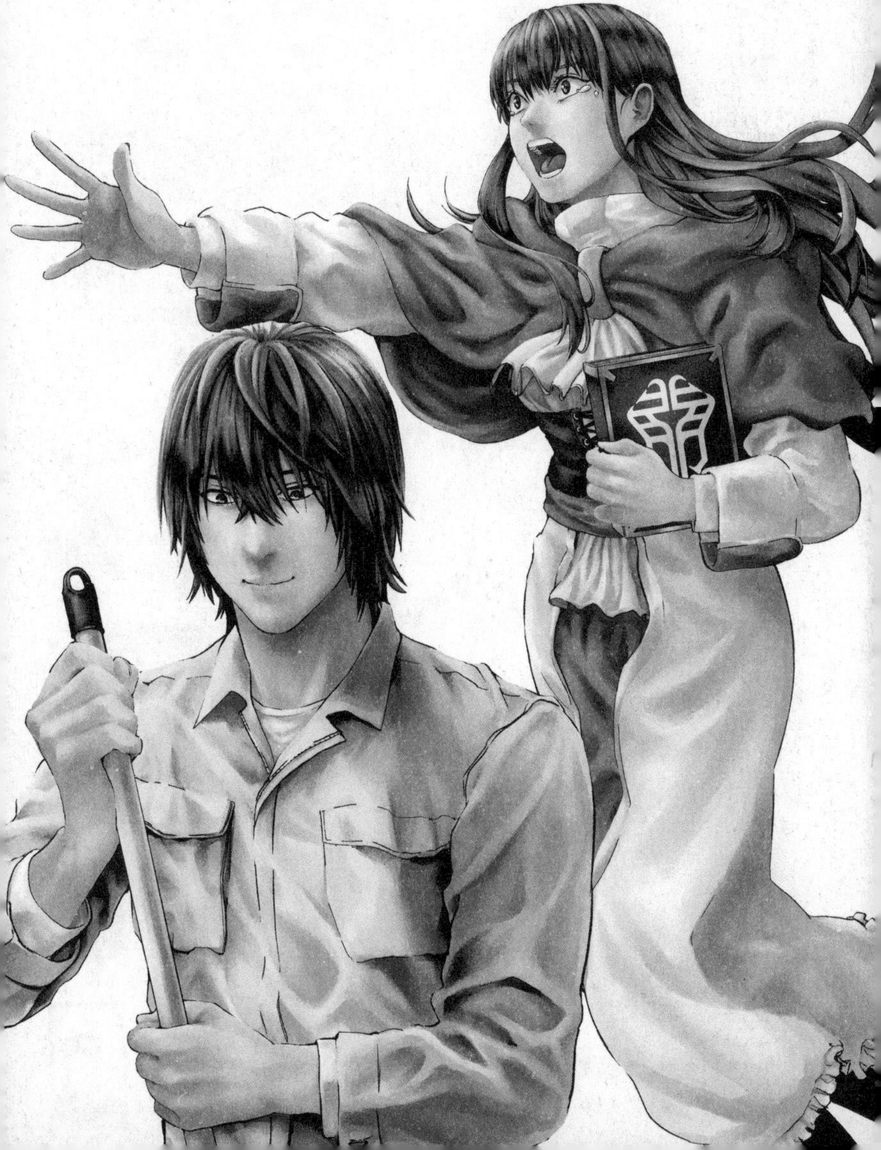

xperience all that SEVEN SEAS has to offer!

SEVENSEASENTERTAINMENT.COM

Visit and follow us on Twitter at twitter.com/gomanga/

SEVEN SEAS ENTERTAINMENT PRESENTS

THE NPCs IN THIS VILLAGE SIM GAME MUST BE REAL!

Vol.3

story by **HIRUKUMA**   art by **KAZUHIKO MORITA**   character design by **NAMAKO**

TRANSLATION
John Neal

LETTERING
Ochie Caraan

COVER DESIGN
H. Qi

LOGO DESIGN
George Panella

PROOFREADER
Brett Hallahan

COPY EDITOR
Dawn Davis

SENIOR EDITOR
J.P. Sullivan

PRODUCTION DESIGNER
Christa Miesner

PRODUCTION MANAGER
Lissa Pattillo

PREPRESS TECHNICIAN
Melanie Ujimori

PRINT MANAGER
Rhiannon Rasmussen-Silverstein

EDITOR-IN-CHIEF
Julie Davis

ASSOCIATE PUBLISHER
Adam Arnold

PUBLISHER
Jason DeAngelis

MURAZUKURI GAME NO NPC GA NAMAMI NO NINGEN TOSHIKA OMOENAI Vol.3
©Hirukuma 2021
©Kazuhiko Morita 2021
©Namako 2021
First published in Japan in 2021 by KADOKAWA CORPORATION, Tokyo.
English translation rights arranged with KADOKAWA CORPORATION, Tokyo.

No portion of this book may be reproduced or transmitted in any form without written permission from the copyright holders. This is a work of fiction. Names, characters, places, and incidents are the products of the author's imagination or are used fictitiously. Any resemblance to actual events, locales, or persons, living or dead, is entirely coincidental. Any information or opinions expressed by the creators of this book belong to those individual creators and do not necessarily reflect the views of Seven Seas Entertainment or its employees.

Seven Seas press and purchase enquiries can be sent to Marketing Manager Lianne Sentar at press@gomanga.com. Information regarding the distribution and purchase of digital editions is available from Digital Manager CK Russell at digital@gomanga.com.

Seven Seas and the Seven Seas logo are trademarks of Seven Seas Entertainment. All rights reserved.

ISBN: 978-1-63858-273-1
Printed in Canada
First Printing: May 2022
10 9 8 7 6 5 4 3 2 1

READING DIRECTIONS

This book reads from *right to left*, Japanese style. If this is your first time reading manga, you start reading from the top right panel on each page and take it from there. If you get lost, just follow the numbered diagram here. It may seem backwards at first, but you'll get the hang of it! Have fun!!

Follow us online: www.SevenSeasEntertainment.com

Experience all that SEVEN SEAS has to offer!

SEVENSEASENTERTAINMENT.COM
Visit and follow us on Twitter at twitter.com/gomanga/